INTERNATIONAL HANDBOOK OF THE OMBUDSMAN

Evolution and Present Function

INTERNATIONAL HANDBOOK OF THE OMBUDSMAN

Evolution and Present Function

Edited by
GERALD E. CAIDEN

GREENWOOD PRESS
Westport, Connecticut • London, England

Library of Congress Cataloging in Publication Data
Main entry under title:

International handbook of the ombudsman.

  Bibliography: v. 1, p.
  Includes indexes.
  Contents: v. 1. Evolution and present function—
v. 2. Country surveys.
  1. Ombudsman—Handbooks, manuals, etc. I. Caiden,
Gerald E.
JF1525.O45O63   351.9′1   81-20190
ISBN 0-313-22685-7 (set)
ISBN 0-313-23715-8 (v. 1)
ISBN 0-313-23716-6 (v. 2)

Library of Congress Catalog Card Number: 81-20190
ISBN 0-313-23715-8

First published in 1983

Greenwood Press
A division of Congressional Information Service, Inc.
88 Post Road West
Westport, Connecticut 06881

Printed in the United States of America

10 9 8 7 6 5 4 3 2 1

To the Memory of
William A. Robson, a pioneer in humane public
administration, whose untimely death prevented
his contribution to this volume.

CONTENTS

CONTENTS OF THE COMPANION VOLUME,

International Handbook of the Ombudsman: Country Surveys

TABLES

ACKNOWLEDGMENTS

IN A PROJECT of this size, it is impossible to acknowledge all those who brought it to fruition. I would like to express my gratitude to the contributors for their speedy responses to my numerous queries, to Bernard Frank (International Bar Association Ombudsman Committee), Ulf Lundvik (International Ombudsman Steering Committee), Randall Ivany (International Ombudsman Institute), and Maxine Vlieland (Hansard Society) for their enthusiastic support and virtual sponsorship, and to the School of Public Administration, University of Southern California, for technical assistance. Readers who would like to keep up to date on the institution of ombudsman should address their inquiries to the International Ombudsman Institute which maintains the most complete collection of data. Its address can be found in Appendix D.

Gerald E. Caiden

INTRODUCTION

THE CONTRIBUTIONS TO the *International Handbook of the Ombudsman* are divided into two volumes: general essays describing the various roles of the institution of ombudsman (*Evolution and Present Function*) and specific essays dealing with the operations of ombudsman offices around the world (*Country Surveys*). The general essays in this volume are arranged sequentially from the ideological and universal to the practical and particular to illustrate not only the variety of roles that the ombudsman performs but also the diversity of views that ombudsmen themselves and scholars hold about the institution and its activities. It will be readily apparent that in true democratic tradition, there is agreement to disagree over the utility, impact, and effectiveness of the ombudsman. At one extreme, there are those who hold that the institution is an essential instrument in the modern administrative state to reduce the gap between the administrators and the administered, to open up the operations of government to public gaze, to protect basic human rights against possible infringements by the public bureaucracy, and to improve the quality of public administration. At the other, there are those who maintain that the institution is merely a public pacifier, a device to assuage public critics of government operations at minimal cost without having to change anything fundamental, and should it attempt to do anything more than mediate between public agencies and complainants, should it criticize the administration and embarrass the government, ways are quickly found to neutralize it. Even the ombudsmen dispute among themselves what should be their role, how best they should perform it, and what measures they should employ to indicate how effectively they perform their role.

Chapter 1, "The Institution of Ombudsman," by Gerald E. Caiden, Niall MacDermot, and Ake Sandler presents a definition of the office of ombudsman along with an overview of the development of the concept, a brief survey of the variety of forms that it has taken, and a look at some evaluations and assessments of the institution. They describe the ombudsman as a unique instrument of human rights who acts both as an arbitrator in

cases of abuse of public power or careless exercise of authority and as a bureaucratic watchdog for areas of chronic maladministration.

The ombudsman, as an independent, nonpartisan officer appointed by one of the principal organs of state, deals with specific complaints from the public and is in a position to research these cases and make public findings and recommendations. Solutions are sought through conciliation, or, where necessary, through exposure of wrongdoing. The ombudsman has no power to reverse administrative decisions or to issue orders but has effective channels of investigation and influence.

The institution of ombudsman has its roots in ancient times, but has only gained worldwide acceptance in the last thirty years. The first constitutionally established office appeared in Sweden in 1809, and Finland instituted the office in 1919. Now there are over ninety offices in thirty countries. In time, diverse forms of the office have developed in response to different needs and forms of government. These can now be seen in effect in the various countries that have adopted the office. Some examples of these variations are presented by Caiden, MacDermot, and Sandler, describing offices in countries that are not studied in detail elsewhere in the *Handbook*.

Concluding Chapter 1 is a survey of some of the assessments and evaluations that have been made of the ombudsman office. While most of the criticism is favorable, it also warns that appraisal of the benefits and costs of maintaining an ombudsman office is difficult and that comparing the various forms that the office has taken is almost impossible. Above all, there is the reminder that the ombudsman is intended only as a supplement to existing institutions, such as courts and legislatures, which ideally should be made more responsive to the complaints of citizens.

In Chapter 2, "The Ideological Foundation of the Ombudsman Institution," H. H. Kirchheiner argues that many countries impressed with the Swedish model have adopted and modified it to suit their own circumstances without fully appreciating its ideological roots. They have regarded it as being largely supplementary to existing legal remedies designed to protect individual rights and strengthen judicial review of public administration, whereas the essence of the institution is to remind public officials of their duties and obligations to the public they serve and their personal responsibility toward the people whose lives they affect. The ombudsman humanizes relations between government and citizen and enlarges personal security by reducing the arbitrary, incorrect, and tardy acts of officialdom. Democracy is not so much correct institutional forms, such as a representative constitutional system, but a state of mind, a way of life, a respect for personal security in its widest sense that includes an individual's feelings of safety, humanity, human dignity, and personal worth. This personal security is the *conditio sine qua non* for a sound democracy as a tolerant society based on natural respect and understanding between individuals. As a set of social relations, democracy is reflected not only in the political sphere but also in the everyday relations between people, between public officials and citizens, between judges and those subject to court jurisdiction. The whole idea of the *justitieombudsman* was to democratize public administration in this sense, that is, reduce the distance between public officials and the public, to get them to respect and understand one another, to conduct public business in such a way that personal security was enhanced.

Kirchheiner shows how the idea of ombudsman evolved during the Swedish Enlightenment when freedom of thought and expression, humanitarianism, and individual liberty were emphasized against state absolutism on the one hand and personal indiscipline or high-handedness on the other. Every man should be concerned with the fate of another. A serious offense against one person should be considered an offense against all. In investigating individual grievances, the ombudsman would be investigating collective grievances. Public officials should be continually liable for incorrectly applying laws, overstepping their authority, being high-handed, and failing in their duties and obligations to their fellow men. Thus, the ombudsman was to be responsible for seeing that all public officials performed their duties with proper consideration for their fellow men, correctness and tact, and fairness and diligence. Officials were expected to see all problems from the viewpoint of those affected. Only when they performed their duties with that sense of responsibility toward the public could an individual's feelings of security be based on confidence in officials. In Sweden, this interpretation of public responsibility has since been extended to include failure to perform when, given their intellectual capabilities, they should have known better or should have done more to find out the appropriate facts. To ensure proper public responsibility, state operations have been thrown open to public access

and knowledge, and the ombudsman has been strengthened as an independent investigator of public administration, capable of identifying with victims of public maladministration and jealous in protecting personal security against possible threats by officialdom.

Kirchheiner warns that, while other countries have copied the form of the Swedish ombudsman, they have not taken over its ideology. They have incorporated the institution into their machinery of government but not the spirit of democratization that goes with it. They have given the office similar powers and functions, but they have not supplied adequate conditions for their performance. They have appointed similarly qualified incumbents, but they have been reluctant to allow them the same independence, freedom of action, accessibility, and modus operandi. They have not understood its democratic elements—those of freedom, trust, personal responsibility and security, sense of humanity, individual dignity, toleration, and conciliation. Without these, they cannot expect the same results.

Baroness B. Serota in Chapter 3, "The Evolution of the Role of the Ombudsman—Comparisons and Perspectives," shares some of Kirchheiner's concerns. She also emphasizes that the form of the ombudsman is less important than the spirit that infuses its operations. She is particularly critical of formalism and some self-satisfied complacency which she detects creeping into the ombudsman fraternity. As an ombudsman herself, she is convinced that regardless of the form it takes, the modern state must incorporate permanent machinery for investigating public complaints against public administration, not only on ideological grounds but also as a practical tool for detecting wrongdoing that escapes attention and keeping public officials on their toes lest they find their actions subject to investigation. She traces the evolution of the institution of ombudsman as a specific form of complaint machinery that has spread from its original Scandinavian home around the world, justifies its growth and extension, and explains the nature of its successful adoption and adaption in different settings. She describes in some detail the variety of ombudsman offices that now exist and compares and contrasts concisely their objectives, forms, powers, place in the polity, relations with other government bodies, jurisdiction, and accessibility. In so doing, she does not flinch from raising basic issues.

Among several problems that Baroness Serota discusses are the restrictive nature of enabling legislation, limitations on public access to the ombudsman office, lack of knowledge within the community about the institution, the political drawback to independence, competition with a formal administrative law system, tunnel vision, the low utility so far to the disadvantaged or underprivileged, reluctance of ombudsmen to use their powers against recalcitrant public officials, and a negative image. She believes that ombudsmen should not content themselves with being efficient complaint handlers within the boundaries set for them. They should be more pro-active. They should seek to remove unnecessary obstacles that impede their performance. They should make themselves more accessible to the public; they should publicize their services more widely; and they should try to reach the disadvantaged and underprivileged. They should seek allies within the political system so that they become a more important force within the machinery of government, a force promoting better government, more efficacious administration, and greater humanity in the relations between state and citizen. They should seek further to fill gaps in protecting individual rights against public maladministration and generally promote the extension of the institution of ombudsman where it is known to have succeeded elsewhere. They should urge public agencies to establish their own complaint-handling machinery. Altogether, they should develop a more positive image of the office, one that is seen not as a check on public administration but as a force for good within the machinery of government. In her own words, the ombudsman "must have a human face." Clearly, Baroness Serota is an activist ombudsman opposed to negative attitudes exhibited by more conservative ombudsmen.

The contrast between the position taken by Baroness Serota and that presumably taken by other ombudsmen of whom she is critical is well brought out by Larry B. Hill in Chapter 4, "The Self-Perceptions of Ombudsmen: A Comparative Survey." Hill records the results of a survey conducted during the 1970s among ombudsmen of their attitudes toward the institution in general, their own particular offices, and the work they did. Many of Hill's findings support Serota's analysis of the contrasts between ombudsman offices from one jurisdiction to another. Hill directs his focus on accessibility, the substance of complaints, operational norms, and degree of political autonomy. He has found that outside of Scandinavia, the ombudsman has become mainly a reactive institution, particularly in British Commonwealth countries, that is, the ombudsmen wait passively for complainants to reach them rather than taking their office to the public or initiating their own investigations. Few support outreach notions. The great majority accept the limitations placed on their accessibility and jurisdiction and narrowly interpret their powers, preferring complainants to exhaust other avenues first. Interestingly, ombudsmen in North America are the most liberal in their perception of their role, tend to be activist, and, unlike offices elsewhere, do not insist that complaints be in written form. Naturally, the volume of complaints received and investigated reflects differences in attitude toward whether or not to encourage

the public to complain about public administration and what constitutes a complaint as opposed to requests for information and services. Ombudsmen in the United States deal with requests as well as complaints and so involve themselves with much administrative minutiae, although no ombudsman office can be said to be constantly involved with weighty matters of public import.

When asked to rank six different operational modes, there was almost total unanimity in selecting the impartial-investigator model first except among U.S. ombudsmen where the enabler-facilitator model was preferred by almost half the respondents. That model was usually the second choice of ombudsmen, with the broker-negotiator model a poor third. A handful, however, did see themselves as citizen-advocates but none as political activists. The great majority tried to keep themselves politically impartial and neutral and to steer clear of both public controversies and lobbying activities. Hill concludes that, despite differences in attitude, there is sufficient commonality to define the ombudsman cross-nationally "as accessible to citizens, as processors of administrative grievance, and as impartial and politically independent investigators."

To flesh out Hill's survey, three notable ombudsmen and an ombudsman observer set out their different views of the ombudsman role in a mini-symposium in Chapter 5, "Four Perspectives on the Ombudsman's Role." The Israeli ombudsman, Izhak E. Nebenzahl, who also is state comptroller, leads off with his address to the 1976 International Ombudsman Conference which has often been quoted since and remains influential in ombudsman circles. Like Kirchheiner, Nebenzahl takes a more ideological and philosophical view of the ombudsman as complaint handler with decided impact on public administration, both directly in helping complainants and indirectly as influential administrative investigator. He does not believe that the ombudsmen deal largely with insubstantial matters and unfounded grievances. For complainants, they are not inconsequential or unreal. For the rest of society, taken together, they have considerable meaning, and every so often a few causes célèbres concern all in their import. None of them is picked up elsewhere in the machinery of government. Yet, there should be far more; ombudsmen only receive a tiny fraction of the number of complaints that could (and should?) be made. The jurisdiction of ombudsmen has been too narrowly drawn and interpreted and, with Baroness Serota and Larry Hill, Nebenzahl does not think that ombudsmen have been active enough in making themselves known and seeking complaints that should be investigated. Nevertheless, he believes that the office has an important deterrent effect on officialdom, a necessary cautioning influence. Above all, it gives citizens a means of influencing public administration, and whether or not they use it personally, they know justice will be done and the quality of life thereby enhanced.

Per-Erik Nilsson, the chief ombudsman of Sweden, in his address to the same organization four years later, sympathized with Nebenzahl's perspective but took issue with him on the matter of power. Nilsson does not believe that influence alone is enough. He would like to see the ombudsman's powers as an administrative critic and reformer strengthened and those powers already possessed actually used. The ombudsman office should not just argue its case but should be able to bring a matter before a competent authority and extort an answer from it. It should be able to advocate changes in legislation as well as changes in administrative procedure. It should act as a citizen's advice bureau, and in seeing that justice is done, it should ensure not only that wrong is righted but also that wrong does not occur in the first place. It should be a more results-oriented institution. It should work to make today's recommendations tomorrow's reality. Nilsson shares Nebenzahl's belief that the office, including his own in Sweden, is underutilized, perhaps because the public and the mass media perceive it (unjustly?) as merely a paper tiger, a weak agency unable to gain proper respect from public administrators. The annual report—for many ombudsman offices the only public document issued by them—is an inadequate instrument for influencing public administration, informing the mass media, and educating the public. The office has to find ways to use the mass media, the public, and the political system to reinforce its work.

Arthur Maloney, QC, formerly an activist Ontario ombudsman and a strong advocate of individual rights against inappropriate bureaucratic behavior, also supports the institution of ombudsman but believes its full potential has yet to be realized. He observes that as the ombudsman offices differ one from another, their effectiveness depends on the character and personality of the incumbents themselves. Regardless of their organizational and legal framework, they are highly personalized institutions. To illustrate, he draws on his personal experiences to show how the same kind of complaint can be viewed and therefore handled differently. He describes how an activist ombudsman can ruffle passive bureaucrats and emphasizes that the ombudsman needs good working relations with the legislature behind him to ensure public backing and adequate resources to do his job as the voice of the ordinary man, whether rich or poor, free or unfree. Altogether, the institution has power to do much good as mediator, reformer, and fighter.

Robert Miewald, the outsider in this mini-symposium, is less sanguine. He believes that the institution of ombudsman has been oversold; enthusiasm for it is waning,

at least in American academic circles where the leading texts on public administration rarely mention it. It has been promoted as a great boon to the citizen vis-à-vis the public bureaucracy, but in fact no one, citizen or not, is denied access to it. The term "citizen" is meaningless, and even the notion of citizenship is questionable in a world dominated by organizations and the organizational imperative. "A citizen, a person who believes that one's welfare is tied in with the welfare of the whole community, is obsolete," Miewald states in contradiction to Kirchheiner and Nebenzahl. Nevertheless, Miewald admits that the ombudsmen can help people, if not as citizens, then as constituents, clients, and victims, but within the confines of the organizational imperative. It is "one more technique . . . which makes reform less likely" because it does not require bureaucrats and outsiders to question the underlying assumptions of the organizational society. Quoting Victor Thompson, he asserts that the ombudsman is a gimmick which substituting for deep analysis leads to formalism. By employing a bureaucrat to control bureaucrats, it is merely another step in the bureaucratization of society, distracting people from meaningful political participation. It makes for a better managed but not a better governed society. Miewald would seem to imply that the more successful it is, the more it imprisons the common man within his bureaucratic cage.

The common man believes that he has gained more from the bureaucratization of society than he has lost. Before the organizational society, he may have been free or freer, but he had little to rejoice about and he was enslaved in other ways, not the least of which was the absence of enforceable basic rights. The organizational society provides machinery whereby basic human rights can be enforced against one's fellow men, against organizations, and against society itself. The ombudsman office is a welcome addition to this machinery because it can expose abrogations of individual rights committed by public officials insofar as it can investigate complaints against most classes of public officials in their official capacity. Much depends on how well the ombudsmen conduct their investigations, which is the subject of William B. Gwyn in Chapter 6, "The Investigations of Ombudsmen." He compares the operations of five offices, those in Denmark, Sweden, New Zealand, the United Kingdom, and Hawaii. Not surprisingly, he finds that they differ considerably in the length and complexity of their investigations, with the British being the most thorough, although tending to make investigation an end in itself instead of concentrating on the rectification of wrongdoing. More important than getting at the facts is their interpretation and evaluation.

Viktor J. Pickl, an insider, substantially agrees with Gwyn but points out difficulties that ombudsmen face when they conduct investigations, difficulties that Gwyn has overlooked. Nobody likes to be investigated, bureaucrats included, and in their case they are mindful of secrecy laws, adverse public image, and mass media sensationalism which inhibit their full cooperation even without their trying to second guess the ombudsman office. The purpose of the ombudsman is not, as citizens' advocate, to find fault with public officials or to place the worst interpretation on their actions, but to report on the facts and if necessary exonerate them when no wrong has been done. Although, in fact, ombudsmen fault public officials much less than they exonerate them, this does not mean that they have been coopted or that they are a needless luxury. They provide essential public education services in explaining to complainants how public administration works, they reduce friction between government and citizens, and they remove lingering doubts about possible injustice. They act more as public relations officers for public agencies than as inquisitors. As lightning conductors for genuine grievances, they protect public agencies from political storms in the long run.

Pickl implies that by being on nobody's side, the ombudsman works for the benefit of all. In Chapter 7, A. W. Bradley closely examines this claim from a British perspective in respect to the ability of the ombudsman to protect citizens' rights. Clearly, the ombudsman is a supplement to such long-established institutions as the courts, administrative tribunals, public inquiries, and political controls, and, given the many restrictions on the parliamentary commissioner's jurisdiction, a rather weak supplement. But the ombudsman provides a process by which principles of good administration can emerge from the casework, and from this viewpoint it can protect citizens' rights. This has already been demonstrated by the National Health Service commissioner who, in dealing with claims by complainants that the hospital service should have provided more efficient or compassionate service, has sought to further the rights and interests of patients in dealing with hospital authorities. Other beneficiaries have included income tax payers, pensioners, social service recipients and prisoners, all vulnerable groups within society when faced with bureaucratic power. The ombudsman office can enforce rights established in law but not fully enjoyed, and can extend rights beyond the point where the law stops. For this reason, it "should be concerned not merely with the law as it is, but also with the law as it might be," something that the Danish office has been more prepared to do than the British office. It might also assume a residual competence in relation to the courts, that is, it might fill gaps in the system of judicial control over public administration, perhaps by referring legal points that arise in investigations to the courts, by possessing the power to seek temporary

injunctions against irreparable actions being taken by public agencies, and by requiring the payment of financial compensation to wronged citizens. Bradley would like the same substantive rules and principles applied to the courts and the ombudsmen. Already in respect of natural justice and fairness, substantial common ground exists, and while the courts would concentrate on enforcing the legal rights of citizens, the ombudsmen could protect their interests in respect to good administration.

Bradley draws attention to areas where basic rights are still being defined and to vulnerable groups in society whose defined rights are, for one reason or another, poorly enforced. The remaining essays largely deal with these issues and show how the institution of ombudsman is well suited to help resolve them. One area that Bradley did not mention is conflict between public access to public records (the public's right to know) and the protection of privacy and personal data (confidentiality). The problems inherent in balancing conflicting rights are described in Chapter 8, "The Ombudsman and Freedom of Information in Canada" by Inger Hansen, the privacy commissioner within the Canadian Human Rights Commission. While governments have gradually extended public access to public records, moving toward Sweden's liberal access, they have also been mindful of the need to preserve secrecy in regard to national security, personal tax statements, medical records, criminal investigations, and corporate data. In Canada, individuals now have the right to examine and obtain copies of records concerning themselves used for administrative purposes by the federal government and to know the purposes for which the records are used. A list of personal information data banks is available at local post offices. Individuals who allege that they have been denied access may complain to the privacy commissioner who acts as an ombudsman in respect to these complaints. Legislation is now pending that would strengthen the ombudsman's role in investigating complaints. Should other countries adopt similar provisions, Hansen warns that the ombudsman office would be treated like any other public agency, but it also would have good claims to assume responsibility for enforcing individual access to public records concerning personal data.

Five groups of people who have consistently been denied access to information about themselves by the public agencies that deal with them are patients, members of the armed forces, prisoners, students, and school children. In each case, they are denied legally or organizationally certain rights accorded to others, and they have considerable difficulty enforcing the rights they possess against authoritarian administrations. More than others, they require special protective mechanisms to suit their particular needs. They need access to outsiders who can deal with the administrators of their organizations on equal terms, who have access to information denied to them, and who cannot be intimidated should they disagree with administrative actions and interpretations. They seek cheap, accessible, speedy means of redress of their grievances. The institution of ombudsman meets these requirements and is flexible to accommodate to the different circumstances of each group. In Chapter 9, "The Ombudsman in Health Care Institutions in the United States," Mildred Mailick justifies the emergence of health care ombudsmen who deal with complaints of patients and other long-term care populations in nursing homes and retirement communities, and she describes federal government schemes to promote the ombudsman idea and patient representatives. Despite shortcomings in current programs, she believes that experience to date justifies their extension.

Citizens conscripted into the armed services come under military codes of discipline which in effect curtail their liberties and rights. Like confined patients, they may have just cause to complain about the treatment they receive. They may appeal through the chain of command, but there are many psychological as well as practical obstacles in exercising their rights and they may fear reprisal or victimization for daring to challenge authority. Because of the peculiar nature of military service, when Sweden extended the right of citizens to complain about mistreatment at the hands of public officials to soldiers in 1915, it created separate machinery. So have Norway, the Federal Republic of Germany, and Israel. Haim Laskov, Israel's military ombudsman, describes his office in Chapter 10, "The Military Ombudsman in Israel," and shows how differently it operates compared with other ombudsman offices. While it cannot intrude into military command, it does investigate to good effect soldiers' grievances against military administration and conditions of service. Like other Israeli ombudsman offices, the military ombudsman is kept quite busy and deals with large numbers of complaints, one-third of which are found to be justified, mostly to do with conditions of service, incorrect payments, statutory privileges, and medical treatment.

The military ombudsman receives written complaints and, in the course of investigations, makes field inspections. Where an ombudsman's jurisdiction extends to prisoners, much the same procedure is followed. In recent years, prisoners' complaints about prison administration in some North American locations have been investigated by a corrections ombudsman. The new offices do not deal with all grievances prisoners may have. There are too many. They do screen them and pass matters they cannot handle to more appropriate bodies such as legal aid offices, social service agencies, and public defenders.

Stanley V. Anderson in Chapter 11, "The Corrections Ombudsman in the United States" describes the operations of the Minnesota office under ombudsman T. Williams and compares its experience with the way prisoners' complaints are dealt with elsewhere. He is very much an advocate for this new role for the ombudsman institution. The value of having the corrections ombudsman actually on prison premises is argued cogently by the Kansas corrections ombudsman Preston N. Barton II, in a companion essay, in which he shows that in contrast with other ombudsman offices, his office tries to investigate and resolve complaints at the lowest possible level within the institutional chain of command. He maintains that this requires a different set of skills, skills that are more personal, more psychological, and more demanding to diffuse highly emotional situations. His personal account of his work dramatically illustrates what it is like to be a corrections ombudsman in the pursuit of truth and justice and the protection of personal worth and dignity.

Whereas prisoners are involuntary inmates, university students are volunteers. Nevertheless, as Donald C. Rowat points out in Chapter 12, "The Campus Ombudsman in North America," they, too, find themselves confronted with an authoritarian bureaucracy that mistreats them and ignores their just complaints. Rowat makes a strong case for a campus ombudsman and describes progress made in that direction in Canada. The campus ombudsman is widely deployed in state universities in the United States, particularly in the mega-versities of Illinois, Ohio, New York, Michigan, Texas, and Wisconsin. The largest of the state universities, in California, have adopted the office on most campuses for over a decade. Geoffrey Wallace, the campus ombudsman at the University of California, Santa Barbara, describes his office and how he sees his role, not so much as a factfinder or administrative critic, but as a student counselor.

University students are not the only members of society who complain about education bureaucracies. School children and their parents are often angered by public school administrators, as are teachers and school employees. Perhaps school boards are not as enlightened as university governors, but the fact remains that there are very few school ombudsman offices. One such office can be found in Wichita, Kansas. The school ombudsman, James Wineinger, describes the functions of his office and how it serves the local school district in Chapter 13, "An American School Ombudsman." Again, in an oft-repeated tale, he recounts the special needs of his clientele and the peculiar nature of their grievances which are not satisfactorily considered by any other channel. The surprise is that so few other school boards have been willing to consider a school ombudsman of their own to deal with the kinds of complaints school children and their parents, teachers, and employees have. The risks seem low, but the potential rewards appear to be high, not only in terms of reducing friction in the administrative system, but also in client satisfaction and as a sensory device to pick up potentially emotional issues that could suddenly explode in the face of school administrators.

Taken together, these essays present an impressive, if not compelling, case for the institution of ombudsman in the modern administrative state. But then their authors, with only one exception, are ombudsmen or strong advocates of the institution. Interestingly, their commitment to truth and justice in society, so often illustrated by their own words, does not permit them to omit the obverse side of the institution, its shortcomings and failures, its imperfections and inadequacies, and the limitations, legal, operational, and personal, of ombudsman offices. Theirs is a cautionary message—proceed carefully, look before you leap, plan properly, avoid exaggerated expectations, and do not expect instant miracles. The ombudsman within its limitations can do much good, but it is only a minor weapon in a vast arsenal that modern society can command to smooth relations between state and citizen, to enforce basic human rights, to improve public administration, and to educate the public about the workings of the public bureaucracy.

INTERNATIONAL HANDBOOK OF THE OMBUDSMAN

Evolution and Present Function

CHAPTER 1

THE INSTITUTION OF OMBUDSMAN

GERALD E. CAIDEN, UNIVERSITY OF SOUTHERN CALIFORNIA, NIALL MACDERMOT, INTERNATIONAL COMMISSION OF JURISTS, AND AKE SANDLER, CALIFORNIA STATE UNIVERSITY, LOS ANGELES

A NEW AND, to many people, a foreign word is being heard more frequently. It is "ombudsman," a term that refers to a special office or officer to whom people can go with their grievances about the way their business with large anonymous bureaucracies has been handled. The ombudsman records public complaints, investigates them, and reports the findings to the complainants and the organizations investigated. Should any wrong be discovered, it is expected that it will be put right, if not to the complete satisfaction of the aggrieved party, then at least better than it would have been without the ombudsman's intervention. For the public, the ombudsman is a welcome device for assuring that justice is done and that bureaucracies treat their clients fairly, promptly, and respectfully. For bureaucracies, it is an additional fail-safe check on their operations to ensure that any mistakes that have not been spotted are eventually caught and rectified, and it also serves to identify unintentional impacts of otherwise well-intentioned procedure. Where wrong has been done, it points to maladministration that needs to be corrected, and where wrong has not been done, it reinforces current operating practices. Thus, it provides additional protection for both public and bureaucracy, something that seems required as transactions between them multiply.

The ombudsman is not a term coined by modern technological society for some new invention like radar, microwave, and transistor. It is an old Swedish word that has been used for centuries to describe a person who represents or protects the interests of another. It gained a more specific meaning in 1809 when the Swedish government appointed a public official to investigate public complaints against public administration. As the word became more frequently used, especially outside Sweden, it was misused and corrupted, and it is now often used loosely for any public complaints officer, that is, for any officer or office of any organization that receives public complaints about the way it conducts its business or how others conduct their business. Thus, radio stations, newspapers, churches, businesses, and other nongovernmental bodies have their own ombudsman offices, and it is difficult for people to distinguish the more specific use of the term to refer to government ombudsman offices established to receive complaints from the public about the administrative actions of public authorities. In this book, the institution of ombudsman refers only to these official, independently constituted ombudsmen and not to their private imitators or to administrators with an intrinsic interest in the operation against which complaints are lodged.

The establishment of these ombudsman offices opens a new chapter in the relations between the governors and the governed, between state and citizen, between public servants and the public. Throughout history, rulers have imposed duties and obligations on the ruled. Despite theories of the social contract and representative, responsible government, rarely have the ruled been able to extract implied duties and obligations from the rulers. On the whole, the machinery of government has been designed to protect the rights of the rulers against the ruled, and not vice versa. There have been some successful attempts to strengthen the right of the ruled against the rulers through constitutionalism, the rule of law, judicial control, administrative law, communal self-government, participative management, and executive self-regulation, but how far rulers can be limited in their claims against the ruled has never been adequately tested, let alone measured, in peacetime. The existence of an independent ombudsman office denotes a clear indication by the rulers that they recognize obligations and duties to the ruled, that the ruled should be treated justly, promptly, and courteously, that they should be granted their due according to the law, and that public business should be conducted honestly and efficaciously.

The most important implication of the ombudsman institution is that, if the ruled feel aggrieved at the way their business has been handled (and aggrieved here refers to complaints that have not been settled by officialdom, unanswered questions, and unheard cries for help), they have the legal right to complain and someone to whom to complain who will in turn have legal rights to investigate their complaints on their behalf without let or hindrance by the rulers, mediate the dispute to resolution, and make the findings public. The ruled are placed on a more equal footing with the rulers and their agents. The ruled do not have to tolerate unjust treatment they receive. If they are offended, they have recourse. They can appeal, protest, or complain to the ombudsman if all else fails. The ombudsman office will use its powers, resources, links, and experience to challenge the actions of the rulers' agents. The ruled have a champion at court, their own defender and protector who can take on public officials and through his good offices attain better satisfaction, even getting public officials to admit mistakes and reverse decisions. The ombudsman reminds them that they are public servants as well as public officials and that they have rights and duties not only to the state but also to the public generally, to their clients as members of that public, and to the individual as such. In Bernard Frank's words, "the right to complain, the right to be heard, the right to have corrective action taken if one has suffered harm from government are human rights."[1]

The existence of the ombudsman formally acknowledges that government though good is fallible and could be improved. Mistakes occur not out of any malice by public officials towards the public but simply in the nature of things. Somebody mixes up some documents and sends the wrong ones to the wrong people. Somebody else misreads a chart or misinterprets figures. Another person, in an irritable mood, speaks out of turn. Sooner or later it happens to everybody. We are the perpetrators of malpractice one day, its victims the next. In the countless daily transactions between the government and the governed, some things slip through unobserved and mistakes

are not spotted in time, or not much can be done about them once they have occurred. A certain portion, quite often surprisingly small, gives just cause for complaint. The ombudsman admits to the imperfectibility of public administration and provides a quick, simple, cheap avenue of redress. It gets to the root of any difficulty by cutting through red tape that may block the citizen's access, circumventing bureaucratic defense mechanisms and puncturing official conceit (and deceit). It can mediate between public servants and aggrieved members of the public. It can propose remedies of its own. And if all else fails, it can publicize malpractice and instances of injustice, misrepresentation, arrogance, illegality, and other similar conduct unbecoming public servants, thereby embarrassing the perpetrators and drawing public attention to correctable wrongs and preventable mistakes.

Not everybody needs this latest innovation in government. Several classes of people can obtain redress of their grievances directly. Many more can use alternative avenues of redress, or they can employ other intermediaries, such as lawyers, politicians, and distinguished public figures, to intercede for them. But within every society, there are the disadvantaged, the underprivileged, the poor, the elderly, the weak, and the frightened who do not understand the ways of bureaucracy, who are terrified at dealing with public officials, and who, no matter what the provocation, are reluctant to complain about the treatment they receive from public authorities. Sometimes they do not know they have been victimized. They need an expert who can articulate their grievances, frame their complaints, and represent them. They need someone who can explain the workings of bureaucracy to them in language they understand, who can interpret official documents, who can obtain advice or knows where advice can be obtained, and who can give them reasons for decisions. In short, they need someone who can personalize bureaucracy and who can humanize public business transactions. The ombudsman is such a person. The office does immeasurable public service by explaining government actions to bewildered citizens and by lowering the barriers between the governors and the governed.

JUSTIFICATION FOR THE OMBUDSMAN

These attractive functions of the institution of ombudsman would lead us to expect that any government serious about upholding the dignity of man and reducing the distance between the rulers and the ruled would support the establishment of an ombudsman office. Yet, until as late as 1950 there were only two such offices in existence, the original Swedish *Riksdagens Justicieombudsman* and a Finnish equivalent that had been established when Finland gained its independence after World War I. Only in the last thirty years has the idea caught on, and only in the last twenty years has substantive action been taken outside Scandinavia. In 1981, there were over ninety ombudsman offices operating in over thirty countries, and few offices had been formally abandoned. This sudden surge of ombudsmania can be attributed in part to the proselytizing activities of ombudsmen and their advocates, but more important was the greater receptivity to the idea by governments who recognized the ability of ombudsmen to advance the cause of human rights, to control the public bureaucracy, to remedy individual grievances against public maladministration, and to draw public attention to administrative maladies in public organizations.

An Instrument of Human Rights

Ubi ius ibi remedium. There can be no right without remedies. Declarations and charters of human rights, as well as several international conventions and covenants on human rights, which have been enunciated since World War II, proclaim many different rights including the right to have all these rights enforced. This universal recognition of basic human rights is something new in world history. It marks a significant shift in human values and provides a measure by which reality can be judged. It changes in a fundamental way the relations between government and the governed. While it places limitations on public power, it raises individual expectations of how public power can or cannot be used and to what purposes. It promises protection for individual rights (against slavery, torture, banishment, penal servitude, collective punishment, genocide, and other government intrusions on privacy) and requires governments to assume the initiative in enforcing and extending individual rights (to express oneself freely, to assemble, to participate in public affairs, to work, to own property, and so on), but it creates no machinery for enforcement, and the machinery that has been created in its wake has not been very effective. It is left largely to national governments and institutions to provide the machinery for implementing or making effective human rights.[2]

The courts, supplemented by administrative tribunals, are usually relied upon as the principal method of enforcing legal rights. For many of the basic human rights and fundamental freedoms, judicial processes can be an effective means of enforcement, particularly in the field of civil and political rights such as freedom of speech, freedom of the press, freedom of assembly and association, security of the person, freedom from arbitrary arrest and the right to a fair trial, at least in countries where the legal restrictions on these rights do not assume greater importance than the rights themselves. But there are many other rights, particularly economic, social, and cultural rights where the ordinary machinery of law, and even administrative law, is not at all well suited to remedying many of the problems confronting individuals. It is too costly, too slow, too inaccessible, too restrictive, too disputive, too formal, too legal, too conservative, and in many instances, it has been deliberately excluded and no alternative is realistic or feasible in the circumstances.

Yet, in all their dealings with government, individuals should be assured that they have the right of appeal to an impartial arbiter. They must feel confident that public power is executed fairly and equitably in accordance with natural justice and the rule of law. If their rights are affected as invariably they must be, they should be "entitled to a fair hearing before a disinterested adjudicator with advice of the case to be made and a fair opportunity in which to meet it. It is this presence of relative certainty as to the scope of the state's authority and the availability of redress in the event of arbitrariness which distinguishes a democracy most significantly and dramatically from a totalitarian regime."[3] The ombudsman not only provides procedural justice but also substantive justice, a shared sense of injustice when any human being suffers needlessly, and a determination that no one should be denied a claim to just treatment by nature of race, religion, sex, or any other discriminatory factor.[4] Its very presence within the machinery of government acts as a deterrent against the misuse and abuse of public power to deny basic human rights by upholding the dignity of the individual and giving people the opportunity to question the legality and fairness of public laws and directions and to challenge official behavior and actions. In Walter Gellhorn's words, ". . . no society worthy of respect can gaily march toward its defined goals (whatever they may be) without caring whom it tramples underfoot en route. That is why country after country has sought protections against oppressive, mistaken, or careless exercises of public authority."[5]

A Unique Mechanism of Democratic Control over Bureaucracy

The ombudsman has certain advantages over other mechanisms of control over the public bureaucracy. It is obligated to investigate the public complaints falling within its jurisdiction, regardless of subject matter and level of bureaucracy implicated. It has sufficient access to the bureaucracy to conduct adequate investigations. It has power to publicize its findings, however embarrassing they might be to the public bureaucracy, the government, and the "establishment."[6] A meaningful ombudsman office takes seriously its role of "citizens' defender, grievance man, or public watchdog"[7] against public bungling and abuses of power, particularly arbitrariness that allows "a citizen's right to be crushed by the vast juggernaut of the government's administrative machinery."[8] Should it fail to meet its public responsibilities and legal obligations, it will decline, like so many other control mechanisms, into just another pacifying defense mechanism, another public relations gimmick that insults the intelligence, another inconsequential charade and self-serving office that should best be avoided.

All that is needed to activate the ombudsman is a public complaint. Any individual aggrieved by a public agency has the right to contact the ombudsman office and lodge a complaint. The rest is up to the ombudsman office, which cannot refuse to investigate if the complaint is legitimate and within the ombudsman's jurisdiction. The use of the ombudsman is very much in the public's hands—the more people avail themselves of its services, the more likely it will influence the public bureaucracy; the less people use it, the more likely it can be ignored, although its powers of initiative and its ultimate reserve power to expose wrongdoing must also be reckoned with. When people do avail themselves, there is no telling what may arise.

Take, for instance, some samples from a country where the ombudsman is widely used. In his ninth annual report (for the year 1979–80), the Israeli ombudsman, Dr. I. E. Nebenzahl, referred to the following complaints.

A businessman living in France who often visited Israel was arrested on arrival on suspicion of having circulated counterfeit money, and suffered a heart attack as a result. On a previous visit he had deposited money in a bank but two bills had later been found counterfeit. He had left the country before he could be questioned although the police said he had passed the bills in all innocence. The police had then obtained a detention order against him, declaring that there was suspicion that he passed counterfeit money. Instead of being arrested, he should have merely been summoned to report to the police in order to testify. The police had failed to tell the magistrate the real reason for requesting the detention order. The ombudsman recommended disciplinary action against those responsible.

The parents of an elementary school pupil hurt while playing in the school yard had sued the local authority for damages but while the case was pending the child was transferred to another school in another district. There he had been called out of class and questioned by a stranger about the accident. His parents' lawyer complained to the Ministry of Education that the principal had acted improperly as a minor could only be interviewed with the consent of and in the presence of his parents. The Ministry of Education had found nothing wrong with the principal's action. Apparently the child had been questioned but only

asked his name and how he felt. The ombudsman found the principal's action wrong because while a pupil was within a school, the staff should protect his well-being, health and privacy. They had no business to enable strangers, even representatives of the Ministry of Education, to contact a pupil without the parents' knowledge except for pedagogical matters.

A civilian driving instructor employed by the Army complained against his suspension pending a police investigation of certain allegations against him. After the district attorney decided not to submit a charge against him for lack of evidence, he was reinstated. The ombudsman found that it was not Army practice to allow an employee to answer allegations before suspension. Further the Army made do with only a summary of the police investigation and the personnel chief did not obtain legal advice even when he planned to suspend an employee who had yet to be charged. The ombudsman recommended that these practices be changed and the Army promised to do so.

What would have happened if none of the complainants had approached the ombudsman? Probably nothing, even though they had used some of the alternative avenues of redress available to them. The bureaucracy would have continued to deny malpractice.

In these cases, the ombudsman had been able quickly and at no cost to the complainants to investigate incidents and to compel the bureaucracy to respond. Dr. Nebenzahl had obtained all relevant documents and had questioned the participants closely, in these cases, the police, the school staff, and the personnel chief of the army. If necessary, he would have gone over their heads if they had not cooperated with him. He would not have stopped until he had exhausted every legal avenue to obtain the facts, and in the last resort, he may well have drawn on his reserve powers to initiate investigation of his own and to have prosecuted wrongdoing. The Israeli ombudsman was demonstrating that the right of individuals to petition for the redress of wrongs committed against them by public authorities is based upon the principle of open government, that is, that individuals have the right to know about official actions that may concern them. As Itzhak Galnoor declares, liberal theory regards secrecy as an evil necessity imposed upon free citizens as a result of imperfection in human affairs.[9] Only regrettable, temporary measures require tampering with the free flow of information. There are few reasons for government to conceal in the public interest. Public information is regarded as a tangible property. Disclosure is the general rule and not the exception. Whatever a government does is public unless legally restricted. Whenever the right to possess information or to gain access is disputed, the burden of proof is shifted from the citizen to the government, from the need to know practice to the need to conceal justification. It must always be remembered that rights can be enjoyed only by those who are aware of them and are sufficiently well informed to ensure their possession.

Although the ombudsman office is bound by legal restrictions in the disclosure of information, it can penetrate undue secrecy, it can provide information previously denied or deliberately secreted, particularly in the ambiguous zones that surround the exercise of administrative discretion, and it can disrupt "the unwritten rules of government secrecy" as far as individuals are concerned. It is no accident that the establishment of an ombudsman and liberalizing public access to official information have usually gone together; they are part of the democratization of government. In Donald Rowat's words,

The principle of open access to administrative information is essential to the full development of democracy. . . . The logic of democracy demands that the long-term trend be in the direction of the principle of publicity . . . for when essential information is withheld from the public, there is a grave danger that the discussion of public policy will be shallow and that the people will be unable to control their government.[10]

After all, public business is the public's business. People should not only be informed but they should also be able to investigate how the government and its administration are handling their affairs and to criticize when discontented.

The ombudsman office is a unique mechanism of democratic control over bureaucracy in a literal sense as well. Its operations embody the concept of free choice and other democratic values. The public can take their grievances elsewhere; they are not compelled to go to the ombudsman. They do so presumably because they expect it to satisfy them. The ombudsman office can choose to align itself with the administration or the public; it is not compelled to take either side. It is independent of both, acting as an impartial intermediary even if both administration and public misunderstand its position. The administration can choose to aid or to stall investigations. With some exceptions and reservations, it usually cooperates. Public agencies are saved public embarrassment and can correct their own mistakes. Finally, the government and the administration can accept or reject the ombudsman's recommendations. A high proportion is accepted and quickly implemented because the proposals are based on concrete instances of malpractice, they emanate from a friendly critic experienced in the ways of public administration, and they have probably been worked out with the guilty party. If not, the ombudsman and administration negotiate further, and if that fails, they agree to disagree. All the participants try to reach unanimous agreement or at least acceptable compromise without resort to threats and power plays. They learn to appreciate each other's point of view and to confess error without losing self-respect.

The ombudsman concept is truly part of what William Riker calls the "democratic vision."[11]

A Formal Avenue for the Redress of Grievances Against Administrative Wrongdoing

The past century has seen an enormous growth in the responsibilities of the state, covering almost all aspects of economic and social as well as political and cultural life. This has necessitated the devolution of power to a growing army of public servants in many matters that intimately affect the daily lives of people. Their entitlement to land, housing, employment, health and welfare benefits, and other social services, their obligations to pay taxes and social contributions, and many other important matters are in the hands of the public bureaucracy. On occasion unreasonable decisions are made, causing a sense of injustice. These decisions may be the result of bias, improper influence, graft, abuse of power, or merely incompetence, neglect, idleness, or other causes amounting to maladministration.

As previously mentioned, the law provides many safeguards to give protection against improper administrative action. Sometimes there is a right of appeal to a higher administrative authority or to an administrative tribunal or to the ordinary courts. At times these procedures are simple, speedy, and effective but as often as not, they are protracted and costly. They will often involve following confusing and intimidating procedures, and sometimes they are too complex for individuals to assert their rights. On other occasions, the complainants feel that decisions against them are unjust, but they lack the means to probe further to discover whether they have been victims of arbitrary or improper decisions. When faced by a professional and monolithic bureaucracy, they become inhibited and believe themselves to be in a weak position because by contrast they are inexperienced, ignorant, or poor. When they seek help from the proper authorities, it comes as a surprise that the authorities are unwilling to deal with their grievances as they are legally precluded from questioning administrative decisions and practices. It is no comfort to them to be advised that nothing can be done, or that the matter is not worthwhile (to whom?) to pursue, or that they should swallow the injustice, or that unfortunately petty tyrants can be found everywhere and in much contemporary government no formal procedures are provided for objecting to official decisions or deciding on objections, particularly complaints against discretionary decisions and complaints against acts of maladministration. They need the help of someone who has greater power than a lawyer or politician to investigate their complaints, if they seem to merit investigation, and to try to negotiate a remedy for them. The ombudsman is such a help, if not so much in respect to objections to discretionary decisions, then certainly in regard to complaints against official wrongdoing. If the ombudsman cannot help or fails to satisfy complainants, the buildup of sullen resentment of authority is detrimental to progress and development in the society. Indeed, Barrington Moore goes so far as to suggest that cultural achievement should be measured by the degree to which protection is offered against arbitrary authority.[12]

In explaining why the New South Wales Law Reform Commission suggested the establishment of an ombudsman office, D. Gressier stated that to such elementary self-evident propositions as

(1)   The powers of public authorities to affect private rights have increased in recent decades and are increasing.

(2)   Problems of administrative justice are causing concern in most parts of the world. . . .

(3)   When objectives of government policy have been determined, these objectives must be attained without unreasonable delay and account must be taken of the needs and duties of public authorities to run the day-to-day administration of the state.

(4)   Any official action of a public authority should have reasonable regard to the balance between the public interest which it promotes and the private interest which it disturbs and it should be fair.

should be added

Any person adversely affected by an official action of a public authority should have the right to question that action simply, cheaply and quickly; and procedures should be available to him which are fair, impartial and open.

The commission had tried to find out who and how many had been adversely affected by official actions and by whom and in what way and to what extent they had been so affected. It would not accept that every official action had been free from error and had not been thought to have gone wrong. Even the best human institutions sometimes went wrong. It found that for every one separate power exercisable by public authorities for which there was statutory right of appeal, there were no less than twenty that were not. It decided to recommend the extension of the statutory right of appeal against official actions because:

(1)   Existing means for correcting wrong official actions are inadequate.

(2)   . . . Appeals have been favored by most legal systems and are part of our legal inheritance.

(3)   Rights of appeal are given in civil and criminal proceedings on the plain and simple ground that for the purpose of correcting errors and miscarriages in the administration of justice the practice is essential. But errors and miscarriages cannot be confined to civil and criminal proceedings; they occur inevitably in the administrative process where the claims of justice are no less demanding.

(4)   We could see no reason why a right of appeal should not be as effective in the field of administrative law as it is in other fields of law, or that giving a right of appeal would be more disturbing to the administrative process than it is to the judicial process, or that disturbance of the administrative process would cause greater public harm than the disturbance now caused to the judicial process by the judicial appeal system.

Where redress was already available, "our conclusion was that neither jointly or severally do those avenues of redress provide adequate protection for the citizen; they fail because they are not available as of right or because they are too expensive or because they are not seen to be impartial or because their field of action is too restricted."

The ombudsman is an appropriate official to deal with cases that are unfit for the more elaborate methods and legal sanctions of the courts or existing appellate bodies. He is a proper recipient of complaints about, among other things, rudeness, delay, partiality, harshness and failure to give reasons. It is open for him to investigate in cases where there is other means of redress. He might do so, for example, where the complainant does not want to incur the trouble and expense of a formal appeal, but wishes to be satisfied that the public authority has given a fair consideration of his representations and has not misconceived the relevant law. In short, an ombudsman has a useful part to play in dispelling imaginary grievances, obtaining redress where a grievance has substance, and pointing out possible improvements in relevant laws and procedures.[13]

Complainants in New South Wales have been gratified that the government supported the commission. They now have an effective avenue for the redress of their grievances against administrative wrongdoing, as do all fellow Australians and people in thirty or so other countries.

An Instrument for Tackling Bureaupathologies

The ceaseless flow of public complaints and the constant round of investigations give the ombudsman a unique opportunity to know at firsthand every possible manifestation of maladministration and to discern problems of bureaupathology. In bringing administrative malpractice or just sheer poor public relations to the attention of public authorities, the ombudsman promotes administrative reform. Its very presence in the machinery of government cautions public servants to behave properly lest they personally and their agencies find themselves the subject of complaint and all that entails—confrontation, investigation, negotiation, unwelcome publicity and possibly government retaliation, professional disgrace, and official disciplinary action. Furthermore, the ombudsman is not a passive observer of public administration. Ombudsmen and their staff are well qualified to comment on administrative practice and to suggest improvements. In France, the *mediateur,* a French variation of the ombudsman, has become a major instrument in the government's administrative reform program.

These functions of the ombudsman have led Larry Hill to conclude that the ombudsman is an ideal type of bureaucratic auditor.[14] Its predominant citizen-orientation is contrapuntal to the other ideal type, the financial auditor's predominant system-orientation. Both share the following characteristics:

1. They hold bureaucratic units accountable and responsible to political instrumentalities and ultimately to the public.

2. They investigate bureaucratic improprieties, such as illegality, unfairness, and incompetence.

3. They are reviewing agencies or appeals agents whose function is to investigate concluded actions.

4. They continuously monitor the bureaucracy and are highly accessible.

5. They use activist methods of investigation.

6. They have unfettered access to information.

7. They are high-status offices.

8. They are autonomous organizations.

9. They audit bureaucracies.

10. They themselves are bureaucracies, that is, they have legal status, their authority is depersonalized, and they operate hierarchically.

11. They are external to and operationally independent of the bureaucratic units subject to their investigations.

12. They are operationally independent of political authorities.

13. They issue detailed reports of their investigations.

14. They cannot reverse administrative decisions; they can only persuade investigated agents to accept their findings and recommendations.

The ideal of the ideal types would be a bureaucratic auditor who combined the qualities of both financial auditor and ombudsman. Such an officer exists in the state comptroller of Israel who also plays the role of general commissioner for the public interest. As has been illustrated, he is probably more outspoken in his criticism of bureaucracy than other national ombudsmen and seems to understand more clearly than others what bureaucratic auditing entails, although he is not as forward in making remedial proposals as the French *mediateur.* For Hill, "the bureaucratic auditor fights fire with fire." In helping citizens resolve their grievances, the ombudsmen fight against mechanized petrification (Max Weber's reference to the ultimate bureaucratic culture initiated by "technicians without souls, sensualists without hearts"[15]) and the "parceling out of the soul" (the exclusive rule of bureaucratic life ideals).[16] Most people would be happy if the ombudsman institution just held creeping bureaucratism in check.

THE EVOLUTION OF THE OMBUDSMAN

Complaint-handling mechanisms are not new to government. Ancient Egyptian kings had complaint officers in their court. Moses appointed grievance officers to deal with complaining Hebrews. During the Roman Republic, two censors both scrutinized administrative actions and received complaints alleging maladministration.[17] The Control Yuan in the Han Dynasty in China undertook similar activities. In the Middle Ages, intermediaries between rulers and ruled, administrators and administered were common in government, church, and business organizations. Absolute monarchs of the emerging nation-states appointed special representatives or agents or officials to see that public officials obeyed the law, carried out their instructions, and generally behaved themselves.

The Swedish monarchs like other monarchs, had difficulty holding on to their kingdom and their authority. Every so often they were forced to compromise with the nobility, church, and burghers who sought to impose limitations and constraints on their rule through the representative assembly (Riksdag). This struggle between king and parliament dominated Swedish history for over four hundred years. In 1709, Charles XII was forced to flee to Turkey after Russia defeated Sweden. There he came to know the Turkish office of chief justice which ensured that officials followed Islamic Law.[18] He thereupon ordered the creation of an office to be headed by his highest ombudsman to ensure that Swedish officials followed the law and fulfilled their obligations. The word "ombudsman" was derived from medieval Germanic tribes which applied the term to a third party whose task was to collect fines from remorseful culprit families to give to the aggrieved families of victims. In time, it came to refer to any kind of agent.[19] Charles XII wanted his agent to see that public officials acted legally. His death in 1718 marked the decline of Sweden as a great power and the end of absolutism. A new Constitution in 1719 brought parliamentary government and ushered in the Enlightenment (*Frihetstid*) in which democratic values were nurtured. The Riksdag forced the office of the chancellor of justice in 1739 to report to it and in 1766 came to appoint the chancellor until 1772 when a coup d'etat restored absolute monarchy and brought this "Era of Liberty" to an end. However, Sweden's defeat in 1809, again at Russian hands, was followed by a coup d'etat, this time by the revolutionary opposition. Gustav IV was forced to abdicate and a new Constitution restored parliamentary rule.

The 1809 Swedish Constitution incorporated a justice ombudsman, a position to be filled by a person of known legal ability and outstanding integrity elected by the Riksdag. The justice ombudsman was to supervise public administration as part of the legislative branch of government (not the executive branch like the chancellor of justice) and was to report to parliament rather than to the monarch. Like the procurator general established in 1722 by Peter the Great, the justice ombudsman would ensure the legality of official actions and would protect the public from excessive official zeal by investigating public complaints of official wrongdoing. He would scrutinize official actions and, if necessary, prosecute officials who "committed an unlawful act or neglected to perform official duties properly." In time, the justice ombudsman evolved more as a citizen-defender, concerned with resolving public complaints against the public bureaucracy, and less as a prosecutor of official wrongdoing. Following the outbreak of World War I, it was decided to separate the function of supervising military authorities. In 1915, an independent military ombudsman (*militieombudsman*) was established and continued to operate until 1968, when the two offices were amalgamated.

In the meantime, Finland, which had been under Swedish rule for centuries until 1809 when it came under Russian rule, had become an independent sovereign state after World War I. In the new 1919 Constitution, it retained the powerful and fairly autonomous executive office of the attorney general (renamed chancellor of justice) as supreme prosecutor to ensure that the government took no unconstitutional or illegal action, but also provided for a legislative counterpart in the ombudsman (which has historically been overshadowed by the chancellor). In 1933, the ombudsman was given exclusive responsibility for investigating military and prison complaints to lighten the chancellor's workload, and in time assumed more of the inspection function. Although the two offices may overlap in function, parliament has been jealous to preserve the ombudsman as its distinctive institution independent of the executive, the judiciary, and the executive administrative law system to investigate complaints of official arbitrariness and wrongdoing. Scandinavia did not further adopt the ombudsman institution on the Swedish-Finnish model until after World War II when Norway introduced a military ombudsman in 1952 and Denmark a general ombudsman in 1953. The Danish ombudsman, appointed in 1955, differed from the Swedish and Finnish ombudsmen in that he was precluded from investigating complaints against the judiciary, his investigations were not made public until after completion, his powers of jurisdiction and of initiating inspections were limited, and he had no power of prosecution.

The first adoption of the ombudsman institution outside Scandinavia came in the Federal Republic of Germany in 1957 with the controversial establishment of a military ombudsman, following the creation of the new German Army, "to maintain parliamentary control over the military and to ensure that the army would develop according to the new democratic spirit of the citizen in uniform."[20] It had been first proposed by a socialist who had spent time as a refugee in Sweden, and it was modeled on the Swedish military ombudsman. The parliamentary commissioner for military affairs did not begin operations until 1959. Its development was affected by controversies surrounding the resignation of the first incumbent in 1961 and the actions of his successor in publicly criticizing the military establishment.

Meanwhile, the Danish ombudsman, Professor Stephan Hurwitz, had been giving the institution publicity of a more positive kind. Indeed, throughout the 1960s, the institution became better known thanks to the efforts of the United Nations Division of Human Rights at seminars in Ceylon (1959), Buenos Aires (1959), Stockholm (1962), Jamaica (1967), and Cyprus (1968), all of which supported the ombudsman idea,[21] and of the International Commission of Jurists at conferences held at Bangkok (1965), Colombo (1966), and Strasbourg (1968).[22] The conferences on World Peace Through Law in Geneva (1967), Bangkok (1969), and Belgrade (1971) enthusiastically supported the ombudsman, and the 1971 conference called "upon states to make every effort towards the establishment of effective national machinery for the protection of human rights including, where appropriate, the institution of the ombudsman or similar institutions." In the United States, the American Bar Association (ABA) created an ombudsman committee in 1967, and the ABA favored the adoption of the ombudsman at the state and local level and recommended experimentation at the federal level in resolutions passed in 1969 and elaborated further in 1971.

Consequently, the 1960s opened a new chapter for the

ombudsman. In 1962, Norway added a general ombudsman, but, more important, New Zealand became the first British Commonwealth country to adopt the institution. The New Zealand office was modeled on the Danish ombudsman with similar limitations except that, while in Denmark the ombudsman investigated complaints of maladministration, that is, with the fairness of procedures, the New Zealand ombudsman could investigate complaints of wrongdoing, which also included the fairness of administrative decisions, or so the New Zealand parliamentary commissioner for administration, Sir Guy Powles, interpreted his jurisdiction.[23] The successful introduction of the ombudsman outside Western Europe intensified pressure for its adoption around the world, and again much credit for its extension goes to the missionary work of Professor Hurwitz, Sir Guy Powles, and Judge Alfred Bexelius of Sweden and the pioneering academic work of Walter Gellhorn, Stanley Anderson, and Donald Rowat.[24] Within eight years, the ombudsman had spread

to Guyana, Tanzania (1966), Canada, Israel, and the United Kingdom (1967), the United States (1969), and Mauritius (1970).

In 1971, the European Parliamentary Conference on Human Rights held in Vienna recommended that it was necessary to "consider favorably the establishment of an organ authorized to receive and examine individual complaints with the right of access to the files of government departments, functioning on the lines of the Ombudsman as known in the Scandinavian countries."[25] Member states were encouraged to establish ombudsman offices. The following year, the Council of Europe supported the creation of an office of ombudsman commissioner of human rights and in 1975, following a conference in Paris in 1974, organized by its Legal Affairs Committee, recommended that governments that had not yet done so consider "appointing at national, regional and/or local level persons discharging functions similar to those of existing Ombudsmen and Parliamentary Commis-

Table 1.1
Legislative Ombudsmen According to Date of First Incumbent

YEAR	AREA	YEAR	AREA	YEAR	AREA
1810	Sweden (national) }1968	1972	Fiji (national)	1975	Alaska (state)
1915	Sweden (military)		Iowa (state)		Kansas (prisons)
1920	Finland (national)		Israel (military)		Michigan (prisons)
1952	Norway (military)		Maharashtra (state)		Oregon (prisons)
1955	Denmark (national)		Minnesota (prisons)		Ontario (province)
1959	Western Germany (military)		South Australia (state)		New South Wales (state)
1962	New Zealand (national)		Western Australia (state)		Berkeley (urban)
1963	Norway (national)		Wichita (urban)		Newfoundland (province)
1966	Guyana (national)	1973	Bihar (state)		Flint (urban)
	Tanzania (national)		Canada (prisons)		Papua New Guinea (national)
1967	Alberta (province)		Connecticut (prisons)	1976	Liguria (region)
	Jerusalem (urban)		France (national)		Portugal (national)
	New Brunswick (province)		Jackson County (urban)		Australia (national)
	United Kingdom (national)		Rajasthan (state)		Austria (national)
1969	Hawaii (state)		Saskatchewan (province)		Trinidad and Tobago
	Northern Ireland (province)		United Kingdom (health)		(national)
	Quebec (province)		Victoria (state)		Uttar Pradesh (state)
1970	Canada (languages)		Zambia (national)	1978	Jamaica (national)
	Jamestown, N.Y. (urban)	1974	Anchorage (urban)		Puerto Rico (territorial)
	Manitoba (province)		Atlanta (urban)—1976		Tasmania (state)
	Mauritius (national)		Detroit (urban)	1979	British Columbia (province)
1971	Dayton (urban)		Haifa (urban)		Guam (territorial)
	Israel (national)		Lexington (urban)		New York City (urban)
	Nebraska (state)		New Jersey (state)		The Philippines (national)
	Nova Scotia (province)		Queensland (state)	1980	Florida (state)
	Seattle (urban)		Rhineland-Palatinate (state)		Ghana (national)
	Zurich (urban)		Tuscany (region)	1981	Ireland (national)
			United Kingdom (regional)		The Netherlands (national)
					Spain (national)

sioners.'' Meanwhile, in 1973 the International Bar Association Council had approved an ombudsman committee headed by Bernard Frank, which in turn created an advisory board and a member organization liaison. This committee and the Ombudsman Committee of the Section of Administrative Law, ABA, jointly issued an annual development report recording nonjudicial complaint-handling mechanisms, with stress on the ombudsman institution. At its 1974 Vancouver conference, the International Bar Association passed a resolution similar to that of the Council of Europe. This worldwide endorsement has led to the rapid spread of the ombudsman, so much so that it is difficult to record every instance. (See Table 1.1.)

The difficulty arises largely from disagreements over what exactly constitutes an ombudsman office. The 1971 American Bar Association resolution recommended

that each statute or ordinance establishing an ombudsman should contain the following twelve essentials: (1) authority of the ombudsman to criticize all agencies, officials, and public employees except courts and their personnel, legislative bodies and their personnel, and the chief executive and his personal staff; (2) independence of the ombudsman from control by any other officer, except for his responsibility to the legislative body; (3) appointment by the legislative body or appointment by the executive with confirmation by a designated proportion of the legislative body, preferably more than a majority, such as two-thirds; (4) independence of the ombudsman through a long-term, not less than five years, with freedom from removal except for cause, determined by more than a majority of the legislative body, such as two-thirds; (5) a high salary equivalent to that of a designated top officer; (6) freedom of the ombudsman to employ his own assistant and to delegate to them, without restraints of civil service and classification acts; (7) freedom of the ombudsman to investigate any act or failure to act by any agency, official, or public employee; (8) access of the ombudsman to all public records he finds relevant to an investigation; (9) authority to inquire into fairness, correctness of findings, motivation, adequacy of reasons, efficiency, and procedural propriety of any action or inaction by any agency, official, or public employee; (10) discretionary power to determine what complaints to investigate and to determine what criticisms to make or to publicize; (11) opportunity for any agency, official, or public employee criticized by the ombudsman to have advance notice of the criticism and to publish with the criticism an answering statement; (12) immunity of the ombudsman and his staff from civil liability on account of official action.

The 1974 International Bar Association resolution read in part:

That the office of ombudsman so established should be in accordance with the following definition: An office provided for by the constitution or by action of the legislature or parliament and headed by an independent, high-level public official who is responsible to the legislature or parliament, who receives complaints from aggrieved persons against government agencies, officials, and employees or who acts on his own motion, and who has the power to investigate, recommend corrective action, and issue reports.

The annual survey issued by its Ombudsman Committee (assumed in 1980 by the International Ombudsman Institute) tried to stick to institutions that incorporated the characteristics spelled out in these two resolutions but confessed that it was no easy task and the results might be questioned. The list usually distinguished between legislative ombudsman and executive ombudsman offices and between them and other government complaint-handling mechanisms, such as legislative petitions committees, correctional investigators and people's councils, chancellors of justice, police complaints boards, vigilance commissions, administrative counselors, public complaints bureaus, citizen's advocates, and a whole host of self-designated ''ombudsman'' offices as well as intergovernmental commissions on human rights which investigate individual complaints against government wrongdoing. The co-editors (Bernard Frank and Peter Freeman) invariably complained that ''the efforts to make the term so broad as to blur the distinction between classical or legislative ombudsman and the executive complaint-finding office does violence to the ombudsman concept.'' Paradoxically, an institution barely known at all in the 1950s had within twenty years become so popular that every office that performed some ombudsman functions wanted to be so titled. Resistance by international associations of ombudsmen to restrict the use of the term only to legislative ombudsmen was rapidly crumbling by 1980 as nonlegislative ombudsmen threatened to set up their own association.

Indeed, the private sector has also adopted the term. For instance, in many countries the news media have their own ombudsmen who receive public complaints, investigate them, and publicize the findings. While some of the grievances received relate to public organizations, most relate to wrongdoing in the private sector. The public sector has no monopoly over bad decision-making and bureaupathologies. The public wants independent complaint-handling mechanisms to deal with private organizations as well, for much the same reasons that it wants ombudsman offices in the public sector, namely, feeling of powerlessness, lack or inadequacy of redress, inability to deal with the bureaucracy, lack of trust in self-regulating administrative systems, and a sense of moral outrage. In response, more and more extrajudicial avenues of redress are being created, among them a variety of third-party complaint handlers which call themselves ombudsmen who operate much like their counterparts in the public sector, but unlike them they are not required by law to report to anyone and they are not accountable to the public. Since there is no law confining the use of the term to the public sector only and within the public sector to the legislative ombudsman only, there is no way to prevent its inappropriate or nonpurist use.

THE VARIETY AND CONSISTENCY OF OMBUDSMEN

The definitions used by the International Bar Association, the American Bar Association, and the International Ombudsman Institute permit a variety of forms. There are private sector ombudsmen and public sector ombudsmen. There are legislative ombudsmen and executive ombudsmen. There are all-purpose ombudsmen, and there are specialized ombudsmen who take only one kind of complaint or deal with only one species of complainant. There are ombudsmen who receive complaints directly from the public and others who receive them only from members of parliament. There are ombudsmen who may only investigate written complaints and others who take oral complaints as well. There are ombudsmen who can investigate all public officials from the highest to the lowest and others who can investigate complaints only against certain classes of public servant. There are ombudsmen who can investigate any wrongdoing in the public sector and others who are expressly limited to specific acts of maladministration. There are ombudsmen who can investigate on their own initiative and others who are confined strictly to grievances of complainants. There are ombudsmen who investigate for themselves and others who rely on somebody else to conduct investigations on their behalf. There are ombudsmen who take a judicial approach to their office and others who see themselves as executive trouble-shooters. There are ombudsmen who report at length and others who issue only brief summaries of their operations. The original Swedish conception has proved remarkably flexible and adaptable; it is cloth that seemingly can be cut to any form. It is found in old countries and new countries, rich countries and poor countries, small countries and large countries, capitalist economies and socialist economies, unitary states and federal states, civil regimes and military regimes, states with strong administrative law systems and states with weak administrative law systems, presidential and cabinet systems, political systems where legislators enjoy constituents' casework and political systems where they do not, efficient and inefficient administrative systems, merit and spoils systems.

Because of these variations, it has been said that "An Ombudsman cannot be bought off the peg; he must be made to measure."[26] But regardless of the differences, there is sufficient commonality to provide a general description. The ombudsman is an independent and nonpartisan officer (or committee of officers as in Nigeria, Tanzania, and Zambia), often provided for in the Constitution, who supervises the administration. He deals with specific complaints from the public against administrative injustice and maladministration. He has the power to investigate, report upon, and make recommendations about individual cases and administrative procedures. He is not a judge or tribunal, and he has no power to make orders or to reverse administrative action. He seeks solutions to problems by a process of investigation and conciliation. His authority and influence derive from the fact that he is appointed by and reports to one of the principal organs of state, usually either the parliament or the chief executive. This ensures both the confidence of the complainant in the ombudsman and the respect of the public service. At first, public officials tend to regard the ombudsman with hostility and suspicion, but in time they come to realize that he can also be an important protection for them against unfair, ill-founded, or malicious attacks.

A complaint may be made by any aggrieved person. It may be made in writing or by telephone, or the complainant may appear for an informal interview. No fee is required, and technical limitations are few. Generally, the complaint has to be made within one year of the action complained of, although some ombudsmen may consider older grievances. Most countries allow direct access by the public to the ombudsman, but in Great Britain and France complaints must be submitted through a member of parliament, who is supposed to act as a filter but rarely does. The ombudsmen usually have complete discretion as to which complaints they will investigate. They are not required to take up those that are outside their jurisdiction or that appear frivolous or misconceived or without foundation. If they consider that the complainant has an available remedy he should pursue, they may so advise and decline to act. Otherwise, they give complainants an expert agent without personal cost, time delay, the tension of adversary litigation, and requirement of counsel.

The ombudsman's jurisdiction is generally sweeping in scope. The Swedish Constitution says simply that the ombudsman should "supervise the observance of laws and statutes." In Denmark, the ombudsman "shall keep himself informed as to whether any person comprised by his jurisdiction pursues unlawful ends, takes arbitrary or unreasonable decisions or otherwise commits mistakes or acts of negligence in the discharge of his or her duties." The People's Assembly Committee in Sudan may investigate complaints alleging "(a) nepotism, corruption, bias; (b) failure to observe sound administrative bases; (c) negligence in carrying out duty; (d) misuse of discretion; (e) incompetence; (f) loss of documents and papers; (g) tardiness and delay; (h) unjust segregation (discrimination); (i) any similar matters.'' Judicial decisions and court proceedings are generally exempt, as are political offices, the armed services and police, and local self-government bodies. Otherwise,

The roll call of action or failure to act ranges from simple clerical errors to oppression, and includes injustice, failure to carry out legislative intent, unreasonable delay, administrative error, abuse of discretion, lack of courtesy, clerical error, oppression, oversight, negligence, inadequate investigation, unfair policy, partiality, failure to communicate, rudeness, maladministration, unfairness, unreasonableness, arbitrariness, arrogance, inefficiency, violation of law or regulation, abuse of authority, discrimination, errors, mistakes, carelessness, disagreement with discretionary decision, improper motivation, irrelevant consideration, inadequate or obscure explanation, and the other acts that are frequently inflicted upon the governed by those who govern, intentionally or unintentionally.[27]

In most countries, the ombudsmen have full powers to investigate complaints. They may see official files and documents, and may question officials involved. In some countries, they have the same power as judges. An exception was the French *mediateur* who initially was dependent on the administration for access to information. Elsewhere, the administration can deny information where it considers that national security and defense may be harmed. The British ombudsman may have full access but may be prohibited from disclosure where ''prejudicial to the safety of the state or otherwise contrary to the public interest.'' Ombudsmen have no powers of enforcement. They reach agreements with public agencies about an alteration or improvement in administrative procedures to avoid repetition of error. Where there is disagreement, the ombudsmen report to the chief executive or parliament or other authority to which they are responsible, for any appropriate decision or action.

Confidentiality is observed by most ombudsmen. Anonymous complaints will usually be ignored, but the identity of complainants will not be disclosed without consent. Inquiries are conducted in private, and reports omit the identity of complainants and public officials involved. Thus, individuals may complain without fear of reprisal, and public servants can learn from their errors without being victimized. Exceptions to the confidentiality rule are Sweden and Finland where the public's right to know is paramount, and upon completion, cases are usually open to public inspection. Confidentiality and anonymity do not imply secrecy about the ombudsmen's activities. The ombudsmen keep the public informed, and their reports are important means of publicity. Mass media exposure serves a useful educational purpose and encourages trust in the institution. Some ombudsmen

have established branch offices, while others regularly tour their territory.

The volume of complaints varies widely, occasionally topping ten thousand a year at peak workload, that is, over thirty complaints a working day, but the average workload is much lower, less than ten complaints a working day and in a few jurisdictions less than ten complaints a month. Compared to the number of people served, the figures are rather low, given the number of daily transactions between public agencies and the public. This may be because public administration is much better than people suspect or because people are reluctant to complain against public agencies or because the ombudsmen are not widely known. Bernard Frank blames ''small staff, lack of publicity, low budget, use of other remedies, restrictions on access, the requirements that complaints be in writing, language problems, distance of office location, fear of reprisals, and lack of branch offices.''[28] Whatever the reason, the ombudsman institution does not seem to be used as fully as it should be by the very groups of disadvantaged who need it most and to whom the incumbents seem more kindly disposed. Complaints of racial or religious discrimination have been rare, perhaps because the ombudsman's powers are too restricted and something much stronger is needed to fight social prejudice.[29] On the other hand, prison inmates, when permitted access to the ombudsman, do avail themselves of the opportunity, and ombudsmen seem keen to protect the rights of prisoners.[30] The same can be said about members of the armed forces and persons aggrieved at police conduct.

The institution depends much on the incumbents of the ombudsman office, their personality, their judgment, their status, their impartiality, and their independence. They should have a judicial temperament, and many statutes insist that the ombudsman should have legal qualifications. They should have knowledge of public administration and government operations. They should be accessible, not offputting in manner. They should have an innate sense of justice, for they symbolize what government ought to do, that is, to cultivate the well-being of the citizen, the preservation of individual freedom, and the equitable treatment of all citizens by the public bureaucracy. The role of the ombudsman is what incumbents make of it. They can be lazy or energetic, formalistic or personal, bold or weak. They can eke out their working days by acting as little more than a post box between complainants and public agencies, or they can set out to right wrong, reform the government apparatus, change laws and policies, and educate the public and officials with ways of good government. They can suppress wrongdoing and act as establishment spokesmen, or they can expose wrongdoing and act as advocates for complaints. They have power to do much good or to hide much evil. How well they perform depends on how well they want to perform and how well they are allowed to perform. They may lack sufficient support in the system and be denied adequate resources and access. In their approach, they may choose to be investigators or inquisitors, to be critics or helpmates, to use power or influence, to adopt force or persuasion, to act on their own initiative or to hide behind alleged legal restrictions.

In studying any ombudsman office, the following questions form a useful guide for quick reference:[31]

- How is the ombudsman placed in office? By appointment or election? How does the legislature participate in the process?

- What control does the ombudsman have over his staff? Is the staff governed by public sector conditions?

- What is the ombudsman's jurisdiction? How are the public agencies within the jurisdiction defined? Does the ombudsman have jurisdiction over local or municipal administration?

- How does the ombudsman receive complaints? Must complaints be signed? Are complaints accepted over the telephone?

- Are there alternative remedies available to complainants? What is the position of the ombudsman?

- Does the ombudsman release reports on investigations other than in the form of an annual report?

- Can the ombudsman initiate investigations and/or inspections?

- What happens to the ombudsman's reports? Are they submitted to a committee of the legislature? If so, how does the committee function?

- How is the office organized?

- How are complaints processed?

- Who complains? What do they complain about? Against whom are most complaints lodged?

- How does the ombudsman office measure and evaluate its services?

- What impact does the ombudsman have on complainants, agencies investigated, and administrative performance?

- What is the public reputation and image of the ombudsman?

Major ombudsman models are described in detail in this volume, and a host of country studies make up the companion volume, *International Handbook of the Ombudsman: Country Surveys.* Their similarities and differences should speak for themselves. Elsewhere, Kent Weeks has conveniently tabulated national ombudsmen,[32] but a useful capsule guide to the variations can be gained from the following examples which are given here because they are not discussed further in this *Handbook.*

Fiji

The 1970 Constitution provided for an ombudsman to be appointed by the governor general after consultation with the prime minister, leader of the opposition, and other political leaders, and to investigate official actions, including police and prisons but excluding political offices and statutory authorities. Justice Moti R. Tikaram, seconded from the supreme court, has been in office since 1972. His ten staff members are public servants, and they deal with about five hundred public complaints annually, about half of which they assist complainants to put in written form. No investigations can be started if other reasonable avenues of redress are available, and the ombudsman cannot initiate investigations on his own motion. An independent and bold person, Justice Tikaram has publicly criticized restrictions on his jurisdiction. He would like an extension to cover statutory authorities and the power to issue special reports as well as an annual report. He personally examines every complaint received, makes decisions on whether they are justified and on what further action should be taken, and signs every letter that leaves his office.

Iowa

The Citizens' Aide Act of 1974 provided for a citizens' aide to investigate public complaints about the "action or inaction" of the state and local government agencies and to "improve administrative practices and procedures." The office can instigate investigations on its own motion and has power to concern itself "with strengthening procedures and practices which lessen the risk that objectionable administrative actions will occur," but it cannot investigate where alternative remedies are available and "when there is no objective standard upon which an opinion ought to be formulated." It has wide powers of reporting and has close liaison with the committees of the state legislature. The citizens' aide is appointed every four years and employs a staff of seven to deal with approximately twenty-seven hundred contacts a year, two-thirds of which are by telephone thanks to a toll-free line to the office. Within the office, a deputy for corrections deals with inmate grievances and another specialist deals with the grievances of American Indians. The office considers itself an intermediary between government and people and has rarely initiated investigations.

Manitoba

The Ombudsman Act of 1970 provided for an ombudsman to be appointed by the lieutenant-governor in council on the recommendation of an all-party committee of the legislature whom he serves. A former police chief, George Maltby, has held the office since 1970, although appointed only for six-year terms, and he employs five civil servants to deal with approximately 650 written complaints a year. He has the power to initiate his own investigation of any administrative decision aggrieving any person, and he assumes jurisdiction in questionable areas until challenged. He has striven to make the office known through publicity throughout the province, and he personally deals with every complaint, although an informal system of specialization has developed within the office.

Northern Ireland

Both the office of the commissioner for complaints and the parliamentary commissioner for administration were created in 1969 by separate enactments of the Northern Ireland Parliament, although since inception the commissioner for complaints has acted in a dual capacity. As commissioner for complaints, he receives complaints directly from the public about alleged maladministration (about five hundred a year), and as parliamentary commissioner he receives complaints through members of the Northern Ireland Assembly (about seventy a year). He has a lifetime appointment subject to retirement at age sixty-five, and he appoints his own staff. Although given wide statutory powers of investigation, the commissioner has refrained from their use, but he has used his powers to recommend redress, including court relief for damages and reimbursement of complainant expenses. Maladministration has been held to cover administrative actions based on improper considerations or conduct (for example, malice, bias, and arbitrariness). Security and criminal matters have been excluded as have medical matters. Any obstructions in the course of investigations can be treated as contempt of court.

Papua New Guinea

At independence in 1975, the Constitution provided for a leadership code specifying rules of official conduct and an ombudsman commission

(a)   to ensure that all governmental bodies are responsive to the needs and aspirations of the people;

(b)   to help in the improvement of the work of governmental bodies and the elimination of unfairness and discrimination by them;

(c)   to help in the elimination of unfair or otherwise defective legislation and practices affecting or administered by governmental bodies; and

(d)   to supervise the enforcement of the Leadership Code.

The commission, appointed by the governor general on the recommendation of an Ombudsman Appointment Committee, has wide jurisdiction over all government levels and may initiate investigations. One ombudsman deals with public complaints, another has primary responsibility for the leadership code, while the chief ombudsman directs the activities of the office. A staff of ten deals with five hundred complaints a year. The first incumbents were appointed initially for three years, a term set for all future noncitizens, but citizens will be appointed for six years.

Quebec

The Public Protector Act of 1968 provided for a public protector to be elected by two-thirds of the legislative assembly for a term of five years, with a staff outside the civil service to investigate public complaints against administrative wrongdoing, gross irregularity, and injustice where other avenues of redress are unavailable. The office is obligated to assist prospective complainants in drafting complaints. The large number of annual complaints (approximately seven thousand) requires a sizable staff and considerable internal specialization and delegation and bureaucratization of procedures rather than personal service by the ombudsman. The office is located in Quebec City, but a branch office operates in Montreal.

Tanzania

The 1965 Interim Constitution provided for a Permanent Commission of Enquiry to investigate the conduct of all public officials and all office-holders of the country's only political party. Complaints may be submitted orally, and the commission, consisting of a chairman and four members appointed for two years renewable once only, may investigate on its own motion. The president may overrule the commission and may prohibit the release of information prejudicial to the security, defense, or international relations of Tanzania. The commission employs a staff of public servants to investigate some two thousand complaints annually.

The ombudsmen in these examples are obliged to submit an annual report relating to the exercise of their functions. In some cases, the annual report is the only source of public information available. Thus, what the ombudsman decides to include determines what is known about the office, and the number of copies of the document determines its availability outside the office and the legislature in the case of legislative ombudsmen. They invariably contain statistical summaries of complaints on cases or contacts (the terminology differs), but some record all complaints received during the year while others record only cases investigated and completed, without necessarily indicating complaints in hand awaiting resolution. Not all record their contacts, only the complaints they decided to investigate. Most reports record the name of the agency a complaint was lodged against, but few say anything at all about the makeup of complainants (by location, sex, age, language of communication, and so on). Similarly, there are differences in classifying whether or not complaints were justified and whether they were resolved satisfactorily. Some do provide a complete list of complaints investigated, together with elaborate summaries of what ombudsmen consider to be their most significant investigations and findings. As a result, the average size of annual reports (including summaries in foreign languages) varies from less than twenty pages to over six hundred pages (Sweden). Consequently, it is difficult to evaluate the ombudsman institution from annual reports alone.

EVALUATION AND ASSESSMENT OF THE INSTITUTION OF OMBUDSMAN

Whenever a new institution appears, especially one such as the ombudsman which promises to revitalize relations between the governors and the governed, the administration and the public, its boosters tend to exaggerate its initial performance. In the case of the ombudsman, it is well to recall that its true role, in the words of one of its leading advocates, "is to supplement the existing institutions—courts, legislatures, executives, administrative courts, and administrative agencies, which institutions must be strengthened and made more responsive to the grievances of citizens."[33] Another warns that the ombudsman is a useful administrative critic but no pathfinder[34] or panacea.

Administrative critics do not produce good government. They cannot themselves create sound social policies. They have no capacity to organize a competent civil service. They are at their best when calling attention to infrequent departures from norms already set by law or custom, at their weakest when seeking to choose among competing goals or to become general directors of governmental activity. . . . No ombudsman can renovate a de-

cayed government or promulgate sound public policies or fill the gaps of a deficient civil service. He can tidy up a well-built house, but he cannot himself build one.[35]

Accepting these constraints, a third advocate agrees that "It may be true, as critics say, that the office is not very well equipped for hunting lions. But it can certainly swat a lot of flies."[36] And, he could have added, there are many flies hovering around the body administrative in the contemporary state that need swatting even by inadequate fly swatters.

The issue is not whether the ombudsman institution works, but how well it works to redress individual grievances against public maladministration, protect basic human rights against official abuse of power, improve administrative performance, reduce citizen alienation from increasingly bureaucratized government, and protect public servants against unfounded criticism.[37] Does it violate constitutional, legal, and political precepts? Does it needlessly duplicate the activities of existing grievance mechanisms? Does it divert public resources from more urgent administrative reforms? When the U.S. Office of Equal Opportunity financed an experimental ombudsman demonstration program in the late 1960s and early 1970s, it expected some definitive answers to such questions, and social scientists were compelled to devise objective evaluative criteria of actual experience in place of speculation based upon the extrapolation of foreign experience then available.

The Ombudsman Activities Project began with an appraisal of the performance of individual ombudsman offices before proceeding to estimate their benefits and costs. Under performance measures, the social scientists placed productivity (number, type, and outcome of cases closed in relation to size of staff and finding), quality control (office supervision and procedures, recordkeeping, spirit of inquiry), publicity, and accessibility. Despite limitations in the data, their study showed that the ombudsman offices investigated (Seattle, Nebraska, Iowa, Hawaii) had "thoroughly investigated complaints received, obtained the timely resolution of complaints found to be justified, and provided complainants with a carefully documented explanation where their complaints are found to be unjustified."[38] Next, they devised criteria for measuring the social benefits of ombudsman offices under such headings as individual (utility to complainants), group (equalizing opportunities for redress, addressing distinctive grievances of groups), community-wide (administrative improvements, better government performance, increased public confidence in public institutions), administrative (alerting officials to shortcomings or grievances, identifying reform needs, improving morale), and political process (reduced burdens on other redress mechanisms, improved government performance). Finally, they devised criteria for estimating the social costs under the same headings, including such items as reduced contact between the public and public officials (both elected and appointed), substitution of palliatives for fundamental changes in public policy, proliferation of grievance mechanisms, and neutralization of the ombudsman through cooperation. But they were unable to apply these criteria in detail because of legal protection of privacy, official secrecy, lack of research resources and data, limited time frame, and various methodological problems. Still, their work provided a solid foundation on which others have been able to build.

Independently, JUSTICE in Great Britain was grappling with similar problems in considering the adequacy of machinery for redressing citizens' grievances against such bodies as the nationalized industries. The criteria which its expert committee used included

(1) *visibility*—the arrangements should be well-known, particularly to those likely to use them;
(2) *accessibility*—likely users should be able easily to put the arrangements into operation;
(3) *independence*—any body (or person) deciding on the validity of a complaint or grievance and the appropriate remedy should have no interest in the way in which the case is decided;
(4) *expertise*—any [such] body . . . should have itself, or easily available to it, the technical competence necessary to the making of a reasonable decision;
(5) *authority*—any body . . . should be in a position to ensure that its decision is effective;
(6) *representativeness*—any body . . . should be reasonably representative of the public at large.[39]

Because existing grievance mechanisms did not meet these criteria, the committee considered various alternative forms, including the ombudsman, but rejected it because it, too, did not conform to the criteria because of its limited jurisdiction and powers and its expense.[40]

In a state of the art assessment,[41] Brenda Danet has pointed out how little has been done to evaluate the institution of ombudsman outside the United States and how difficult it is to compare the different offices. She raises questions about who uses the office, what happens to the users, and what impact the office has on public administration. Above all, she stresses how subjective judgment is unavoidable, simply because such terms as "assessibility," "efficiency," and "effectiveness" are themselves so subjective, let alone "redressing a wrong" and "pursuing justice." Borrowing Larry Hill's six major objectives of the institution, namely, (1) to right individual wrongs, (2) to make bureaucracy more humane,

(3) to lessen popular alienation from government, (4) to prevent abuses by acting as a bureaucratic watchdog, (5) to vindicate civil servants when unjustly accused, and (6) to introduce administrative reform,[42] she suggests three sets of measures, six related to clients, six to public administration, and seven to the ombudsman office, as follows:

(a) Client-related measures
   - rate of complaining or petitioning
   - knowledge of availability of the ombudsman's help
   - knowledge of the ombudsman's jurisdiction
   - representativeness of the general public or profile of complainants compared to the general adult population
   - nature of complaint—whether individual or collective in nature
   - appropriateness of form, content of complaint, and the extent to which complainants observe bureaucratic norms

(b) Public administration system
   - target of complaint
   - subject of complaint
   - overall fairness
   - fairness to subgroup
   - response to ombudsman's recommendations
   - targets of reform

(c) Ombudsman office
   - annual caseload
   - staff workload
   - degree of investigation
   - efficiency
   - ability to help
   - fairness to subgroups
   - impact on administrative reform

Danet then applies these measures to the fragmentary evidence available and concludes with Hill that the ombudsman idea "is an extraordinarily successful institutional innovation." She does warn, however, that evaluation studies tend to stress the positive, functional aspects rather than the negative, dysfunctional ones, and the easily documented help to individuals rather than the longer term goal of improving public administration.

The studies presented in this book generally concur

with Danet's assessment. Given its constraints, the institution of ombudsman has fulfilled limited expectations. It has done many of the things that its advocates promised it would do. Its obvious successes have brought about a veritable "ombudsmania" among enthusiasts who probably promise more than they have any right to do. This book sounds a more cautionary note because, among the many undoubted successes, there are some disquieting features. First, some ombudsman offices receive few complaints, barely enough to justify their existence. It is doubtful whether public agencies within their jurisdictions are that good. Probably they are little known and discourage people from using their services. Second, some offices have exceedingly restricted jurisdiction, excluding many areas that people would like to complain about, and others take a deliberately narrow view of their powers. They are reluctant to deal with such big issues as political and administrative corruption; fraud, waste, and abuse of public resources; arrogant use of public office; and intimidation of dependent clients. Third, some offices are unable to investigate complaints for themselves or as thoroughly as they should. They are denied the necessary resources and cooperation. The administration delays response, hoping that the substance of the complaint will get buried under the ombudsman's impossible workload. Fourth, some offices conduct themselves too formally. They are themselves too bureaucratic, too legalistic, too cumbersome to deal with, possibly because in reality they constitute protection for the administration, not the public. Fifth, some offices cannot publicize themselves by law, or they feel it is unbecoming and improper to appear to be searching for business. As a result, there are probably far fewer complaints than there should be, and more remediable injustice and wrongdoing escape notice than need be. Finally, ombudsmen who have publicly challenged the government or have figured prominently in public controversies with high ranking public officials have not been reappointed at the end of their terms of office, and in some cases they have been forced to resign before completion of their terms. The implication is that the ombudsman should avoid publicly embarrassing the powers that be, but if the ombudsman avoids offending them, is the position not compromised?

Even so, compared with the performance of complaint-handling mechanisms in the private sector, the ombudsman shines, even the worst of them (and there are very few of them). Laura Nader, in her study of such mechanisms in the United States,[43] concludes that extrajudicial alternatives generally fail. They are rarely used, and they have a low success rate. In contrast with the ombudsman office in the public sector, most complainants remain dissatisfied and feel cheated, deprived, and insulted by the complaints process. Their unsolved grievances feed frustration, anxiety, and friction, and they resent a system that condones chicanery, petty exploitation and unethical business practices, and only reconfirms their powerlessness against injustice and wrongdoing. "In many cases, neither knowledge nor persistence nor calm rationality [sic] serves to win redress."[44] Government did little better than business; bureaucratic circumlocution rather than resolution seemed to characterize citizens' experiences with both elected and appointed officials in the absence of an ombudsman office and action lines. The onus of proof is pushed on the complainant, not on the offending organization, a quite unequal affair as the complainant does not have the time, resources, know-how, and access to justify the complaint, whereas the offending organization has the power of intimidation, suppression, privacy, and absolute discretion whether or not to listen. She looks to government to redress the imbalance by providing new forms of regulation that would tackle the causes and not the symptoms of social injustice. Whatever its shortcomings, the ombudsman institution has proven superior in the public sector to anything provided in the private sector for the redress of grievances.

In the final analysis, we must agree with Bernard Frank[45] that undoubtedly the ombudsman has much real and potential value in protecting the public against public maladministration. Its uniqueness may tend to overglamorize the concept, especially in a world where big government is an established fact and people find themselves at a great disadvantage in dealing with officialdom. But it is only a supplement to existing institutions, which in turn must be strengthened and made more responsive to people's grievances. But none of this

is a substitute for a committed, intelligent and vigilant citizenry. Our times have taught us that the greatest danger to good government comes not from without but from within; the most dangerous tyranny has always been apathy. In the end, good government, the protection of individual freedoms, is the responsibility of every citizen, and cannot be delegated to any single official.[46]

NOTES

1. Bernard Frank, "The Ombudsman and Human Rights—Revisited," *Israel Yearbook on Human Rights*, Vol. 6 (Tel Aviv: Faculty of Law, Tel Aviv University, 1976), p. 122.

2. I. al-Wahab, *The Swedish Institution of Ombudsman: An Instrument of Human Rights* (Stockholm: Liber Förlag, 1979).

3. Arthur Maloney, *Blueprint for the Office of the Ombudsman in Ontario* (Ontario: 1979), pp. 13–14.

4. Stanley Anderson, *Ombudsman Papers: American Experience and Proposals* (Berkeley, Calif.: Institute of Governmental Studies, University of California, 1969), pp. 6–7.

5. Walter Gellhorn, *When Americans Complain: Govern-

mental Grievance Procedures (Cambridge, Mass.: Harvard University Press, 1966), p. 4.

6. Donald C. Rowat, *The Ombudsman Plan: Essays on the Worldwide Spread of an Idea* (Toronto: McClelland and Stewart, 1973), p. viii.

7. Ibid., p. vii.

8. Ibid., p. 46.

9. See Itzhak Galnoor, "Government Secrecy: Exchanges, Intermediaries, and Middlemen," *Public Administration Review* 35, No. 1 (1975): 32–42.

10. Donald C. Rowat, "The Problem of Administrative Secrecy," *International Review of Administrative Sciences* 32, No. 2 (1966): 105.

11. William H. Riker, *Democracy in the United States,* 2d ed. (New York: Macmillan, 1965).

12. Barrington Moore, "Reflections on the Causes of Human Misery and Upon Certain Proposals to Eliminate Them" (Boston: 1972), p. 114, quoted by D. Hyman and D. Griffiths, *An Advocate for the People* (University Park: Pennsylvania State University, 1976), p. 175.

13. D. Gressier, "Appeals in Administration," *Public Administration* (Sydney) 33, No. 1 (March 1974): 1–8.

14. Larry B. Hill, "Bureaucracy, the Bureaucratic Auditor and the Ombudsman: Ideal Type Analysis" (Seventeenth Bicentennial Conference of the International Bar Association, Sydney, September 1978).

15. Ibid., quoting from Max Weber's *The Sociology of Religion,* Vol. 1 (Boston: Beacon Press, 1964), p. 206.

16. Hill, "Bureaucracy," quoting from A. Mitzman, *The Iron Cage* (New York: Alfred A. Knopf, 1970), p. 232.

17. C. Ferris, B. Goodman, and G. Mayer, "Brief on the Office of the Ombudsman" (Report of the Ombudsman Committee, International Bar Association, Seventeenth Conference, Sydney, September 1978; Edmonton, International Ombudsman Institute, 1979).

18. al-Wahab, *The Swedish Institution of Ombudsman,* pp. 24–25.

19. Anderson, *Ombudsman Papers,* pp. 2–3.

20. See Rowat, *The Ombudsman Plan,* p. 40.

21. *Seminar on Judicial and Other Remedies Against the Illegal Exercise or Abuse of Administrative Authority,* Peradeniya (Kandy), Ceylon, May 4–15, 1959 (ST/TAO/HR/4); *Seminar on Judicial and Other Remedies Against the Illegal Exercise or Abuse of Administrative Authority,* Buenos Aires, Argentina, August 31 to September 11, 1959 (ST/TAO/HR/6); *Seminar on Judicial and Other Remedies Against the Abuse of Administrative Authority, with Special Emphasis on the Role of Parliamentary Institutions,* Stockholm, Sweden, June 12–25, 1962 (ST/TAO/HR/15); *Remedies Against the Abuse of Administrative Authority—Selected Studies, 1964* (ST/TAO/HR/19); *Seminar on the Effective Realization of Civil and Political Rights at the National Level,* Kingston, Jamaica, April 25 to May 8, 1967 (ST/TAO/HR/29); *Effective Realization of Civil and Political Rights at the National Level—Selected Studies, 1968* (ST/TAO/HR/33); *Seminar on Special Problems Relating to Human Rights in Developing Countries,* Nicosia, Cyprus, June 26 to July 9, 1969 (ST/TAO/HR/36).

22. *The Dynamic Aspects of the Rule of Law in the Modern Age* (Report on the Proceedings of the South-East Asian and Pacific Conference of Jurists, Bangkok 1965), p. 184; Working Papers, Ceylon Colloquium on the Rule of Law, Colombo, Ceylon, January 10–16, 1966, International Commission of Jurists (Ceylon Section); European Conference of Jurists on the Individual and the State, *The Essential Legal Elements to Ensure the Protection of the Individual,* Strasbourg, 26–27, Conclusion 17 (October 1968); see also *Bulletin of the International Commission of Jurists* 36 (December 7–8, 1968).

23. Guy Powles, "The Office of Ombudsman in New Zealand," *Journal of Administration Overseas* 7, No. 1 (1968): 287–92.

24. See Stanley Anderson, *Canadian Ombudsman Proposals* (Berkeley, Calif.: Institute of Governmental Studies, University of California, 1966), Anderson, *Ombudsman Papers;* S. Anderson: *Ombudsman for American Government?* (Englewood Cliffs, N.J.: Prentice-Hall, 1968); W. Gellhorn: *Ombudsmen and Others: Citizens' Protectors in Nine Countries* (Cambridge, Mass.: Harvard University Press, 1966); Gellhorn: *When Americans Complain;* N. Jain, *Lokpal: Ombudsman in India* (New Delhi: Academic Books, 1970); *The Ombudsman or Citizen's Defender: A Modern Institution,* a symposium in *Annals of the American Academy of Political and Social Science* 377 (May 1968)); D. Rowat, ed., *The Ombudsman: Citizen's Defender* (London: Allen and Unwin; Toronto: University of Toronto Press; Stockholm: Norstedt; 2d ed., 1968).

25. Bernard Frank, "The Ombudsman—Revisited," *International Bar Journal* (May 1975): 52.

26. S. A. de Smith, Constitutional Commissioner for Mauritius, *Mauritius Legislative Assembly Sessional Paper, No. 2 of 1965,* para. 39.

27. Frank, "The Ombudsman and Human Rights—Revisited," p. 134.

28. Ibid., p. 141.

29. Ibid., p. 147.

30. New Zealand Ombudsman Sir Guy Powles has been quoted by B. Frank, "The Ombudsman—Revisited," p. 148, as stating "whatever an inmate has done, he remains a person, and has the right, and not merely the privilege, to be treated as such."

31. Maloney, *Blueprint for the Office of the Ombudsman,* pp. 165–66.

32. K. Weeks, *Ombudsmen Around the World: A Comparative Chart,* 2d ed. (Berkeley, Calif.: Institute of Governmental Studies, University of California, 1978).

33. Frank, "The Ombudsman—Revisited," p. 60.

34. Gellhorn, *Ombudsmen and Others,* p. 225.

35. Gellhorn, *When Americans Complain,* pp. 53–54, 132.

36. Rowat, *The Ombudsman Plan,* p. 138.

37. J. E. Moore, "Evaluating American Ombudsman Offices in Theory and Practice," address at the Annual Meeting of the American Political Science Association, Chicago, 1974, p. 4.

38. Ibid., p. 9.

39. JUSTICE, *The Citizen and the Public Agencies: Remedying Grievances* (London: 1976), pp. 5–6.

40. Ibid., pp. 46–47.

41. Brenda Danet, ''Toward a Method to Evaluate the Ombudsman Role,'' *Administration and Society* 10, No. 3 (November 1978): 335–69.

42. Larry B. Hill, *The Model Ombudsman: Institutionalizing New Zealand's Democratic Experiment* (Princeton, N.J.: Princeton University Press, 1976).

43. Laura Nader, *No Access to Law: Alternatives to the American Judicial System* (New York: Academic Press, 1980).

44. Laura Nader, ''Complainant Beware,'' *Psychology Today* (December 1979), p. 51.

45. Frank, ''The Ombudsman and Human Rights–Revisited,'' pp. 157–58.

46. Maloney, *Blueprint for the Office of the Ombudsman*, p. 29.

CHAPTER 2

THE IDEOLOGICAL FOUNDATION OF THE OMBUDSMAN INSTITUTION

H. H. KIRCHHEINER, DISTRICT COURT JUDGE, AMSTERDAM

THE INSTITUTION OF the parliamentary ombudsman, which originated in Sweden, has now been established in many countries throughout the world, although at times with considerable changes. Relatively little attention has been paid to the ideas that preceded its establishment and formed the basis for its underlying principles. The original institution of the *justitieombudsman* (JO) is quite distinct from legal measures designed to uphold existing rights and bring about change in the juridical situation.[1]

The JO institution should be seen principally within a context of democratic values, where the personal responsibility of the official towards the citizen is of primary importance. As long as the official or judge, in his contact with the citizen, is not fully aware of his responsibility towards the individual, the danger remains that the individual's *feelings of security* will be adversely affected by an official who, for example, exceeds his authority or acts arbitrarily, incorrectly, or tardily. The feelings of security, based on the right to freedom of thought, include not only feelings of security in the narrow sense of the word, but also feelings of safety, humanity, and human dignity. The individual's feelings of security are a *conditio sine qua non* for a sound democracy.[2] In this sense, democracy is not so much a representative constitutional system, although this aspect of the JO institution is of utmost importance, but rather democracy is an ideal. In this sense, democracy is a state of mind, a way of life, a challenge to be faced and dealt with continually. An essential element therein is mutual understanding and respect between citizens. As a way of life, it is reflected not

only in the political sphere, but also in the normal relations between people, between the official and the citizen, between the judge and those subject to the jurisdiction of the court.[3] This chapter traces the importance of the democratic principles underlying the JO institution to Sweden.

The introduction of the institution of the *justitieombudsman* in Sweden in 1809 was preceded by the Enlightenment in its Swedish form, or the *Frihetstid* as it is called, which lasted from 1719 to 1772. This period clearly left its mark on many areas of Swedish life and is still noticeable today. Of course, Sweden has also had periods of strong authoritarian rule in which human rights were curtailed, but one must also acknowledge that the democratic thread in Sweden has repeatedly been taken up and woven into the pattern of life.[4]

During the *Frihetstid,* when old Swedish ideas were reexamined and enlarged upon, inspired among other things by currents of French thought, modern literature, modern science, and the press came into existence. It was believed that by enlightening the human mind one could create a better world. The right to freedom of thought was regarded more highly than ever, and humanitarian views of life, with their closely related sense of personal responsibility, took a prominent position. The concept of freedom and the desire to participate in determining one's own fate gained new dimensions. The right to individual freedom became the right to an individual personality, to recognition of and respect for human dignity.[5] No longer could the concept of individual freedom be separated from the idea of personal responsibility. However, according to Swedish historian L. Stavenow (1864–1950), the concept of freedom had two enemies: on the one hand, absolutism or the existence of a stronger power and authority than laid down by or allowed for in the Constitution, and on the other hand, lack of self-discipline or high-handedness.

It was of utmost importance during the *Frihetstid* that the true concept of individual freedom or the right to an individual personality be protected against these enemies. The concept of responsibility demands that positive consideration be given to one's fellow citizen, so that the concept of freedom gains the democratic feature of respect for one's fellow man, for the autonomy of others. In this way, the concern of one person with the fate of another can be explained. A serious offense committed against one person becomes, in fact, an offense against fellow citizens, against large groups in society.[6] This is the explanation for the *actio popularis* which Sweden incorporated into the *justitieombudsman* institution.

It is this positive aspect of the concept of freedom that later formed the basis for the criminal liability of judges and state officials, as specified in Section 17, Chapter 25, of the Swedish Criminal Code of 1864 (revised repeatedly since then).[7] Judges and state officials were liable to criminal punishment if, in addition to incorrectly applying laws and ordinances by overstepping their authority or being high-handed, they failed to fulfill their task properly.

Lack of proper consideration (*oförstånd*) and lack of tact and correctness (*oskicklighet*) in carrying out their duties were subjective elements in their liability, later to become designated as "breach of duty." The standards established for state officials in the Criminal Code of 1864 can already be found in the Swedish Code for the Rules of Procedure from 1734, although in vague form, and in the literature of the *Frihetstid,* where it was stated that the ombudsman (at that time still appointed by the king) was "responsible to see that every state official performed his duty with due consideration ("förstånd"), correctness and tact ("skicklighet"), fairness and diligence."[8]

Thus, in the *Frihetstid* the idea already existed that the state official's abuse of the freedoms allowed for in his position should be checked by requirements of *förstånd* and *skicklighet*. In this way, it was intended to curb excessive arbitrary and high-handed conduct, and lack of self-discipline. Along the same line of thinking, the official was considered to have fulfilled his task properly only if he was at all times conscious of his personal responsibility to his fellow citizen. This in turn implied that he see all the problems with which he was confronted from the point of view of the actual situation in which his fellow citizen found himself. The citizen's feelings of security were thus based on a confidence in the official, who performed his duty properly in society with a sense of responsibility towards the public. Hence, the Swedish concepts of *förstånd* and *skicklighet* also embody an aspect of security.

At a much later date, these subjective elements in the standards required of judges and state officials were objectified, although they retained the element of security. In 1929, Olof Barklind wrote that *oförstånd* should be seen as a "failure on the part of the official to assess the facts or interpret or apply the regulations, when, given his intellectual capacities, he could have known better."[9]

An example can be found in the JO's 1961 *Ämbetsberättelse* (annual report). A judge in Stockholm had rendered legal assistance to several persons, in some cases for a fee. The *justitieombudsman* thought that this was a "breach of duty." He considered the nature of a judge's function to be such that he was bound to refrain from any activities that might undermine *trust in him as a judge or in the administration of justice in general*. According to the *justitieombudsman,* the extent of the services rendered by the judge to the persons involved was such that he had acted irresponsibly and brought the *aforementioned trust into jeopardy*. The pronouncement stated that the judge, in his lack of proper consideration (*oförstånd*), had been derelict in the duties of his profession.

According to Barklind, *oskicklighet* should be regarded as a lack of rational insight into existing law and the general regulations or into the technical skills required for the responsible execution of one's duty. This assumes that the official's shortcoming could at least be considered as *culpa,* which is the case when he fails to acquaint himself with the facts to the best of his ability, or at least fails to keep informed of them.

Take for example a case in the JO's 1949 *Ämbetsberättelse* in which the committee of a Methodist church in Märsta had filed a complaint against a police officer. During a church service, the officer had drawn his firearm in order to arrest a mentally disturbed person sought by the police who had hidden himself among the churchgoers. In the *justitieombudsman*'s investigation, it was established that several officers, dressed in civilian clothes, had followed the mentally disturbed person into the church where he was seeking to hide. He had situated himself at the altar during the service and shouted out that no one could touch him there. An officer had drawn a weapon and had aimed it at him. The *justitieombudsman* was of the opinion that the officer concerned had acted incorrectly and tactlessly (a demonstration of *oskicklighet*), in view of the norm by which police were bound not to use any more severe measures than necessary for a given situation.

While the JO's critical judgments were originally based on the foundation of criminal liability already described, this situation changed in 1975 as a result of the ideas of decriminalization prevailing at that time. Although the offense of "breach of duty" was deleted from the Swedish Criminal Code, a democratic attitude to life has continued to dominate the JO's judgments.

The *Frihetstid* made another outstanding contribution to Swedish culture. By one of Sweden's constitutional laws, the Law on Press Freedom (*Tryckfrihetsförordningen*) was enacted on December 2, 1766, and introduced the principle of public access to official documents. The censorship previously in existence was abolished. This law, which accorded every Swede the right to examine all official documents except for those specified in the law and to publicize their contents, again with exceptions, represented an outstanding basis for the full development of Swedish democracy in the widest sense of the word. The Swedish principle regarding free access to official documents was based on the assumption that documents received or drawn up by the public authorities (allowing for exceptions) should be freely accessible to anyone and that the official concerned has a duty to grant access, without the person who makes the request having to specify the motive. The press has made ready use of this access since 1766 and has kept the public quite adequately informed. The great importance of the principle of free public access to official documents is noticeable to this day.

The spirit of the *Frihetstid,* together with the principle of public access to official documents, has provided an excellent basis for the development of the independent-thinking and responsible citizen. It is true that freedom of the press was abolished and censorship reintroduced during the absolutist reigns of Gustavus III and Gustavus IV, but following the revolution of 1809, in which Gustavus IV was overthrown, the *Regeringsform* (Constitution) of 1809 restored freedom of the press (Section 86) and created the institution of the *Riksens Ständers Justitiae Ombudsman* (Section 96) as it was then called, to be the mandatary of the Estates of the Riksdag,[10] thereby providing two constitutional guarantees for intellectual freedom and the dignity of the individual, the first by preventive and the second by repressive control over the judiciary and state officials.

It is quite understandable that problems arise when an institution originating in one country with its own history and culture is introduced into another country with a quite different cultural tradition, but the Swedish institution of the *justitieombudsman* is so unique that everything should be done to retain as faithfully as possible its democratic elements—those of trust, personal responsibility, and security. For it is only if this is done that optimal results can be expected from the activities of the *justitieombudsman:* a behavioral norm becomes a mental norm, an appeal to one's sense of humanity. So too is the *justitieombudsman*'s task a conciliatory one: frustrations are eliminated, conflicts are resolved, communication problems are removed, and confidence in one's fellow man is restored.

NOTES

1. Kurt Hans Ebert, "Der Ombudsman in Gross Britannien," *Recht und Staat in Geschichte und Gegenwart* (Tübingen: J. C. B. Mohr, 1968), p. 9.

2. Alf Ross, *Hvorfor demokrati?* (Copenhagen: Ejnar Munksgaard's Forlag, 1946), pp. 191 ff. and 216–19.

3. Werner Kägi, "Studien im Prozess der Demokratie," *Schweizer Monatshefte* (Zurich), No. 2 (May 1957): 99 ff.; and Nils Herlitz, *Elements of Nordic Public Law* (Stockholm: Norstedt, 1969), pp. 19 and 193.

4. Nils Herlitz, *Svensk Självstyrelse* (Stockholm: Hugo Gebers Förlag, 1933), pp. 15 ff.

5. L. Stavenow, *Frihetstiden, dess epoker och kulturliff* (Göteborg: Wettergreen and Kerber, 1898).

6. Kai Thaning, *Menneske først* (Copenhagen: Gyldendal, 1963), pp. 342 ff. and 373 ff.

7. Section 17 of Chapter 25 reads as follows: "Visar ämbetsman vårdslöshet, försummelse, oförstånd eller oskicklighet i sitt ämbete och är ej särskilt ansvar därå satt; straffes med böter eller mistning av ämbetet på viss tid. . . ."

This reads in translation: "Should a state official show carelessness, negligence, thoughtlessness and lack of tact in discharging his duty, he will be punished by means of a fine or dismissal, unless he is criminally liable by another means. . . ."

8. Niklas von Oelreich, *En ärlig Svensk* (Stockholm: n.p., 1755), p. 462.

9. O. Barklind, "Ämbetsbrotten i det svenska förberedande utkastet till Strafflag," *Svensk Juristtidning* (May 1929): 126–27.

10. By 1550, a society of "estates" had developed in Sweden, with representative bodies being created for the *Ständers* ("estates") of the nobility, clergy, burghers, and peasants, which together formed the Riksdag.

CHAPTER 3

THE EVOLUTION OF THE ROLE OF THE OMBUDSMAN— COMPARISONS AND PERSPECTIVES

BARONESS B. SEROTA, Chairman of the
Commission for Local Administration in England

THIS CHAPTER SEEKS mainly to look forward rather than back, except to the extent that what is past is often prologue to what lies ahead. It does not pretend to examine and compare the origins and forms of the many ombudsman systems throughout the world. They are already well documented. Briefly, the 1809 Swedish Constitution is usually regarded as providing the first modern ombudsman. While the establishment of the Finnish system in 1919 followed naturally from the new state's historical connection with Sweden, the arrival of the dynamic Professor Stephan Hurwitz as Danish ombudsman in 1953 signaled the beginning of a crusade to many countries and widespread acceptance of the ombudsman concept.

There were, of course, a number of milestones along the road from 1953 to 1980. The New Zealand Ombudsman Act of 1962 has rightly been described as a benchmark providing a model for ombudsman legislation in the English-speaking and/or common law countries. In Great Britain, a nine-year campaign by JUSTICE (the British Section of the International Commission of Jurists) led to the Parliamentary Commissioner for Administration Act of 1967, and in the same year the first provincial ombudsmen were appointed in Canada. In 1971, the first state ombudsman—Oliver Dixon—was appointed in

Australia, and the post of commissioner for complaints was created in Israel as an extension of the role of the state comptroller. In the same year, Bernard Frank's challenge to the International Bar Association to concern itself with the ombudsman concept resulted in a worldwide wave of interest and action on which many offices have ridden. The impetus of that wave should not be allowed to fade away.

Explosions of this kind do not occur simply because of the zeal and enthusiasm of individuals, and this one was no exception. No government will move in advance of public pressure or opinion (although there are some notable exceptions to prove that rule). There can be tides in the affairs of men, but new constitutional developments do not suddenly emerge, especially in highly developed countries with long-established and well-entrenched government institutions. It has to be clearly demonstrated that newly recognized needs cannot be met by existing institutions. And chance can sometimes play an important part. In 1954, in the United Kingdom, for example, the spur was provided by a single administrative mistake by the government—the well-known Crichel Down affair—concerning a failure to offer back to the original owner land released from military use. It involved complaints of mis-

Address to the Second International Ombudsman Conference, Jerusalem, October 28, 1980.

behavior by civil servants, resulted in the resignation of a minister, and threw up in sharp relief an area that the courts and other complaint-handling mechanisms could not cover. As a result, the Franks Committee on Administrative Tribunals and Inquiries was set up and concluded that "over most of the field of public administration no formal procedure is provided for objecting or deciding on objections." The JUSTICE campaign already mentioned followed from that, and eventually the creation of an ombudsman service began in the United Kingdom.

The situation was different in newly independent states such as Fiji, Guyana, Mauritius, and Papua New Guinea, where new constitutions and new forms of self-government were replacing former colonial status. Many ombudsman systems were created in this climate of radical change when the rights of full citizenship were being experienced for the first time. These countries may equally experience their own particular problems. The Ombudsman Commission of Papua New Guinea, for example, recorded rather ominously in its 1976 report that the ombudsman system "is an idealistic institution" and in its 1979 report that it received too little cooperation from "the powers that are" and that there had been calls in parliament for the commission to be abolished.[1] It is heartening that the latest view is that the ombudsman concept has struck root in that country and is there to stay.

To summarize, in the words of Sir Guy Powles, "communities have felt the need for Ombudsmen, have demanded the system and have got it."[2] Or, in the words of a British educational administrator:

The whole national climate of opinion, from consumers' rights through the new employment legislation to race and sex equality, pointed to the abandonment of a benevolent administrative autocracy as an acceptable technique. It was, I suppose, the advent of the Ombudsman which finally put an end to that management style.[3]

While one may doubt whether that style has indeed disappeared, it is certainly more frequently challenged, not least by the activities of ombudsmen on behalf of those who complain to them.

In his 1971 challenge to the International Bar Association, Bernard Frank set down the reasons for having an ombudsman.[4] It may be useful here to summarize his statement which remains valid. In being comprehensive, however, it may not be totally applicable in the circumstances of all countries.

1. The modern state has assumed many functions as the result of social and welfare legislation affecting the lives and property of everyone. Extensive powers and discretion have been given to all types of individuals, boards, agencies, and departments. The possibilities of friction between officials and citizens have greatly increased. Protection of the individual is required against executive and administrative mistakes and abuse of power.

2. Concern to guarantee the legal rights of the individual has grown. But the growing activities and power of the bureaucracy mean that the legal status of the individual needs additional protection.

3. The legislature traditionally concerned with the observance of laws and rulings by public officials has extensively delegated powers to administrative authorities. The ombudsman can help the legislature in supervising the executive and administrator.

4. Existing mechanisms for adjusting grievances are inadequate.

   a. The legislator's role in investigating complaints is frequently limited because of lack of funds, staff, and access to files and information. He must rely in most cases on a reply from the agency or department he is investigating.

   b. The courts everywhere play a major role in correcting government abuses. But litigation is expensive, tension-creating, protracted and slow and, in many cases, the citizen bears with injustice because he cannot afford or does not wish litigation.

   c. Where administrative courts exist, even using procedures that are as informal as possible, they still follow adversary procedures, and legal representation is the normal rule. Such courts frequently move slowly, and there is great delay in executing their judgment.

   d. The executive may have a grievance procedure but is in essence investigating itself and is relying on the reply from the agency or official against whom the complaint was made. Complaint procedures within agencies likewise lack impartiality.

5. The ombudsman gives the citizen an expert and impartial agent without personal cost to the complainant and without the tension of adversary litigation. The citizen has confidence that there is a watchdog who will hold government accountable.

One other factor needs to be added to this list. Citizens' expectations of government increase, particularly as universal education spreads. Many more people are now articulate in making their needs known. In contrast, however, the socially disadvantaged and the handicapped remain much less articulate and less able to cope, although they are likely to be especially affected by the increasing complexities of government. They need special help with their problems.

COMPARISONS OF OMBUDSMEN SYSTEMS

Although there are obviously common factors behind the very rapid expansion of ombudsmen over the last twenty years, there are wide differences in systems. To appreciate why some countries have provided particular restrictions on ombudsmen's jurisdictions, or why different ombudsmen have adopted different ways of doing their job, requires a close understanding of the legal and administrative systems of the countries concerned and of the vested interests. Ombudsmen cannot easily be compared one with another in isolation from their national background: the outsider may not immediately appreciate nuances of a particular country's administrative systems and the importance of the nation's history. It is much easier to appreciate the constraints which, for example, geographical facts can impose on how the particular ombudsman system operates. An ombudsman in a populous city obviously has scope for greater personal contact with complainants than, say, the ombudsman for Denmark where water provides a considerable barrier. Other ombudsmen will be constrained by the sheer distances over which their writ runs.

Objectives

There is a danger of assuming that all ombudsmen are in the same game and working toward the same ends. Only very broadly does such a generalization stand up. There is a fairly clear procedural distinction between those systems, as in the United Kingdom, where the ombudsman can only respond to a complaint from an individual, and those where the ombudsman may himself initiate action as in Scandinavia and has an inspection role. But behind that procedural distinction lies a difference of philosophy between those systems where the ombudsman's prime task is to seek satisfactory action for the individual with a grievance, and those like Sweden where the primary objective is the very much wider one of keeping a general watch on the efficiency and fairness of the administration.

The philosophical difference may in turn lead to different methods of working, just as can the externally imposed procedural requirements of the originating legislature. Thus, if the primary objective is to procure

satisfactory action for the individual, this may be achieved without any real investigation of the administrative act that led to the complaint. A telephone call to a particular official might produce a solution without the need to establish whether the official's previous action should be criticized. But if the ombudsman's primary objective is to investigate the administrative actions of the official, then the quick settlement approach will not be enough.

To an extent, the objectives of the ombudsman are self-evident from considering the reasons for having an ombudsman in the country concerned. The English Local Commission, which covers 450 local authorities varying in size from populations of 7 million to thirty thousand and providing a wide range of services including housing, planning, education, and personal social services directly affecting 46.8 million people, is currently considering the following draft statement of objectives:

Primary objective
To investigate complaints that injustice has been caused by alleged unfair treatment by authorities within jurisdiction with a view to securing redress and more efficient administration by those authorities.

In addition there are:—

Supportive objectives (which need to be achieved to allow the primary objective to be fulfilled)

(a) to secure remedies for those whose complaints are found to have substance;
(b) to make the Local Ombudsman system known;
(c) to help people to make their complaints.

Subsidiary objective
To give advice and help to those with complaints outside jurisdiction.

Not unnaturally, it is easier to put fine words to paper than to assess whether the objectives are being achieved.

Access to the Ombudsman

Only in the United Kingdom and France (coincidentally the countries with the largest populations, 55 million and 53.2 million, respectively) is there no right of direct access to the ombudsman. The French *mediateur* can normally be approached only through a member of either house of parliament—the National Assembly or the Senate. The U.K. parliamentary commissioner can be approached only through a member of one house—the House of Commons. The U.K. local commissioners must normally be approached through a member of the authority against which the complaint is made, but direct access is possible if a member has been asked to send in a complaint but has not done so. As with most systems, all complaints must be in writing.

These systems contrast sharply with the ease of access to the ombudsman which exists, for example, in the Canadian provinces. As Frank Stacey has expressed so well in describing the Quebec public protector,

Any member of the public can telephone the Public Protector's office in either Quebec or Montreal to state his complaint. The assistant who answers will often, early in the conversation, ask the caller to give his number and then ring him back. The main conversation therefore takes place at public expense and allows the assistant time to take down fairly full details of the complaint. He will then ask the caller to send in documentary evidence to substantiate the complaint. Such evidence is necessary since the Act states that complaints to the Public Protector must be written. But the assistant does not wait for the supporting letter and other documents from the complainant before beginning his investigation. He will normally telephone the government department concerned as soon as possible and ask it to look into the case.[5]

Without detailed knowledge of the debates that preceded the creation of ombudsmen in the various countries, it is impossible to say whether the question of access loomed large. It has been considered carefully in the United Kingdom in recent years, and the current view of the majority of existing ombudsmen is that complaints should come *either* direct *or* through a member of the legislature or local authority (as the case may be), whereas the view of a majority of the elected members is that complaints should come only through them.

The difference in view (and in access system) no doubt stems from traditional views of the role of the elected member. In the United Kingdom, members of parliament represent single-member geographical constituencies, and members of local authorities similarly represent closely defined areas, although there is often more than one member (but not more than three) for each electoral area. Members of parliament and of local authorities are expected to take account of the views of their constituents and to be ready to pursue their grievances. Many complaints are solved by elected members, and there are some who see the pursuit of constituents' grievances as a major task. The usefulness of the member cannot therefore be underrated in countries with a strong and deep-rooted tradition of member involvement with constituents' complaints. But if the member channel always worked, there would be no work for the ombudsman—and patently there is. Apart from the fact that a member's investigative powers are limited, for example, in not having the ombudsman's right of access to the source material on which decisions have been made, the fact is that the service that elected members can provide is at best uneven, whereas

the service that the ombudsman provides should at best be extremely even. Some members will care deeply about constituents' problems; others will find them the least attractive part of their work in parliament or in the local authority.

Moreover, local authority elected members have disadvantages from the complainant's point of view. Although they will be closer to the grass-roots than the member of parliament, they may not be as well known to constituents if only because they change more frequently and generally represent multiple member areas. A recent survey in a London borough of over two hundred thousand people showed that fewer than one in five could correctly name one of their sixty-four borough councillors, and only 6 percent could correctly name two or more of them. Yet, more than two-thirds of those questioned had had cause to complain to the council about something and almost half *had* heard of the ombudsman. Whether or not people know the name of a member of a local authority, members are often regarded by complainants as representatives of the body against which they wish to complain. Rightly or wrongly, they see little logic in being told that they can approach the ombudsman only through such a representative.

Discussion of this subject would not be complete without reference to the unique petitions system in the Federal German Republic where the role of the Bundestag member operates to the exclusion of an ombudsman system. A chairman of the Petitions Committee of the Bundestag, Lieselotte Berger, has described the system thus:

In contrast to most countries of the world, there is in the Federal Republic of Germany basic provision for comprehensive judicial control of administrative decisions. Thus a broad range of tasks which are performed in other countries by Ombudsmen is already taken care of in Federal Republic of Germany by the administrative courts. All that remains is the handling of those cases which are not, or to a limited extent only, subject to judicial examination. These are, in particular, decisions for which the authorities are allowed room for discretion or where the application of the law results in unacceptable hardship for the citizen. There is no need for a special extra parliamentary body to deal with these cases.

In addition, some hesitate to create a "fourth power" which would supplement the three traditional powers—the legislature, the executive and the judiciary. There are significant reasons why citizens' requests and complaints should be examined by the elected Parliament itself, for it is part of its job to uphold the citizens' interests vis-a-vis the authorities and to keep a check on the government. In addition, the work in the Petitions Committee produces a "feedback" effect: the members of the Petitions Committee can establish more directly than would be possible by the roundabout way of an Ombudsman's annual report what difficulties the citizen has, where there are problems with the authorities or where laws cause injustice and hardship. They are able to make use of this experience in their work in the technical committees of Parliament as well as in the working groups of the parliamentary parties.[6]

Thus, systems for investigating complaints range from one where the members of parliament control the investigations to those—the vast majority—where the elected members may know little or nothing about individual complaints and have no formal part to play in the ombudsman operation.

Supervising the Ombudsman, or Who Watches the Watchdog?

Frank Stacey has said:

All national or provincial Ombudsmen are responsible to their legislature and may report to a committee of the legislature. But none has a committee which takes such an active interest in the work of the Ombudsman as is taken by the House of Commons Select Committee on the British Parliamentary Commissioner.[7]

He did not go into the reasons for this situation, one of which no doubt is that the longer an ombudsman office has existed, the more it is accepted and is thought not to need close control. Regardless of whether his conclusion is totally correct (the Select Committee in Ontario took a very close interest in their ombudsman), there are undoubtedly variations in the methods laid down for the ombudsman to report to the legislature on the operation of the ombudsman service. Even where, as in West Germany, that service is actually provided through a committee of the legislature, the committee's chairman has written: "For a more effective performance by the Petitions Committee it is also important that the members of the Bundestag themselves attach greater significance to the Committee than they have done hitherto."[8]

Ombudsmen are divided into those who are grateful that the legislature does not pay too much attention to their work and those who wish they did have a body that was interested and to whom they could turn for guidance, advice, and, if necessary, support. Individual ombudsmen move from one group to another from time to time, especially when they feel they need allies in a fight.

This is a field that would merit, first, some research to establish the present position in factual terms and, second, some careful thought about the need for "supervision" and the most effective way of providing it. Objective research would establish not just whether there exists a committee of the legislature but how in practice it operates and whether existing requirements, for example, about annual reports, help or hinder. Sometimes one is

bound to wonder whether reports of six hundred and fifty pages plus appendices or of eight hundred pages contribute more to the revenues of the printers and the postal service than to the accountability of the ombudsman office. Careful thought about supervising the ombudsman service would also need to cover the precise functions of any supervising body and the relevance of other matters such as the feelings of dissatisfied complainants and of administrative agencies who felt they had cause to complain about the outcome of an investigation.

The Ombudsman and the Courts

There are two facets to this subject. The first is that some ombudsmen have the duty of supervising the law courts. This is the case in Sweden, for example.

The aim of the Ombudsman's supervision over the courts is to ensure that cases are tried and judgement rendered within a reasonable time and without abuses or breach of duties on the part of officials. The Ombudsman is empowered to intervene if it appears there were faults or malpractices during the proceedings of the trial such as if the parties or witnesses were mistreated in the court. Moreover the decisions of the courts may also fall within the purview of the Ombudsman's supervision even though he normally does not intervene except when an obvious error has been committed.[9]

The courts are equally covered by the Finnish ombudsman, but this duty in respect of the courts is not common among ombudsmen. This is not to say that it would not be useful to have in other countries an independent person to scrutinize the work of the courts and consider individual complaints about the way they have operated. There is, incidentally, an equal need to consider the relevance of an ombudsman to the work of administrative tribunals which are, to good effect, within the jurisdiction of ombudsmen in, for example, the Scandinavian countries and the Canadian provinces.

The second facet of the relationship between the ombudsman and the courts is perhaps more universally relevant to existing ombudsmen. It concerns the extent to which the ombudsman's role has been restricted because of the existence of the courts, and the possibility of establishing a formal link between the two institutions. On the latter point, the fact that, quantitatively, there is more "administration" year by year has once again aroused concern in Britain at the state of administrative law. An ombudsman must constantly say what is and what is not good administration. The main duty of the existing courts is to say whether or not the rule of common law or statute has been broken. Their concern is with the infringement of a legally enforceable rule—albeit by bad administration—whereas the ombudsman's concern is primarily about administrative action that may or may not infringe a rule of law but that falls short of a standard the ombudsman subjectively applies.

Despite the somewhat different concerns of ombudsmen and the courts, there is a common interest in ensuring that individual complainants secure a remedy if they are so entitled. In 1966, the Law Commission in England began a general inquiry into the possibilities of administrative law reform and, in 1969, recommended the establishment of a Royal Commission to carry out a detailed investigation. However, successive governments have refused to do more than consolidate the old forms of action, as opposed to introducing a new one. There has been no statutory extension of the courts' power to remedy administrative failure, although there have been some small changes in common law.

One wonders whether there will be growing pressure for the work of the ombudsmen and the work of the courts in the sphere of administrative law to be consolidated as an Administrative Division of the high court. In May 1979, JUSTICE and Oxford University began a joint review of British administrative law. The long French experience with *Droit Administratif* and the *Conseil d'Etat* seems to be the precedent, and as the work of the courts of the European community develops, applying largely French law, the impetus in that direction may accelerate.

On the other hand, the creation of the office of *mediateur* in France in 1973 was most significant in this context. To many British observers it was a surprising development, particularly to critics of the ombudsman idea who argued that a well-developed system of administrative justice provided more effective redress for the citizen against public authorities than could be provided by an ombudsman. Since France, with its *Conseil d'Etat* and subordinate *tribunaux administratifs,* had the most admired system of administrative courts in the world, it was surprising to find that the French Parliament had decided to set up an ombudsman to complement the work of the *Conseil d'Etat.* Some thought that the office would not have an effective role. But experience has shown that this is far from being the case and that the ombudsman can be very necessary, despite the existence of administrative legal systems.

Moreover, there can be what Frank Stacey describes as ''an almost obsessive shunning of provision for alternative channels of complaint.''[10] He especially applies this criticism to the British ombudsman system, pointing out that it is not found to the same extent in, for example, the Swedish ombudsman system. In Sweden, the aggrieved citizen often has a choice of several different channels of complaint, and the fact that he has already used one channel does not necessarily prohibit him from using another. Indeed, when a citizen has complained to an om-

budsman and has received a finding in his favor, he can use the ombudsman's report as evidence in a court of law. Reference was made earlier to the drawbacks, as summarized by Bernard Frank, of courts and court procedures in relation to dealing with citizens' complaints. Those drawbacks plus, for example, the French experience support the belief that the extension of jurisdiction of the courts would be no substitute for having an effective ombudsman system and that citizens should not be barred from turning to the ombudsman merely because some other channel of complaint is open to them.

Reference is made later to the JUSTICE view that the ombudsman's findings should be enforceable through the courts at the suit of the complainant. This is indeed the system in Northern Ireland, and the fact that the courts there have rarely been called to act in that way may indicate that the possibility is a useful deterrent for those who might not accept the ombudsman's findings. It could also be an effective way of linking the ombudsman to the courts in countries where up to now a very clear distinction has been drawn—not necessarily in the interests of the citizen.

Extending the Role of the Ombudsman

In some countries, the jurisdiction of the ombudsman is wide. The Swedish and Finnish ombudsmen, for example, cover all agencies of government, both central and local, and the courts, and can investigate complaints against the police and wholly state-owned industries, as well as complaints from members of the armed forces, prison inmates, and government employees. Other countries have separate ombudsmen for particular services; for example, there are ombudsmen for the armed forces in Israel, the Federal German Republic, and Norway. In some countries, the total ombudsman service is very wide, whereas in others it is confined to investigating complaints against the central, provincial, or local government.

In countries where ombudsmen deal only with complaints against government, there remain other large, and probably growing, areas of public administration that can provoke complaint from the citizen. In Great Britain, where the jurisdiction of the total ombudsman service is relatively narrow, these include postal, police, electrical, gas, transport, and broadcasting services. At present, there are varying arrangements (but not ombudsmen) for dealing with citizens' grievances about such services, just as there are separate statutory arrangements for pursuing complaints of sex discrimination and racial discrimination. Size of population and size of the area of public administration are important factors. But the simple question remains: if the ombudsman is a good idea in certain contexts, may it not be equally good in others? And wherever the creation of an ombudsman system is contemplated, the extent of jurisdiction has also to be settled. A multiplicity of complaints systems can be as confusing to citizens and as difficult to penetrate as the service they wish to complain against.

Existing ombudsmen are not necessarily best able to judge whether their service is working effectively, let alone whether a similar service should be extended to other areas of public administration. But they do surely have a duty to interest themselves in that possibility. In the English context, consumers of publicly supplied water can complain to a local ombudsman, but consumers of publicly supplied gas and electricity make their complaints to local consultative committees that are independent of the suppliers and broadly represent the range of consumer interests. Is the difference logical or efficient? The fact that those committees received some fifty-three thousand complaints in 1979–80 suggests that an individual ombudsman, or even a small "college," would be a hard-pressed substitute for the committees. But is there a role for an ombudsman, as JUSTICE has proposed, to whom the complainant can turn if the committees do not provide a satisfactory outcome?

There are other fields of perhaps wider interest. For example, the idea of an ombudsman to consider complaints against the police was specifically rejected in the United Kingdom, and a separate statutory body, the Police Complaints Board, was created instead to provide a measure of independence in the consideration of such complaints. Over seventy-five hundred complaints were submitted to the board in 1979–80, and, again, an individual ombudsman might have been overwhelmed.

The International Year of the Child aroused interest in England in having an ombudsman for children; that interest may grow because the trail has already been blazed in Scandinavia. A campaign in England aims "to try to make it possible for children and young people who are placed in the care of local authorities to have more say in planning and organising their own lives."[11] Thus far, it has led to the establishment of a conciliation service for children in care who have a problem. Such an initiative is close enough to the ombudsman's concern to deserve interest and support.

The relevance of the ombudsman system to the rights of prisoners is perhaps the field where existing ombudsmen have much experience to pass to those countries where prisons are outside the ombudsman's jurisdiction or where the creation of an ombudsman is proposed. Stanley Anderson has clearly shown the important role that the ombudsmen play in contributing to what he summarizes as "fairness within prisons."[12] As the chairman of JUSTICE recently pointed out, "a custodial sentence is ac-

companied by deprivation of most of a prisoner's civil rights."[13] In some countries at least, there is a balance to be redressed, and discussion of how to do that would be the poorer without a contribution from the ombudsmen. In Europe, for example, the growing influence of the European Commission on Human Rights in this field is very welcome, but reform is likely to be slow unless an active interest is shown in the individual countries where reform is overdue.

The ombudsman's role in the freedom of information is also relevant in considering extension of the ombudsman system. So, too, is the question of preserving confidentiality of information about individuals. Details about millions of people in many countries are now lodged in computers; does the individual need a means of redress if that information is incorrect or is misused and, if so, is there a role for an ombudsman? Eight European countries have some form of data protection legislation, but only in Sweden, as well as in the United States and New Zealand is there access to or public accountability for security and police files. Sweden also has a Data Inspection Board (within the jurisdiction of the ombudsman) with powers in respect of all public and private computer systems which include personal details. In New Zealand, the ombudsman also has a role in this field. The Wanganui Computer Centre Act of 1976 empowers a commissioner, in practice the ombudsman, to examine and correct personal security and police files on behalf of concerned citizens. Not for the first time New Zealand may have created a milestone.

To sum up, many areas of public administration provide much scope for citizens' complaints, and there are varying arrangements for considering them. The extent to which an ombudsman system is or might be the most effective means for investigating those grievances is a subject that the International Ombudsman Institute might well wish to consider, not as a substitute for action in individual countries but as a valuable source of information for such action. But where an ombudsman is thought appropriate, one of many questions to be considered is the precise form of the system in terms of numbers of ombudsmen and their relationship to each other. Some factors to be taken into account will be size of population and likely workload, geography, the need to have a system acceptable to those who may be investigated, and, last but not least, the need for a system that will not confuse the citizen. Sweden, for example, where the jurisdiction of the ombudsmen is very wide, has progressed from one *justitieombudsman* to a separate military ombudsman, to three ombudsmen (plus two deputies) in a combined office, and finally to four ombudsmen, one of whom is the administrative chief.

In Papua New Guinea, from the relatively recent start

there have been three ombudsmen, one of whom is the chief. In New Zealand, the system has moved from the single ombudsman to (with the extension of the office to cover local government) provision for the appointment of more than one ombudsman in addition to the chief. In Great Britain, when the government decided to create an ombudsman to deal with complaints against central government departments, they settled for an office largely on the then New Zealand model—a single officer responsible to parliament. A separate office was created later for the Health Service ombudsman, although in practice the same person has always held the two offices.

In England and Wales, it was decided not to extend the existing parliamentary commissioner's office to investigate complaints against local government. Instead, these countries opted for a number (at present three in England and one in Wales) of separate local ombudsmen, each covering a geographical area but forming commissions for each country. A formal statutory link was established with the parliamentary commissioner who is a member of both commissions (although there is no such link with the Health Service commissioner), but he has no role in the investigation of individual complaints against local authorities. This separate system was chosen because the local authorities were far more numerous and far-flung (compared with the central government departments, all with their head offices in London) and, perhaps, because it was thought that there would be far more complaints than could possibly be handled by a single ombudsman. Most of all, there is little doubt that the long-established and fiercely independent local authorities both separately and collectively would have been strongly opposed to what they would have regarded as "central supervision."

Although the commissions of local ombudsmen created in England and Wales can be termed "colleges," there is no statutory provision for collective responsibility in individual investigation matters, although each commission has a duty annually to review the way the system is working and may make recommendations to the government. There are undoubtedly certain advantages in a "college," namely, consultation; spreading the workload; deputizing when necessary; and avoiding the danger of overpersonalizing the office of ombudsman. When an ombudsman's personal workload can be kept within manageable proportions through sharing with colleagues, he should be able to become more involved in the individual complaints with which he deals—none of which advantages a single ombudsman enjoys. There are, of course, the natural disadvantages arising from the fact that a group of people is involved in operating a service that should be consistent in its policies and practices. In countries with large populations and numerous public agencies, "colle-

giate" or "collective" ombudsmen systems merit careful examination.

Differences between Central and Local Government

Systems of local government vary widely between countries; each has developed from different circumstances and to meet different needs. The common factor is that every local authority exists only to serve those who live in its area. It provides services of importance to citizens, and it must answer to them for doing the job efficiently. The jurisdiction of some ombudsmen extends to local government. In some cases, there are separate ombudsmen to consider complaints against local authorities. In other countries, local government is not covered, and no doubt in some there is still resistance to its inclusion.

While the ombudsman concept is as relevant to local administration as to central administration, experience from various quarters, particularly where an existing ombudsman system has been extended to cover local government (as in New Zealand in 1975), suggests that there are important differences that need to be appreciated in advance of introducing or extending the system. The position of the elected local member has already been mentioned in relation to access to the ombudsman. Unlike members of parliament or of provincial legislatures, they will be often closely involved in the administrative decisions and actions of the authority. Unless, as in New Zealand and Victoria, for example, their decisions are excluded from investigation, the ombudsman will be seen by local members not just as a person to whom citizens' complaints can be directed, but as an outsider who may well investigate their own actions. Some will adopt a defensive, if not hostile, attitude, compounded perhaps by a feeling that an official, however eminent or impartial, from the national or state capital cannot possibly judge what is unreasonable action in a local situation.

In short, the virtues of an ombudsman system have to be sold harder to local than to central government. This process has equally to be extended to the staff that serves the local authorities. By and large, the departments of central government seem to find it easier to adapt to the introduction of an ombudsman, however hard they might have fought against that introduction. A wide scattering of independent, directly elected local authorities with different traditions and problems and with staff who vary widely in calibre, will find it much more difficult, first, to accept that their citizens need an ombudsman and, second, to cooperate sensibly with the ombudsman service when it has been introduced.

It follows that an extra burden is placed on the ombudsman and his staff, and it is a burden that may have to be carried for a long time because of the bush fire nature of the exercise. No sooner will good and understanding relations be established with one local authority which has been investigated, than another authority in another part of the country may erupt at the outcome of an investigation of a complaint against it. The test is to restore calm and cooperation without slipping into the cosiness that destroys the impartiality and credibility of the ombudsman in the eyes of the citizen.

In making comparisons between how the ombudsman system can operate in respect of different tiers of government, as in judging whether the ombudsman idea can sensibly be extended into wider areas of public administration, the realities of different situations and "cultures" have to be defined and their significance assessed, before judging that what is sauce for the goose will also be sauce for the gander.

PROBLEMS AND PERSPECTIVES

At the beginning of this century, there were about 1.6 billion people in the world, of whom one in a hundred lived in a city. By the end of this century, according to a recent United Nations report, the population could be 6 billion, of whom more than half will live in cities. Already there are some twenty-six cities with more than 5 million people each and a combined population of 252 million. The citizen in the large city faces problems in relation to authority that may be quite outside the experience of the rural citizen.

In saying something of English experience on some subjects, the hope is that others will be able to make comparisons with their own experience, to put the problems into perspective, and to point to possibilities for future action. The points covered in this section are based largely on research done in 1977 by the staff of the English Commission for Local Administration and, in 1979, by Dr. Wyn Grant and Bob Haynes of the University of Warwick in support of a study of the local ombudsman service by JUSTICE (published by them in July 1980). Both surveys sought the views of those who had complained to the local ombudsmen, and they provided much consumer feedback.[14]

Dealing with Complaints Locally

As "government" impinges more and more on the individual and he or she becomes more affected *and* more inclined to question, so the scope and likelihood of complaint increase. What does the complainant do? Overwhelmingly, and perhaps not surprisingly, people take their complaints either to the office of the authority against which they are complaining or (rather less often) to an elected member of that authority. Seldom do people first turn to another quarter, for example, an advice agency or a lawyer, or direct to the ombudsman office.

This finding naturally reinforces two views: that emphasis should always be placed on seeking to have complaints raised and settled locally; and that England at least is not full of people ready to rush to the ombudsman without first giving the responsible authority a chance to settle the matter. If these views are to remain valid, the authorities must be willing and have the means to receive complaints and to consider them properly. With that in view, the English local ombudsmen prepared and issued jointly with representatives of authorities in February 1978 a Code of Practice setting out guidelines for dealing with complaints. It included a checklist by which authorities could judge their own arrangements.

As others will know from their experience, publication of the code did not herald a new deal for all would-be complainants, or the rapid demise of the ombudsman as a necessary institution. When the scene was surveyed in November 1979, the conclusion was that, while the authorities had made marked progress in introducing or reviewing local complaint procedures, some regrettably did not propose to introduce them, relatively few procedures were well-publicized, and some were overelaborate and complicated. The "culture" of an authority or public agency influences the arrangements they make for considering citizens' complaints. Moreover, the "good" ones will pay heed to a Code of Practice; the "bad" ones will ignore it.

It was accepted, as all ombudsmen no doubt do, that the road would be rockier in respect of some agencies with which they would deal than with others. The code therefore sought to establish a benchmark from which movement would more likely be forward than backward.

The most effective solution may lie in imposing on every department or authority that provides a public service a duty to have procedures for investigating complaints. It is significant that the relevant British minister is proposing to take the power to direct a local authority about the information it should provide to citizens. The power would only be used if the authority did not follow an agreed code of practice on the information to be provided, a code that incidentally includes giving information about the existence of the local ombudsman.

Publicity for the Ombudsman

The best possible arrangements for considering complaints will not always lead to solutions. The English citizens surveyed, faced with disappointment locally, did turn to the ombudsman. How did they know he existed?

Just over one-half knew from the media—newspapers, radio, and television—and it is helpful that local newspapers give good coverage to reports on investigations in their area. The rest knew from various other sources. It is potentially disturbing that only 12 percent said they were told by an employee or elected member of the authority about which they were complaining.

The "culture" of the authority is again significant, and the survey findings emphasized how important it is to secure the support and understanding of authorities for the ombudsman's work. Sir Guy Powles has referred to the natural reluctance of legislators to allow other people to receive complaints from their constituents. To which must be added the equally strong reluctance of the administrator to say "if you do not accept my decision you can of course go to the Ombudsman." The public library close to the local ombudsman's London office displays posters telling citizens how to complain about a wide range of agencies, but not about the local authority that runs the library.

The need is to convince authorities that they can rightly claim credit because there is an ombudsman. Leaving citizens to find out for themselves that they have an independent person to whom they can turn with their complaints will increase their belief that injustice has been done. Once a complaint has reached the ombudsman, the cooperation of authorities is in English experience generally very good. The same helpful spirit needs to be applied to the individual citizen.

The English local ombudsmen have so far deliberately not embarked on a generalized publicity campaign about the service. In keeping with the philosophy already described, authorities have instead been urged that *they* should inform those who might need the ombudsman. For that purpose, they have been kept supplied with booklets for citizens explaining the scope of the service and the procedure for making complaints. The booklet has also been widely distributed to advice-giving agencies and, although relatively few complainants say they learned of the service through such an agency, the percentage in the lower socioeconomic groups was higher—15 percent compared with 2 percent for the highest group.

Whether or not to publicize and how to publicize are subjects of regular debate in ombudsman offices. The 1979 report of the New Brunswick ombudsman, for example, records that the traditional view of his office against a publicity campaign has been changed, and an advertising budget and program established. The 1979 report of the Israel ombudsman states that such a campaign doubled the number of complaints to him. On the other hand, the Alberta ombudsman reported an 18 percent decrease in complaints received in 1979, despite the fact that circumstances provided plenty of publicity for the service

during the year. The experience of Alberta, although interesting and worth investigating, is likely to be untypical. It is more likely that publicity will increase the number of complaints received, but the charge of "drumming up business" can be easily dismissed. The ombudsman has a duty to publish information about the procedure for making complaints, and that job must be done effectively, which means, for example, being open with the media. The problem is to hold the balance between urging authorities to be positive in trying to resolve complaints themselves and urging them to tell the individual of his right to go to the ombudsman.

Do the "Right" People Complain?

The types of people who complain to an ombudsman may well vary from country to country depending perhaps on the subjects within jurisdiction. Those who complain to the English local ombudsmen are older than the population at large and have received more formal education. The "top" socioeconomic class predominates; semi-skilled and unskilled people are particularly underrepresented. Complaints about planning—mainly from those who own their houses—have always formed over one-third of the complaints in the country as a whole. Complaints about the social services normally account for only about 3 percent of the total; they have led to some of the most difficult investigations. While 30 percent of complaints are about housing, there were only 682 such complaints in the year ended March 31, 1980, although there are nearly 5 million local authority-owned dwellings in England.

This problem is not confined to the ombudsman service but is true of the "take up" of many social services in the developed countries. A 1976 survey in Britain on the provision of health care concluded that, although what are broadly called the "working classes" suffered more illness than the "middle classes," the National Health Service spent up to a third more per head on middle-class than on working-class patients. This finding was broadly confirmed in a government-sponsored survey published in August 1980. The quality of care received by the lowest social classes, and especially the amount of preventative medicine like antenatal care, is far lower than that received by the top social class. Currently, for example, the most underprivileged areas of the country have the largest proportion of vacancies for senior hospital doctors.

There are many facets to the problem of getting through to those who might have cause to complain but do not. It is of interest to record a finding from the JUSTICE report about the treatment of complaints by authorities at the stage before they came to the ombudsman:

The results suggest that if you are well educated and in a non-manual occupation, your chances of "success" in the sense of getting your complaints seriously considered (and discussed, not merely answered) are much greater than if you are working in a manual occupation and left school at the statutory school leaving age. Local authorities are not being accused of persistent social bias in the way in which they handle complaints. It is simply more difficult for the less well educated and less socially skilled to persist with their complaint in an effective way until they obtain satisfaction from the council concerned.[15]

In statistical terms, the people most successful in securing a positive response from an authority were those who had completed their education at the age of nineteen or over. The JUSTICE report records certain qualifications but concludes that, those aside, "the handling of complaints by local authorities is prone to social biases which may to a large degree be unavoidable."

The finding adds a further dimension to the problem of the disadvantaged groups:

- They are more likely to be housed by the local authority or be receiving help from local authority social services. They can therefore have potential cause for complaint in very sensitive areas.

- They are more likely to have difficulty in putting their complaint to the authority and in persisting with it and thus in obtaining satisfaction.

- They are less likely to know of the existence of the ombudsman.

- They are more likely to be diffident about taking their complaint to an elected member of the authority.

- They are more likely to have difficulty in putting their complaint in writing.

- They are more likely to have difficulty in doing justice to their complaint when they do set it down. (It is significant that one in three of those questioned who *had* been educated to age 19 or over said that *they* had difficulty in putting their complaint in words on paper. The proportion was two in three for semi- and unskilled manual workers.)

This list would not apply universally. The great majority of ombudsmen can, for example, be approached directly. On the other hand, some operate over far greater distances than in England, so that meeting a complainant to clarify an ill-formed complaint may well be quite unrealistic. Moreover, literacy rates are lower in some other countries, and language barriers may operate for newly arrived immigrant groups.

Just as the ombudsman is not a universal panacea for all administrative ills, it is never going to be equally accessible to all citizens. But may the time not have come to redress the balance? This must start with the authority—hence, the importance of an administrative "culture" that firmly believes in helping citizens—and not just in helping them to complain. Ombudsman's offices have plenty of scope to help redress the balance. In the English experience a complaint is likely to be more fully investigated if the complainant has been met. In systems where the ombudsman can exercise discretion to decide whether to pursue a complaint with the authority concerned, more complainants should be seen where geography does not make that impossible and particularly those whose submissions suggest they might not be doing justice to their case.

The ombudsman needs strong links with local advice-giving agencies where they exist. There is, however, a danger, because of heavy workloads and limited resources, that ombudsmen and their staffs will tend to rely on "establishment" sources of publicity and advice, whereas in England, for example, the last two decades have seen a rapid growth in grass-roots agencies for advising the citizen and fighting his battles, and the use made of some traditional sources of advice has fallen. It is much more difficult to get through to the grass-roots—and to convince the agencies there of the value of the ombudsman—than it is to tap into established networks. One way tried in England is to invite workers from these advice agencies to come to seminars held in the office to discuss the work of the local ombudsmen and its relevance to the problems with which the agencies are dealing.

Moreover, effective help from the media is not gained easily. It requires less effort to get coverage in newspapers read mainly by those who know very well how to complain than to get coverage in the newspapers that most people buy. It requires less effort to get time on a radio or television program with a small audience than to get time and gain attention on a program with wide popular appeal.

Relevant to the problem of getting through to the disadvantaged is the proposition that the ombudsmen should themselves go out in an informal but well-publicized way so that, in addition to speaking at local meetings and doing a local radio program, time is specifically set aside for people to come to the ombudsman with their complaints. This is done by a number of ombudsmen who have large geographical areas to cover or minority groups who require special attention. The views of individual ombudsmen vary, but if only to combat the "God syndrome" one can see sound sense in the ombudsman personally going out and about and not confining those travels to formal meetings. Radio phone-in programs can be useful, but they are relevant only to those who can listen to the program and who have ready access to a telephone and the confidence to use it, a confidence that even now a surprisingly large number of people lack. The fact that in some complaint systems the ombudsman office is regarded as the last resort should not mean that to know of it and to reach it is the most difficult task of all.

Delivering the Goods

The ombudsman has no point unless a finding supporting a complaint is followed by action to set matters right, or, to be realistic, unless *most* of such findings are followed by remedial action. What if the ombudsman is satisfied by the remedy offered by the authority but the complainant is not? For example, in the six years up to March 31, 1980, the English local ombudsmen expressed their satisfaction with the remedial action in 563 cases and dissatisfaction with only thirty-five, or 6 percent. On the face of it, this is an admirable record. Yet, while a majority of those questioned in the JUSTICE survey were satisfied with the ombudsman's investigation and findings, a majority were not satisfied with what happened afterwards. As a result, JUSTICE recommended that the local ombudsmen's findings be enforceable through the courts at the suit of the complainant. JUSTICE reasoned (based on survey findings) that in deciding whether or not the ombudsman was satisfied with the remedy provided, he was making a discretionary decision for which he was not accountable to any other person or body.

But the discussion should not be primarily about "teeth" for the ombudsman or about the need for a relationship between the ombudsmen and the courts. If there is a credibility gap between ombudsmen and some injured complainants, is such a gap perhaps inevitable? Does it detract from the usefulness of the office? Let us take an extreme example. The ombudsman finds that an authority has mishandled a planning application for a house extension that will slightly reduce the privacy of, and thus cause some injustice to, the complainant who lives next door. The authority agrees to apologize and to revise its working methods to try to avoid similar mistakes. The ombudsman is satisfied with that remedy; the complainant bitterly protests that the injustice will only be removed if the house extension is removed. The ombudsman is right to stand firm in such cases but on the understanding that he will try to convince the complainant that the remedy is reasonable in the circumstances. It may, for example, seem cold comfort to stress to a complainant that the main outcome will be improved administration in the future, although more complainants than we may think may gain satisfaction from having that point made to them.

The more difficult situation arises when the ombudsman has worked hard to get a remedy from a reluctant authority and when the remedy finally offered still falls somewhat short of his ideal expectations. Bearing in mind the time that will have passed in striving for a remedy, and the ever-present workload of other cases, is the ombudsman wrong to be satisfied with less than perfection? There is a delicate balance to maintain here. But the remedy should be examined through the complainant's eyes, even though the eventual decision may be that he should not see all that he wishes to see.

Authorities, too, have an important part to play. A remedy will be the more acceptable if it is quickly given in a generous spirit. The begrudged remedy contains the built-in likelihood that, though reasonable in itself, the injured party will not be satisfied with it.

Making a Wider Impact

As the direct impact of any ombudsman is necessarily very limited, there is a spur to increase the indirect impact of the ombudsmen's findings. Moreover, the possibilities of more efficient public administration are especially attractive in times of economic difficulty when there is pressure for reduced public expenditure. The remedies sought after investigation are always twin-headed: to dissolve the injustice to the individual and to improve administrative methods so that the same complaint does not arise again. While the resources needed to pursue the second objective are usually limited, only an ombudsman office can know all the lessons learned from all the investigations it has completed.

In the individual case, one must rely on the authority to learn the lessons from the investigation of the complaint against them, and actually to apply them. The average ombudsman has no power, and probably insufficient resources, to undertake a continuing efficiency audit. All he can do is make it clear that failure to correct a faulty system after a complaint has been lodged will simply create a great furor in the future. But the ombudsman office is the logical place from which the lessons can and should be disseminated to a wider audience. In England, this has been done by feeding views to government departments, for example, on the information to be given to parents about the schools to which their children might go and about the best arrangements for settling disputes about allocations to schools. A good relationship has been established with the professional planning organizations which are inevitably concerned that so many complaints reflect on the work of their members. Every qualified planner is now receiving guidance on the lessons derived from the ombudsmen's work and the standard of practice necessary to reduce the danger of maladministration.

This process needs to be a continuous one if it is to have impact, and the ombudsman office should regularly consider whether its resources are being used judiciously. For example, it is correct to investigate individual complaints about the way public housing has been allocated to individual citizens. But what of applying the ombudsmen's experience to secure an overall improvement in systems for allocating houses? A recent survey in an area of London revealed that four out of five tenants in public housing had problems inside their homes. Does the ombudsman not have a responsibility at least to consider whether experience of individual investigations enables him to help with the wider problem of the repair and maintenance of public housing? Such a task requires not only the effort of codifying experience but also persistence, perhaps over a long time, to secure effective reform.

Apart from the resource problem, and the problem of balance between the different facets of the ombudsman's work, it is necessary to guard against thinking that an impression has been made when perhaps it has not. Ombudsmen's annual reports seek to draw attention to bad practices (and sometimes to good practices) revealed by investigations. But it would be unwise to assume that those reports are eagerly awaited by those who receive them or that they will reach those willing *and* able to pass the message down the line and secure action. In short, hard and thoughtful effort is needed to secure the indirect impact, and experience suggests that there is very much a personal role for the ombudsman to play in this field. Some barriers will never be removed, and others can be surmounted only if the office has achieved real regard and if the holder is persistently persuasive with a well-argued case.

The aim of the indirect impact should be not just to improve practices in particular areas but to establish benchmarks to which authorities can relate their practices. The Code of Practice on complaint procedures was such a benchmark in England. A next step should be to seek to establish a Code of Good Administrative Practice. The idea is by no means original. In 1971, a JUSTICE committee recommended that the British Parliament enact a ''Statement of Principles of Good Administration'' as a framework for all government departments, local authorities, and publicly owned bodies and industries. A draft statement was prepared which was perhaps too legalistic and formal, but its principles were designed to ensure that

(a) people likely to be particularly and materially affected by a decision of an administrative authority are told about it beforehand, and are given a reasonable opportunity of being heard;

(b) the authority will ascertain all material facts before taking the decisions;

(c) decisions are taken promptly, the reasons for them are stated, and are made known to people likely to be affected by them;

(d) authorities will give information about what they are doing promptly and accurately whenever it is reasonably asked for.

The statement has not yet been enacted, and there are deeply conflicting views about the need for it and its effectiveness if it were endorsed. No one would underestimate the difficulties of implementing it. But no ombudsman would doubt that its application would be greatly welcomed by many complainants and by those who may have cause to complain but do not.

More progress has been made in other countries. For example, Part II of the Barbados Administrative Justice Bill set down provisions to apply the principles of natural justice, including a duty to supply statements of the reasons for administrative decisions. The ground is also covered, among other matters, in, for example, the Swedish Administrative Procedures Act of 1971 and in the Australian Administrative Decisions (Judicial Review) Act of 1977. This is indeed a field where the International Ombudsman Institute has a role to play. It can inform ombudsmen of the progress that others are making in establishing the benchmarks derived from work and experience that is common to all. The series of Occasional Papers will be used for this purpose, and Paper 4—''A Note on Common Administrative Errors'' by Sir Guy Powles—is a good example of a contribution of universal value. Ombudsmen should also see themselves partly as public relations men for the bodies within their jurisdiction since in the majority of cases they find no fault in the matters they investigate. This is not a casual thought; standards of administration can be improved, and the morale of administrators uplifted, if an impartial investigator both praises the good and criticizes the bad.

SUMMARY

The objectives derived from ombudsman legislation vary. It is important to know what those objectives are, but one should not feel inhibited by them. Legislation seldom anticipates all the realities and cannot easily be changed to reflect changing circumstances. Moreover, many ombudsmen at times operate on the fringe of their statutory responsibilities. For example, the fact that an act does not say that the ombudsman office *must* seek to reform administrative practices generally does not mean that it should not seek to do so. Indeed, it will uniquely gather experience and could be blamed if it did not apply that experience in the wider interest. But some objectives may deserve more priority than others, especially when there is pressure on resources. It is often tempting to do the easy thing and to postpone the more difficult.

Access to the ombudsman is only one example of the

obstacles between the complainant and the ombudsman office. The subject is closely related to that of publicity, and views on it may sharply vary. Some ombudsmen may see themselves as a last resort whose existence is discovered only after other avenues have been explored. They may well look askance at visits to rural areas or advertisements for the ombudsman on milk cartons. Others will see little point in the institution unless its existence is widely known, so that from the start the would-be complainant knows that he has an impartial person to whom he can ultimately turn, and the administrator knows that his actions are open to independent investigation.

Supervision for the ombudsman is a two-sided coin. Those who feel that they require minimum supervision may question the usefulness (to citizens more than to ombudsmen) of a supervisory body that can support the ombudsman as well as supervise him. Such a body has a place especially in countries where the office is relatively new and where hostile interests are strong. The ombudsman must largely fight the battles. He will be the first to see, for example, the defects in practice in the ombudsman legislation, but without friends in the right places the battles will be longer than they might be and may not always lead to victories. It must be wrong if "Ombudsmen are mostly ignored by their parent legislatures."[16]

The courts have severe limitations from the point of view of the aggrieved citizen who wishes to complain against administrative defect. The position is scarcely better in those countries that have a system of administrative courts. Even in the Federal German Republic where the existence of such courts is one argument used for not having an ombudsman, it is not used as an argument against having a separate system for dealing with citizens' complaints on matters not subject to judicial examination. A role for the courts may well develop to ensure remedies for complaints where authorities are reluctant to give them. But the drawbacks of the courts—cost, tension, delay, and formality—point to the need for an ombudsman and also demonstrate features that should be avoided in the way the ombudsman operates.

If the ombudsman office is a good idea in certain contexts, may it not be an equally good idea in others? There are still in some countries, and on some subjects, gaps in the provision made for safeguarding citizens' legitimate rights. The ombudsman who believes that his office performs a useful function in one field has a responsibility to make others aware that other fields may benefit from an extension or creation of the system.

The task of local ombudsmen is different from that of investigating the actions of central government departments. An ombudsman system needs to be adapted according to the activity to which it is applied, just as it will need adapting to cultural, constitutional, geographical, and historical circumstances. The demand for an ombudsman system cannot be met by taking one "off the shelf" or by putting existing legislation through the photocopier.

Authorities should be constantly pressured to solve complaints locally and to have clear and well-publicized systems for considering citizens' complaints. In that sense, the ombudsman should be the last resort (but not an unknown institution). But there are two related tasks. First, the ombudsman must take a leading part in maintaining the pressure. He will after all be in an excellent position to see not only cases that could easily have been settled locally if the will and the system had existed, but also cases where the citizen has had to engage in an extraordinary battle to pursue his complaint locally because the local arrangements for dealing with complaints are defective. The second task is to be vigilant that local settlement of complaints does not become an easy option to disguise defects in administration. For example, a complaint that someone has not been allocated a house can be met by allocating one to that person. But that action may not ensure the improvement of a defective allocation system and may indeed create injustice to others still on the waiting list for houses.

If there are obstacles to knowing about the ombudsman and to making a complaint to him—the obstacle of having to make a written complaint, for example—those obstacles can be especially formidable for those least well equipped to fight their own battles. Moreover, these same people are more likely to have cause for complaint because they are more dependent than others on public services—housing, social welfare, education. The obstacles need to be minimized for all citizens. Help to surmount them is particularly needed for those who already have disadvantages. This means regularly looking at publicity and procedures from the point of view of the disadvantaged and seeking the advice of those who work directly with such groups. For example, a full report of an investigation in a local newspaper is helpful to the ombudsman and to many citizens, but it will have small relevance for the minority who cannot read or for the majority who never buy or read that newspaper.

A task for the ombudsman is to minimize the number of disappointed complainants. The time may well come when the agencies subject to investigation will have to be told either to cooperate reasonably to remedy injustice or accept that powers of enforcement will be given either to the ombudsman or to the courts.

There is no point in investigating individual complaints if the knowledge gained from such investigations is not applied to the wider purpose of improving administrative practices. The whole ombudsman concept can be considered a failure if the ombudsman is seen as a deterrent causing officials to become overcautious and pedantic. Rather, his reports must be widely studied by officials who want to improve their administrative methods. As objective observers, ombudsmen are in an excellent position to see what standards should be set and, as reformers or fighters, to campaign for action to get them.

An examination of how the ombudsman's role evolved and of future possibilities for development cannot be complete without discussing the impact of the personalities of the ombudsmen themselves. The individual nature of the appointment makes it inevitable that the individual will shape the "culture" of the service. In England, for example, the appointment as the first parliamentary commissioner of Sir Edmund Compton, who had previously been comptroller and auditor-general, meant that the parliamentary ombudsman system was modeled on the office of which he had previous experience. Dr. Nebenzahl in Israel was similarly influenced when he became commissioner for complaints in addition to being state comptroller. In both cases, the reputation and background of the appointees enhanced the prestige and credibility of the new office.

However the ombudsman office is defined, its achievements depend upon its public standing with complainants and with the authorities investigated, and will be derived from the reputation the office gains in practice. The best reputation will never be a reality if the office succumbs to what has earlier been called the "God syndrome," whereby the ombudsman suffers from delusions of grandeur and infallibility. If one had to single out just one practical point, it would be to emphasize that the ombudsman office must have a human face and not be hidden by the development of its own bureaucracy, which would create the sort of dissatisfaction the ombudsman is there to dispel. Ombudsman letters, for example, must be written in terms plain to the recipient. Complaints that arise from poor communication can only be compounded by letters written in officialese of the worst kind. To achieve this clarity, the staff must not only have a natural skill in writing but also be constantly reminded to put themselves in the position of those who will read what they write.

The spread of the institution of the ombudsman has been, and will continue to be, a response to a genuinely felt need. Ombudsmen will never please everyone, but they should never forget that those who feel the need for them and whom they exist to serve expect them to work hard to fulfill their expectations.

NOTES

1. Ombudsman Commission of Papua New Guinea, Annual Reports, 1975–76 and 1978–79.

2. Sir Guy Powles, "Citizen's Hope: Ombudsmen for the 1980s" (Alberta: 1978).

3. Jack Springett, "Education," London, February 8, 1980.

4. Bernard Frank, "The Ombudsman—A Challenge," *International Bar Journal* (November 1971).

5. Frank Stacey, *Ombudsmen Compared* (Oxford: Clarendon Press, 1978).

6. Lieselotte Berger, "The Administered Citizen—Experience and Findings from Parliamentary Work" (Berlin: 1977).

7. Stacey, *Ombudsmen Compared.*

8. Berger, "The Administered Citizen."

9. Ibrahim al-Wahab, *The Swedish Institution of Ombudsman* (Stockholm: Liber Förlag, 1979).

10. Stacey, *Ombudsmen Compared.*

11. "A Voice for the Child in Care," London, 1980.

12. Stanley Anderson, "Ombudsmen and Prisons in Scandinavia" (Copenhagen: 1978).

13. JUSTICE, *Annual Report,* London, June 1980.

14. Commission for Local Administration in England, Annual Report, 1977–78; and JUSTICE, *The Local Ombudsmen—A Review of the First Five Years* (London, 1980).

15. JUSTICE, *The Local Ombudsmen.*

16. Stanley Anderson, *American Journal of Comparative Law* 26 (1978).

CHAPTER 4

THE SELF-PERCEPTIONS OF OMBUDSMEN: A COMPARATIVE SURVEY

LARRY B. HILL, University of Oklahoma

IN THE PAST quarter of a century, the institution of ombudsman has spread beyond Scandinavia. Can self-styled ombudsman offices be profitably compared on an interstate or intrastate basis? If so, can a generic type be discerned? What are its distinctive characteristics? How do ombudsmen compare with similar complaint-handling institutions? To find answers to such questions, ombudsmen were surveyed during 1975 to 1977. Scholars have suggested several definitions of the institution.

Walter Gellhorn lists the "common attributes" of ombudsmen:

1. All are instruments of the legislature but function independently of it, with no links to the executive branch and with only the most general answerability to the legislature itself. 2. All have practically unlimited access to official papers bearing upon matters under investigation, so that they can themselves review what prompted administrative judgment. 3. All can express an ex officio expert's opinion about almost anything that governors do and that the governed do not like. 4. All take great pains to explain their conclusions, so that both administrators and complaining citizens well understand the results reached.[1]

John E. Moore identifies these "distinctive attributes or capacities" of the office: "An Ombudsman is an independent, impartial, and easily accessible expert in government who receives and investigates individual complaints of bureaucratic abuse. He reports on them, and

may publicize his findings, but has no power to change administrative decisions."[2]

Donald C. Rowat points to the office's "essential features":

(1) The Ombudsman is an independent and non-partisan officer of the legislature, usually provided for in the constitution, who supervises the administration; (2) he deals with specific complaints from the public against administrative injustice and maladministration; and (3) he has the power to investigate, criticize and publicize, but not to reverse, administrative action.[3]

Stanley V. Anderson contends that the ombudsman's "essential characteristics" require the incumbent to be: "(1) independent, (2) impartial, (3) expert in government, (4) universally accessible, and (5) empowered only to recommend and to publicize."[4]

And finally, there is the following definition of the "classical" ombudsman as:

(1) legally established, (2) functionally autonomous, (3) external to the administration, (4) operationally independent of both the legislature and the executive, (5) specialist, (6) expert, (7) nonpartisan, (8) normatively universalistic, (9) client-centered but not anti-administration, and (10) both popularly accessible and visible. The institution's mission is to generate complaints against government administration, to use its extensive powers of investigation in performing a postdecision administrative audit, to form judgments which criticize or vindicate administra-

tors, and to report publicly its findings and recommendations but not to change administrative decisions.[5]

Despite differences of emphasis, these definitions have many common features; furthermore, the academician's definition of the ombudsman and the International Bar Association (IBA) definition are strikingly alike:

An office provided for by the constitution or by action of the legislature or parliament and headed by an independent, high-level public official who is responsible to the legislature or parliament, who receives complaints from aggrieved persons against government agencies, officials, and employees or who acts on his own motion, and who has the power to investigate, recommend corrective action, and issue reports.[6]

Thus, the IBA-recognized offices were used as the survey's universe of *classical ombudsmen*. In addition, for comparative purposes, a number of *quasi-ombudsmen* were included; these complaints officials (sometimes called "executive" ombudsmen) share many of the classical ombudsman's characteristics, but lack at least one fundamental structural feature—usually some compromise has been made concerning the offices' independence.[7]

Nearly all of those surveyed returned the questionnaire; many respondents provided elaborate replies. The responses of the forty-seven classical ombudsmen analyzed below include nine from the Scandinavian countries, twenty-two from British Commonwealth countries, six from other European countries, and ten from the United States.[8] The replies of several special-purpose ombudsmen from around the world are excluded, as are those of several quasi-ombudsmen. Large numbers of quasi-ombudsmen exist only in the United States, which is the point of origin of the seventeen responses reported below from this type of office (seven have statewide jurisdiction, and ten have local jurisdiction only).[9] The survey analysis is organized around the following dimensions:

1. *Accessibility to citizens*—Are ombudsmen anxious to serve, deeply involved in the local community, and highly accessible; or are they distant, Olympian creatures who occasionally deign to accept complaints from mere mortals?

2. *Substance of complaints*—Do ombudsmen deal with dramatic grievances against "administrative injustice and maladministration" (Rowat), or do they listen to tales of garbage not picked up?

3. *Operational norms*—Are ombudsmen impartial and nonpartisan, or are they the people to see when you need an advocate or a favor?

4. *Degree of political autonomy*—Is the ombudsman really independent, or does the office, in fact, have to pay close attention to the desires of the executive and the legislature?

ACCESSIBILITY TO CITIZENS

For the most part, the early Swedish ombudsmen operated much like the Eastern European procurator or the inspector-general, a relatively independent position found in many armies. That is, ombudsmen were heavily involved in the inspection of such governmental facilities as prisons. The inspection role became less important as citizens began to lodge increasing numbers of complaints, but ombudsmen continued to inspect. They initiated some complaints that they learned about through the mass media or other sources.[10] Most of the extra-Scandinavian agitation for an ombudsman has focused, however, on the institution's role as an investigator of grievances presented by citizens. Some offices, for example, those in the British Isles, do not even have the authority to take up complaints on their own motion.

Offices' Operational Modes

Two principal operational modes for ombudsmen can be postulated: one is an *aggressive* mode in which the office seeks out matters of concern, inspects, and initiates investigations; the other is a *reactive* mode in which the office simply waits for citizens to judge complaints and then acts on whatever has been brought forward.

The data in Table 4.1 record answers to the following question about the offices' operational modes: "Is the posture of your office: 1. almost entirely passive in that you wait for complaints to be brought to you; or 2. do you take up a substantial number of complaints on your own initiative?" The responses reveal that outside of Scandinavia the ombudsman has become mainly a *reactive* institution; this is almost exclusively so of the Commonwealth officials.[11] These answers make it clear that the new ombudsmen function chiefly as citizens' service organizations of a type to be revealed by subsequent questions.

The concept of "outreach" has recently become popular in such client-service fields as social work. The notion is simply that many of the most needy clients may be intimidated by transportation problems, by inchoate fears of going to a centralized office that may seem forbidding, or by ignorance of the services available. According to outreach theorists, the solution is to take the service to the clients through establishing a local delivery system. In

Table 4.1
Ombudsmen's Principal Operational Modes (in percentages)

OPERATIONAL MODE	SCANDINAVIA (N=9)	COMMONWEALTH (N=22)	OTHER EUROPE (N=6)	UNITED STATES (N=10)	U.S. QUASI (N=17)	TOTAL CLASSICAL (N=47a)
Mainly passive	11	95	67	70	88	70
Many initiatives	89	5	33	30	12	30
Total	100	100	100	100	100	100

a The responses of the quasi-ombudsmen were excluded from these totals.

order to measure the extent to which the outreach philosophy has affected the ombudsman institution, a question asked: "Does your office have any branch offices to provide 'outreach' services to citizens in local areas?" None of the Scandinavians replied affirmatively; only about one-fifth of the U.S. classical and the quasi-ombudsmen reported they had such branch offices, but 33 percent of the Other European and 27 percent of the Commonwealth officials said they possessed them. Apparently, ombudsmen in general have not, as yet anyway, been greatly influenced by the outreach movement. A few offices, however, spontaneously reported that they periodically "rode a circuit" through their jurisdiction; that is, they traveled to various towns, announcing in advance that they would receive complainants in some location such as a post office.

Barriers to Access

Although the data thus far presented indicate that few ombudsmen are very aggressive either in developing their own complaints or in actively soliciting them from citizens, the degree to which the offices are open to the approach of clients may vary considerably. The most extreme limitation on accessibility is the requirement of the French and the British offices that complaints be filtered through legislators—although the parliamentary commissioner for administration, in his role as health service commissioner, accepts complaints directly from the public. In order to assure that the office was not swamped with trivial complaints, the New Zealand ombudsman was required, until 1975, to charge a $2 fee. Such barriers to citizen access have not been erected for any other offices.

Legal limitations on jurisdiction may, of course, be significant barriers for clients, even though everyone included in the present analysis answered the following question positively: "Does your office have general jurisdiction over the levels of administration to which it applies?" Ombudsmen were not in complete agreement that

their jurisdiction, spatially conceived, was entirely satisfactory. In fact, 32 percent of the total agreed that "My office's jurisdiction should be expanded so as to include more administrative agencies." Only 13 percent of the Scandinavians concurred, but 40 percent of the Commonwealth and 50 percent of the Other European groups endorsed the statement. The U.S. rates of agreement were 20 percent for the classical offices and 29 percent for the quasi-ombudsmen.

Jurisdiction can also be identified in analytical terms, and the following question was intended to facilitate some analytical differentiations: "It is often said that complaint-handling offices should confine their attention to 'administrative' matters and should stay out of 'political' or 'policy' matters. Is your office's jurisdiction limited to searches for maladministration or errors, etc., involving administrative matters or functions?" Nine out of ten of the Commonwealth offices reported their jurisdiction was thus limited, and it is well known that some of those offices (willingly or unwillingly) construe "maladministration" in very narrow terms. Four out of five of the Other European respondents, five out of seven of the U.S. classical officials, and three out of four of the Scandinavians are also limited to quests for maladministration. But less than half (47 percent) of the U.S. quasi-ombudsmen had their scope of investigation constrained in this manner.

Another way in which access to the ombudsman may be limited is through requiring that other appeals be utilized before the office will investigate. Lawyers call such a requirement "exhaustion of remedies"; sociologists are more likely to call it "cooling out the mark." Seventy-two percent of the total ombudsmen agreed with the following statement: "Our office usually demands that clients exhaust whatever other appeals channels are available before we will investigate." Four-fifths of both the Other European and the Commonwealth respondents and three-fourths of the U.S. classical ombudsmen reported such a restriction, but only half of the Scandinavians and 47 percent of the U.S. quasi-ombudsmen did. Thus, most

Table 4.2.
Clients' Principal Method of Approach to Ombudsmen (in percentages)

PRINCIPAL APPROACH	SCANDINAVIA (N=8)	COMMONWEALTH (N=21)	OTHER EUROPE (N=5)	UNITED STATES (N=10)	U.S. QUASI (N=17)	TOTAL CLASSICAL (N=44a)
Correspondence	100	76	100	10	6	68
Telephone	—	14	—	90	94	27
Interview	—	10	—	—	—	5
Total	100	100	100	100	100	100

a The responses of the quasi-ombudsmen were excluded from these totals.

of the world's ombudsmen, with or without legal direction, restrict their role to that of a court of last resort and deny or discourage access to citizens who may have other appeals options.[12]

Methods of Access

According to law, most ombudsmen must require that complaints be lodged in written form. This condition apparently disciminates against those clients who are poorly educated, who have difficulty expressing themselves in writing, or who are not highly motivated. This requirement has been dropped for some of the United States and other recently appointed ombudsmen, and many offices to which it applies get around it by encouraging telephoned or personal approaches. After investigation has proceeded, they assist the client in developing a formal, written complaint.

Table 4.2 records the responses to an inquiry about methods of client access: "Please rank the frequency with which citizens who contact your office utilize the following means of interaction: telephone, correspondence, interviews." The differences among the groups are dramatic. Whereas all of the Scandinavian and Other European and three-quarters of the Commonwealth respondents ranked correspondence first, nearly all of the U.S. classi-

cal and quasi-ombudsmen reported that contacts by telephone were most common. Only two ombudsmen, from the Commonwealth, ranked interviews as the most frequent means clients used to complain. According to a further analysis (not included in the table), personal interviews were ranked second by about one-third of the ombudsmen, and most of that group was composed of the U.S. officials. Eighty percent of the latter grouping reported that interviews were second in importance to telephone calls as a means of citizen access, but a similar percentage of the quasi-ombudsmen said that letters ranked second to telephone calls. Thus, the U.S. classical ombudsmen have gone further than the others in promoting the more personalized forms of citizen access.[13]

Complaint Volume

How accessible are the ombudsmen as measured by the volume of complaints received? The three categories in Table 4.3 were defined to fit the actual reported distribution of complaints. The results are not adjusted to control for the various jurisdictions' population levels. Although very roughly one-third of the classical offices fit into each of the table's classifications, there are some important differences among the groups. Most notably, none of the Scandinavian offices and only one of the U.S. offices

Table 4.3
Annual Volume of Complaints to Ombudsmen (in percentages)

VOLUME	SCANDINAVIA (N=4)	COMMONWEALTH (N=22)	OTHER EUROPE (N=6)	UNITED STATES (N=10)	U.S. QUASI (N=17)	TOTAL CLASSICAL (N=47a)
High (above 2,000)	75	23	33	50	53	38
Medium (1–2,000)	25	32	33	40	24	34
Low (under 1,000)	—	45	33	10	24	28
Total	100	100	99b	100	101b	100

a The responses of the quasi-ombudsmen were excluded from these totals.

b The totals are greater or less than 100 percent because of rounding.

receive fewer than one thousand complaints each year, and these groups also have proportionately more offices that receive in excess of two thousand annual complaints than the other groupings. It is also noteworthy that so many of the Commonwealth offices fall into the low category and that few are high-complaint-volume offices. Furthermore, over half of the U.S. quasi-ombudsmen receive more than two thousand annual complaints, but it is not true—as one might conclude from some of the writing about such offices—that they are all high-complaint-volume operations.

Clients' Socioeconomic Status

What types of clients have suceeded in gaining access to the ombudsmen? Social class is an especially important variable, and the ombudsmen's perceptions of their clients' class origins are recorded in Table 4.4. Respondents were asked to think of their clients as being divided into two broad segments: an "affluent and middle and upper class"; and a "poor and lower class." Then they were asked to estimate which of five alternatives best represented their clients' backgrounds: 1. nearly all *affluent;* 2. about 75 percent *affluent*—25 percent *poor;* 3. approximately even distribution; 4. about 75 percent *poor*—25 percent *affluent;* 5. nearly all *poor.* (Alternatives 1 and 2 and 4 and 5 are collapsed in the table.) The most obvious finding is that the vast majority of every group of officials believed they served at least as many poor as affluent people; the fact that two-fifths of the total ombudsmen believed they served mainly poor clients is highly interesting. Because there may be important cultural, as well as individual, differences in the meaning of "affluent" and "poor" between Sweden and Fiji, for example, it is probably unwise to subject the findings to intensive analysis. But why the U.S. classical ombudsmen should feel they serve proportionately fewer affluent citizens and more poor ones than their quasi-ombudsmen colleagues is not readily apparent.

Officials' Attitudes Toward Accessibility

As a final measure of accessibility, how receptive do the ombudsmen *want to be* to citizens' complaints. In reacting to the statement, "It is best for a complaints office to adopt a low profile so that it does not become inundated with grievances," 20 percent of the total ombudsmen agreed; 11 percent were neutral or had no opinion; and 69 percent disagreed. Probably reflecting the circumstance that their offices are older than most others, none of the Scandinavians agreed; three-quarters of them and four-fifths of the U.S. classical ombudsmen disagreed that it was wise to keep a low profile. Not much more than half of the U.S. quasi-ombudsmen—a proportion lower than any of the groups of classical officials—disagreed with the item, however. Of course, the statement under consideration expressed an extreme position, but it is noteworthy that the vast majority of the ombudsmen opted for accessibility and disagreed that they should restrict their availability to clients.

THE SUBSTANCE OF COMPLAINTS

Since the data indicate that nearly all ombudsmen nearly always adopt a reactive posture, it is apparent that the essential character of the office is shaped by the kinds of complaints received. The composition of the intake sets parameters that delimit the accomplishments of any particular ombudsman.

Services versus Grievances

A first question investigating the content of the complaints inquired:

If all the citizen inquiries to your office could be divided into the following two types, please indicate the relative proportions of each—(A) Requests for the actual provision of government services or for information about them; (B) Requests for investiga-

Table 4.4
Ombudsmen's Perceptions of Their Clients' Class Origins (in percentages)

CLASS	SCANDINAVIA (N=8)	COMMONWEALTH (N=20)	OTHER EUROPE (N=6)	UNITED STATES (N=10)	U.S. QUASI (N=17)	TOTAL CLASSICAL (N=43[a])
Mainly affluent	—	5	—	10	18	5
Even distribution	38	65	67	40	47	55
Mainly poor	63	30	33	50	35	41
Total	101[b]	100	100	100	100	101[b]

[a] The responses of the quasi-ombudsmen were excluded from these totals.

[b] The totals are greater than 100 percent because of rounding.

Table 4.5
Content of Complaints to Ombudsmen (in percentages)

COMPLAINT TYPE	SCANDINAVIA (N=8)	COMMONWEALTH (N=22)	OTHER EUROPE (N=6)	UNITED STATES (N=10)	U.S. QUASI (N=16)	TOTAL CLASSICAL (N=46a)
Mainly services	—	9	—	40	56	13
Even distribution	—	9	33	30	38	15
Mainly grievances	100	82	67	30	6	72
Total	100	100	100	100	100	100

a The responses of the quasi-ombudsmen were excluded from these totals.

tion of personal grievances against administrative actions: 1. nearly all concerning provision of *services;* 2. about 75% provision of *services*—25% investigation of *grievances;* 3. approximately even distribution; 4. about 75% investigation of *grievances*—25% provision of *services;* 5. nearly all concerning investigation of *grievances.*

Many of the non-U.S. officials were puzzled about this question. "Doesn't this fellow know that ombudsmen specialize in the investigation of administrative grievances?" they may have wondered. As indicated in Table 4.5, very large majorities of the Scandinavian, Other European, and Commonwealth groups believed that most of their intake consisted of administrative grievances.[14]

This question was asked in the hope of revealing important differences between the U.S. and other ombudsmen. This occurred. Only three of the U.S. classical ombudsmen believed their intake consisted mainly of grievances, but four thought theirs was composed mainly of requests for services or information. The finding is even more pronounced for the U.S. quasi-ombudsmen. A large majority reported that their caseload consisted mainly of service and information matters, and only one felt grievances were preponderant.[15] *The principal implication of these data is that most of the U.S. offices are dual-purpose agencies.* Whereas the ombudsman traditionally has been largely involved with the investigation of complaints against administrative actions, the workload of only a minority of the U.S. ombudsmen consists mainly of such matters. From personal conversations with several of these officials, I know that many of them consider the winnowing out of the information-and-referral and service-oriented contacts to be a major burden, and they are anxious to get to what they consider their "real" work—grievances.

As John Moore has pointed out, distinguishing among inquiries, requests for service, and complaints about faulty service is sometimes a tenuous process:

A resident who asked how to get his discarded refrigerator picked up would be making an inquiry about bulk-item collection; if

he said, in effect, "I want you to get someone down here to pick up that refrigerator," he would be registering a complaint requesting service; and if he stated that he had been trying for a month to get the appropriate agency to collect the damned thing, he would be complaining about a service failure by which he was personally aggrieved.[16]

Furthermore, ombudsmen do discover administrative grievances among both the inquiries and requests for services, and the value of the latter types of citizen approaches should not be disparaged.

Nevertheless, William B. Gwyn is on the mark when he observes that "a request to the executive ombudsman to have a dead cat removed from a backyard is very different from a complaint to a classical ombudsman that an administrative agency had abused its authority in deciding to deny the complainant some social service."[17] To reiterate: The salient finding of Table 4.5 is that the *U.S. classical ombudsmen* are deeply involved with the processing of requests for services and information.

Inefficiency versus Malfeasance

Not all grievances are alike, and the following question was designed to distinguish between two basic types:

If the complaints which ask for investigations of an administrative grievance are divided into the following two types, please indicate the relative proportions of each—(A) Allegations of inefficiency—including delay, misplaced records, and other minor procedural errors; (B) Allegations of malfeasance—including substantive error, abuse of authority, discrimination, arrogance, and other injustice: 1. nearly all concerning allegations of *inefficiency;* 2. about 75% allegations of inefficiency—25% allegations of *malfeasance;* 3. approximately even distribution; 4. about 75% allegations of *malfeasance*—25% allegations of *inefficiency;* 5. nearly all concerning allegations of *malfeasance.*

The responses, arrayed in Table 4.6, reveal that the ombudsmen are far more likely to become involved with an investigation into inefficient procedures, delay, and the

Table 4.6
Content of Grievances Brought to Ombudsmen (in percentages)

GRIEVANCE TYPE	SCANDINAVIA (N=8)	COMMONWEALTH (N=20)	OTHER EUROPE (N=6)	UNITED STATES (N=10)	U.S. QUASI (N=17)	TOTAL CLASSICAL (N=44[a])
Mainly inefficiency	—	55	83	80	94	55
Even distribution	63	35	17	20	—	34
Mainly malfeasance	38	10	—	—	6	11
Total	101[b]	100	100	100	100	100

[a] The responses of the quasi-ombudsmen were excluded from these totals.

[b] The total is more than 100 percent because of rounding.

like, than with investigating charges that administrators were guilty of malfeasance—bias, abuse of authority, and so on. The Scandinavians claimed to investigate more allegations of malfeasance than others. Some of this response may be attributable to Sweden and Finland's very tightly drafted systems of administrative law that can escalate civil servants' minor lapses into occasions for prosecution.[18]

Although it is striking that none of the U.S. officials reported they were deeply involved with investigations of supposed malfeasance, it is not true that hardly any of these more serious administrative infractions are brought to their attention. The table collapses the question's first two and last two options; when the responses to the former are examined, some interesting differences among the groups are revealed. Only 10 percent of the U.S. classical and 29 percent of the quasi-ombudsmen indicated that "nearly all" of their clients demanded investigations of inefficiency; the corresponding percentage for the Other European was 33, and for the Commonwealth respondents, 25. Thus, a considerable preponderance of all of the groups surveyed reported that at least one-quarter of their grievances involved allegations of official malfeasance. Nonetheless, it is clear from the table that the extra-Scandinavian ombudsmen are preoccupied with investigations of the administration's efficiency rather than

with its justice. It should not be forgotten, however, that administrative inefficiency may result in a type of injustice.

Offensive versus Defensive Perspective

In an attempt to probe further into the substance of complaints, the ombudsmen were given the following request:

If the perspectives of those complaints that ask for an investigation of a grievance are divided into the following two types, please indicate the relative proportions of each—(A) Complaints from an offensive perspective (client appeals for a review of administration's decision not to grant him something he wants, e.g., a welfare benefit); (B) Complaints from a defensive perspective (protection asked against damaging actions, e.g., decisions to raise taxes, to incarcerate, and to lower or eliminate a welfare benefit already being received): 1. nearly all complaints from *offensive* perspective; 2. about 75% *offensive* complaints—25% *defensive;* 3. approximately even distribution; 4. about 75% *defensive* complaints—25% *offensive;* 5. nearly all complaints from *defensive* perspective.

Table 4.7 indicates that, except for the Scandinavians, from one-half to three-fifths of the other groups believed their grievances were mainly offensive. Presumably,

Table 4.7
Perspective of Grievances Brought to Ombudsmen (in percentages)

GRIEVANCE PERSPECTIVE	SCANDINAVIA (N=7)	COMMONWEALTH (N=20)	OTHER EUROPE (N=6)	UNITED STATES (N=10)	U.S. QUASI (N=16)	TOTAL CLASSICAL (N=43[a])
Mainly offensive	14	50	50	60	50	47
Even distribution	14	45	17	20	38	30
Mainly defensive	71	5	33	20	13	23
Total	99[b]	100	100	100	101[b]	100

[a] The responses of the quasi-ombudsmen were excluded from these totals.

[b] The totals are more or less than 100 percent because of rounding.

some of the Scandinavians' reported high incidence of defensive complaints would be due to their traditional involvement with prison matters, but most of the other officials also have jurisdiction over prisons or jails. Historically, most discussions about the need for ombudsmen have centered around situations in which citizens were trying to escape from the clutches of a grasping bureaucracy. In analyzing the New Zealand complaints, however, it was apparent that most complaints did not seem to be of this type. Dividing the sample of complaints into offensive and defensive types revealed that nearly three-quarters were lodged from an offensive perspective.[19]

If detailed studies of other ombudsmen were conducted, a relationship between the two types of client perspectives similar to the New Zealand one would be found in many cases. Since this is not a subject ombudsmen are likely to think about in quantitative terms, however, they would not be expected to be very aware of the actual distribution of complaints between the perspectives. It is interesting that two-fifths of the Commonwealth respondents, about one-fifth each of the Other European respondents and the U.S. quasi-ombudsmen, but none of the U.S. classical or the Scandinavian ombudsmen believed their complaints were "nearly all" offensive. (These findings are not shown in the table, which again collapses options 1 and 2 and 4 and 5.) At least, it is considerably more likely that an ombudsman's client will demand greater benefits *from* the government than that he or she will ask for protection *against* its damaging actions.

OPERATIONAL NORMS

Role Models

The preceding data indicate that ombudsmen are driven by their intake, which encompasses all of the citizens' myriad experiences with public bureaucracy. Because the complaints are highly variegated, a standard response is impossible. An ombudsman must be an educator, a facilitator, a negotiator, a proponent—all in a day's work, depending on the nature of particular complaints received. Sometimes such roles are played serially in dealing with the same complaint as the investigation unfolds.

Even though a single label cannot be used to describe thoroughly the activities of a given office, two individuals receiving the same complaints might behave quite differently, depending upon their conceptions of their role. The following question was designed to probe generalized role perceptions:

Following is a list of role models that have been suggested as descriptive of the orientation toward clients of complaint-han-

dling offices. Please place a 1 before the model that best describes your conception of your primary role, and place a 2 before the one that is your secondary role:

____ the impartial investigator model
____ the enabler-facilitator model
____ the broker-negotiator model
____ the arbitrator model
____ the advocate model
____ the political activist model

These models were developed from several possibilities suggested by a review of the complaint-handling and the social work literatures.[20] According to tradition, the ombudsman is supposed to be mainly an "impartial investigator." But if every ombudsman would at one time or another be involved in activities that fall within the scope of each of the role models, which one would they rank as their primary choice?

The responses indicate that ombudsmen believe they act as "impartial investigators," or they know their tradition very well: *96 percent—all but two—of the classical officials chose the "impartial investigator" as their primary role model.*[21] One Scandinavian thought of himself principally as an advocate, and one U.S. official viewed his major role as that of an enabler-facilitator.

The U.S. quasi-ombudsmen responded very differently. Nearly half (47 percent) said they thought their primary role was that of an "enabler-facilitator." Only 35 percent chose the "impartial investigator" model; 12 percent chose the "broker-negotiator model"; and 6 percent chose the "arbitrator" model. It is not surprising that so many of these officials should view themselves as enablers and facilitators. Often the offices' literature extolls their virtues at cutting red tape and bringing citizens and agencies together. And if, as we have seen above, much of their intake consists of requests for information and services, it follows that fewer actual "investigations" would be conducted and that more efforts at facilitation, brokerage, or conciliation would occur. Although we saw above that the intake of the U.S. classical officials actually is similar to that of their quasi-ombudsmen brethren, it is noteworthy that all but one of the former group perceive of their job as being that of the traditional ombudsman and list their principal role as impartial investigator.

As indicated in Table 4.8, the two classical ombudsmen who did not choose "impartial investigator" as their primary role did identify it as their secondary role—as did 18 percent of the quasi-ombudsmen. Four of the Scandinavians did not choose a secondary role model; two of them volunteered that "impartial investigator" said everything there was to say about their role. The most popular secondary role model for every group was that of "enabler-facilitator." The "citizen advocate" model

Table 4.8
Ombudsmen's Secondary Role Model (in percentages)

ROLE MODEL	SCANDINAVIA (N=5)	COMMONWEALTH (N=20)	OTHER EUROPE (N=6)	UNITED STATES (N=10)	U.S. QUASI (N=17)	TOTAL CLASSICAL (N=41[a])
Impartial investigator	20	—	—	10	18	5
Enabler-facilitator	80	50	67	40	35	54
Broker-negotiator	—	15	17	20	12	15
Arbitrator	—	25	17	10	12	17
Advocate	—	10	—	20	24	10
Total	100	100	101[b]	100	101[b]	101[b]

[a] The responses of the quasi-ombudsmen were excluded from these totals.

[b] The totals are more than 100 percent because of rounding.

was the least popular for all but the U.S. officials: "advocacy" tied with "brokerage" as the second-ranking secondary role model among the U.S. classical officials,[22] and the quasi-ombudsmen ranked "advocacy" second. It is of interest that no respondent chose "political activist" as either a primary or secondary role model.[23]

Universalistic versus Particularistic Norms

The significance of the finding that ombudsmen virtually unanimously select from an assortment of role models those identifying their job in universalistic terms is underscored by the reactions to the following statement: "A complaints office should perform investigations that are neutral and impartial; it should not be an advocate of the client's interests." When faced with a direct conflict between citizen advocacy and impartiality, 91 percent of the ombudsmen opted for impartiality. Of the remainder, two respondents replied "neutral, don't know" (both were from the United States), and two "disagreed" (one was from the United States [it was he who chose the enabler-facilitator model as his primary role], and one was from the Commonwealth). The U.S. quasi-ombudsmen enjoyed less consensus: only 69 percent of them agreed; 6 percent chose "neutral, don't know"; and 25 percent "disagreed."

The following statement attempted to measure a similar attitudinal dimension: "Even though a complaints office may have a reservoir of political influence, it should not use such influence to obtain preferment for a client." The distribution of the ombudsmen's replies was exactly the same in percentage terms as for the previous question. But one of this question's "neutrals" was Commonwealth; one was Other European. And the same U.S. ombudsman who reacted negatively to the previous question and who had selected as his primary role the enabler-facilitator

model also "disagreed" with this statement. A Commonwealth colleague—not the one who "disagreed" with the previous statement—joined him. The pattern of responses of the U.S. quasi-ombudsmen, most of whom are closely linked with the political executive, was similar: they, too, staunchly refused to condone preferment. Over 75 percent of them "agreed," 18 percent marked "neutral, don't know," and only 7 percent "disagreed."

According to the reactions to another statement, the occasion to deal with requests for preferment arises infrequently for most offices. Presuming that the ombudsmen would respond to the items discussed previously in this section as they have actually responded, the statement contended: "Clients often ask for preferment without realizing that my office is an impartial, neutral bureaucratic mechanism." Only 22 percent of the ombudsmen "agreed" that they often had to deal with requests for preferment; none chose the "neutral, don't know" category. This response, which provides further information about the offices' intake, indicates that the matters brought to ombudsmen apparently differ significantly from those often received by legislators. According to studies of the caseloads of legislators in several countries, it is common for citizens to request that they be treated better than the existing rules allow. Analysis of the New Zealand ombudsman's cases indicated, however, that preferment was rarely sought: only 10 percent of the clients sought preferential treatment.[24] The pattern of responses of the various groupings of ombudsmen did not deviate greatly from the totals: the Commonwealth respondents had the lowest rate of agreement—14 percent; the highest rate belonged to the Other Europeans—33 percent.[25] Asking politicians for preferential treatment in the United States is quite common,[26] so it may be surprising that only three-tenths of the U.S. ombudsmen agreed that their clients often sought preferment. It is even more surprising that only 18 percent of the quasi-ombudsmen—all of whom have close political linkages—reported their clients often sought preferment.

Thus, to a striking degree, all of the groups of complaint offices surveyed favored impartiality—at the expense of client advocacy—and opposed particularistic "fixing"—for which they reported receiving relatively few requests.

POLITICAL AUTONOMY

In political life, only a totalitarian dictator is truly autonomous. But relative independence has been generally accepted as a defining characteristic of ombudsmen. Donald Rowat, for example, contends that an ombudsman "is politically independent, even of the legislature."[27] On the other hand, according to Alan Wyner, an "executive Ombudsman" is "a centralized complaint-handling officer who has been appointed to office and who serves at the pleasure of an elected or appointed chief executive." Furthermore, Wyner asserts that "appointment by the chief executive stands as the most prominent difference between the executive Ombudsman and the classical model."[28]

In beginning to explore the ombudsman's autonomy, let us examine four questions: What is the basis of the office's authority? Who appoints the ombudsman? Who can give him orders? Who can fire the ombudsman?

Office's Basis of Authority

As a response to the question "Upon what authority does your complaint-handling function rest?" 38 percent of the ombudsmen indicated their reliance upon a "provision in government's fundamental document—constitution, city charter." The highest percentage indicating such a foundation was 75 for the Scandinavian offices; the lowest was 9 for those in the Commonwealth (the Other European figure was 50 percent, and that for the U.S. officials was 40 percent). With one exception, all of the remaining members of the IBA's Ombudsman Advisory Board are founded upon a statute. The exception is the Dayton/Montgomery County, Ohio, Joint Office of Citizens' Complaints, which is chartered as a corporation and contracts to provide complaint-handling services.

One of the reasons the term "quasi-" may be preferable to "executive" ombudsman is that some of the offices in question are legally founded. Hence, they have a certain stability that may thwart the caprice of any particular executive. Thirty-five percent of the quasi-ombudsmen answered that their authority was buttressed by a legal provision of some sort; in half of the cases a local charter or state constitutional provision, rather than an ordinary law, provided the foundation.

Method of Appointment

Unfortunately, the responses to the question "Who was responsible for your appointment?" are not very useful because the question did not discriminate between the situation regarding formal responsibility and the actual political processes involved. Thus, if a Commonwealth respondent thought of the formal process, he might indicate that the queen or her governor general appointed him (a "nonelected public official" in terms of the question's options); or if he thought of the political process, he would know that "an elected official"—usually the prime minister—made the actual choice and parliament only endorsed it. In real terms, an ombudsman who is acceptable to all major factions is normally sought. The initiative may come from the executive or, less often, from the legislature, and the process will vary depending upon whether a parliamentary or presidential governmental structure exists. Except for three U.S. offices in which some sort of public commission chooses the incumbent, the legislature plays a major role in the appointment of all ombudsmen.

The quasi-ombudsmen indicated that they were, in the main, appointed by "an elected official": 71 percent said that governors or mayors appointed them; the remaining 29 percent were appointed by a "civil servant," usually a city manager. Although none of the quasi-ombudsmen was appointed by the legislature, 18 percent of them said their legislative body played some role in the appointment. Ordinarily, it ratified the governor's, mayor's, or city manager's choice.

Identity of Superior Authority

Since political autonomy is a relative concept, no negative replies were expected to the following question: "Can anyone exercise direct authority over your office—making binding rules or issue orders which must be followed?" The data in Table 4.9 reveal, however, that just over half of the classical respondents felt there was no such authority over them.

In actuality, ombudsmen must always pay attention to input from some political and administrative constituencies. In almost every instance, the executive and the legislature could combine to make rules for the office or change the law. Further control could often be exercised through the ability to regulate the ombudsman's budget.[29] Although none of the classical officials reported that civil servants could give them orders, 29 percent of their quasi-ombudsman colleagues did. And over half of the latter group said they were controlled by elected officials. In a few instances, allegiance was owed to both a mayor and a city manager. Surely, the two quasi-ombudsmen who as-

Table 4.9
Who Exercises Authority over Ombudsmen? (in percentages)

AUTHORITY'S IDENTITY	SCANDINAVIA (N=9)	COMMONWEALTH (N=22)	OTHER EUROPE (N=6)	UNITED STATES (N=10)	U.S. QUASI (N=17)	TOTAL CLASSICAL (N=47a)
No authority	11	45	100	70	12	51
The legislature	78	50	—	10	—	40
An elected official	11	5	—	—	53	4
A special commission	—	—	—	20	6	4
A civil servant	—	—	—	—	29	—
Total	100	100	100	100	100	99b

a The responses of the quasi-ombudsmen were excluded from these totals.

b The total is less than 100 percent because of rounding.

serted that they had no master were guilty of exaggeration, but it is possible that they usually are allowed to operate as if they had none.

Security of Tenure

A major indicator of an institution's political autonomy is, of course, its security of tenure in office. As far as is known, the Finnish official is the only legally irremovable ombudsman, but one Commonwealth respondent claimed that status in answering this question: "Whose action is required for you to be removed?" Most of the remaining ombudsmen (76 percent) answered that the legislature had the power to dismiss them; 4 percent (one Commonwealth and one Other European respondent) said they could be fired by an elected official; 7 percent (two Commonwealth and one U.S. respondent) reported that action by both an elected official and the legislature was necessary to break their tenure; and 9 percent (three U.S. and one Commonwealth official) said a special commission could end their career.

One supremely confident quasi-ombudsman testified that he was irremovable. But the majority of his colleagues (53 percent of the total) admitted that an elected official could cashier them; another 18 percent said it was necessary for the legislature to concur with the governor's or mayor's recommendation; and finally, 24 percent acknowledged that a civil servant could terminate their employment.

Orientations toward Autonomy

Thus far, the questionnaire responses concerning the basis of the office's authority, the identity of the appointing institution, whether or not anyone could issue orders to the office, and how the official could be removed have confirmed and expanded the scattered knowledge about

these matters. At the same time, some indicators of the ombudsmen's perceptions of their independence have been given. The responses in Table 4.10 enable us to explore more fully the officials' attitudes toward political autonomy.

Statements 1 and 2 attempted to probe the ombudsmen's interactions with politicians, singly and corporately. Two-thirds or more of all groups but the U.S. officials agreed they received few complaints on referral from politicians. Substantially more of both the U.S. classical and the quasi-ombudsmen indicated that autonomy was at least somewhat compromised in that they were asked to be a "mop-up" complaint handler for politicians. Of course, from another perspective this can be viewed as an enviable opportunity for interaction with an important constituency. A large majority of all groups agreed that the legislature was not very important in the actual performance of their jobs. This finding may be shocking to those who have assumed that the ombudsman-legislature linkage is close, an assumption that is especially prevalent in parliamentary countries.

The quasi-ombudsmen, however, indicated a lesser degree of autonomy, measured thus: a scant majority of them agreed. This finding actually could be an index of relative autonomy for these officials, however. If nearly half of them felt that their city council or state legislature did have a substantial impact upon them (only one had no opinion), this can be interpreted as meaning they are not merely creatures of the mayor or governor. Instead, they have multiple constituencies, as do classical ombudsmen.

There was complete consensus among the ombudsmen about the desirability of conducting nonpolitical investigations (statement 3), and four-fifths of them "strongly" agreed. Only one quasi-ombudsman responded neutrally, and none "disagreed." The classical officials were also unanimous in their desire to be "as independent as possible of elected officials" (statement 4); 89 percent agreed

Table 4.10
Ombudsmen's Orientations Toward Political Autonomy (in percentages)

STATEMENTS CONCERNING POLITICAL AUTONOMY	SCANDINAVIA (N=8)	COMMONWEALTH (N=21a)	OTHER EUROPE (N=6)	UNITED STATES (N=10)	U.S. QUASI (N=17b)	TOTAL CLASSICAL (N=45c)
1. Politicians refer few complaints to me for investigation.	100	68	67	40	35	67
2. I find that my legislative body (council, legislature, parliament) has little impact upon my job.	75	57	67	60	53	62
3. It is important to the success of a grievance office that its investigations be utterly nonpolitical in character.	100	100	100	100	94	100
4. It is of cardinal importance that a grievance office be as independent as possible of elected officials.	100	100	100	100	69	100
5. Having and cultivating close political connections and having them generally known can increase the effectiveness of a complaints office.	75	86	67	60	47	76
6. Offices such as mine should not be filled by former politicians.	100	76	50	70	47	76

Note: "Agreement" is defined as the autonomous response except for statement 5, where "disagreement" is so interpreted. The usually very small "neutral, don't know" category was included in computing the percentage of agreement.

a Twenty-two respondents reacted to statements 1 and 4.

b Sixteen respondents reacted to statement 4.

c The responses of the quasi-ombudsmen were excluded from these totals. Forty-six respondents reacted to statements 1 and 4.

"strongly" with this sentiment. Three of the quasi-ombudsmen chose the "neutral, don't know" response, however, and two "disagreed."

About three-quarters of the classical respondents reaffirmed their desire to be independent of politicians by disagreeing that "cultivating close political connections" (statement 5) could increase their effectiveness. The Commonwealth respondents were the most displeased by this suggestion; more than half of them disagreed "strongly." The American classical officials were the least upset at the notion of "buttering up" politicians. Of course, one of the advantages of the quasi-ombudsman is supposed to be his "ability to draw upon the power and prestige of the chief executive to facilitate his work."[30] Nevertheless, nearly half of the quasi-ombudsmen asserted their independence and disagreed that it was desirable to capitalize upon their political connections. On the

other hand, one-fifth of the group agreed "strongly" that it was wise to cultivate such linkages.

Finally, three-quarters of the classical officials agreed that former politicians should not be appointed as ombudsmen (statement 6). The Scandinavian respondents (none of whom had political backgrounds) and the Commonwealth respondents (86 percent of whom had never run for public office) were most adamant; a majority of each group agreed "strongly." A large majority of the U.S. classical respondents (70 percent of whom had never thrown their hats in the electoral ring) also were convinced that political backgrounds were inappropriate. Only 19 percent of the total classical ombudsmen had backgrounds as politicians; their experience apparently led them to trust politicians more than their colleagues did who were "uncontaminated" by political associations. Only one of the former group believed politicians should not be chosen as ombudsmen. Perhaps surprisingly, four-fifths of the quasi-ombudsmen did not have political backgrounds. According to the table, however, fewer than half of that entire group believed such backgrounds were undesirable for incumbents of such offices as theirs.

CONCLUSION

It should be apparent to those interested in such matters that the coinage of the term ''ombudsman'' has become somewhat debased. Currently, many individuals who are in any way involved with the handling of complaints consider it fashionable to advertise themselves as ombudsmen. Sometimes it is obvious that the offices, which actually may be involved with public relations or client advocacy, have only the most tangential involvement with the functions performed by the traditional ombudsmen. Questionnaires were also sent to many of the former officials, who may be called ''pseudo-ombudsmen.'' Their replies are not analyzed in this chapter, but it is interesting to note that they virtually unanimously answered positively the questionnaire's initial item: ''Do you consider that your office is an Ombudsman Office?'' The same is true of the officials whose answers are analyzed above: all of those dubbed ''classical ombudsmen'' and all but one of the ''quasi-ombudsmen'' asserted they were ombudsmen. Let us briefly consider what light the findings reported above throw on the ombudsman's definition and the extent of its variability.

Accessibility to Citizens

The usual operational mode of most extra-Scandinavian ombudsmen is reactive, and few of the offices surveyed are much involved with outreach activities. Whereas Stanley Anderson reports that the practice of what he calls ''active access'' and what in the present article is called an ''aggressive'' operational mode, coupled with outreach activities, was becoming characteristic of the styles of ''executive'' ombudsmen, few quasi-ombudsmen respondents in the survey were much involved with either activity.[31]

For a variety of reasons, some barriers to complaints (such as restricting jurisdiction, demanding that alternative appeals be exhausted before complaining, and requiring that complaints be put in writing) have been erected. These barriers separate the ombudsmen, to a greater or lesser degree, from their potential clients. The barriers are especially high among the Commonwealth officials. As a reflection of one of the barriers to access, most ombudsmen receive the bulk of their complaints through correspondence. But the accessibility of the U.S. classical and quasi-ombudsmen has been greatly increased: both kinds

of offices receive most of their contacts through the more personal medium of telephone calls.

As one would expect, the number of citizens who actually gain access to each ombudsman varies, but it appears that enough do to justify the offices' continued existence. Mirroring some of the barriers to access, the proportion of offices with low complaints was the greatest among the Commonwealth group. From the viewpoint of social equity, it is interesting that the preponderance of every group reported they serve at least as many poor as affluent clients. Furthermore, an overwhelming majority of the ombudsmen indicated their orientation toward complaints by refusing to agree with ''adopting a low profile'' to avoid grievances.

When we consider collectively the items related to accessibility, the ombudsmen seem generally to be quite open to the receipt of grievances. While most offices are not aggressive in seeking out grievances, they are also not aloof. Despite expectations to the contrary, the results of most items depicted the quasi-ombudsman as less accessible than the U.S. classical officials.

The Substance of Complaints

William B. Gwyn maintains that ''the classical ombudsmen of Scandinavia, New Zealand, and the United States . . . are primarily concerned with investigating complaints against alleged abuses of administrative authority.''[32] The findings indicate that this contention is correct if it is revised to exclude the U.S. officials. Furthermore, the intake of the quasi-ombudsman consisted largely of requests for the provision of governmental services or for information about them rather than of requests for investigations of alleged administrative grievances. The U.S. classical ombudsmen are dual-purpose agencies involved with requests for services more than with grievances. Furthermore, except for the Scandinavians, most of the world's classical ombudsmen deal mainly with a particular *type* of grievance: grievances alleging administrative inefficiency rather than more consequential matters involving malfeasance. Such supposed inefficiency is the cause of almost all the grievances lodged with the quasi-ombudsmen. In addition, the citizens who proffer complaints to ombudsmen are more likely to do so from an offensive rather than a defensive perspective; that is, they want some benefit from government instead of demanding protection against government.

This discovery that the substance of complaints commonly brought to ombudsmen is not as weighty as may have been expected could cause some to question the office's social utility. Further thought may indicate, however, that the intake reflects reasonably well the kind of relationship citizens have with modern government. Increasingly, we are dependent consumers of government services.

Operational Norms

Definitions of the ombudsman ordinarily mention the institution's impartial character as a central feature. Indeed, nearly all of our classical respondents chose from a list of six models the "impartial investigator" as their primary role, whereas the quasi-ombudsmen were more likely to think of themselves as "enabler-facilitators." Overwhelmingly, when faced with a choice, all of the groups surveyed—including the quasi-ombudsmen—felt they should be impartial rather than an advocate for clients, and few reported that many clients sought preferential treatment.

Of course, this pattern of response may be influenced by the desire of the officials to give the "right" answers; admitting that they sometimes show partiality might seem to be bad form. Stanley Anderson indicates that his "executive" ombudsmen are sometimes partial toward certain constituencies.[33] From a different perspective, some critics suggest that ombudsmen are biased and "establishment oriented." The ones examined for this study seem to operate impartially. At the very least, the questionnaire responses indicate that the understandings are very likely shared about what the "proper" role perceptions are for ombudsmen.

Political Autonomy

The principal structural criterion used in defining the universe to be surveyed was *independence*. Although there were some variations, only highly autonomous officials had been asked to become members of the IBA's Ombudsman Advisory Board. The quasi-ombudsmen were thought to be much like the classical officials in other respects, but the former were less independent.

The responses to the items concerning independence confirmed expectations: the officers generally thought of themselves as being independent of politicians. Most prized this independence and also thought they were not much affected by their legislatures. Some evidence of attitudinal and structural autonomy was also found among the quasi-ombudsmen. The existence of one-third of them reportedly is based upon a law, city charter, or state constitutional provision.[34]

In conclusion, this attempt at institutional definition indicates strong grounds for believing that such a thing as an ombudsman does exist cross-nationally. Furthermore, the officials studied can be described as accessible to citizens, as processors of administrative grievances, and

as impartial and politically independent investigators. At the same time, however, each of the concepts just mentioned is a relative term. Although there was remarkable uniformity of opinion about certain key issues, the institution certainly is not invariable. Some ombudsmen are more accessible than others, some are more independent, and so on. It may seem a cliché to call for further research, but on most matters discussed above the surface has hardly been scratched thus far. Then too, many of the offices under discussion are in the preliminary stages of institutionalization. Fundamental decisions must yet be made about the role they actually play in political life.

NOTES

1. *When Americans Complain: Governmental Grievance Procedures* (Cambridge, Mass.: Harvard University Press, 1966), pp. 9–10.

2. "Ombudsmen and the Ghetto," *Connecticut Law Review* 1 (December 1968): 246.

3. "Preface to Second Edition," in Donald C. Rowat, ed., *The Ombudsman: Citizen's Defender*, rev. ed. (Toronto: University of Toronto Press, 1968), p. xxiv.

4. *Ombudsman Papers: American Experience and Proposals* (Berkeley, Calif.: Institute of Governmental Studies, University of California, 1969), p. 3.

5. "Institutionalization, the Ombudsman, and Bureaucracy," *American Political Science Review* 68 (September 1974): 1077.

6. Quoted in Bernard Frank, "The Ombudsman—Revisited," *International Bar Journal* (May 1975): 50.

7. See the papers in Alan J. Wyner, ed., *Executive Ombudsmen in the United States* (Berkeley, Calif.: Institute of Governmental Studies, University of California, 1973).

8. The origins of the replies from the classical ombudsmen may be further subdivided: *Scandinavia*—Sweden (six responses, including two from retired officials), Finland, Denmark, Norway; *Commonwealth*—New Zealand, Canada (Alberta, Quebec, Manitoba, Nova Scotia, Saskatchewan [two responses], Ontario, Newfoundland), Britain (parliamentary commissioner, commissioner for local administration in Scotland, commissioner for local administration in Wales), Northern Ireland, Australia (Victoria, South Australia, Western Australia, Queensland, New South Wales), Mauritius, Fiji, India (Maharashtra); *Other Europe*—France, Switzerland (Zurich), Italy (Tuscany), Israel (commissioner for complaints from the public, Jerusalem, Haifa); *United States*—Hawaii; Iowa; Nebraska; Alaska; Dayton/Montgomery County, Ohio; Seattle/King County, Washington; Jackson County (Kansas City), Missouri; Atlanta, Georgia; Detroit, Michigan; Wichita, Kansas. Because the Other Europe category is small and unevenly distributed—half of its members are Israeli—its results are reported in the tables or the text but they are not ordinarily discussed.

9. The replies of the U.S. quasi-ombudsmen having statewide jurisdiction originated from the following states: Illinois, North Carolina, South Carolina, New Jersey, Maine, New Mex-

ico, and Montana. Those quasi-ombudsmen limited to local jurisdiction whose replies are used came from Houston, Texas; Columbus, Ohio; Raleigh, North Carolina; Jamestown and Mineola, New York; Omaha, Nebraska; Charleston, South Carolina; Peoria, Illinois; Portland, Oregon; and San Diego, California.

10. For a brief account of this role transformation, see Larry B. Hill, "International Transfer of the Ombudsman," in Richard L. Merritt, ed., *Communication in International Politics* (Urbana, Ill.: University of Illinois Press, 1972), pp. 296–97.

11. Indeed, my own research in Scandinavia leads me to conclude, with Walter Gellhorn, that these ombudsmen, too, are in actuality less involved with own-initiative complaints than might appear from these responses. See *Ombudsmen and Others: Citizens' Protectors in Nine Countries* (Cambridge, Mass.: Harvard University Press, 1966), pp. 218–27.

12. Sixty-one percent of the total ombudsmen agreed with the following statement: "Usually, my office is a court of last resort for clients who have already exhausted most available avenues of appeal." By far, the highest rate of agreement was among the U.S. classical ombudsmen—90 percent. A similar proportion, 87 percent, of the U.S. quasi-ombudsmen agreed.

13. According to another measure of clients' telephonic access to ombudsmen, such access seems extensive. Half of both the Scandinavian and the Other European groups and three-quarters or more of each of the remaining three groups responded affirmatively to this question: "Can citizens telephone your office from anywhere in your jurisdiction at little or no expense to them?" (Offices that possess only local jurisdiction, whose clients could make calls at minimal expense, were excluded from this analysis.) Unfortunately, the question does not discriminate between offices with toll-free lines and offices with the authority only to accept reversed charges.

14. The question's options 1 and 2 as well as 4 and 5 are collapsed in the table. One-half of the Commonwealth, one-quarter of the Scandinavian, and one-sixth of the Other European respondents chose option 5: "nearly all concerning investigations of grievances." Offices known to be purely information-and-referral bureaus were not sent questionnaires, and none of the respondents—including none of the U.S. quasi-ombudsmen—chose option 1: "nearly all concerning provision of services."

15. John E. Moore found that the top five requests for services brought to Honolulu's Office of Information and Complaint concerned dead animal removal (the leader by a large margin), cesspool service, road maintenance, bulk-item-collection service, and abandoned vehicles. The leading matters about which information was sought included city bus service (the leader by more than a five-to-one majority), auto registration, bulk-item-collection service, marriage licenses, traffic violations, and consumer protection. "Honolulu's Office of Information and Complaint," in Wyner, ed., *Executive Ombudsmen in the United States*, p. 54.

16. Ibid., p. 55.

17. Review of *Executive Ombudsmen in the United States* in *American Political Science Review* 70 (March 1976): 231.

18. Successful prosecutions normally result in very minor penalties.

19. Larry B. Hill, *The Model Ombudsman: Institutionalizing New Zealand's Democratic Experiment* (Princeton, N.J.: Princeton University Press, 1976), pp. 93–99.

20. References to such models abound, especially in *Social Work,* the official journal of the National Association of Social Workers. See, for example, Charles F. Grosser's seminal article, "Community Development Programs Serving the Urban Poor," *Social Work* 10 (July 1965): 15–21.

21. An Other European official reported that the "broker-negotiator" role was tied with the "impartial investigator" role for first place.

22. Several ombudsmen explained that it was their job to be a complaint advocate *after* an impartial investigation revealed cause for complaint.

23. Elaborations of the models and illustrations of ombudsmen performing functions under each, including the political activist model, are found in Larry Hill, "Ombudsmen, Bureaucracy, and Democracy" (Unpublished manuscript).

24. Hill, *The Model Ombudsman,* p. 133.

25. Included in the Other European category are the Israeli ombudsmen. In their society, *proteksia,* "pulling strings," is well known as a traditional method of appeal to officials. See Brenda Danet and Harriet Hartman, "Coping with Bureaucracy: The Israeli Case," *Social Forces* 51 (September 1972): 7–22.

26. See Gellhorn, *When Americans Complain,* pp. 58–73.

27. Donald C. Rowat, "The Spread of the Ombudsman Idea," in Stanley V. Anderson, ed., *Ombudsmen for American Government?* (Englewood Cliffs, N.J.: Prentice-Hall, 1968), p. 7.

28. Alan J. Wyner, "Executive Ombudsmen, and Criticisms of Contemporary American Public Bureaucracy," in Wyner, ed., *Executive Ombudsmen in the United States,* pp. 10–11.

29. See Alan J. Wyner, "American Ombudsmen and Their Political Environment" (Paper delivered at the 70th Annual Meeting of the American Political Science Association, Chicago, August 29–September 2, 1974).

30. Wyner, "Executive Ombudsmen, and Criticisms," p. 11.

31. My measure of outreach is imperfect, however. See Stanley V. Anderson, "Comparing Classical and Executive Ombudsmen," in Wyner, ed., *Executive Ombudsmen in the United States,* pp. 307–10.

32. Review of *Executive Ombudsmen in the United States,* p. 231.

33. "Comparing Classical and Executive Ombudsmen," p. 310.

34. In general, the "quasi-ombudsmen" appear to be somewhat less accessible but somewhat more impartial and politically independent than the "executive ombudsmen" surveyed in *Executive Ombudsmen in the United States.* Many of the reported differences are probably due to the circumstance that rather different populations were surveyed. Whereas Wyner included some offices that were not complaints specialists, such as lieutenant-governors and information-and-referral officers, they are excluded here.

BIBLIOGRAPHY

Anderson, Stanley V. "Comparing Classical and Executive Ombudsmen." In Alan J. Wyner, ed. *Executive Ombudsmen in the United States*, pp. 305–15. Berkeley, Calif.: Institute of Governmental Studies, University of California, 1973.

_____. *Ombudsman Papers: American Experience and Proposals*. Berkeley, Calif.: Institute of Governmental Studies, University of California, 1969.

Danet, Brenda, and Hartman, Harriet. "Coping with Bureaucracy: The Israeli Case." *Social Forces* 51 (September 1972):7–22.

Frank, Bernard. "The Ombudsman—Revisited." *International Bar Journal* (May 1975):48–60.

_____. "State Ombudsman Legislation in the United States." *University of Miami Law Review* 29 (Spring 1975): 397–445.

Gellhorn, Walter. *Ombudsmen and Others: Citizens' Protectors in Nine Countries*. Cambridge, Mass.: Harvard University Press, 1966.

_____. *When Americans Complain: Governmental Grievance Procedures*. Cambridge, Mass.: Harvard University Press, 1966.

Grosser, Charles F. "Community Development Programs Serving the Urban Poor." *Social Work* 10 (July 1965):15–21.

Gwyn, William B. Review of *Executive Ombudsmen in the United States*. *American Political Science Review* 70 (March 1976): 230–32.

Hill, Larry, B. "Bureaucracy, the Bureaucratic Auditor, and the Ombudsman: An Ideal-Type Analysis." In Benjamin Geist. *State Audit: Developments in Public Accountability*, Chapter 4. London: Macmillan, 1981.

_____. "Bureaucratic Monitoring Mechanisms." In Charles T. Goodsell. *The Public Encounter: Where State and Citizen Meet*, Chapter 9. Bloomington, Ind.: Indiana University Press, 1981.

_____. "The Citizen Participation-Representation Roles of American Ombudsmen." *Administration and Society* 12 (August 1981).

_____. "The Ideal Ombudsman and American Ombudsmen." In Larry B. Hill, ed. *American Ombudsmen* (forthcoming).

_____. "Institutionalization, the Ombudsman, and Bureaucracy." *American Political Science Review* 68 (September 1974): 1075–85.

_____. "International Transfer of the Ombudsman." In Richard L. Merritt, ed. *Communication in International Politics*, pp. 295–317. Urbana, Ill.: University of Illinois Press, 1972.

_____. *The Model Ombudsman: Institutionalizing New Zealand's Democratic Experiment*. Princeton, N.J.: Princeton University Press, 1976.

Moore, John E. "Honolulu's Office of Information and Complaint." In Alan J. Wyner, ed. *Executive Ombudsmen in the United States*, pp. 45–69. Berkeley, Calif.: Institute of Governmental Studies, University of California, 1973.

_____. "Ombudsmen and the Ghetto." *Connecticut Law Review* 1 (December 1968): 244–62.

Riggs, Fred W. "The Comparison of Whole Political Systems." In Robert T. Holt and John E. Turner, eds. *The Methodology of Comparative Research*, pp. 73–122. New York: Free Press, 1970.

Rowat, Donald C. "Preface to Second Edition." In Donald C. Rowat, ed. *The Ombudsman: Citizen's Defender*, rev. ed., pp. v–xxiv. Toronto: University of Toronto Press, 1968.

_____. "The Spread of the Ombudsman Idea." In Stanley V. Anderson, ed. *Ombudsmen for American Government?*, pp. 7–36. Englewood Cliffs, N.J.: Prentice-Hall, 1968.

Wyner, Alan J. "American Ombudsmen and Their Political Environment." Paper delivered at the 70th Annual Meeting of the American Political Science Association, Chicago, August 29–September 2, 1974.

_____. "Executive Ombudsmen, and Criticisms of Contemporary American Public Bureaucracy." In Alan J. Wyner, ed. *Executive Ombudsmen in the United States*, pp. 1–15. Berkeley, Calif.: Institute of Governmental Studies, University of California, 1973.

_____, ed. *Executive Ombudsmen in the United States*. Berkeley, Calif.: Institute of Governmental Studies, University of California, 1973.

CHAPTER 5

FOUR PERSPECTIVES ON THE OMBUDSMAN'S ROLE

A. THE DIRECT AND INDIRECT IMPACT OF THE OMBUDSMAN

IZHAK E. NEBENZAHL, State Comptroller of Israel

By THE DIRECT impact of the ombudsman is meant the benefit that accrues to his clients—the complainants—from his operation; the indirect impact of the ombudsman refers to the benefits accruing to others, including the public at large. This distinction is easier to draw than to apply, but it at least seems reasonably clear.

The most obvious form of direct impact of the ombudsman is achieved when an administrative shortcoming is rectified as a consequence of his intervention. Two examples from Alberta conveniently illustrate this. A couple wishes to adopt a child, but the authorities reject their application; they contact the ombudsman, and subsequently are allowed to become foster-parents. A prisoner will soon leave jail, but nobody can find the suitcase of clothes he brought with him when he entered; he writes to the ombudsman, and the suitcase suddenly reappears.

These very short stories are reasonably typical of a multitude of cases reported on by all ombudsmen every year. In these cases, where the ombudsman helps to rectify matters, there can be two types of development: either the administration changes a decision, or it is prompted to make a greater effort to accommodate the complainant.

Still, these two alternatives can be seen as representing a single pattern: the ombudsman steps in, the administration changes its behavior, and the complainant receives a benefit that he desires and was entitled to, but otherwise would not have received. Such cases are basic to ombudsman work.

Nevertheless, it is clear that this sort of direct impact is not to be achieved in the majority of ombudsman cases. After all, most complaints that ombudsmen receive turn out to be unjustified. The Israeli office has found almost half the complaints it investigates justified, but the rate for many other ombudsmen is nearer 20 percent or even less.

When he believes a complaint is unjustified, the ombudsman can hardly be expected to press the administration to change its behavior. His direct impact in these cases can lie nowhere else than in the satisfaction that the complainants get from having their complaints heard, investigated impartially and thoroughly, and the merits of the situation explained to them. Presumably, the satisfaction of the complainant for whom the ombudsman has helped to obtain a refund of $100 from the government is usually greater than that of the complainant to whom it

Address to the International Ombudsman Conference, Edmonton, Canada, September 9, 1976.

was explained that the $100 he paid were indeed due. But this does not mean that the ombudsman has not psychologically been of help in the latter case.

Every ombudsman will have some disappointed clients. These clients are not only the fringe of "habitual complainers" or the few who, in the words of the Saskatchewan ombudsman, "simply cannot accept a state of facts which does not coincide with their beliefs"—their psychology can only be accommodated in Alice's Wonderland. They are mainly those complainants who in all sincerity cannot bring themselves to accept the ombudsman's decision. Sometimes the ombudsman himself finds a case hard to decide, but since he must make a decision he concludes that the arguments against finding the complaint justified tip the scale. The public purse does not have means to alleviate every hardship. Parliament, whose responsibility it is to allocate public resources, has not seen fit to provide for cases like that of complainant x. So the ombudsman rules his complaint unjustified, but cannot help seeing that x is unfortunate and the outcome unsatisfactory.

This disappointed minority of complainants sometimes writes to the ombudsman and suggests that his staff did not deal with their case thoroughly or speedily enough. They may even get in touch with the mass media. A very small number of disappointed complainants may achieve rather wide publicity and thereby have a lingering, and detrimental, effect on the ombudsman's image. The ombudsman's credibility with the public is of highest importance, not least for his influence on the administration. But he can only strive to minimize the number of disappointments; it is unlikely that he can eliminate them altogether.

Psychological satisfaction is the only direct impact of the ombudsman in a further type of case, that where a complaint is justified, but no remedial action is taken, because this is impossible in the circumstances. A complaint about the rudeness of a clerk, if found justified, may well improve the lot of those who will have to deal with the same clerk or his department in the future. Sometimes the complainant will specify that this is his motive in complaining. However, if the complainant does not have recurrent contact with the organization concerned, the ombudsman's intervention achieves nothing for him but self-vindication, and perhaps receiving an apology. Nevertheless, the number of complaints of this type is substantial.

Another type of ombudsman case confronts us where neither the direct impact of a remedy nor that of removal of doubts and their replacement by confidence is attained. These are the cases, hopefully few in number but of great importance, where the ombudsman finds a complaint justified and suggests a remedy, but the administration re-

fuses to accept his ruling and implement his recommendation. This happens to most ombudsmen, if only rarely. Particularly in cases where some real benefit is at stake for the complainant, the administration may find itself tempted to disagree with the ombudsman and to brave the secondary sanction he commands.

The question is often asked, in Israel as elsewhere, whether the ombudsman's lack of power of enforcement does not detract from the effectiveness of his operations. The fundamental constitutional answer is that the authority, but with it also the responsibility of the administration must not be divided or diluted. Only the law—or rather parliament which gives it, and the courts which enforce it—can give binding orders to the administration. The ombudsman, who neither creates standards with the authority of a legislative body, nor restricts himself to the application of legally binding norms, cannot and must not lay claim to powers of enforcement.

At the same time, the task of the ombudsman is not to be resigned to any lack of influence, but to be so convincing in his ruling on the individual case, and generally to acquire so strong a status in public esteem, that the sanction of his disapproval, with the parliamentary and other public consequences this is likely to entail, becomes a very effective instrument. In this sense the city ombudsman of Zurich could hardly have been paid a more telling compliment than when the *Neue Zuricher Zeitung,* one of the free world's great dailies, captioned its writeup of Dr. Jacques Vontobel's first annual report: "Ein Amt ohne Macht setzt sich durch"—an office without power has its way.

The analysis so far has implied that the direct impact of the ombudsman depends on the end result of his work— how many complaints he found justified or unjustified, and how often remedy was possible with regard to those complaints that were found justified. In a more basic sense, however, it is not mainly the final result—the disposition of complaints—but at least as much the raw material—the complaints themselves—that determine what the direct impact of the ombudsman can be. It could be said that the subject matter of the complaints which the ombudsman receives is not very impressive. The Swedish ombudsmen speak of "the rare occurrence of cases where an individual's rights or freedom are really at stake. Most complaints concern defaults of a not very serious nature." The ombudsman's direct impact cannot be very strong if the subjects he deals with are not serious.

"Not very serious" cannot mean trivial in the eyes of the complainants. It could conceivably mean uninteresting in the eyes of the general public, and it is certainly true that the vast majority of ombudsman cases do not excite public interest nor do they deserve to. The Swedish ombudsmen mean that most complaints objectively do not concern very serious matters. In their view, the importance attached to complaints by those aggrieved should not be decisive. They say: "The continually growing number of complaints has made it necessary for the JO to dismiss immediately such complaints as seem to be of minor importance or are obviously unfounded. . . ."

However, not only does the law in many countries not permit the ombudsman to decline complaints which seem of minor importance, but there are also valid reasons for this. "Trivial" matters make up a good part of the life of almost all citizens. The German military ombudsman, Dr. Karl Walter Berkhan, puts it very eloquently: "The soldier frequently and rightly considers his sorrows and complaints to be his fate in life, however small they may sometimes look as seen from this report. A family separated, insufficient leave granted—such things do not as a rule inflict wounds which cannot be healed. But for those affected they appear a misfortune which they alone have to bear."

The ombudsman can exist even if those few citizens who are rich enough, powerful enough, or philosophical enough not to be bothered at all with trivial matters remain outside his clientele. However, he can hardly fulfill his function successfully if he is unaware of the immense agitation that small matters may cause the ordinary citizen, and fails to show the administration that the objectively unimportant is important enough for him. True, the ombudsman cannot live on bread and butter cases alone. His analytical capacity and prestige, in other words the essential conditions of his future success, are enhanced by sometimes coming to grips also with difficult cases involving substantial sums of money, questions of principle or basic civil rights—the Sachsenhausen camp case in Britain, the Swedish case of private homes being bugged for security reasons, perhaps in Canada the case of the expropriations for the Forillon National Park in Quebec. A prominent example is Ontario ombudsman Arthur Maloney's Pickering investigation. The broad base of everyday complaints and the apex of causes-célèbres are equally vital in the pyramid of the ombudsman's work.

But will a sufficient, if not really large, number of important cases reach the ombudsman? Will they not rather be brought before the law courts? It is true that the ombudsman must be willing to deal with many matters that do not deserve the cost and effort of formal court procedures, and at the other end must leave alone those that require an authoritative legal ruling—because of lack of guiding precedent, or perhaps conflicting legal views. However, this does not mean that there is some definition that all important matters necessarily go to the courts and all unimportant ones to the ombudsman. Even in countries with a system of administrative courts or easy access to the ordinary courts on administrative matters, many

important matters are best brought before the ombudsman, who is empowered to deal with them by standards of good administration and fairness, which are broader than the standards of strict law.

We have yet to come to what may be the most important factor of all in judging the direct impact of the ombudsman, in a way more important than the proportion of complaints that are justified and the seriousness or triviality of the bulk of complaints. This factor is the number of complaints the ombudsman receives. The analysis of figures on this subject leads to the conclusion that the direct impact of the ombudsman is necessarily very limited.

Figures from Israel are used to illustrate this point, but the line of argument seems applicable elsewhere also. Israel's population is about 3.5 million. There must be at least six hundred thousand households in the country. If we remember that trivial matters are expressly included, it is safe to assume that each household has at least one grievance every year on average against the central or local government, schools or universities, or the public utilities—in short, against one of the bodies subject to the ombudsman's jurisdiction. In fact, even the far bolder assumption that each household has one *justified* grievance on average against the authorities every year would by no means be exaggerated. However, the more cautious assumption is enough for our present purposes.

I receive between five and six thousand complaints a year. In other words, at the most about 1 percent of the grievances that could come before the ombudsman do in fact reach him. Even criminologists, who emphasize the big difference between actual and reported crime rates, have not pointed to such a gap between them. Considering the statistics on other ombudsmen's caseloads and the popular feeling that bureaucracy is rampant, it can be assumed that these statistics are fairly representative. This cannot be proven by exact methods, but precision is not needed. It is the order of magnitude that should bear out the point that the ombudsman in practice receives only a tiny fraction of the number of complaints that could be made to him.

For any ombudsman in any particular territory, it would be possible to make a more refined analysis of the grievances of citizens of that area against public administration which do not reach him. Grievances against some units of public administration in the area may not fall within his jurisdiction. If there is no complaints-handling mechanism to deal with these grievances, then the disproportion between the number of citizens' grievances and the number of complaints they register will tend to be more marked; if there is such a mechanism, then the gap will be slightly closed. Then again, some grievances against bodies subject to the ombudsman's jurisdiction may reach other complaints-handling mechanisms. There is, for instance, a considerable amount of overlap between my jurisdiction and that of several internal ombudsmen—in cities, in central government units, like the police or the Ministry of Housing, and others. This type of overlapping competence is very welcome. It is natural and helpful that a public authority should try to divert complaints about its functioning and deal with them before and without the intervention of an outside ombudsman. However, even the additional grievances taken care of by others will not substantially narrow the vast gap between potential complaints and complaints actually made. It is this gap first and foremost that makes it necessary for the ombudsman's direct impact to be supplemented by a weighty indirect one.

But before considering in more detail the indirect impact of the ombudsman, let us add one more thought concerning his direct impact. It is axiomatic that the ombudsman, as a holder of public office, should wish to increase this direct impact. One means to achieve this end which he cannot afford to neglect is publicity. Ombudsmen are, of course, aware that, on principle, a public service ought to be publicized by those supplying it, unless it automatically publicizes itself, as does the existence of public schools or public mass transport, for instance. Most ombudsmen report use of the mass media, lectures, and other activities for this purpose. Our Ministry of Education, at my request, circularized all elementary school teachers, drawing attention to the existence of the ombudsman service. Especially in rural or poor regions, the teacher often has occasion to talk to his pupils or their parents about a problem facing the family; in suitable cases, the teacher's suggestion to turn to the ombudsman may be helpful and welcome.

Publicity can be a means not only for increasing the number of complaints the ombudsman receives, but also to influence the content of the complaints that reach him. Publicity efforts should also be so planned that they help to ensure that the ombudsman fulfills his proper social function. He must succeed in bringing his service to the notice of the really unfortunate members of society, a group that exists in all countries. These people may have learned from unpleasant experiences to see as normal a more shoddy type of administrative behavior than others would be willing to put up with. They may be unable to recall at the right moment that the ombudsman exists to help them and how they can reach him. In order to bring down this barrier, the ombudsman's publicity should be constant and easily understood.

True, there is often another side to publicity, as the ombudsman of Saskatchewan frankly admits: "The workload has been such that there was a fear that an extensive advertising campaign might flood the office

with complaints. . . . The excuse for not advertising, to permit the staffing of the office and gaining of experience, would perhaps be valid for a year or two in any new office. . . . " But, as Dr. Edward Boychuk himself implies, this just will not do for any longer period. Mind you, I say this not as his critic, but as a fellow culprit.

The most obvious way of having an indirect impact—always in the sense of achieving something beyond what concerns the individual complainant in the matter of his specific complaint—is the drawing of some general lesson from the particular instance. A case in point will be when the authority complained against is advised by the ombudsman to change some general practice or even the administrative regulation establishing that practice, and actually makes the change. At best, such a result can be obtained over a broad front, comprising not only the unit complained against, but also other units within the ombudsman's jurisdiction. In one of my cases, a woman who could not walk was to appear before an administrative panel of the Ministry of Health. Their office was on the second floor of an office building without an elevator— we have many such buildings. Since then, outside all buildings where such hearings are held there has to be a conspicuous notice saying that persons unable to mount the stairs may ask their prospective interviewers to transfer to a ground floor room to hear them.

In their periodic reports, all ombudsmen try to draw attention to general aspects of administrative practice revealed, and sometimes sharply high-lighted, by complaints. It may depend on the subject matter or on the taste of the individual ombudsman whether in a particular instance this is made part of a case presentation or of the general introduction to a report. The annual reports of the French *mediateur* are an outstanding example of analyzing problems incurred down to their fundamental aspects of principle.

Sometimes the ombudsman points out a general problem, but has no specific proposal for its solution. Policy questions are involved, perhaps of a political nature, or priority claims regarding the allocation of funds. One case of this kind from Hawaii concerns the problem of administrative boards made up of unpaid members with large backlogs of applicants to be heard. Another involves the long waiting list for hangar space for private planes at an airport—for once a matter not especially affecting the socially underprivileged. In this kind of case, the ombudsman can often only call attention to an unsatisfactory situation, hoping that as a result there may be some movement.

The most far-reaching, visible, and lasting effect of handling individual complaints is the bringing about of new legislation to prevent the occurrence of future cases like those already complained about. Most ombudsmen function, in one style or another, on behalf of parliaments. A special committee, and in some instances the whole house, deals with their reports. There is a good chance that an issue well presented will in suitable cases engage enough sympathy from some of the legislators that legislative action will be seriously considered and initiated where merited.

Sir Guy Powles over several years conducted an energetic and on most points successful campaign, which eventually led to important legislation in his country. As the outcome, the Social Security Commission in New Zealand is no longer bound to insist on the repayment of amounts overpaid to beneficiaries of social security and received by them in good faith, if they have altered their economic position in reliance on the overpayments.

In Israel, a district town planning commission had authorized the building up of an area to the extent of an aggregate floor space equal to 138 percent of the ground area, while the legal limit was 105 percent, with a tolerance up to 116 percent. As a result of our investigation, the government initiated an amendment to the Planning and Building Act, rendering criminally liable any member of a town planning authority who knowingly disregards binding legal restrictions. Overdense building is an important ecological issue in areas of quick development.

In this matter of initiating legislation, a parliamentary petitions committee fulfilling ombudsman-like functions is, of course, particularly well placed. The outstanding example is the Petitionsausschuss of the German Bundestag. For instance, having dealt with many cases of delay in social security payments, the committee brought about special legislation—ahead of the enactment of a planned social security code—under which all delayed payments of social benefits are to be made together with interest from the day on which they were due.

At this point, it should be stressed that the two-way relationship between parliament and the ombudsman has many facets, and most of them have a bearing on the ombudsman's impact. Legislation, in which the role of parliament needs no explaining, as an outcome of ombudsman work is only one such facet, though a very important one. The general subject of this two-way relationship undoubtedly deserves review on some future occasion.

Some ombudsmen are, by law, expressly charged to go beyond responding to the individual complainant with regard to his complaint. In Finland, for instance, where the main duty of the parliamentary ombudsman is general supervision of the legality of the action of officials and authorities, he calls complaints from the public his most important source of information; but he also conducts inspections and investigations on his own initiative. The

Victorian ombudsman believes, and in this belief he certainly is not alone, that it is his duty to visit places where persons are confined, or without being confined, suffer from some common disadvantage. The Swedish Parliament, when recently adopting a reform of the ombudsman office, found it necessary to reduce the number of routine inspections. However, this was done only because of the need to diminish the ombudsmen's workload. Their right to undertake inspections whenever they think this necessary has remained unaffected.

In Israel, where in my other capacity as the state comptroller I am charged with supervising public administration in general, the ombudsman section of my office is instructed always to look out for possibilities of general improvements as an outcome of our investigation of individual complaints. The ombudsman section may see to this themselves, but the law also expressly authorizes the state comptroller to take up matters in this capacity where he left them off as ombudsman, and this is often done.

The possibility of extracting a wider benefit from the handling of complaints also helps to assuage my financial conscience. Contrary to what might be feared, even as a state comptroller it does not bother me in the least, when I find a complaint justified, on legal grounds or grounds of moral justice, that I have to tell the authorities to pay out whatever sum is involved. But it does bother me that the average cost of our dealing with a complaint is not much less than $100, while the subject matter of many complaints is $20 or less. The additional indirect impact is a valid answer to this worry.

Finally, there is the impact of the very existence of the ombudsman function and its exercise generally, regardless of the individual cases and the lessons learned from them. Of great general importance is the deterrent effect that ombudsman activity has on officialdom. The fact that citizens can complain, and their complaint will be fully dealt with, goes to influence public servants to act so properly that there will be little cause for complaints, and none for justified complaints. For fear to be found in the wrong, perhaps reprimanded, perhaps unfavorably mentioned in a published report, officials will do their work with more consideration for the public, and will instruct and guide their staff in this sense. This indirect effect of ombudsman work is perhaps hard to quantify, but it should not be beyond some verification by way of empirical studies. Anyway, the better ombudsmen discharge their duties, the more anxious bureaucracy will be to avoid becoming involved with them.

This deterrent function is not without problems. It raises a question, with which not only ombudsmen are familiar, but also state comptrollers and generally all those who are charged with expressing criticism of the public service, and more particularly those whose criticism is published. Does the service improve for fear of criticism, or does it deteriorate because officials become overcautious and pedantic? In their comprehensive study of the British parliamentary ombudsman, Roy Gregory and Peter Hutchesson deal with this problem. On the basis of what they were told by civil servants they tend to be pessimistic. Presumably, both types of influence, the desirable and the undesirable, exist side by side, in varying degrees in different countries, even in different parts of the bureaucracy of the same country. There may also be changes over time. After a big scandal, brought to light by the ombudsman or comptroller, officials have been known to take to writing numberless memoranda to each other, in order to keep their direct responsibility for actions and decisions circumscribed and the limitation well recorded. But there must be many places, times, and kinds of activity, in which the need and urge to act, to get things done and to exercise authority prevail sufficiently to overcome undue cautiousness—though hopefully not that measure of caution and propriety which is desirable.

Much depends quite obviously on whether ombudsman relations with the authorities are handled at the right pitch. Ombudsmen cannot afford excessive collaboration, lest they jeopardize the interest of the complainant. But excessive confrontation may indeed paralyze or unduly frighten the administration, quite apart from being counterproductive in the fulfillment of their direct mission. An ombudsman institution that has exercised an overall undesirable, or perhaps only an excessive effect, could even find itself downgraded in the choice of who is to head it or by a narrowing of the terms of its charter. However, there is no need to speak at length against excess, which is by definition wrong. If the ombudsman acts properly and with due wisdom, he is bound to have a desirable preventive effect against shortcomings in the dealings of public officials with citizens and their affairs.

Not least important is the meaning which the existence of the ombudsman institution has for the general well-being of the citizen. In West Berlin, I participated in a seminar on the protection of the citizen against bureaucracy. The invitation to me to address the seminar spoke of Kafka, Orwell, Huxley, and Parkinson as the true prophets of the modern era, and they wrote before the prime of His Majesty the Computer. One does not have to subscribe to their gloomiest forebodings and may still sense something frightening and oppressive, at least for the ordinary man, in the power of officialdom facing him in those many confrontations modern life entails. The fact that this machine contains another part designed to stand by his side, to defend him against the apparatus itself, that there is an office of high standing in the hierarchy with no other mission to justify its existence and with no other challenge to the ambitions of its office-holders—this fact, if sufficiently brought home to him, should be of comfort to the individual. Many of those people who have cause for lodging a complaint but do not do so may still have felt reassured by the knowledge that they could have claimed to be heard, even though in fact, for their own reasons, they chose not to.

Today's ombudsman is a profoundly democratic institution. With the right to complain, the individual citizen is given a means of directly influencing the administration more specifically and, in its own time and place, more powerfully, than by casting his vote as one of many in an election. This element of direct democracy may account for some of the appeal of the ombudsman idea. But here again the citizen is not only interested by what affects him personally. It is part of a good man's well-being and peace of mind to know that the society to which he belongs also does justice to his fellow men. Many young people care, but not only they. We may not all fully live up to the commandment to love our neighbor like ourselves. But some of this love there certainly is, and it carries over into our demands on, and expectations from, organized public life. Therefore, the existence of an institution that helps citizens to obtain justice in their dealings with the powerful authorities has a value for us, even while we do not need it ourselves.

With all this in mind, it seems to me we ombudsmen have been given a chance to have a deep impact on the quality of life in our communities. The affairs of human society are hardly anywhere in such good shape that the potential of a blessing can be permitted to be redundant. Our function is a young one, and often we are still groping to find our way. This can be for the good, adding a dynamic element in an age that anyway does not permit standing still.

God gave man the task of conducting an everlasting struggle for moral advancement, not only in his individual soul but also in his society. In this a meaningful role is assigned to us.

B. THE OMBUDSMAN AS MEDIATOR, REFORMER, AND FIGHTER? (1)

PER-ERIK NILSSON, CHIEF PARLIAMENTARY OMBUDSMAN, SWEDEN

THE INTERNATIONAL BAR ASSOCIATION defines the ombudsman institution as

an office provided for by the constitution or by action of the Legislature or Parliament and headed by an independent, high-level public official who is responsible to the Legislature or Parliament, who receives complaints from aggrieved persons against government agencies, officials, and who has the power to investigate, recommend corrective action, and issue reports.

This definition succeeds quite well in indicating the minimum demands that should apply to the use of the designation "ombudsman": an official who does *not* possess the right to investigate a matter, may *not* make recommendations as to what a government agency or official should do to right something that has gone wrong, and who *cannot* publish an account of his doings and findings—such a person should *not* properly be entitled to call himself ombudsman.

The definition, like all good definitions, is one of principle and is general. Quite obviously, of course, the role and functions of the individual ombudsman vary—and quite a lot from one country to another, variations that are due to what the legislature or parliament has decided about his activities, what tasks and what functions have been assigned to him. But bearing this in mind, one may recognize that the definition nevertheless depicts fairly correctly the factual situation in most countries that possess an ombudsman institution. Having said that, it is another—and very essential—matter that the concrete content of the ombudsmanship is determined to no mean extent by the person or persons functioning at any time as ombudsmen. In this office in particular, the person exercising it undoubtedly determines both how it functions in practice and how it is regarded.

The measures that ombudsmen practically everywhere can take—severally or in combination—are

- to *recommend* to a government agency or official to do or refrain from doing something,
- to *submit* a matter in respect of which a fault or "illegality" has been found to the body or bodies that have to decide in such cases,
- to *report* observations to the body or bodies that have the constitutional means to rectify what may be unsatisfactory or to improve what is not altogether as it should be,
- to *request* notification of what has been done or of what is intended to be done by reason of recommendations from the ombudsman.

At the same time, the possibilities or duties to reject complaints are also largely the same practically everywhere. Thus, most ombudsmen can or should reject a complaint if

- the possibilities to obtain redress offered by the totality of the system have not been exhausted,
- the person who applies to the ombudsman is not the person directly concerned by the matter complained of,
- the complaint relates to a mere triviality.

Address to the Second International Ombudsman Conference, Jerusalem, October 28, 1980.

I, too, work in principle on this basis, but I have also a possibility that most other ombudsmen lack: I can prosecute before a court of law an official who is considered to be guilty of a serious fault or—in less serious cases—commit an erring or remiss official to a disciplinary procedure. During the institution's first one hundred years, the ombudsman was primarily a prosecutor. In the last decades, this function has lost some of its significance, if I translate significance by the number of prosecutions and disregard the effect that lies in the *threat* of these measures! In the past few years, the number of prosecutions has been between five and ten per annum. Prosecution has been superseded by more or less sharp criticism of the agency or official and indications as to how the matter *should* have been handled.

If I regard the function of the average ombudsman strictly formally—that is, if my judgment is based exclusively on the constitutional conditions he has to abide by—only very few have the means for real mediation between a complainant and the agency he complains of. Even fewer—if any— have the possibility of fighting *for* their opinion or for an individual person *against* an agency or its representatives. By "fighting" I mean that the ombudsman has wider powers than merely to argue his cause (and to hope that those who have the powers of decision and action will be convinced by his arguments and do as he wishes). An ombudsman who cannot decide a matter substantively (and the predominant number of issues are such) must, in order to be classed as a fighter, have the right, or at all events not be forbidden, to bring a matter before a competent authority—and to extort an answer from it.

If it appears, therefore, that there is little scope for mediators and fighters in the ombudsman circle, there is at any rate no lack of reformers. This assertion stands, however, only if one is also prepared to classify as reformers the persons who merely *suggest* reforms and do not demand that they also carry out what they suggest.

What I have stated is a recognition of factual circumstances. It embraces no value-judgment and should not be taken as any form of criticism. I would also say that I am fully aware *both* that there are cases when the ombudsman's formal possibilities to act are greater than I have indicated as average *and* that the practical reality not seldom has wider limits than the formal. There are certainly numerous examples when formal legislation gives the ombudsman considerable scope for personal initiative and action. Whether this room for maneuver is utilized, and how, will obviously depend in the last resort on the ombudsman himself, on his disposition and his view of his task, and on how he wishes to carry it out.

To return to my own country and my own conditions, I must say that my scope is perhaps less than in most other countries, and this is because of the Swedish administrative structure. We differ from most other countries in the following respects:

- The central power of the state (the government, the ministries) has nothing to do with the factual implementation of decisions that itself or parliament has made. That task (the executive authority) rests with an independent body—an agency—which on its own responsibility executes what government and parliament have decided. This agency may, in turn, have both a central, a regional and a local organization.

- Both the central power of the state and the government agencies almost always act on the basis of statute more or less detailed in its formulation. The administrative statutes in the various fields are in turn supplemented by an Administrative Procedures Act covering the entire administration. The Administrative Procedures Act lays down how government agencies shall deal with the matters under their jurisdiction. There are rules governing communication, the statement of reasons for decisions, appeal, and so on.

- The system of independent, executive agencies is supplemented by a separate court organization for administrative questions. The administrative court organization is based on the same model as that for the ordinary courts—a triple instance system with a supreme administrative court at the top. In principle every administrative decision can be appealed and the action carried through all three instances.

In an administrative system with this structure, there is little or no scope for mediation. There is actually nothing for an ombudsman to negotiate or compromise about—at all events theoretically. Statutes say, or are assumed to say, how a given situation will be resolved: how large a pension Mr. A will have, what sickness benefit Mrs. B is entitled to, and when Mr. C will get back the driving license he lost when intoxicated. Since the agencies that make the concrete decisions are independent, and thus do not take orders either from the government or from a superior authority, if any, there is in principle only one way to bring about another outcome than that which the agency decided on: to appeal against its decision. All one can do is to demand changes of the legislation—that it be reformed—to prevent a repetition of something considered to be bad. *That* the ombudsman can fight for!

Before going on to the question of whether today's ombudsman office—in Sweden and elsewhere—is what it should be, two points should be considered. First is an aspect of the ombudsman's work that does not usually receive much attention, namely, what he signifies for the agencies that come under his supervision and against which he can take action if they are at fault or remiss, and second is something about the Swedish ombudsman's tasks and functions.

Government agencies are often presented in the media as insensitive, hard-hearted, impersonal bodies concerned not with the individual's good but with their own. In their striving to strengthen their own position, to demonstrate their power and infallibility, these "bureaucratic hydras" are, it is said, not above cheating the individual by adopting various tricks and dodges. In their more beneficent moods, the media may depict the ombudsman as the small man's only friend—his shield. In both cases, the picture is oversimplified. As regards the agencies it is undoubtedly also false. If it were not, the overwhelming majority of complaints that the ombudsman receives would be justified. But they are not—neither in Sweden nor anywhere else. An international average would show that the number of justified in relation to unjustified complaints is in the proportion one to four. Our Swedish statistics show that about 15 percent of all complaints may be denoted as justified; some sectors, for example, the taxation sectors, show a few percentage points higher. Why so many complaints prove to be unjustified is a matter worth separate study. While such an analysis is not attempted here, it may be supposed that many complaints are due to the fact that the individual cannot penetrate and understand the agency's way of expressing itself. Often, quite simply, he cannot grasp what the agency wishes to say to him. And what a person doesn't grasp, he is suspicious of and has reason to question. We, the Swedish ombudsmen, have, therefore, to devote quite considerable trouble to explaining in simple language what has happened and why things went as they did. I think we are fairly successful in that respect, but it is both regrettable and alarming that we should need to spend time on such matters.

The ombudsman undeniably plays an important role for the agencies and their officials. He supervises and inspects them; he advises them as to how to handle a case or a situation; he sometimes criticizes them and, perhaps more seldom, commends them. They often do as the ombudsman says, but they also use his decisions as shield and defense against criticism from the public or media: "the ombudsman has looked at what we have done or not done and had no fault to find." Although they are indeed entitled to do so in most cases, it often happens that agencies refer to the ombudsman's "verdict of acquittal" even in cases that have little in common with the one decided by the ombudsman. If the ombudsman's "acquittal" is used in that way more frequently, it may give people the

idea that there is no use in addressing the ombudsman or—what is worse—that the agencies and the ombudsman stick together against the little man, that is, that they are in collusion with one another.

The Swedish ombudsman institution was created as a parliamentary control organ to ensure that the agencies which at that time were constitutionally subordinate to the Crown (and today to the government) followed the laws decided by parliament and applied them correctly. If an agency or official failed to do so, it or he was criticized; if the ombudsman judged the fault or negligence to be serious, he could prosecute the offending party. In such a case, the ombudsman himself acted as prosecutor before the court. Prosecution was common up to the middle of this century. It is now rare, not because the rules of conduct for the ombudsman have been changed, but because the manner of their application has been altered.

In rather simplified terms, one may say that the Swedish ombudsman's task is to keep a watch on behalf of parliament on the administration and to take action to ensure that an acceptable quality level is maintained. Complaints from the public—as also the ombudsman's own observations at inspections on the agencies' premises—become gauges of the standard of administration. To stretch the point a bit, one may say that the object of the ombudsman institution is not to ensure that what has gone wrong in the individual case is put right; its object is rather to ensure that no mistake is made. The work of the Swedish ombudsman is directed to that "indirect impact." It has been said that the most important aspect of this institution is that it is; what it does is of minor importance.

Does the ombudsman institution today, in general, have the form and the powers that are proper, reasonable, and adequate for the foreseeable future? Or should one strive for a more result-oriented institution?

As already stated, the Swedish ombudsman (and undoubtedly several others with him) has few possibilities of acting as mediator and even fewer of taking on the role of fighter. He may propose changes and hope that his proposals will be followed. This, many consider, is an acceptable state of affairs. I do not unconditionally adhere to their ranks. There are undeniably reasons to *discuss* whether the ombudsman should be given greater means to enforce his views. Why should not today's recommendations be tomorrow's reality?

Having a long tradition may be a handicap for an organization. The Swedish institution has existed for a long time and today functions largely as it did 170 years ago, but the society does not. The question of whether changes are needed is therefore perhaps more warranted in Sweden than elsewhere. To recognize this fact is not, however, to question the institution as such. On the contrary, an institution of this kind is necessary from all points of view, but it is also necessary to raise the issue so that the institution is as well adapted as possible to the society in which it operates. It is true that investigations have been made of the Swedish institution, and changes have been brought about in it. On the whole, however, the investigations and changes have related to internal, organizational questions. We have not actually had any proper debate on the role and forms of work of the institution in a complex society, and on its relation to other official institutions and agencies and to other ombudsmen such as the consumer's ombudsman. That debate is needed. It is hoped that the evaluation of the 1976 organizational changes, an evaluation that the Swedish Parliament promised when the changes were made, will soon be effected and that the institution will be discussed in a broader perspective. A thorough study of the institution, of its role and forms of work, while needed in Sweden, is probably not warranted in countries where the institution is relatively new.

There are other and perhaps more solid reasons for discussing the institution in Sweden, and in several other countries, not only from the points of view mentioned here, but also concretely to ask whether the "instruments of power" possessed by the ombudsman today are sufficient.

The Israeli ombudsman Dr. Nebenzahl presumes that only about 1 percent of the complaints that *might* have reached him actually did so. With regard to Sweden, a figure of 1 percent is probably not too high; a figure of one per thousand would be more likely. Of the complaints received in Sweden, about 15 percent prove to be justified. These are, in their way, strange figures that undoubtedly merit special analysis; I can merely speculate about them. One among several possible explanations of this latter figure has already been indicated. The 1 percent figure might be explained by the fact that Swedish officials are of such high calibre that they practically never commit any error—or, if one will, that the Swedish ombudsmen have succeeded well in their efforts to improve administrative standards. This explanation would admittedly be comforting to all concerned, and not least to the ombudsman, but it is not quite true. The small number of complaints is likely due to the fact that people think there is no use in turning to the ombudsman. "He can do nothing for me: he cannot alter the decision that has gone against me or see that I get back the tax that I consider I have paid in excess," and so forth. People are, after all, more interested in getting what they consider themselves entitled to than being treated only as victims of maladministration. This statement ignores the few who are out for revenge and who find their desire satisfied when an official is criticized or, even better, prosecuted by the

ombudsman. The Swedish ombudsman is not uncommonly called a "paper tiger" in the press and in other quarters as well. Some describe the complaints procedure as "formless, costless—and useless."

There is a third explanation of the surprisingly low number of complaints: People in general do not dare complain for fear that the agency will, for instance, badger them in other matters out of some sort of revenge. If this explanation should prove true, then the situation in Sweden is undeniably serious. Then it will be all the more urgent to restore or strengthen both the position of the public against the agencies and confidence in the ombudsman institution.

This is not to say that the role and working conditions of the ombudsman *must* be changed. The idea here is to stimulate debate rather than present any proposals as to what the new role should be, what means should be made available, or what form his work should take. It would be quite presumptuous to make any proposals in that direction. What can and should be done is partly a constitutional and partly a political question. We must be content here with the virtually self-evident remark that ombudsmen should closely follow developments, improve their knowledge of society and of its inhabitants' views and attitudes, and not hesitate in face of the changes which this knowledge warrants or renders necessary.

Proclamations of this kind may have a fine ring, but they do not provide much guidance for those who may one day have to bring about the necessary changes. The ombudsman of the twenty-first century will have to be more of a fighter than his twentieth-century counterpart. As already intimated, I am not a priori against the idea of giving the ombudsman more "power," of giving him the means to ensure that his recommendations do not remain "pia desideria," but practical, concrete action. What is more important is to establish a new way of operating—to change from today's rather defensive to a more aggressive attitude towards the administration. The principle upon which the Swedish institution is based is reasonable: If you cannot give real and immediate help to the individual, the second best thing is to help raise the general standard of the administration. Ombudsmen do not do that, at least not to a reasonable extent. I have a feeling that I deal too much with what went wrong and with who is to blame, and too little with what I can do to help prevent that wrong from reoccurring—often to people who for various reasons would not dream of writing to me. It would be helpful to have recurrent decisions—based on and illustrated by individual complaints—for every sector of the society in which ideas of improvement are presented and specific recommendations are made for the benefit of the individual and the agencies concerned.

But giving the activity this general direction does not exclude more specific measures. Serious consideration should be given, for instance, to

- empowering the ombudsman to bring about a special examination of an agency's decision by an administrative court of law of not too low instance (for instance, a court of appeal for administrative matters) in a situation when an appeal is no longer possible because the set term for it has elapsed and no third-party interest exists in the matter;

- empowering the ombudsman to demand from an agency a statement outlining what it has done about an ombudsman's report and, in the event of an unsatisfactory reply, to submit the matter to the government for action;

- empowering the ombudsman to direct that a decision not be implemented as long as the matter is under examination by the ombudsman.

Finally, a comment on "the power to issue reports" is in order. As judged from documentation, some people have not been particularly impressed by the results of reports. Justice Carl Clement noted that as the annual report to the legislature was the only method by which the ombudsman's work became known, few other than legislators would be able to read the report and others would only learn about it through the media. He pointed out that this was in contrast with the public nature of the courts. To this rather gloomy picture can be added an even more depressing one, which is that some ombudsmen are becoming skeptical about the value of preparing reports at all. They feel that no one reads the reports or cares to implement their recommendations.

Ombudsman reports with accounts of special cases usually have extremely little to give the ordinary decision-maker or individual. Their significance as "standard-raiser" appears to be moderate. I am currently considering what ought to be done to make ombudsman reports more usable and of greater value than they are today.

In this regard the annual report, in the form it assumes in Sweden, is a questionable means of disseminating information and knowledge about ombudsman activities and about how we think agencies should behave and act in various situations. I do not question the principle of issuing reports. In the Swedish system, as undoubtedly in most others, it is imperative that we spread knowledge of our decisions as widely and as quickly as possible. The best aid we have for this purpose is the mass media, particularly the press. The press can expedite the ombudsman's decisions, or at least assist in getting them executed. The regional and local press especially devotes great attention to those decisions concerning their own region or locality. Through the press, not only those directly affected by a decision but also the broad public learn what has happened and what they may demand from authorities and officials in fact and in behavior. The authorities and officials are aware that the public knows this and, it is hoped, are guided accordingly. This is one of the chief ways of indirectly influencing the administration and of raising or maintaining its standard. Cooperation with the mass media in mutual confidence is a "must" in ombudsman's work. We in Sweden have no more effective and cheaper weapon at our disposal than the press, which spreads what we think about the government agencies and their manner of fulfilling their tasks.

C. THE OMBUDSMAN AS MEDIATOR, REFORMER, AND FIGHTER? (2)

ARTHUR MALONEY, QC, FORMER ONTARIO OMBUDSMAN

THE MAN OR WOMAN who combines the functions of a mediator, reformer, and fighter is gifted with all the attributes that will make him or her fully successful and effective as an ombudsman. Mediation of a citizen's complaint against the action of a bureaucracy is an important and familiar part of the ombudsman's role. Many complaints must be denied; many complaints will be upheld, but, during my tenure of office, I had a feeling that the majority of the cases that came across my desk were resolved by a compromise that may have given the citizen less than he had hoped and the bureaucrat more than he intended. As a reformer, the appointment of an ombudsman unquestionably inspires the public servant to improve the service being given to the people. The calibre of service which the public receives from the civil servant is enhanced whenever an ombudsman is appointed, simply because the public servant understandably seeks to render unnecessary an ombudsman's intervention in his decisions. By improving the quality of service he gives, his conduct generates far fewer complaints.

The ombudsman has the power to criticize a law or a statutory provision that is unreasonable, unjust, oppressive, or improperly administered, although he does not otherwise encroach on matters of government policy. An ombudsman must always be sensitive to laws that fall into these categories, and as a result of his recommendations in the great variety of cases that come before him, a reform of such laws is bound to follow.

An ombudsman is not the citizen's lawyer or advocate. He has a duty of objectivity which would be incompatible with such an approach. The ombudsman investigates a complaint and if he finds that a case has merit, he must give leadership to the fight for justice in which the citizen may then be required to engage. He is not the citizen's lawyer for the simple reason that if his investigation vindicates the actions of the civil servant, he must not hesitate to uphold him.

The ombudsman who acquires a reputation for being willing to challenge the bureaucrat is better able to mediate and to bring about a suitable result in cases in which he feels an injustice has been done. The ombudsman who shows the bureaucrat his or her ability to act objectively and fairly then maintains confidence in this area as well.

The position of ombudsman was born out of the need for an agency that could cope with the problems that resulted from the intervention of government, growing ever bigger, in the lives of ordinary citizens and of the huge bureaucracies created to administer laws that governments felt were required to meet the needs of the people. The size of government has increased to such an extent that, according to Sir Guy Powles: "The fact is that in most advanced countries today the citizen feels himself oppressed by the organs of the State. He feels compelled to assert his rights. He is on the defensive. He feels the possibility of being smothered by authority." Not surprisingly, the institution of ombudsman has become widespread. Ombudsman offices are now found in Europe, Asia, Australasia, and North America. The fact that the institution has taken hold in so many countries demonstrates that it is aiding millions of people all over the world in their fight against acts of public maladministration.

When I took my oath of office as Ontario's first om-

Address to the Second International Ombudsman Conference, Jerusalem, October 28, 1980

budsman, I undertook to prepare a blueprint for the office which I felt would be best suited to the needs of the province. In fulfillment of this undertaking, I visited and studied a number of ombudsman offices around the world. These visits proved to be of great value to me. I found that no two ombudsman offices were identical; each has peculiarities in its legislation and each has differences in its conception and in the context within which it functions. Nonetheless, much can be learned by examining another office in actual operation and by meeting with one's counterparts, discussing their approach, and drawing from their experience. The key to the effectiveness of any ombudsman office is the character and personality of the ombudsman himself. I found all of the offices which I studied to be extremely personalized institutions, regardless of the organizational and legal framework within which an ombudsman might operate. They take their stamp from the individual ombudsman.

During my three years' experience as Ontario's ombudsman, I was immensely impressed with the amount of good the ombudsman office can do for the people. There is a real need for it, and it is important that it continue strong and independent in the people's service. There is no appointed public function that belongs more especially to the people than that of the ombudsman.

The ombudsman office is the only office or agency that is totally independent of the massive structure of government. The ordinary individual can rely on this source to obtain help when he feels he has been dealt with unfairly by the bureaucracy. If, upon investigation of a complaint, the ombudsman finds that it has merit, it will be pursued with vigor and no effort will be spared to ensure justice.

The welfare state has brought about many programs at every level all over the world. In Canada, such programs are manifested in the fields of education, health, unemployment insurance, mothers' allowances, workmen's compensation, and many other areas. Effective administration of these great programs requires a huge bureaucracy of men and women. From time to time, the ombudsman is called upon to review and survey the actions of these appointed officials. It follows, therefore, that the idea of the ombudsman as an official who sits alone in an obscure office answering his own telephone, unaided by qualified staff, is truly incompatible with the function as it must be seen. An ombudsman is only as effective as the staff and resources he is able to call upon to assist him in the performance of his duties.

A poorly staffed operation attempting to operate on the proverbial ''shoestring'' is only a front. The citizen may think he has a crutch to lean on when, in fact, he has nothing at all. To be effective, an ombudsman office must have adequate funding. It must engage staff of high calibre who are just as knowledgeable and competent as the civil servants whose actions are, from time to time, under scrutiny.

His Eminence Cardinal Flahiff, the archbishop of Winnipeg, commented on the ombudsman's qualifications in remarks he delivered at Toronto during the National Conference of Canadian Ombudsmen in 1977:

Certainly the ombudsman must be technically and professionally competent and must strive for fairness and even-handed dealings whenever it is necessary to correct or to supplement the provisions of law or their administration. It seems to me, nevertheless, that the very highest and most mandatory qualification is to be, besides all this, profoundly interested in and committed to the humanness of the human individual. The Ombudsman to my mind must be able to say—and adequate provision must be made for the Ombudsman to say effectively—with the ancient Roman leader—''I am a human being and nothing human is foreign to me.''

The province of Ontario, with a population of approximately 8.4 million people, has a civil service of ninety-five thousand. As a province, it has a land mass of 415,000 square miles. While much of the population is concentrated in large urban centers such as Toronto, Windsor, Hamilton, Ottawa, and London, a great deal of it is located in rural areas hundreds of miles distant from Toronto. There are at least twenty-five ministries of government and several hundred boards, agencies, and other commissions. There are eighty correctional and psychiatric facilities which house over seven thousand involuntary inmates or patients. The province's total budget for 1981 was over $17 billion, and some ministries command huge budgets.

In 1980, the Ontario ombudsman, the Honorable Donald Morand, received 10,572 new complaints and information requests.

The attorney general defrays the cost of prosecutors and judges; the solicitor general pays just part of the police cost; the Correctional Services Ministry the costs for those incarcerated in prisons or jails under provincial jurisdiction; and the Ministry of Revenue the cost of those who collect our taxes. Each of these has a budget in excess of $145 million.

The Ontario ombudsman provides none of these services. He does not prosecute or try or imprison anyone. Nor does he police or tax anyone. He serves simply as the people's watchdog over the bureaucracy. Yet, the Ontario ombudsman's budget is only $4.5 million, or less than one thirty-fifth of the provincial budget. Considering the millions that governments spend annually to investigate the citizen, this is a small fraction to set aside to enable the citizen to investigate government agencies that he feels have been unfair to him. The people are surely entitled to no less.

The ombudsman is involved in a number of relationships to which he must be especially sensitive. The first is his relationship with the news media—the press, radio, and television. In Ontario, there is a special sensitivity, insofar as the news media is concerned, to matters that are within the realm of civil rights and therefore the media show a keen interest in the ombudsman's activities. This interest is beneficial not only to the office but also to the civil service and to the public. The news media's access to the courts and their exposure of the courts to the bright glare of publicity usually help ensure fair trials. The press's interest in the ombudsman's activities is bound to have the same result. Even more important is the knowledge the people acquire about the existence of the office and its ability to serve them.

During my tenure as Ontario ombudsman, the members of the news media were very supportive of the office. As a result of coverage in the press, radio, and television, the public came to view the office as ready to fight for the rights of any individual who felt he or she had been wronged by bureaucratic action. The office was publicized in many ways. I accepted many public speaking engagements that brought me all over the province, and I encouraged members of my staff to do likewise. We were frequently invited as guests to the regular meetings of some of the well-known service clubs from which I encouraged invitations to the office. I urged high schools and universities to invite members of the office staff to address them about the role the ombudsman played in the lives of the people.

During the debates on the Ombudsman Act in 1975, members of the legislative assembly in Ontario suggested that the ombudsman tour the province explaining his mandate to the people and also enabling citizens to whom Toronto was not accessible to discuss their problems with representatives of the office in their own community. Morand has continued this practice. By March 1980, the ombudsman office had held a total of 156 private hearings around the province.

The philosophy behind these hearings is that the ombudsman office should be taken to the people; one should not wait for the people to come to the office. These tours represent one of the most important activities of the Ontario office. They produce a twofold benefit since, not only are the citizens able to meet personally with representatives of the office in their own locale, but also members of the staff are given an opportunity to meet the people they serve. They become personally acquainted with the problems of those within their jurisdiction. In addition, the interest in the local news media generated by these tours further educates the public as to the existence of the ombudsman office and popularizes it.

The relationship between the ombudsman and the elected members of the legislature is very important. The ombudsman's objective must be a good working relationship. I always considered the elected members to be ombudsmen in their own right. I had the experience of handling constituents' problems as a member of the federal parliament between 1957 and 1962. The advantage which the ombudsman enjoys over the ordinary elected member is that, as a result of the powers delegated to him by parliament, he has at his command the staff, expertise, financial resources, and access to the inner workings of government which are unavailable to the ordinary members of parliament and which they could not, realistically, make available to themselves.

I always thought of the elected members as fellow ombudsmen and accordingly always invited them to participate in the private hearings held throughout the province. Increasing numbers referred their constituents' problems to the ombudsman office, particularly toward the end of my term. We worked together in good accord, thereby assisting them and their constituents. It is fundamental to the ombudsman concept that the office remain totally independent of the executive arm of government—the cabinet, the civil service, and the political arm of the legislature. That the ombudsman must be subject to legislative control is basic; however, this is accomplished by giving the legislature power to fix the ombudsman's budget and to dismiss the incumbent for cause. Beyond that, the legislature should not interfere with the ombudsman's day-to-day performance.

In Ontario, a Select Committee of the legislature made up of members of all political parties was created, giving the ombudsman real access to the legislature in that his reports and his recommendations could be discussed, debated, and voted upon in a way for which the original legislation did not make adequate provision. But a Select Committee should avoid the temptation to regard itself as an "appellate tribunal" in its dealings with the ombudsman. The committee should work in close partnership and accord with the ombudsman. It must be careful to refrain from even appearing to usurp the ombudsman's function.

During my term in office, I received a complaint from a member of the provincial parliament about the actions of two members of my staff. One of these individuals, quite wrongly, appeared on a television program with a candidate who had been nominated by the opposite political party in the member's constituency. The member alleged that the appearance of my staff officer with the nominated candidate had seriously impaired the credibility of my office and raised questions in the minds of his constituents as to the ombudsman's partisanship. The member recommended that the officer who had arranged the interview and the other office staff member who had appeared on the program should be dismissed. Upon receipt of his complaint, I immediately conducted an investigation of the matter. After a full and detailed review of the circumstances, I concluded that the members of my staff had made errors of judgment. However, I did not consider their errors to be so serious as to warrant dismissal. I reported my findings in detail to the member in question. His attitude was unfair and unreasonable.

The Select Committee of the legislature to which he complained also wanted to investigate the complaint. I maintained that the committee lacked jurisdiction to deal with the matter and that if the member seriously wished to press the matter, he should report his dissatisfaction to the speaker of the assembly who, if he chose to, could refer the matter to the Procedural Affairs Committee. I advised the chairman of the Select Committee that I believed the principle of impartiality in the future operation of the ombudsman office would be threatened if the Select Committee involved itself in the member's complaint. It would involve the committee in the day-to-day operation of the ombudsman office, and, in effect, such an action would open wide the door to the creation of a far different ombudsman function in Ontario than that envisaged by the legislature when it unanimously adopted the Ombudsman Act in 1975. I contended that the ombudsman must remain free from the control of any body except for the legislature itself, which alone could dismiss him for cause and receive his reports. Notwithstanding the position I took on the complaint, the matter was placed on the agenda of the Select Committee and the chairman called the case in my presence. Consequently, my only alternative was to withdraw from the committee, together with the members of my staff who were present.

Examples of some of the cases I saw during my period in office are as follows:

> The father of a seventeen-year-old boy complained that his son had been subpoenaed to appear as a prosecution witness in court on a date that coincided with the date on which his school was to be brought to Toronto on a conducted tour. The boy's parents had been given the impression by the police that it would not be necessary for their son to attend court on that date. The case proceeded while the young man was in Toronto, and the judge issued a bench warrant for his arrest. When the boy later appeared in court, he explained the situation to the judge. He was nonetheless found guilty of contempt of court and fined. The boy's father engaged a lawyer in Toronto to appeal the judge's decision. In an attempt to keep down the legal costs, the lawyer suggested that the attorney general's ministry consent to the appeal being allowed, as indeed it subsequently was, and the contempt of court conviction was quashed. After obtaining a number of character references for the boy, I requested that the attorney general reimburse the father for the legal costs he had incurred. As a result of our request, the deputy attorney general

agreed that the young man had been the victim of a miscarriage of justice, and the attorney general authorized the reimbursement of the legal fees.

In another case, the father of a seventeen-year-old girl complained that his daughter, who had not previously been in difficulty with the law, was to be detained in custody for three weeks while a provincial court judge considered the sentence he would impose following her plea of guilty on a charge of mere possession of a small quantity of marijuana, an offense for which an offender would normally receive a small fine or a discharge. I contacted the young girl's lawyer and advised him that it was his right, in order to secure her release from custody, to appeal both conviction and sentence and obtain bail. The lawyer followed this course, and the young girl was released from custody.

The provincial court judge wrote to me and complained about my intervention. In his letter, he said the situation raised "very significant issues as to the due administration of justice and the division of function between this Court and the Office of the Ombudsman." In my reply to the judge, I pointed out that it is basic to the successful functioning of the ombudsman office that citizens who approach it be advised as to their rights and as to how they go about asserting them if they choose to. I indicated to him that where a matter raised by a complainant is outside his jurisdiction, the ombudsman must never send the complainant away in ignorance of where he goes to have his rights determined. I concluded my letter as follows:

> Quite often the actions of officials which I am asked to review are outside the scope of my jurisdiction. The policy of my Office in such cases is to inform the claimant as to where the remedy lies and as to how to go about obtaining it. If I were to have refrained from advising the accused and her counsel as to the remedies by way of appeal and bail that were open to her in the unusual circumstances of her case, I would have left myself open to serious censure. I trust this will serve to clarify your understanding of the role the Ombudsman in this Province is required to play and will continue to play so long as I am the incumbent.

I should add that the young girl appeared before the judge and was sentenced to a substantial fine.

Another case related to the owner of a cottage situated in a provincial park. This complainant's problem was that his lease did not contain an option to renew clause, and this was unknown to him as he had failed to read the fine print. A number of his neighbors whose leases had been renewed at the same time as his did have option to renew clauses. He had been assured by the former park superintendent that it was the policy of the department to permit the leases to be renewed. On the basis of this assurance he made extensive and costly improvements to his cottage. Departmental officials admitted to me that they may have made an error when they renewed the complainant's lease. Following my office's investigation and my recommendation to the department, the complainant's lease was renewed for an additional twenty-one years.

In another case involving a cottage owner, the complainant purchased a small cottage from a friend. He paid the yearly taxes to the government for eight years until he was informed that the cottage was located on government land. Upon learning this fact, he contacted the ministry and requested an opportunity to purchase the land. The ministry refused to sell the land to him, and he was asked to relocate his cottage. Following my office's investigation, the ministry arranged to have a survey of the land conducted. The survey disclosed that, in fact, the cottage was not on government land. As a result, the ministry did not require him to relocate his cottage.

None of these cases would sound strange to ombudsmen throughout the world. If one were to study the annual reports of every ombudsman in the world, one would find a striking sameness in the cases that come from many different jurisdictions. That is why an ombudsman is nourished by the support and encouragement he receives from his counterparts. That is also why the International Ombudsman Institute is playing and is going to continue to play such a vital function in the continuing evolution of the ombudsman concept.

It is often said that the ombudsman is the voice of the ordinary man. Indeed, the great majority of cases that come to the ombudsman's attention involve people who are poor and disadvantaged. Their cases are given top priority. We do not, however, apply a means test in the ombudsman office. As will be noticed from the specific cases mentioned here, often a man who is well-to-do can be the victim of unfair treatment at the hands of the bureaucracy, and he has every right to avail himself of the office. He must be made to feel absolutely certain that his case will be taken up as well.

A former member of the Ontario Legislature once wrote to me on behalf of a former constituent who had a complaint against the Workmen's Compensation Board. The legislator, a former cabinet minister, thought we had showed a lack of interest in his constituent's complaint. The fact was that it was one of those cases we were unable to resolve. He phrased his criticism as follows: "My impression from news reports is that the Ombudsman Office has become not the defender of the weak but the vehicle for prosperous individuals." His criticism is not substantiated by the facts.

When I left the ombudsman office of Ontario, increasing numbers of citizens who were well-to-do financially were availing themselves of the office's assistance. They did not regard the office as an agency they were required to pay taxes to maintain but from which they would derive no benefit. Rather, they saw it as an office to serve all the people.

A man is "little" or "ordinary" because he has no one else to speak for him. And on occasion, the ordinary man happens to be well-to-do. It must not be forgotten that the ombudsman office is designed to serve everyone regardless of race, color, class, or creed, or economic circumstance. It is not an agency of the welfare system serving only those who are on welfare or relief. It is not an extension of the Legal Aid Plan.

As ombudsman in Ontario, I devoted a great deal of my attention to the specialized complaints of workmen's compensation and correctional services. Because of the unique nature of these complaints, I set up two specialized investigative directorates to deal with complaints from injured workers, inmates in provincial correctional institutions, and persons held involuntarily in provincial psychiatric facilities.

Perhaps the most important impact which the ombudsman office in Ontario may have had on the field of workmen's compensation during my tenure as ombudsman lies in a general recommendation I made in my fourth report. In dealing with complaints against the Ontario Workmen's Compensation Board, I had become concerned that the claimants before the board had no means of informing themselves of the operative law governing their cases, for the board published neither its adjudicative policies nor its past decisions. Although the board officials had always been most cooperative with my office, it was my belief that the publication of its policies and past decisions would permit claimants to inform themselves and to address their evidence and arguments to points and issues which the board considered relevant in adjudicating their claims. I therefore recommended that the board publish and make available to the public its adjudicative policies and manuals and that it publish an index without reference to the names of the parties or witnesses of its Appeal Board decisions and reasons therefor.

My recommendation was initially resisted by the board, but it was ultimately accepted. This recommendation will have a real impact on the entire field of workmen's compensation, because those who advocate the cases of injured workers before the board will no longer be ignorant of the operative law of workmen's compensation. They will also be able to ensure that the board is operating within the limits of and fulfilling the purposes of the Ontario Workmen's Compensation legislation. The ombudsman office in Ontario has also had a significant impact in the field of workmen's compensation as a result of recommendations made by the Honorable Donald Morand. In my view, Morand's recommendation to the Workmen's Compensation Board that it clarify its policy with respect to extending the "benefit of reasonable doubt" to injured workers will greatly benefit the many injured workers who appear before the board seeking compensation. The success Morand achieved in encouraging the board to succinctly define its policy on "benefit of doubt" will undoubtedly have a most beneficial effect in the area of workers' compensation in the province.

The ombudsman stands in a special relationship to prison inmates, the other specialized area to which I have referred above. Citizens who are incarcerated lose all their civil liberties, and outside the prison system, the ombudsman is often the only person in authority who can speak for them. I became increasingly convinced that the ombudsman's role in the correctional system is vital. A prisoner derives psychological benefit from being able to air his grievances within an independent agency with assurance of absolute confidentiality.

As a result of many complaints from prisoners, my office embarked upon a major investigation that resulted in a report relating to Ontario's adult correctional institutions. I am especially proud of this report. It contained a total of 144 recommendations, and the Ministry of Correctional Services was favorable to the vast majority of them. A great many of them have since been implemented.

Without doubt, the existence of an ombudsman office in any jurisdiction helps suppress volatile situations in jails and prisons. This surely must be what the former minister of correctional services, the Honorable Frank Drea, had in mind when he said that the office of the ombudsman in Ontario had saved his ministry millions of dollars annually. He cited three points to support this claim: first, the right of the inmates and staff to write confidentially to the ombudsman, which makes it more possible for the corrections ministry to avoid costly confrontations; second, that the ombudsman allows institutional programs to function more effectively, thus facilitating the use of community programs; and third, that vandalism and the amount of deliberate damage inside correctional institutions has dropped due to the "safety valve" of the presence of the ombudsman's services.

D. OMBUDSMAN AND CITIZEN: A CRITIQUE

ROBERT MIEWALD, University of Nebraska, Lincoln

In this age of high anxiety, with a bugaboo lurking around every corner, it is perhaps remarkable that the ombudsman has not become the object of some organized fear and loathing. At least no group has identified this concept as a threat to civilization as we know it. This may mean that ombudsmen are perceived as exceedingly benign or exceedingly harmless; perhaps they are not perceived at all.

At any rate, it must be a very belligerent or hypersensitive person who would object strenuously to the creation of the office of ombudsman. It would seem to be rather difficult to get worked up about an institution that promises the sort of good works any inhabitant of the modern world should be able to appreciate. In our attempts to cope with the bureaucratic age, surely we can agree that we need all the allies we can get. In a situation where the odds are stacked against the individual, only a fool would reject a useful means of fighting back.

So it is that the word "ombudsman" has quickly entered the English language without a great deal of critical examination, and just as quickly it has been bent into several shapes. Department stores have renamed their complaint offices, and garages have assigned their less surly mechanics as ombudsmen. Universities now hope that the office will stop students from occupying the dean's office. Television reporters claim the title, and disc jockeys scream that, "This is your ombudsman station!" The word has even suffered the linguistic indignity of being neutered into "ombudsperson." Much to the dismay of some political scientists, who thought they at last had possession of an esoteric concept that no one else understood, the ombudsman idea has been accepted, and perhaps passed by.

That is to say, the terms of the discussion of the idea in the United States have changed over the last decade. In 1970, the ombudsman was still a novel idea at a time of considerable hope, however naive, that the administrative state could be brought under control. By 1980, we may have become a little more skeptical, and the ombudsman, in the minds of many, was another one of those great ideas that had been oversold. Therefore, if we are to comment critically on the role of the ombudsman in the American political system (instead of rehashing the theoretical pros and cons of the institution), we must first identify what that role is.

One might assume that the increasingly self-conscious profession of public administration, as it works toward the status of a closed corporation, ought to have a fairly clear vision of this aspect of its trade. In view of the proliferation of textbooks in public administration in the past few years, someone unfamiliar with the discipline will surely believe that here is a group with a definite body of knowledge. Without pushing that premise too hard, let us use as a starting point the position of the ombudsman in current American administrative doctrine, as that doctrine is expressed in the textbooks.

Twenty-two general introductory textbooks in public administration were published in the United States between 1975 and 1980. If these books somehow represent the codification of the wisdom about the art, science, or craft of administration, it might be expected that the ombudsman, now no longer a novelty, would find a place. If the indexes are accurate, nine of the textbooks make no mention of the ombudsman. In those describing the idea, the coverage consists of a page or two. To be precise, in approximately ten thousand words of prose, only twenty-six pages are devoted to the ombudsman (and that number would have been much smaller but for a book co-authored by a leading authority on the subject). Obviously, the ombudsman is still on the periphery of the discipline of public administration.

All thirteen books containing references to the ombudsman cover the subject in chapters with "control," "responsibility," or "ethics" in the title. The ombudsman idea is listed as one among several means of ensuring administrative control, responsibility, or a sense of ethics. The writers do not appear overly enthusiastic about the ombudsman, nor do they make extravagant claims for the concept. Since most of the coverage is mere descriptive material covering structural aspects, it is hard to get a feel for the substantive content of the idea, that is, what are the larger implications? Insofar as there is a consensus in this regard, it is that the ombudsman may make life a little easier for individual citizens. The emerging conventional wisdom in American public administration is very much like that given an official stamp by the Advisory Commission on Intergovernmental Relations in its massive document on "citizen participation." Through the use of the ombudsman, "the individual is not left alone in his quest for justice and fair play at the hands of government."[1] If that is the political substance of the idea, let us explore its significance.

THE CITIZEN

In the literature, "ombudsman" and "citizen" form an inseparable pair, like ham and eggs or salt and pepper. The titles of books and articles contain such phrases as "citizen-advocate," "the citizen's defender," and "the citizen's protector." We are assured, in short, that the ombudsman has been a great boon for the citizen, but how are we to evaluate that claim if there is no definition of citizenship? In the writings on the ombudsman, the idea of citizenship is devoid of content.

We see this immediately when we inquire whether the status of citizen refers to some sort of legal qualification for assistance. Obviously not, for it is inconceivable that resident aliens or some other form of noncitizen would be denied access to the ombudsman. Indeed, in many situations, these would be the sorts of persons most likely to have serious problems with an unfamiliar government. And, of course, we know that many ombudsmen specialize entirely in the cases of those people who do not enjoy all the rights of citizens—felons and the mentally incapacitated within public institutions. Ombudsmen are not likely, then, to shoo away people who cannot produce the proper papers identifying them as legal citizens.

In that case, what meaning can we attach to citizen? It is a purely ornamental term, a classy word, to describe those unfortunate members of the polity who feel, rightly or wrongly, that they have been pushed just a little too far by the bureaucratic machine. It carries no real weight and consequently removes the political implications of the ombudsman from consideration. Rather than protecting

citizenship, the ombudsman may in fact contribute to the progressive debasement of what was once an honorable estate.

Because the advocates have not taken time to describe this citizen they are so intent on defending, I will claim the right to put forth a definition of my own, a definition that, I hope, has meaningful content and that distinguishes a citizen of a free community from the subject of a bureaucratic regime. Mark Roelofs captures the essence of citizenship when he speaks of "membership and then status within a community."[2] Its most cherished form, a form for which people have often been ready to make extraordinary sacrifices, requires a special status within a special community. To think in terms of citizenship is to agree that the members of the community enjoying that status are living together within a system that will permit individual growth while maintaining some sort of social harmony. Citizenship is conferred on those who have some capacity for development.

We can see this more clearly when we look beyond those who have citizenship and consider those, past and present, who have been denied the benefits of full citizenship. In our past, slaves, the propertyless, felons, the mentally ill, and, not too long ago, women suffered greater or lesser degrees of deprivation. Insofar as any of these exclusions were based on philosophical grounds, they stemmed from a feeling by the dominant group that the excluded did not have the full capacity to develop, that they suffered, as a class, from defects of judgment that made their participation in public affairs of little value, either for the individual participant or for the community.

In this deepest sense, then, a citizen is a frighteningly volatile element within the polity. Those societies that have consented to give meaning to the status must be honored for their collective courage, for to confer citizenship is to say that these people are of such worthy material and so valuable to the whole that we cannot afford to beat them into a standard mold. Through the free exercise of their judgment they shall continue to grow and through them the entire community. How much safer and more comfortable it must seem, for an order-loving species, to regulate serfs with the knout than to negotiate harmony within a mass of contentious citizens.

Citizenship is a license for those who wish to march to the beat of a different drum in the lonely search for meaning, either in cooperation with other citizens through participation in public affairs or through contemplation within the private life. Citizenship implies a subtle rhythm of participation and withdrawal based upon the individual's perception of what is meaningful. But today, unlike the situation in ancient Greece, the public forum, when we venture out into the world, is not filled with essentially equal fellow citizens. Instead, we meet only big, bureaucratic organizations that must regard the unfettered citizen as a source of unpredictable trouble.

By their very nature, organizations are not hospitable marketplaces of ideas, and when all social space is taken up by the organization, there is little room left for individuals to discuss openly the nature of reality or to work on the reconstruction of the social world. With the continuing ''disenchantment of the world,'' the political arena becomes less significant as a place where free citizens can meet to discuss their common future. What William Scott and David Hart call the ''Organizational Imperative''[3] must persist in driving out all competing perceptions if the system is to function well. Citizens cannot be permitted to exercise that intrinsic intellectuality which ''includes the human potential to reject and review given parameters, to say 'no' to established epistemologies, to introduce qualitatively new ideas.''[4]

Of course, as Scott and Hart admit, we are not first-class citizenship material since, as we grudgingly concede the end of the era of abundance, ''the American people have settled into a mind-numbing routine of trying only to preserve the status quo.''[5] Preservation is best guaranteed, we are promised by the managerial elite, by further submission to the organizations that brought us to such a state. The organizational ethos does not need citizens; it needs loyal workers, docile consumers, and, in the most advanced forms of technocratic utopias, items of administration who by their spasms of behavior give off data to be aggregated into manageable abstractions. Eugene Lewis is correct in writing that ''citizenship as an interactive means for insuring that the will of the people is translated into policies and laws has lost much of its meaning.''[6] Instead, he argues, the hallowed status of citizen has been parceled out into the roles of constituent, client, and victim. These roles are then further fragmented among the functional organizations, with the constituent of one bureaucracy being the client of another and a victim of a third. A citizen, a person who believes that one's welfare is tied in with the welfare of the whole community, is obsolete.

THE OMBUDSMAN

It is evident that the ombudsman can be of assistance to constituents, clients, and victims. Constituents can insist that their voices be heard in the distribution of benefits within their functional fiefdoms. Clients, naturally, are assured by the ombudsman of the receipt of legal entitlements to goods and services. Victims, those injured deliberately or accidentally by the operation of the machine, may seek some redress. However, citizens who carry no credentials other than that status will not find much help in the ombudsman office.

Friends of the ombudsman will immediately object that the office was never designed to effect a political revolution. As the former Seattle/King County ombudsman put it, ''the ombudsman is certainly not a platform upon which major reforms should be launched.''[7] But the indictment implied here is that the ombudsman is one more technique required by the organizational imperative which makes reform less likely. Or, in Ralph Hummel's terms, the ombudsman is part of the grammar of bureaucracy, a language ''so constructed as to prevent both bureaucrats and outsiders from ever formulating questions that might attack the underlying assumptions of the bureaucracy itself.''[8] Those objections which citizens might make about the prevailing reality are translated into the ''cases'' of clients for the manipulation of still another bureaucrat.

Herbert Kaufman concludes that, ''apparently, it takes a bureaucrat to control a bureaucrat.''[9] And why not? If we are concerned only with eliminating vexing little irregularities in a society that is seen as the end station of history, one might as well bureaucratize the function. The bureaucratization of compassion, as Victor Thompson notes, ''only changes the locale of the problem.''[10] The ombudsman, he writes, is ''the gimmick approach,'' which ''takes the place of deep analysis and understanding of the problem and so leads to formalism.''[11] With the ombudsman, the citizen, as compared to an abused client, is given no lever with which to move the underlying foundations of bureaucratic reality.

In this vein, Theodore Becker uses a medical metaphor to critique the ombudsman idea. It is, he asserts, a little first aid applied to a patient in a terminal state. Its fatal flaw is ''that the ombudsman is just one more step in the bureaucratization of society;'' it ''is just another, more sophisticated, way to rob people of involvement in the most crucial issues of the system that menaces them.''[12] Citizens are distracted from trying to revive a political system that would allow them the opportunity for a more thoroughgoing program of improvement in their government.

These critics of the ombudsman, while not demanding that it be abolished, agree that the concept is more of an addition to the science of management than to the art of statecraft. We may thus be better managed but not better governed. But as Lewis remarks, ''to manage is not to govern.''[13] Politics, as the art of governing, has been greatly weakened by the bureaucratic state and is unlikely to benefit from the idea, nor are citizens likely to experience a wider range of alternatives because of its existence.

Becker's medical terminology is questionable, simply

because no critic is qualified to state that society is on its deathbed. A video analogy might be better. The ombudsman is like the fine tuner on the television. It can do nothing to change the channel. In fact, because the picture is made more bearable, we citizens may continue to stare dumbly at "All-Star Championship Wrestling" rather than make an effort to search for more meaningful fare. Ombudsmen may serve as a means of habituating us to our usual perceptions of the world, thus allowing free citizens to forget that grand responsibility of exploring alternative realities.

NOTES

1. Advisory Commission on Intergovernmental Relations, *Citizen Participation in the American Federal System* (Washington, D.C.: U.S. Government Printing Office, 1980), p. 71.

2. Mark Roelofs, *The Tension of Citizenship: Private Man and Public Duty* (New York: Rinehart, 1957), p. 6.

3. William Scott and David Hart, *Organizational America* (Boston: Houghton Mifflin, 1979).

4. Marlis Krueger and Frieda Silvert, *Dissent Denied: The Technological Response to Protest* (New York: Elsevier, 1975), p. 14.

5. Scott and Hart, *Organizational America*, p. 14.

6. Eugene Lewis, *American Politics in a Bureaucratic Age: Citizens, Constituents, Clients and Victims* (Cambridge, Mass.: Winthrop, 1977), p. 9.

7. Paul R. Meyer, "The Effect of an Ombudsman," *The Bureaucrat* 8 (Winter 1979–80):21.

8. Ralph Hummel, *The Bureaucratic Experience* (New York: St. Martin's Press, 1977), p. 147.

9. Herbert Kaufman, "Administrative Decentralization and Political Power," *Public Administration Review* 29 (January–February 1969):6.

10. Victor Thompson, *Without Sympathy or Enthusiasm: The Problem of Administrative Compassion* (University, Ala.: University of Alabama Press, 1975), p. 62.

11. Ibid.

12. Theodore Becker, *Government Anarchy and the POGONOGO Alternative* (New York: Stein and Day, 1972), p. 225.

13. Lewis, *American Politics in a Bureaucratic Age*, p. 172.

CHAPTER 6

THE CONDUCT OF OMBUDSMAN INVESTIGATIONS OF COMPLAINTS

A. THE INVESTIGATIONS OF OMBUDSMEN

WILLIAM B. GWYN, TULANE UNIVERSITY

DESPITE A LARGE scholarly, official, and journalistic literature on the institution of ombudsman, little has been written about the ways in which ombudsmen investigate allegations of maladministration. There are no extended comparative accounts, and even detailed, accurate descriptions of the investigative methods of particular offices are rare. Yet,

Investigation is the backbone of complaint handling by the ombudsman. Once a complaint has been received, nothing can be resolved until there has been the gathering of facts and information from all the people and things involved, along with ascertaining the relevant laws, policies, procedures, and practices nomative [*sic*] to the fact.[1]

The comparative exploration of the subject presented in this essay is itself limited. Several important aspects of ombudsmanic investigations are ignored, such as the backgrounds and training of investigators and their degree of specialization in particular areas of administrative activity. Only five offices, albeit very important ones, are considered in some detail, and the relevant information about them is not as full and as exact as one would desire. The five offices are those in the United Kingdom, Denmark, Sweden, New Zealand, and Hawaii.

The wide variation in the investigative methods of ombudsmen can readily be detected by comparing the average annual ratios of the number of investigative staff of each of the five offices to (1) the total number of cases closed and (2) the total number of cases closed after full investigation.[2] (See Table 6.1.) These ratios are startling. If we assume that the investigative staffs of all five offices are fully occupied with official duties and that the regular investigators spend most of their time investigating complaints, then it seems likely that the ratios, especially those for fully investigated complaints, reflect significant differences in the ways the five offices investigate complaints.

Given frequent statements by all five ombudsmen about how hard their staff members work and about their need for more staff when their complaint loads increase, the first assumption seems justified. One might, however, challenge the second assumption, since investigative staffs engage in other operations besides investigations.

Originally presented to the International Ombudsman Conference, Edmonton, September 1976, and since revised with the helpful comments of ombudsmen Herman Doi (Hawaii), Ulf Lundvik (Sweden), and Sir Guy Powles (New Zealand), and Professors Larry Hill and John Moore.

Table 6.1
Average Annual Ratios of Staff to All Cases and Investigated Cases

OMBUDSMAN OFFICE	ALL CASES	INVESTIGATED CASES
United Kingdom	1/20	1/10
Denmark	1/500	1/60
Sweden	1/120	1/85
New Zealand	1/180	1/80
Hawaii	1/400	1/180

There are five and sometimes six phases of activity that must be undertaken before an ombudsman office can close a case of alleged maladministration:

1. Receive complaint (or in self-initiated cases, become aware of possible faulty administration through some other means).

2. Establish whether the complaint comes within the office's jurisdiction and is deserving of investigation and inform the complainant.

3. Investigate the matter at issue to establish the facts in the case.

4. Decide whether or not the facts as established lead to a conclusion that (a) the complaint was justified and (b) the government agency involved should modify its practices or procedures to prevent further maladministration.

5. Notify the complainant and the government agency of the opinion and recommendations in the case.

6. If the government agency rejects the recommendations further communicate to attain acceptance.

Staff members who take an important part in investigations are usually also engaged in the other phases of the office's operations. Thus, it is possible that the variations in the above ratios result only partly or not at all from variations in investigations. The only way to determine whether or not this is the case is to compare not only investigations but also those other phases. In addition, staff involved in investigations may spend much time not only handling complaints but also simply dispensing information to people seeking it. The five case studies that follow indicate that, while some of the difference in the ratios can be attributed to noninvestigative work, much of it is the result of the different kinds of investigations carried on by the ombudsmen offices.

The ratios suggest certain groupings of ombudsmen that might become the basis of a typology. Denmark, Sweden, and New Zealand form a cluster of offices quite different from Britain on one hand and Hawaii on the other. The Norwegian and Finnish ombudsmen and the offices in the Canadian states of New Brunswick, Manitoba, Nova Scotia, and Saskatchewan also appear to belong to the central cluster in terms of fully investigated cases per staff member. The Alberta ombudsman, on the other hand, falls somewhere between the central group and the British ombudsman, while the Quebec ombudsman and the Nebraska ombudsman resemble the Hawaiian office.[3] One might hypothesize that the time taken in investigations and the complexity of the investigative process are by and large greatest in the United Kingdom, least in Hawaii, Nebraska, and Quebec, and somewhere in between for the central cluster.

HAWAII

The Hawaiian ombudsman's office is able to handle far more complete investigations per staff member than any of the other four offices. The procedures that have been established by Ombudsman Herman Doi for investigating complaints do not in themselves suggest a speedy process. Each day a different investigative staff member is assigned to receive and handle all incoming complaints. The flowchart included in annual reports describes five steps in an investigation:

1. Staff member obtains facts from the complainant and any witnesses. Preliminary review of laws, rules, regulations, and procedures of the affected agency.

2. Inquiry to appropriate State or County agency for information and documentation.

3. Agency responds with facts and documents.

4. Review of all facts. If discrepancy in facts, verify facts by further investigation, interviews or review of records.

5. Research laws and rules, regulations and procedures of affected agency.

Following the investigation of facts, the investigator recommends to the ombudsman "what the opinion and/or recommendation, if any, should be." Doi then reviews the case file and his investigator's recommendation and renders his own opinion. In addition to these investigative steps, Doi also requires "that all cases are scrutinized by more than one person and at several points in time." These checkpoints normally include:

1. Each Monday, all professional staff members meet with the ombudsman and his first assistant to discuss cases newly received during the previous week. As each member explains his new cases, others present offer information and advice to assist in resolving them.

2. Each Tuesday, each investigator meets individually with the ombudsman to discuss problems and the progress of current cases. In addition, investigators are encouraged to consult informally with Doi whenever they encounter problems.

3. All correspondence by an investigator with complainants and government administrators is reviewed and possibly amended by the ombudsman, his first assistant, and a senior staff member.

4. A case is closed only after a final review of its file by the ombudsman and his first assistant.[4]

These elaborate procedures of the Hawaiian ombudsman's office have not prevented it from carrying a very large caseload. One reason for this is that "most of our cases do not require extensive research or investigation."[5] Although Doi emphasizes the need for "thoroughness of fact-finding and research," some of his cases are so simple as hardly to require an investigation at all. Thus, he has written, "It may take only a day to expedite the processing of an unemployment compensation or welfare check, the delayed processing of which seemed unwarranted."[6] If the experience of one month in 1973 is typical, up to a quarter of the complaints received by the Hawaiian ombudsman relate to alleged unreasonable delays in government services.[7] Other "routine" complaints concern such annoyances as "a broken water sprinkler on the grounds of the state building" or "a school fence which has fallen on a neighbor's yard." According to the 1974–75 annual report, "These complaints are considered 'routine' because the calls you make to the appropriate agencies should provide quick resolutions to the problems."[8] Such cases may, of course, lead to fairly lengthy and complex investigations, but available evidence suggests that most do not. A review of the office's files for fiscal years 1970–71 and 1971–72 has indicated that between 35 and 40 percent of the complaints coming within the ombudsman's jurisdiction are disposed of within a week, about one-half within two weeks, and about two-thirds within a month.[9] In striking contrast, simply getting through the first stage of the British parliamentary commissioner's investigation (that is, obtaining a report from the agency complained about) almost invariably takes over two weeks. Although the large majority of Doi's complaint cases are closed within a month, a few require very extensive investigation

sometimes lasting up to two years, with reports sometimes being secured from several government agencies, their files examined, officials interviewed, and sites inspected.

The relative simplicity of many of the complaint cases coming to Doi only partly accounts for the great difference between the staff/investigations ratio of his office and that of the British parliamentary commissioner for administration. A second cause is the difference in their investigative methods.

Before Doi began operations in 1970, he visited the Scandinavian ombudsmen and the British parliamentary commissioner to observe their procedures. Following the visits, in his first annual report, he commented,

We are emulating the system and methods of the Scandinavian countries, for they appear to better suit our purposes. For example, we depend on the departments to do most of the investigating work—to respond to the complaints after a search of their records and to provide us with documentary evidence to substantiate their reasoning. This enables our office to operate with a small, highly professional, legally oriented staff.[10]

In practice, the type of investigation employed by Doi's office varies according to the complexity and significance of the complaint. His office makes greater use of the telephone than the other four offices, and his seems to be the only office to conduct some investigations solely by phone.

Use of the telephone to gather information is a valuable time-saver both for the office and the agency. However, notes made of the phone call and the facts gathered immediately after termination of the call are essential. These notes are filed in the case file. The telephone is usually used for simple cases or for preliminary fact gathering. In complex or controversial cases, a written inquiry and a written response are required. Review of the administrative files is also conducted where the facts are in dispute.[11]

Doi has argued persuasively that the time and methods used by his staff to investigate complaints do not affect the quality of the result. He illustrates his point with a case involving a delay in receiving unemployment compensations. Only an hour after the arrival of the complaint by telephone, the staff member receiving it had phoned the relevant state agency to inquire why the complainant's checks had been held up, phoned the complainant for further information, reviewed pertinent legal rules, reviewed all of the evidence, and met with Doi to recommend that the agency be asked to review the complainant's file and to change the administrative practice that had caused the delay. After listening to his investigator's account of the case (there had not been time for written notes or a case file to be prepared) and examining relevant statutes, the same day Doi concurred in the recommendation and phoned its contents to the agency. The agency reviewed the complainant's file, consulted the claims examiner who had originally handled the case, and phoned the ombudsman the next morning to say that the complainant's checks were on the way to her. Although the complainant was now satisfied, Doi was not and therefore urged the agency to review the procedure that had led to the delay. About a week later, the agency reported back to him that the troublesome procedure had been revised. In this simple case, an hour's investigation carried out by telephone and in the office's library had resulted not only in a complaint remedied but in a poor procedure being revised.[12] A more complex case might have the same result but only after months of elaborate investigations relying mainly on written communications.[13]

The ability of the Hawaiian ombudsman to handle so many complaints per staff member is effected not only by the simplicity of many of his complaints and the extensive use of the telephone to investigate complaints but also by the character of other phases of his operations. Unlike many other ombudsmen, including the other four examined in this essay, Doi is allowed to receive complaints by telephone. In recent years, about 90 percent of complainants have reached him through that medium, with only about 4 or 5 percent by letter to him. According to Doi, complaints by phone allow his office

to pinpoint the concern of the complainant and to secure the necessary relevant facts to immediately start investigating the complaint. On the other hand, complaints received in writing may not clearly specify the issue that the complainant is concerned about, nor contain the essential facts necessary for the commencement of an investigation. In such a case, it would necessitate further contact with the complainant after receipt of the complaint before investigation may be commenced.[14]

Once a complaint has been investigated and a decision made by the ombudsman, further time is saved in Hawaii by reporting the results in simple cases, by telephone to complainants and involved agencies. In more complicated cases, written findings and conclusions are sent to complainants and agencies.[15]

Before a complaint can be investigated by any ombudsman office, a decision must be made as to whether it comes within its jurisdiction. Statutory rules for determining jurisdiction differ considerably from one office to another. The exclusions from the Hawaiian ombudsman's jurisdiction are few and very easy to interpret, with the result that the investigator receiving the complaint can usually make a jurisdiction decision immediately, subject to review by Doi. It appears that about 85 percent of exclusionary decisions are taken on the day they arrive.[16]

The other four ombudsmen all appear to take more time and effort in deciding whether or not to reject a complaint for jurisdictional or other reasons. For example, in New Zealand during the 1960s, the decision as to whether or not to accept a complaint was made on the day of its arrival in only 25 percent of cases, with a further 60 percent taking between two and six days.[17] The British ombudsman has found the application of his jurisdictional rules so difficult that he has created a special "screening" unit of five officers who examine all complaints to determine the jurisdictional question but take no part in actual investigations. During the 1970s, this unit alone was about the size of the entire professional staff of Doi's office!

NEW ZEALAND

Another ombudsman who explicitly distinguished his investigative methods from those of the British parliamentary commissioner was Sir Guy Powles of New Zealand, who has written of their "radically different methods of work."

The first British Ombudsman came to the office from holding the position of Comptroller and Auditor-General and was steeped in the traditions of that office and its methods of work. He consequently thought in terms of sending out investigating teams, themselves to do their fossicking in departments, studying the files on the spot, and producing their own reports. This is what he did and how he worked. On the other hand, in New Zealand the practice of securing and indeed relying upon the co-operation of the departments was adopted from the very beginning. This has meant that a substantial part of the routine investigation of a complaint is in fact carried out by the department itself, prodded, if necessary by the Ombudsman.[18]

Professor Hill's painstaking account of the New Zealand office has shown that between 1962 and 1969 about three-quarters of Powles' investigations were limited to sending a complaint or a precis of it to the relevant department with a request for a report. Forty-eight percent of the cases were closed after receiving only one letter from an agency, the average number being roughly two letters. Agency files were called for in about 20 percent of his investigations, usually to relieve an agency of the need to prepare a report on an obvious matter and not to pursue an investigation beyond the agency's report. Interviews with officials were held in less than 10 percent of investigations and an inspection of an agency's premises in less than 5 percent. Complainants were interviewed in about 10 percent of investigations, usually at their own request. By far the greatest number of the New Zealand ombudsman's investigations are, then, carried out by the agencies complained against. One should not conclude, however, that this heavy reliance on agency reports is evidence that the investigations are not thorough enough. A sample of cases investigated between 1962 and 1969 reveals that in only 19 percent did the agencies dispute the facts as presented by complainants; indeed, this percentage fell to 11 percent for the period 1965–69.[19] In such cases, it appeared that the ombudsman usually saw no need to go beyond an agency report.

Although the New Zealand ombudsman office investigates more complaints each year per investigator than his British counterpart, he investigates fewer than the Hawaiian ombudsman. The New Zealand ombudsman also employs the telephone in his investigations but to a lesser extent than the Hawaiian office. All complaints in New Zealand must be in writing, and Hill's research shows that the ombudsman's office telephoned a public agency in only 13 percent of investigations. Most calls were made by the ombudsman himself, usually to agency heads.[20] The variation between the two offices in this respect may be attributed to a cultural difference. Sir Guy Powles believed that the "telephone habit" was not so prevalent in New Zealand as in Hawaii,[21] and Herman Doi has mentioned that Hawaiian officials usually prefer to be approached by his office by phone rather than letter. Besides this difference in method, some evidence suggested that the New Zealand ombudsman received a larger proportion of complex complaints requiring lengthy investigations than did the Hawaiian office. Up to a quarter of the complaints received by the Hawaiian office involved delays in government services—normally simple, routine cases—but only about 5 percent of the complaints going to the New Zealand ombudsman alleged unreasonable delay.[22] Systematic comparison of complaints received by the two offices is needed to confirm this difference.

DENMARK

Available evidence indicates that in Denmark, Sweden, Norway, and Finland the ombudsmen go beyond agency reports in far more cases than in Hawaii and New Zealand. In Denmark, after the ombudsman decides that a complaint should be investigated, the relevant agency files are always sent for, and in most cases the agency is also asked to send a report on its actions. Under a practice initiated by Ombudsman Nordskov Nielsen, copies of these agency reports, unless they are very brief and uninformative, are always sent to complainants for comment. Although this practice adds two or three weeks to an investigation, Nielsen believes it is necessary if complainants are to be treated fairly. The complainant's written comment or the office's examination of an agency's files may result in further correspondence with the agency in question or with the complainant. "Written pro-

cedure," as Nielsen has remarked, "is the normal procedure." Under certain circumstances, however, "oral procedure" is followed: (1) When a complainant asks to make an oral statement, he is always allowed to do so. In these instances, it is usual for a professional staff member rather than the ombudsman himself to conduct the interview. (2) Even when a complainant does not ask for an interview, on infrequent occasions he is invited to give oral evidence if the ombudsman's office believes it to be important. Interviews of complainants occur in less than 10 percent of cases and are always conducted at the ombudsman's office rather than in the complainant's home. (3) In about eighty to one hundred investigations a year (roughly one-eighth of the total), meetings are held with representatives of the agencies complained against either at the ombudsman's office or at the agencies. The great majority of these talks, which take place more frequently under Nielsen than under his predecessor, are initiated by the ombudsman, although occasionally a department may request one. Sometimes complainants also attend these meetings, which then take on a somewhat judicial character.[23]

With complex investigative procedures being used more frequently than by the Hawaiian ombudsman, greater difficulty in deciding jurisdictional questions, and considerably less use of the telephone, the cases investigated by the Danish office take longer to close. Five to ten days may pass between receipt of a written complaint and a letter being sent to the complainant reporting whether or not his complaint will be investigated. In 1974, Nina Anderskouv estimated that it took two or three months to complete a majority of investigations, while a few took only about a month or a much longer time. Agencies took at least a month and sometimes as much as two or three months to send reports to the ombudsman. Another two or three weeks would elapse before the office would receive a complainant's comment on a report. It is not difficult to understand how a number of months would be needed to complete a case involving complex issues.

SWEDEN

In Sweden, as in Denmark, normal procedure is "written" rather than "oral." As Bertil Wennergren, one of the three Swedish ombudsmen between 1968 and 1976, has remarked, "The vast majority of the office's work is carried on by mail along with some telephone calls to speed things along."[24] In an essay published in 1968, the former Swedish ombudsman Alfred Bexelius noted, "The first step taken in handling a complaint which cannot at first sight be judged to be unjustified is to request the documents in the case from the authority concerned." Frequently, the ombudsman could arrive at a decision on the strength of this evidence. In cases where "the contents of the complaint give sufficient ground for the assumption of a fault" or where an investigation of agency files does not reveal the complaint to be unfounded, "an explanation in writing is usually demanded from the particular authority or official." If still unsatisfied that he has received sufficient information for a decision, the ombudsman can sometimes go a step further and hold a hearing with officials, or ask the police for a further investigation, or request information from other persons including interest groups.[25] Although in 1968 the office of ombudsman in Sweden was considerably restructured with three ombudsmen specializing in different areas of government replacing the single official, investigative methods remained very much the same.

In many cases the first step is to request the documents from the authority concerned. Often it is possible to judge from these documents alone whether there is sufficient cause for complaint. The next (sometimes the first) step will be to ask for an explanation in writing from the particular authority or official. If necessary, further correspondence may take place and opinions of experts and interested bodies may be requested. If the written material does not constitute sufficient foundation for the J.O.'s decision, he can order a closer examination by means of oral hearings. In very important cases these hearings are held by the J.O. himself, often combined with an inspection of the authority concerned. More frequently, the J.O. instructs a lawyer on his staff to make an examination. He can also ask the police to investigate the matter.[26]

The first step mentioned is the only one in a majority of investigations. Requests for explanations from officials in writing occur in about 30 percent of investigations, but hearings with officials are much rarer. Ombudsman Ulf Lundvik roughly estimated in 1976 that oral hearings with officials by the ombudsman or a member of his staff took place in only about 4 percent of investigated cases. In his opinion, one reason for the greater use of hearings in Denmark was the small size of that country. Ombudsman Wennergren's estimate in 1974 of about thirty hearings a year suggested an even lower percentage of hearings. Complainants were very rarely interviewed; Lundvik estimated they took place in only about 2 percent of cases. As in Denmark, however, written explanations from officials are always sent to complainants with an invitation to comment by correspondence.[27]

As one would expect, although hardly up to the Hawaiian rate, the time the Swedish ombudsman takes to close investigated cases is similar to and probably shorter than the time taken by the Danish office. We can arrive at a rough notion of the time required in Sweden by analyzing the disposal of 129 complaints received by the office in January 1974. By the end of January, 47 percent of these

cases had been closed. Since at that time about 38 percent of complaints were being dismissed without investigation, it is probably safe to assume that a large majority of the cases closed during the first month were not fully investigated. This would leave about 15 percent of investigated cases closed in the month they were received. Assuming that all eighteen of the January cases closed in February were fully investigated, during the first two months a little over a third of investigated cases were closed. The same assumption for the seventeen cases closed in March suggests that about 60 percent of investigated cases were closed in three months. With thirteen of the January cases closed in April and May, it appears that three-quarters of the investigated cases were completed in five months.[28]

THE UNITED KINGDOM

Judged in the light of other ombudsman offices, the British parliamentary commissioner for administration (PCA) has an extremely large staff in relation to his case and investigation load. When Sir Edmund Compton, the first PCA, began operations in 1967 he had expected between six and seven thousand complaints a year, which, had they materialized, would have given him a staff/complaint ratio similar to that in Sweden and Denmark. In fact, until the second half of the 1970s, the commissioner had never received more than 1,120 complaints in any one year (1968), and in 1971 they fell to as low as 548.[29] One might think that such a discrepancy between expectations and reality would lead to a considerable reduction in the size of the PCA's staff. In fact, despite British government efforts to reduce the size of the central bureaucracy, the size of the PCA's office has remained much the same at between fifty and sixty employees.

When asked in December 1967 whether he found the size of his staff (which he declared to be fifty-nine) sufficient, Compton replied, "I think that in number almost by luck this remains right. What has happened is that the case load in terms of number of cases has been a good deal less than I had planned on at the start. . . .On the other hand, the amount of work per case is considerably more than I had expected, so it is working out about right."[30] The Parliamentary Select Committee to which the commissioner reports has not seriously raised the question of why his cases require so much work, and it apparently is unaware or unconcerned that the commissioner's staff/investigation ratio is so very different from that of other ombudsman offices.

Part of the explanation for the PCA's exceptionally large investigative staff may be a tendency in organizations generally to resist reduction in size by finding some kinds of activities for their existing staff to perform. But a major contributory factor seems to be that previously mentioned, namely, the influence of the comptroller and auditor-general's office on the procedures instituted by the first parliamentary commissioner. Sir Edmund Compton was appointed after a number of years as auditor-general, where his job had been to direct a large staff to ferret out by very careful investigations possible misuse of public funds by government agencies. As ombudsman, he saw his major role as similarly uncovering official maladministration of other sorts. "My function," he told his Select Committee, "is to investigate the action taken by a department and decide whether there has been maladministration by the department. So my primary job as investigator—and I am sure this must be right—is to ascertain by inquiry inside the department what those department actions were." It was very important "to go in depth into those parts of the case which seemed to merit investigation." Such investigations could not rely on reports from departments on their own investigations of the complaints. "I would think that it is an absolute principle of investigations, as I understand it, that I investigate at first hand. I mean that the evidence that I am getting, if I am investigating a case, is from the person who did this thing complained of, or where the action is recorded, at first hand, not as reported by someone else."[31]

The investigative procedures followed by the PCA's office are partly determined by statute. Section 7(1) of the PCA Act requires the commissioner to begin an investigation by allowing the principal officer of the agency involved to comment on the allegations in the complaint. This "stage 1" of the investigation, as Compton called it, in effect sets in motion an investigation by the government agency complained against similar to that which would have taken place had a member of parliament taken a constituent's complaint directly to a minister rather than to the PCA. According to Compton, "The principal officer's comments to me usually contain a full statement of the facts known to the department and of the department's view of the case, often with supporting evidence."[32] As has been shown, in about three-quarters of the new Zealand ombudsman's investigations this is the only type of evidence relied upon for a decision. In the United Kingdom, on the other hand, only 5 or 10 percent of investigations appear to be limited to an agency inquiry and report.

The vast majority of investigations proceed to "stage 2." In 90 to 95 percent of investigations, the investigator sees the relevant agency files, which in the large majority of cases are sent to the commissioner's office. In a substantial number of investigations, after the files are seen, the officials involved are questioned orally, usually by a team of two consisting of the investigator who had examined the files and a more senior member of the office.[33] In 1971, the secretary to the commissioner estimated that teams were sent to interview officials in about half the cases in which the files were seen. An examination of the commissioner's reports for two quarterly periods during 1973–74 suggests a somewhat lower figure of 40 percent. Still, interviewing officials does appear to consume a sizable amount of investigative staff time, especially when the officials involved do not work in London. Even more often than interviewing officials, the PCA's staff visits the homes of complainants. A member of the PCA's staff estimated in 1976 that such visits occur in 60 percent of all investigations, which is about the same percentage which can be computed from the 1973–74 reports.

This frequent interviewing of complainants appears to distinguish the PCA from all other ombudsmen. The practice, begun by Compton, has been continued by his successors. As stated by Sir Alan Marre, the second commissioner, in his annual report for 1971,

I am continuing the practice of sending my investigating officers to visit complainants in their homes whenever, during the course of an investigation, it seems that the complainant may have additional information that will help me to reach the right conclusion. This is a procedure I follow more than my counterparts in other countries, both because I find it helpful and because it is often satisfying to the person visited.[34]

Note the dual motivation behind this development. On the one hand, it is desirable when there is a discrepancy between the "facts" as presented by the complainant and by the agency or where relevant information is unknown to the agency but known to the complainant. On the other hand, the visit itself brings a certain amount of comfort and assurance to the complainant. The PCA has been criticized for not being sufficiently a "father-figure" for the British public, but for those complainants visited in their homes by his investigators the office has a direct personal touch absent in Scandinavia or New Zealand.

The final step in the PCA's investigation occurs after the commissioner has accepted a draft report on the results of the investigation. Before the report is sent to the member of parliament referring the complaint, the commissioner sends it to the agency for a comment on the accuracy of its factual aspects. This practice has been adopted for two reasons. First, it gives ministers an opportunity to exercise their authority under Section 11(3) of the PCA Act to prevent information appearing in the report which they believe to be prejudicial to the public interest. Second, as a final check on the accuracy of the facts of the case, it assures that, if the agency is criticized, it cannot later argue that the commissioner had his facts wrong.

The very elaborate investigative procedure of the PCA's office not surprisingly consumes a great deal of time and staff. According to a memorandum prepared by the office for the author in 1976,

It is rarely possible to complete an investigation and for the Commissioner to submit his report to the referring MP in under two months. Until fairly recently it has been the intention to complete all stages of an investigation within six months, unless the enquiries were particularly time-consuming, but an increase in the number of complaints received in the last two years has caused this period to be lengthened. At the present time, the shortest period for completion of an investigation is probably about three months and the longest about twelve months, with an exceptional case taking even longer than that. The average time in the present rather unusual circumstances is probably about eight or nine months.

When faced with the problem of investigations taking more time to complete, Sir Alan Marre commented, ''I have felt that it is better to accept that consequence, unfortunate though it is, rather than depart from the thoroughness with which I have tried to make a point of carrying out my investigations.''[35]

No other ombudsman seems to devote so much investigative time and effort to the general run of cases as does the British parliamentary commissioner. In this respect, the commissioner and the Hawaiian ombudsman are extraordinarily different. The major reason for the exceptional character of the British office would seem to be role perception of the original incumbent which has become institutionalized. As has been shown above, the legislation providing for the office has also been influential. These two factors probably account for most of the difference between the British and the Danish, Swedish, and New Zealand ombudsmen. In the case of Hawaii, there may well be the additional important factor of the general run of the PCA's cases being more complex and therefore requiring longer scrutiny than those of the Hawaiian ombudsman.

CONCLUSIONS

It is clear that ombudsmen differ considerably in the length and complexity of their investigations. Ombudsmen, scholars who study them, and government policymakers who create and regulate them would do well to ponder the question, ''What type of investigative procedure is best for an ombudsman's office?'' If one places great importance on the accuracy and impartiality of an ombudsman's empirical findings, then the British system would appear to be superior to the others. Some other ombudsmen are prepared to admit the superiority of the British investigations. In comparing the Danish office with the British, Nordskov Nielsen has remarked, ''The procedure we use is not a completely good procedure in

order to reveal every aspect of the facts of the case. I'm completely sure that the procedure followed by my British colleague is more thorough.''[36] Proponents of British investigative practices have also argued that should the PCA rely merely on reports to him from the agencies complained against, he could do no more for complainants than members of parliament, who are able to secure the same sort of investigation for complainants.

There are, on the other hand, cogent arguments against this line of reasoning. First, protecting citizens against improper administrative actions and improving administrative practices would seem to be more important goals for an ombudsman than a very thorough independent search for the facts in every case investigated by him. Indeed, getting the facts straight is simply a means of achieving the first two mentioned goals, and to treat the investigation of complaints as an end in itself rather than as a means leads to a displacement of an ombudsman's proper goals.[37] While one would hardly go so far as to suggest that such a displacement has occurred in Britain, there does seem to be a tendency for the PCA's office to employ full-scale investigations for just about all the complaints deemed worthy of any investigation at all. Other ombudsmen tend more to vary the thoroughness of their investigations according to the significance and complexity of the complaints.

Second, evidence from New Zealand suggests that, in some ombudsman systems, most complaints do not require intensive investigation to establish the facts, since government agencies do not in most cases dispute the facts as presented by complainants. If such a pattern exists in other systems,[38] then in a large majority of complaints handled by ombudsmen, the issue is not at all what happened to the complainant but whether what happened should be considered as proper or improper administrative action. In these cases, what is crucial for the success of the ombudsman office is not its ability to reveal facts but its interpretation and evaluation of those facts, which depend on its knowledge of government administration and of proper administrative practices and procedures. In saying this, one, of course, should not forget that in a minority of cases the firm establishment of facts by long and careful investigation is vitally important for their successful resolution.

Third, unless in each case the PCA goes well beyond what a member of parliament can do in investigating a case, there is no need for the institution in Britain. Should the PCA follow the New Zealand pattern and rely mainly on the government agency complained against to provide him with the facts of his cases, he would still be able to do several important things a member of parliament cannot do. (1) He can bring to bear on the interpretation and evaluation of the facts in all cases his considerable expertise in government administration. (2) Through a combination of his expertise and status, he is much better equipped than the member of parliament to influence agencies to correct past mistakes and to take steps to assure that they will not recur in the future. (3) He can carry out his own thorough investigation and not rely on the agency when in his judgment such an investigation is needed. Awareness of this possibility may make agency investigations on the ombudsman's behalf more careful and scrupulous. For an ombudsman always to use the full arsenal of investigatory methods would amount in many cases to using cannon to kill flies.

NOTES

1. Larry Guillot, *Ombudsmen Investigative Procedures: A General Guide Adaptable for Use by Individual Offices* (Edmonton: International Ombudsman Institute, 1979), p. 1.

2. The ratios are approximate averages and are based on data gathered on the five offices for the period 1968–75 for the United Kingdom and New Zealand, 1968–74 for Denmark and Sweden, and 1970–75 for Hawaii. Although ratios for a particular office may fluctuate considerably from year to year, the general pattern of similarities and differences among the systems remains much the same. In calculating the size of investigative staff, I have included the ombudsmen themselves, who are always to some extent involved with investigations, and any of their senior officers who also take some part in investigations. In every case except the United Kingdom, the number of investigative staff is equal to the number of professional, nonclerical staff. In the United Kingdom, several staff members take no part in investigations, four being concerned solely with handling jurisdictional questions and one with internal personnel matters. In offices with part-time staff as in Denmark, I have counted two part-time staff as one full-time.

3. The data on which these generalizations are based were drawn mostly from the following sources: "A Brief Survey of the Ombudsman Institution in Norway" (February, 1971), a mimeographed essay provided by the Norwegian ombudsman's office; Michael Hiden, *The Ombudsman in Finland: The First Fifty Years* (Berkeley, Calif.: Institute of Governmental Studies, University of California, 1973); Karl A. Friedmann, "Canadian Ombudsmen," a paper presented to the International Ombudsman Conference, Edmonton, Alberta, September 7–10, 1976; and Allan J. Wyner, *The Nebraska Ombudsman* (Berkeley, Calif.: Institute of Governmental Studies, University of California, 1974).

4. *Annual Report of the Hawaiian Ombudsman (No. 8), Fiscal Year 1976–77*, pp. 8, 119–21.

5. Ibid., p. 7.

6. *Annual Report of the Hawaiian Ombudsman (No. 6), Fiscal Year 1974–75*, p. 6.

7. Computed from the *Annual Report of the Hawaiian Ombudsman (No. 4), Fiscal Year 1972–73*, pp. 3–6.

8. *1974–75 Hawaiian Ombudsman Report*, p. 10.

9. See the table in Herman Doi, "The Work, Staffing and Administration of an Ombudsman's Office," *Conference of Australasian and Pacific Ombudsmen, Wellington, New Zealand, 19–22 November 1974* (Wellington: Office of the Ombudsman, n.d.), p. 87A. The same table indicates that the average time for closing complaint cases during the early 1970s was forty days.

10. *Annual Report of the Hawaiian Ombudsman (No. 1), Fiscal Year 1969–70*, p. 32.

11. *Annual Report of the Hawaiian Ombudsman (No. 5), Fiscal Year 1973–74*, p. 48.

12. *Annual Report of the Hawaiian Ombudsman (No. 7), Fiscal Year, 1975–76*, pp. 6–9.

13. For an example of such an investigation, see ibid., pp. 1–6.

14. Letter from Herman Doi to the author, November 15, 1976.

15. *1976–77 Hawaiian Ombudsman Report*, p. 114.

16. Conference of Australasian and Pacific Ombudsmen, p. 87A.

17. Larry B. Hill, "The International Transfer of Institutions: A Behavioral Analysis of the New Zealand Ombudsman" (Ph.D. dissertation, Tulane University, 1970), p. 517.

18. Review article in *New Zealand Listener* (April 3, 1972), reprinted in *Report of the New Zealand Ombudsman for the Year Ended March 31, 1972*, pp. 125–27. In his annual report for 1975, Sir Guy has written:

The cooperation of the departments in the work of the office has been another outstanding feature [of the New Zealand ombudsman's office], and has indeed meant that, compared with many Ombudsmen offices overseas, the New Zealand office has been able to operate with a comparatively small staff and yet deal with a comparatively large case load. The general principle of inviting departments to cooperate in the investigation of complaints against themselves has proved itself time and time again—it has lightened the load of the Ombudsman's office and it has served to build a firm structure of confidence between the office and the departments which has undoubtedly been in the national interest (p. 13).

19. Hill, "International Transfer of Institutions," Chapters 7–8; and Larry B. Hill, *The Model Ombudsman: Institutionalizing New Zealand's Democratic Experiment* (Princeton, N.J.: Princeton University Press, 1976), pp. 172–79. This account of the New Zealand ombudsman refers to the period before his jurisdiction was extended in 1975 to include local administration. Even before 1975, some change in investigative methods appears to have taken place, although we have no quantitative evidence of the extent. In a memorandum prepared in 1976 for Sir Guy Powles by his legal counsel D. E. Paterson in response to an earlier version of this essay, the opinion was expressed that the number of interviews with complainants was "somewhat higher" at that time than in 1962–69 and that "the office now calls for files in a much higher percentage of complaints than 20%." In several areas, "files are requested with every single investigation; e.g., State Insurance Office claims files."

20. Hill, *Model Ombudsman*, p. 173. After visiting the Ha-

waiian ombudsman in 1973, Powles commented in his 1974 annual report, "The telephone and modern office machinery play a very important role in his office, and while I am not sure that they could be used here to quite the same extent with equal effect, I believe more advantage could be taken of the telephone as a means of communication with the parties to a complaint." *Report of the [New Zealand] Ombudsman for the Year Ended 31 March 1974*, p. 14.

21. Letter from Sir Guy Powles to the author, July 13, 1977.

22. Hill, "International Transfer of Institutions," p. 458.

23. Information for this paragraph was derived from interviews by the author with Nordskov Nielsen on July 4, 1974, and Mrs. Nina Anderskouv of his office on August 19, 1974, as well as a letter to the author from Nordskov Nielsen dated July 19, 1971.

24. Interview by the author with Bertil Wennergren, July 9, 1974.

25. Alfred Bexelius, "The Origin, Nature, and Functions of the Civil and Military Ombudsmen in Sweden," *Annals of the American Academy of Political and Social Science* 377 (May 1968): 15–16.

26. *The Swedish Parliamentary Ombudsman*, 2d ed. (Stockholm, 1976), pp. 9–10.

27. Wennergren interview; an interview by the author with Carl Norstrom, Wennergren's head of division, on July 9, 1974; and a letter to the author from Ulf Lundvik, December 1, 1976.

28. Data for this analysis were given to the author by Ombudsman Wennergren.

29. In 1978, a new high was set with the receipt of 1,259 complaints. These figures refer to complaints handed on to the PCA by members of parliament, the system prescribed by the PCA Act. Each year, the British ombudsman also receives a large number of complaints directly from the public which he is precluded from investigating.

30. *Second Report from the Select Committee on the PCA, Session 1967–68* (HC 350), p. 10.

31. *First Report from the Select Committee on the PCA, Session 1970–71* (HC 240), p. 23; *Second Report from the Select Committee on the PCA, Session 1970–71* (HC 513), p. 6; and *Report from the Select Committee on the PCA, Session 1968–69* (HC 385), p. 9.

32. *Fourth Report of the PCA, Session 1967–68* (HC 134), p. 5.

33. Since agency files are usually quite complete, often the commissioner's investigators feel no need to question officials. On the other hand, the investigators of the Health Service commissioner, an office held jointly with that of the PCA, interview officials in hospitals much more frequently since the files kept on patients are often very incomplete. Interview by the author with Sir Idwal Pugh, July 22, 1976.

34. *Second Report of the PCA, Session 1971–72* (HC 116), p. 10. "Increasingly," Compton remarked in 1971, "we do spare effort, not necessarily required for arriving at a conclusion, for interviewing complainants in order to make sure we have their full story, or, if necessary, so that they can check on an alternative version of that story that the department gave." *Second Report from the Select Committee on the PCA, Session 1970–71* (HC 513), p. 11.

35. *Second Report from the Select Committee on the PCA, Session 1975–76* (HC 480), p. 42. Complaints received through members of parliament had risen from 571 in 1973 to 704 in 1974 to 928 in 1975.

36. Nielsen interview, July 4, 1974.

37. L. B. Hill, *Ombudsmen, Bureaucracy and Democracy*, forthcoming, Chapter 2.

38. Ulf Lundvik believes that the percentage of cases where facts are in dispute is higher in Sweden than in New Zealand. This is an important question requiring further comparative research.

B.   INVESTIGATING COMPLAINTS:
A COMMENT

VIKTOR J. PICKL, DIRECTOR, VOLKSANWALTSCHAFT OF AUSTRIA

CLEARLY BECAUSE OF differing constitutions and legislation, all ombudsman offices have to operate in different ways. There are wide variations in the way they operate and seemingly little common ground other than the fact that they deal with complainants and the public bodies that people complain about. Complainants expect some service from the ombudsman—at the very least, sympathetic reception of their complaints and promise to expedite the matter. Public bodies have no such expectations. To them, the ombudsman has nuisance value. It interferes with their normal operations and demands that special attention should be given to a particular incident, one of hundreds and thousands that occur in the daily life of their organization. What may be important to complainants and through them, to the ombudsman, may be seen by their organization as quite trivial and unworthy of special attention, certainly not worth halting the whole process of government to deal with. The best they can hope for is that the matter be reviewed quickly and settled to their satisfaction never to recur, that is, buried and forgotten. Although most investigations in practice end up this way, they can never know which will involve a serious charge of maladministration, a long protracted investigation, a serious disagreement over the facts and over possible resolution, and a public rebuke by the ombudsman that might be seized upon by the mass media to their deep embarrassment and with perhaps serious personal repercussions for those implicated. No wonder that in every jurisdiction there are officials who look at a communication from the ombudsman as an unwelcome intrusion into their domain or a challenge to their authority.

How ombudsmen conduct their investigations and how in the course of their investigations they deal with public officials depend on the role the ombudsman plays within public administration, the constitutional, legal, and political status of the ombudsman office, and public understanding of the institution of ombudsman. For example, the Austrian federal ombudsman—*Volksanwaltschaft*—is a supreme state agency, and its recommendations are directed at federal government ministers. This high level of communication coupled with its strong constitutional, legal, and political status obviously eases communications at lower levels. Usually, the ombudsmen have been prominent in public life, and they are well known within their jurisdiction. If they have sufficient supports, their personality can shape the operations of the office, and the reputation of the incumbent, the office, and the staff go together.

By law, the ombudsman is guaranteed independence and cannot be told what to do. By law, too, the ombudsman is given full powers of investigation and full access, with certain limitations, to that part of public administration within the jurisdiction. Some ombudsmen can initiate their own investigations, while others can be ordered to investigate certain matters. In Sweden, the ombudsman is enjoined to supervise the observation of the law by all public authorities and officials and to see that they properly fulfill their obligations. In general, however, ombudsmen tend to be reactive rather than proactive—they instigate investigations only after receipt of complaints from individuals. In a country with a short experience of an ombudsman, the incumbent symbolizes and represents the institution. Complainants want to call him, to talk with him, and especially to see their complaint studied and investigated by him personally. In this case, the ombudsman operates personally in public and is in frequent contact with the mass media as a result. Consequently, his behavior is different than if his operations were conducted in private, and probably more difficult, particularly if television is involved. It demands a higher degree of cooperation between the ombudsman, public officials, and complainants. But even with the best intentions, the ombudsman cannot personally investigate all complaints, and, while many can be handled by telephone or interview, he must delegate investigations to his staff. Nevertheless, the hallmark of the office should always remain availability, flexibility, and informality.

Bureaucrats prefer compliant citizens, people who accept authority without much question and rarely complain about the service they receive. They do not like people who complain, especially those who champion public complaints, insist on the public's right to know, and demand reasons and explanations for official actions. To them, the ombudsman is clearly a people's advocate, a defender of lost causes, a protector of hopeless cases. But even bureaucrats have come to recognize that formality, systematization, mechanization, impersonality, and professionalism can be carried too far, that mistakes do occur within the vast complexity of modern government and individuals are harmed despite regulatory and management controls, and that many of their fellow citizens are mystified by modern public administration and do not know what their rights and entitlements are or where to go for help when aggrieved by official actions. They, too, find increasingly that they cannot understand decisions that affect them as bureaucrats, and they often do not understand officialese, especially when relayed by computer. They also worry about the loss of direct contact between the administrators and the administered.

When the ombudsman opens an investigation, quite often public officials, bureaucrats among them, do not know how to respond. They do not know, for example, how much they ought to say or release. They are mindful of secrecy laws and other official restrictions on disclosure. They are aware of public hostility toward them and the gross misrepresentations of them in the mass media. They do not want to provide grist for the mill, but they cannot expect to be passive when accused by complainants of a whole slate of offenses that they know or believe are just not true. They would like to cooperate with the ombudsman, but they are never sure which side he is on (of course, he should be on nobody's side but none of the protagonists really believes that), whether he really understands and appreciates the difficult conditions under which they work, and what is likely to be made out of their response and the manner in which they respond. If they believe the ombudsman is biased against them or is fishing for popularity at their expense or has shown evidence in the past of unreasonableness, they will not cooperate readily or willingly. The ombudsman should evidence no bias.

Ombudsmen have wide latitude in conducting their investigations simply because every complaint requires different treatment. Rarely are complaints identical. Each complaint has its own peculiarities. Nonetheless, they do fall into similar categories of maladministration such as delay, negligence, discrimination, misapplication of the law, individual error, and so forth, or the point of contention is offensive behavior, such as rudeness, indifference, and intimidation, or at fault may be the administrative system itself, being so complicated as to baffle the officials as well as the public, or being outmoded or inadequate. For instance, tax and social security benefit systems are often complicated and rigid and slow to accommodate legal changes. In a special category altogether are complaints from prisoners who are in a weaker position to protect themselves than other complainants, but some of their grievances center on the nature of the penal system and public prejudices rather than prison administration or the conduct of prison officials.

The plight of prisoners and others unable to exercise their full rights is a good reminder that the purpose of the ombudsman in investigating complaints is not to find fault with the administration but to uncover the facts and if necessary exonerate the administration when no wrong has been done to the complainant. Most often, no wrong can be found, but the fact that the ombudsman explains what has transpired in individual cases is a valuable service to complainants mystified by the way public business is conducted in the modern administrative state. More than ever before, people do not understand how public administration works and they want to be enlightened about administrative actions that concern them. Public education is an essential function of the ombudsman apart from fault-finding.

Because only one in ten investigations may actually fault the administration, the ombudsman system might be considered relatively unproductive or wasteful. But in the other nine cases, the ombudsman is still doing something. He explains to complainants why the official action was correct, even if it was misunderstood and a sense of injustice still lingers. It is as important to remove lingering doubts as it is to correct wrongdoing. In all investigations, the ombudsman is reducing friction between government and citizen. Government bodies are in general good at avoiding mistakes but not so good at explaining themselves. In nine out of ten cases, they have in the ombudsman a public relations officer who justifies their actions to persons who feel aggrieved at them. They ought to consider the ombudsman a colleague rather than an inquisitor. He acts as a lightning conductor for bona fide grievances and keeps them out of political storms in the long run. He cannot (and should not) be their friend, for that would compromise him in the eyes of the public. On the other hand, he cannot (and should not) be a protagonist of the public bureaucracy, for that would lessen official cooperation and undermine the credibility of his office in the eyes of officialdom. It does help, however, to be well known publicly, to be well known in the public service, and to have good personal contacts with major public figures.

In some countries, ombudsmen are not completely free to conduct their investigations as they choose. Besides legal restrictions imposed on them and limitations on their jurisdiction, they may be subject to judicial challenge. They may be restricted in their access to public documents by official secrets legislation, political convention (safeguarding the reputation and freedom of action of elected officials), and official tradition and habits. For instance, the ombudsman may be obliged to return any documents he has requested "as quickly as possible, but no later than 48 hours after receipt of the request (for return of documents)." Furthermore, to safeguard reputations, ombudsmen are usually enjoined or compelled to observe confidentiality in their investigations, a provision deemed essential to protect public officials from unwarranted and unjust accusations and criticisms. Every restriction on the ombudsman's ability to investigate shows lack of confidence in the institution or in the office or in the incumbent. But it must be remembered that the ombudsman office is still relatively young, and it has not been able to demonstrate that it can be trusted to operate without restriction. All major parties involved—public, public service, and ombudsman—are still finding their way, and as they come increasingly to know and appreciate one another, confidence in the ombudsman will grow and many of the restrictions initially imposed to protect the administration or parts of it from outside inquisition or interference may in time be abandoned both formally and informally. Perhaps this may best measure the acceptance of the institution—when it is trusted to conduct its investigations with minimal restrictions and maximum latitude.

CHAPTER 7

THE OMBUDSMAN AND THE PROTECTION OF CITIZENS' RIGHTS: A BRITISH PERSPECTIVE

A. W. BRADLEY, UNIVERSITY OF EDINBURGH

IN HIS BOOK *Taking Rights Seriously,* Professor Ronald Dworkin has argued that the institution of rights against the state is justified "because it represents the majority's promise to the minorities that their dignity and equality will be respected."[1] But he also stresses the difficulty of ensuring that these rights are respected:

The institution of rights against the Government is not a gift of God, or an ancient ritual, or a national sport. It is a complex and troublesome practice that makes the Government's job of secur- ing the general benefit more difficult and more expensive, and it would be a frivolous and wrongful practice unless it served some point.[2]

Now Dworkin was primarily concerned with the prob- lems presented in a democratic system of law and govern- ment by a serious commitment to fundamental political rights, such as freedom of speech and the disputed right of civil disobedience. He did not directly consider the in- terest which the individual may have in maintaining good

government in matters that affect him. One object of this chapter is to consider whether it is worthwhile to relate the debate about citizens' rights to an assessment of the Om- budsman system and, since no one would claim that the ombudsman should be the sole protector of citizens' rights, another is to examine the relationship between the ombudsman and other agencies for the protection of the citizen in his dealings with the administration. Although the material is drawn from the British experience of the parliamentary commissioner for administration, aspects of the discussion may be relevant to the experience of ombudsmen in other countries.

Today it is not uncommon for the ombudsman idea to be discussed in the context of human rights.[3] In the mid-1960s, when the institution of ombudsman was being received into the British system of government, the lan- guage of rights was far from dominating political debate. It is true that legislative steps were being taken which were likely eventually to promote the public awareness of

This chapter is based on a paper given to the 1978 Ditchley Park conference, "The Ombudsman System—The Record and Future Possibilities," organized by the Hansard Society and revised for publication in the *Cambridge Law Journal* 139, Part 2 (1980): 304–32, with the kind permission of whose editor this chapter now appears.

rights. Thus, the first, limited Race Relations Act was passed in 1965. But, compared with the 1970s, little was done at that time to further the rights of women, students, prisoners, and other such groups. In the field of social welfare, the Ministry of Social Security Act of 1966 introduced into the supplementary benefits system the notion of a right to residual financial assistance from the state. But closer examination of the law and the way in which it was administered indicates that the right to supplementary benefit was more of a reality for old people than it was for single parents or the unemployed. In the immigration field it was not until 1969, and only after stricter controls over Commonwealth immigrants had been introduced in 1962 and 1968, that a right of appeal to a tribunal was introduced against the discretionary decisions of immigration officers.[4]

Not until 1966 did the British government accept for the first time the right of the individual to petition to the European Commission on Human Rights, as well as the compulsory jurisdiction of the European Court of Human Rights. Within the European Economic Community, the case-law of the European Court of Justice did not get far into human rights questions until the 1970s.[5] Prophetically, Lord Denning in his maiden speech in the House of Lords in 1958 had urged that the provision of a remedy for official maladministration should be the "third chapter" of a new Bill of Rights.[6] But the speeches of the Labour ministers proposing the Parliamentary Commissioner Bill in parliament were not phrased in the language of rights.[7]

RIGHTS AND THEIR PROTECTION

The phrase "citizens' rights" has many meanings; it may be used variously with the narrow precision of a lawyer, the rhetoric of a politician, or the generous enthusiasm of a social reformer. Thus, the notion of citizens' rights may refer, for example, to a citizen's fundamental rights and freedoms, guaranteed by the Constitution and protected in a supreme or constitutional court. Again, it may refer to the economic, social, and political rights, interests and claims of the people that are protected and advanced in a democratic political system by parliament. For the lawyer, the individual's rights are those rights under the existing law that are protected by the judicial system and the machinery of law enforcement: on analysis, these rights are found to include privileges (or liberties), powers, and immunities as well as rights.[8]

Today, the individual has many rights that were unknown to the common law, that originate in legislation and are often typically enforced within a hierarchy of specialized tribunals rather than in the ordinary courts. Again, in the modern administrative state, with its strong corporatist tendencies, economic benefits are often con-

ferred on individual persons and companies by means of departmental rules and policies that lack the force of formally enacted law. Where this is the case, an individual's claim or "right" to a particular benefit depends not on the decision of a court or tribunal duly constituted, but on whether officials consider the claim to be well founded and within the policy of the scheme in question. In a more general sense, the citizen's rights may be thought to include his expectation of receiving fair, equitable, just, and considerate treatment at the hands of officials who wield public power.

While the notion of right in a strict legal sense remains important, in the present context the subject of good administration is approached from the viewpoint of the private individual: his interest in the matter is made up of diverse elements such as a political right or interest in maintaining his status as a citizen, specific legal rights to certain public benefits, as well as a claim to a good many benefits conferred on him by administrative decision. One important issue with which analysis of the ombudsman system must deal is precisely the issue of whether an individual derives any kind of subjective "right" to the maintenance of fair and efficient standards of administration. At present, many public agencies seek to maintain such standards all or most of the time, but a proposal has been made that those principles of good administration should be codified and made of universal application.[9]

According to one view, these principles have as their sole purpose the efficient conduct of administration and the maintenance of good relations between the agency in question and those with whom it deals, including other agencies and the public. It can be argued that public agencies should in their own interests be concerned to administer their affairs well; in this view, the ombudsman serves as a general auditor, inspector, or management consultant. In contrast, it may be argued that the citizen has a direct and immediate interest in seeing that principles of good administration are observed in his case. Accordingly, the ombudsman serves as a structural link between the officials who are required to attain these standards and the individual who may be prejudiced if these standards are not observed. It is the courts which can give an authoritative and impartial ruling on what abstract rules of law require in a concrete situation, when a citizen complains to them that his legal rights have been infringed. So, too, when a citizen claims that he has been unjustly treated by the administration, the ombudsman may similarly give a ruling on whether the agency in question has acted properly.

Two further comments may be made on the wide range of meanings that may be attached to the notion of citizens' rights. The first comment is that much debate about reform in the rights area concerns proposals that a particular subject (for example, the right to be housed or the right to supplementary benefit) should be moved from one category of "right" into another category which it is thought will give the individual better protection: for example, to remove a claim to benefit from a departmental scheme of rules to a legal scheme administered by tribunals or courts; or to elevate a right such as free speech from the level of ordinary law (where it is subject to the legislative mercies of parliament) to the status of a right protected by a constitutional court. The second comment is that the range and diversity of the rights that the citizen may reasonably wish to enjoy makes it difficult to generalize about the relative merits of different constitutional means for the protection of the citizen. Some rights are better protected by the courts. Others may be better protected by the activities of politicians in parliament. Others may depend essentially upon the standards of conduct observed by administrators in the field. It is therefore important not to look at different means of protecting the citizen in isolation from each other.

According to a recent report of the House of Commons Committee on the Parliamentary Commissioner, "the primary responsibility for defending the citizen against the executive rests with the Member of Parliament."[10] Similar statements are sometimes made about the parliamentary commissioner himself. Yet, as the 1965 White Paper proposing the ombudsman made clear, the new form of protection was intended to complement, and not to take over from, the existing means of courts, tribunals, public inquiries, and parliamentary questions.[11] Quite apart from surgery work in their constituencies, members of parliament have a legislative responsibility for seeing that government policies are based on law and are expressed in published rules capable of being applied by administrators without the constant necessity of political intervention. It would be inefficient and haphazard to administer the affairs of government by relying on pressure being applied by individual members of parliament upon the minister. Thus, to give one example, a good tribunal system that enables the citizen to appeal to an impartial and expert body against official decisions which directly affect him seems at least as important to good government as an ombudsman system.[12] The safety valve is indeed essential in the design of an engine, but it is scarcely meant to be used as the means of propulsion.[13]

ESSENTIALS OF THE PARLIAMENTARY COMMISSIONER SYSTEM

It is a commonplace of comparative public law that the legal systems in the United Kingdom and continental Europe present evidence of two contrasting approaches to the protection of rights. On the continent emphasis is laid on the formal enactment of abstract rights (as in the famous Declaration of the Rights of Man in 1789, or in Part I of the Constitution of the Federal Republic of Germany). By contrast, under the influence of the English common law as well as of Bentham, the British tradition has emphasized the provision of an effective procedure for enforcement of rights, such as the ancient remedy in English law of habeas corpus. As the high priest of the English tradition, A. V. Dicey, declared, "the Habeas Corpus Acts declare no principle and define no rights, but they are for practical purposes worth a hundred constitutional articles guaranteeing individual liberty."[14] Although the conditions that enabled this tradition to flourish in the nineteenth century are no longer all present, there is little doubt that the Parliamentary Commissioner Act of 1967 fitted easily into the British pragmatic tradition.

Although the act did not provide a set remedy for aggrieved citizens, it did provide a procedure for investigation of their complaints by the ombudsman. Moreover, by deliberate decision it nowhere defined the rights that the new procedure was to protect. The meaning of "injustice in consequence of maladministration" was not defined in the act; yet, this is what the citizen must claim that he has suffered in order that the ombudsman may have jurisdiction to investigate the complaint. It is also significant that the British ombudsman may act only at the complaint of a private person, and not on his own initiative.

The feature of the British scheme which is most important in the present context is not merely the strong links with the civil service which the ombudsman enjoyed from the start, but in particular the almost total lack of recourse to legal techniques, the legal profession, and judicial process.[15] Indeed, the powers of the English high court are mentioned in the 1967 act only in relation to the ombudsman's right to compel the attendance of witnesses and production of documents, and to refer to the court cases of unlawful obstruction of his investigation. It necessarily follows that the British ombudsman has no power to extend the area of his investigations arbitrarily into such forbidden pastures as local government, the nationalized industries, the police, and the universities, since any such attempt would quickly lead to a high court ruling on the extent of his powers.[16] But within the area of investigation into central government which parliament conferred on him, the British ombudsman enjoys a wide discretion as to how he is to use his powers.[17]

The creation of the office of parliamentary commissioner may well be compared with the growth of the equitable jurisdiction of the lord chancellor in England during the fifteenth and sixteenth centuries. Then the rigidity of the law and the defects of procedure in the common law courts required the exercise of an overriding discretion by the lord chancellor if justice and equity were to prevail. In

1967, at a time when the system of administrative law was failing to give the individual effective protection, the creation of an ombudsman was needed to make possible the development of a new equity, suitable for a much governed nation. According to the American legal philosopher Roscoe Pound, the essential thing in following an equitable approach to dispute-settlement is that within wide limits the judge "should be free to deal with the individual case so as to meet the demands of justice between the parties and accord with the reason and moral sense of ordinary men."[18] The same author also referred to the widespread revival of executive justice in this century as being "one of those reversions to justice without law which are perennial in legal history."[19] The earliest reports of the British ombudsman did indeed often suggest that he was seeking to achieve justice without law (for example, in failure to explain the law relating to the administrative act on which he was reporting). Yet, from legal history there is much evidence that "what appeared at first as an arbitrary discretion wielded by an irresponsible official, gradually crystallised into a body of known, ascertainable and consistently applied law."[20]

The process by which the exercise of discretion develops over time into a set pattern occurs in both judicial and bureaucratic decision-making. It was to be expected that "arbitrary discretion" of the kind which the 1967 act vested in the British ombudsman should evolve into a more or less settled body of ascertainable principles that might even eventually harden into rules. More recent reports of the British ombudsman suggest that this process is under way, for example, in what is now quite a frequent practice of referring back in his reports on individual cases to earlier investigations into similar complaints.[21] Successive holders of the office and their staff have benefited from increasing experience of the administrative performance of government agencies, especially of those (notably the Inland Revenue and the Department of Health and Social Security) against which the most numerous complaints are received. There can be little doubt that an index or digest of his casework exists within his office for internal use, so that previous decisions may, where relevant, serve as informal precedents to be borne in mind and possibly to be followed in like cases that arise in the future.[22]

Thus, inevitably, the British ombudsman has developed principles, standards, and rules of what he believes to constitute good administration, since otherwise no notion of maladministration could have emerged.[23] As the process of investigation and report continues in every fresh case, so the individual complainant receives the benefit of the ombudsman's enforcement of the rules and principles that have emerged from the previous casework.

And it may not be pressing this analysis too far to conclude that the individual citizen thus acquires what may properly be called new rights to the maintenance of a certain quality of administration.

A French observer of public administration, M. Debbasch, has remarked that control over the administration provides a check on whether the administration actually conforms with the basic norms laid down by the authority having political power over the administration.[24] If this is so, then the British ombudsman, supported by the Select Committee of the House of Commons, helps both in the process by which these basic norms are laid down and in the process by which the norms are enforced. Examples of basic norms that may easily be extracted from the ombudsman's casework include the need to handle a citizen's affairs with reasonable speed, particularly in a situation where it is known to the administrator that delay will be harmful to the citizen's interests;[25] the duty to give correct advice to a citizen about his dealings with government and to refrain from giving incomplete or misleading advice;[26] and, when new benefits are created by parliament to meet the needs of particular groups, to take effective steps to bring information about the new rights to the attention of those concerned.[27] A further instance of the process of developing general norms from an individual case occurs when the investigation of a citizen's complaint leads to a review of the position of many others who are in the same category: fairness and justice require that like cases should be treated alike.[28] So, too, when a citizen complains of discriminatory treatment, the ombudsman may look at decisions concerning other citizens which are cited by the claimant as evidence of discrimination.[29] Similarly, the virtual impossibility of treating a citizen's complaint as if it were a unique event is illustrated by the ombudsman's preparedness to refer to findings in earlier investigations.[30]

It is therefore possible to discern in the ombudsman system a process by which, as principles of good administration emerge from the casework, administrators are able to know what is generally required of them and the public derives benefit from the observance of these principles. It is on such grounds that the Scandinavian ombudsman has been described as "a precious protector of the rights of citizens."[31]

THE OMBUDSMAN AND GROUP RIGHTS

This process of protecting the citizen's rights against oppressive or inefficient administration is not spelled out in the legislation, and it takes time for the fruits of the process to be appreciated. One witness told the Select Committee on the Parliamentary Commissioner in 1978:

"Clearly the office (of parliamentary commissioner) is not that of an official exercising on behalf of the public, their rights against the administration."[32] Now sometimes official committees and commissions are remarkably self-effacing about their role in protecting the citizen's rights. Examples of this are to be found in the work of the Council on Tribunals and above all in the first report of the Police Complaints Review Board.[33] In the case of the ombudsman, the judgments expressed in particular reports have not always gone far enough to satisfy the claims of committed rights campaigners, residents' associations, and other pressure groups.[34] It would, of course, be impossible for an impartial ombudsman to accept the views of all who complain to him. But what seems important is that over a period of time it should become established that the ombudsman can give support and assistance to categories of individuals in circumstances in which they are particularly vulnerable to defects in the administrative system on which they depend. In fact, much of the ombudsman's recurring casework is concerned with the interests of a group of claimants affected by a particular branch of government.

The specialized work of the National Health Service commissioner is the clearest example of this. The great bulk of the ombudsman's work in this role has dealt with the claims by patients (or their relatives) that the hospital service should have provided them with a more efficient or a more compassionate service. Despite the fact that the ombudsman is barred by the statute from considering matters of clinical judgment,[35] there can be no doubt that his recent reports as National Health Service commissioner have sought to further the rights and interests of patients in their dealings with hospital authorities. Other large groups that have plainly benefited from the ombudsman's work include the payers of income tax and the war pensioners: important improvements in the administration of income tax and of war pensions can be linked directly with his reports.[36] Social security recipients, another large group of complainants, have also benefited from the ombudsman's findings in individual cases, although in this field it is harder to link general improvements in the system with the ombudsman's casework. The same comment could be made about the treatment of complaints from prisoners, although some individual instances of official errors causing injustice have been discovered[37] and some improvements in prison rules have been encouraged by the ombudsman.[38] For those who are affected by British immigration control, much less benefit has been derived from the office of ombudsman than might have been expected.[39]

What is common to these various categories of cases is that the complaints are coming from a vulnerable group of individuals, usually in a position of some personal, social, or economic weakness, faced with the power of a large bureaucracy where the wrong functioning of the system, for whatever reason, may cause particular harm to the individual. If the position of individual members in these groups is to be strengthened, (1) there should be better means of enforcing rights that are already established in law but that in practice are not fully enjoyed; and (2) the individual's rights and interests should be extended beyond the line at which the law has hitherto stopped. The ombudsman is in a unique position to contribute to both these objects. A striking example occurred in 1977 when, as National Health Service commissioner, the ombudsman established that a mental patient had been compulsorily detained, for one day unlawfully and for a further twenty-eight days unjustly. The hospital authority was prepared to compensate the patient for the single day of unlawful detention, but both the ombudsman and the House of Commons committee agreed that compensation should also be paid for the twenty-eight days of unjust detention.[40]

THE OMBUDSMAN AND DEVELOPMENT OF LAW

In these situations then, the ombudsman should be concerned not merely with the law as it is, but also with the law as it might be. In 1962, the Danish ombudsman was prepared to recommend an extension in the rights of prisoners to include the right to vote in parliamentary elections.[41] But his British counterpart has not always taken such a broad view of his role, even as regards areas of the law of special concern to him as arbiter of citizens' complaints against officialdom. Two examples will be given. First, in regard to open government and the problems of official secretiveness, the ombudsman's power to investigate is itself of outstanding importance: he is entitled to look at departmental records, procedures, and instructions to which the citizen has no legal right of access.[42] But, in order that the ombudsman himself should not reinforce existing protection of secrets, it seems important that the information acquired by the ombudsman should, subject to any overriding consideration (such as the confidentiality of another citizen's dealings with government or the public interest in prison security), be generally made available to the complainant and his member of parliament.[43] Yet, at least in some of the earliest reports, the ombudsman sometimes used a formula of the following kind: "This decision was taken in accordance with departmental instructions which I have seen."[44] In the Compton Bassett case, possibly the most absurd example of excessive official secrecy to have featured in the ombudsman's reports, it is unfortunate that the ombudsman did not criticize the treasury for keeping secret a significant change to a policy that had earlier been announced to parliament—an omission that was left to the Select Committee to remedy.[45]

The second area of legal development of particular concern to the ombudsman involves the European Convention on Human Rights. Although the right of individuals in the United Kingdom to petition to the European Commission on Human Rights is recognized by the government, the convention itself has not been incorporated into national law. There is judicial authority to the effect that immigration officers at least are not required to take account of the convention in exercising their powers under the Immigration Act of 1971.[46] Even though the convention has not been incorporated into national law, the government is under an international obligation to ensure that enjoyment of the rights protected by the convention is not denied in the United Kingdom. It is at least arguable that the interests of good administration require officials of central government to take the convention into account in the exercise of their discretionary powers, and in consequence that the ombudsman should also take the convention into account where it may be relevant.

Hitherto, issues relating to the convention seem to have been raised in few cases, possibly because the convention concentrates on certain rights that are of special importance in the procedures of criminal law, and the acts of the police, public prosecutors, and the courts are not subject to investigation by the ombudsman. But it is not difficult to imagine that the acts of social security investigators, immigration officials, Value Added Tax inspectors, administrators in mental and other hospitals, and prison officers might in some circumstances impinge upon the individual's protected rights. Already some such cases have arisen out of the treatment of prisoners. In the Golder case in 1975, the European Court of Human Rights held that a prisoner's right of access to legal advice had been infringed by action taken under prison regulations.[47] Previously, similar facts in Knechtl's case had been considered by the ombudsman before the complainant petitioned the European Commission, but in his report on that case, the ombudsman failed to consider the implications of the European Convention for Knechtl's complaint of maladministration.[48] More recently, in 1976, when another prisoner complained of interference with his correspondence and suggested that this interference was contrary to the European Convention, the ombudsman rejected the suggestion on the ground that action taken under statutory prison rules was unlikely to be held to be a breach of the convention.[49] This reasoning failed both to grasp one of the main underlying purposes of the European Convention and to appreciate the direct relevance of the Golder

case. On this evidence, it is not possible to be optimistic about the ombudsman's ability to deal adequately with the impact of the European Convention on other areas of public administration.[50]

RELATION OF THE BRITISH OMBUDSMAN TO OTHER AGENCIES

In order to assess the role of the British ombudsman today in defending the citizen's rights and interests, we must consider the operation of the other constitutional procedures for the protection of the citizen which the ombudsman was intended to supplement, both as they were in the mid-1960s and as they are today. The four relevant procedures are those provided by (1) parliament (in particular the House of Commons); (2) administrative tribunals; (3) public inquiries; and (4) the courts. Since the courts and the general rules of administrative law raise the most difficult questions, these will be treated much more fully than the rest.

Since parliament is regarded as a means of protecting the rights and interests of individual citizens, its strengths and weaknesses are well known. Before the office of ombudsman was created, they included the difficulty under parliamentary procedure of making a reality of ministerial responsibility for the administrative acts of civil servants; the lack among members of parliament of independent, investigatory powers; and the difficulty and unsuitability of building up political pressure over alleged administrative defects. In these respects, the case for having an ombudsman remains the same today as in 1967, and it has not been affected by the weakening of the two-party system and the existence of minority governments. Nor have developments in the use of select and specialized committees by the House of Commons since 1967, including the system of select committees established in 1979, been of such a kind as to compete with the ombudsman's investigatory powers. To give but one example of the additional power which the ombudsman gives to members of parliament, in the famous Sachsenhausen case of 1967–68, over half the members of the Commons supported the claim of the complainants that injustice had been done, but it was the ombudsman's report that enabled the facts to be established and a remedy to be provided.[51]

In 1967, the constitutional position of *administrative tribunals* was already clear, largely because of the Franks Report on Tribunals and Inquiries in 1957. This report had concluded that tribunals "should properly be regarded as machinery provided by Parliament for adjudication rather than as part of the machinery of administration. The essential point is that . . . Parliament has deliberately provided for a decision outside and independent of the Department concerned.''[52] The general recommendations in the report in favor of strengthening the independence of tribunals were incorporated in the Tribunals and Inquiries Act of 1958, including the creation of the Council on Tribunals. Tribunals were and are specialized judicial agencies created to decide specific disputes arising out of the administration of social legislation. The disputes may arise between citizens, for example, a rent dispute between landlord and tenant, but they often may arise between a citizen and a government agency, for example, when a citizen disputes the amount of social security benefit he has been awarded. Generally less formal than the courts, tribunals are nonetheless subject to the supervisory jurisdiction of the high court in England and Wales and of the court of session in Scotland. Since tribunals are created for specific purposes, and each has its own procedure and expertise, citizens should make use of them and their functions should not be usurped by the ombudsman. Hence, the Parliamentary Commissioner Act of 1967, Section 5(2)(a) provides that the parliamentary commissioner shall not investigate any matter in respect of which the individual has a right of appeal to a tribunal, except when the commissioner is satisfied that in the particular circumstances it is not reasonable to expect that right of appeal to be used. In practice, this discretion has very rarely been exercised; indeed, the commissioner has often advised individuals of their right to appeal and has encouraged them to do so.[53]

It must also be noted that the ombudsman has no statutory power to investigate the operation of tribunals, since the members of tribunals are typically not civil servants. Moreover, in the light of the conclusions of the Franks Report, it could scarcely be said that the decision of a tribunal is action taken ''in the exercise of administrative functions'' of a government department.[54] Yet, the ombudsman does have power which he exercises when necessary to investigate the administrative acts of civil servants that precede or follow tribunal decisions. This is particularly valuable in the social security field since, at least as regards supplementary benefits, the immediate effect of a claimant bringing an appeal against a decision is to cause that decision to be reviewed administratively at a higher level. But since the ombudsman has no power to investigate the acts of tribunals as such, what remedy is there when an individual wishes to complain about the behavior of tribunal members during a hearing? This problem is particularly acute when, as with the supplementary benefits scheme, there is no right to appeal on the merits of the case beyond the local tribunal and the quality of tribunal adjudication has been called into question.[55] Although such complaints are within the scope of the Council on Tribunals, the council has inadequate resources for the proper investigation of complaints. Since

complaints by citizens about the quality of justice may also extend to magistrates' courts, the county court, and so on, one way of filling the present gap in the complaints system would be to establish a Judicial Complaints Commission. This commission could deal with both courts and tribunals. This solution would seem preferable to extending the ombudsman's powers into the field of judicial decisions.[56]

Public inquiries are plainly an aspect of the administrative process, and they are fully subject to investigation by the ombudsman. He may look at the administrative procedures that lead up to the inquiry, the actual conduct of the inquiry by the inspector, the writing-up of the inspector's report, and the subsequent process of decision-making within the department. Thus, the ombudsman may be asked to consider whether the period of notice given of any inquiry was adequate,[57] whether an interested party was misled by the department into not pressing his objections,[58] whether secret assurances were given by the department to one party that should have been revealed to other parties,[59] and whether there was excessive delay before a decision was finally reached.[60]

The public inquiry process is particularly likely to lead to complaints to the ombudsman from objectors to a planning decision who allege maladministration but who in reality wish to challenge the merits of the decision. In such cases, the ombudsman may well state at the end of his report that he may not question the merits of a discretionary decision that has been taken without maladministration,[61] but this does not mean that the ombudsman has not first given close scrutiny to the process of decision-making and to the factors taken into account by the department. In two important Scottish cases, concerning the new runway at Edinburgh Airport and the oil refinery at Nigg Point, respectively,[62] the decision in each case was cleared by the ombudsman but not without criticism of some aspects of the procedures. Complaints often come to the ombudsman concerning the refusal by an agency to award costs to those who have taken part in public inquiries.[63] Here the role of the ombudsman is usually to check whether the established policy for the award of costs has been observed.

All these matters of complaint to the ombudsman concerning public inquiries potentially fall within the jurisdiction of the Council on Tribunals.[64] In fact, the ombudsman has resources for the investigation of complaints which are denied to the council. As a result, he has assumed the role of receiving complaints about inquiries which before 1967 was played by the council. Only rarely does the ombudsman report that a certain matter is the responsibility of the Council on Tribunals, for example, when it concerns the making of statutory rules of procedure for inquiries.[65]

Another wide area of potential overlap in respect of public inquiries arises between the work of the ombudsman and the jurisdiction of the courts. Many agency decisions that relate to town planning, compulsory purchase, housing, and other environmental matters are in law subject to challenge in the high court on grounds of *ultra vires,* or defective procedure, within a six-week period from the date on which the agency's decision is made known. Allegations of improper procedure and abuse of power could be the subject both of complaint to the ombudsman and of challenge in the courts. This overlap of controls will be examined below. While access to the ombudsman is not subject to the very strict and absolute time limit of six weeks that restricts use of the judicial remedy, the ombudsman does not have power, as the court has, to suspend the operation of the order pending investigation.[66]

Despite this overlap with the Council on Tribunals and the courts, investigation of complaints about public inquiry procedures plays an important part in the casework of the ombudsman. Although the ombudsman has no power to overrule an agency decision, he can penetrate further into the decision-making process than can either the courts or the Council on Tribunals.

RELATIONSHIP BETWEEN THE OMBUDSMAN SYSTEM AND JUDICIAL CONTROL OF ADMINISTRATION

When they are working at their best, the courts would seem to be the most suitable constitutional forum for the declaration, protection, and enforcement of the rights of individual citizens. Between July 1975 and December 1976, for example, the court of appeal, led by Lord Denning, ordered the Home Office in effect to grant a certificate of patriality to two Asian women who thereby became entitled to enter the United Kingdom; held the Home Office to have issued unlawful threats in an attempt to recover television license fees to which it was not entitled; restored the license of a Barnsley stall-holder whose livelihood had been taken away from him by the market committee; and declared that the secretary of state for trade was acting unlawfully in seeking to obstruct the Laker Skytrain from getting into the air.[67]

In these decisions, the court was exercising authority of a kind that has not been entrusted to the ombudsman. Yet, one important reason for the creation of the British ombudsman was stated to be found in the limitations of the courts as an agency for controlling the administration. Since the early 1960s, there has been a resurgence of activity by the courts in administrative law, and procedural reforms in judicial remedies in English law were made in 1977.[68] The achievements of the ombudsman have therefore to be assessed against a changing background of developments in administrative law. One particular point of intersection is provided by the 1967 act, which in Section 5(2)(b) provides that the ombudsman shall not investigate any administrative action "in respect of which the person aggrieved has or had a remedy by way of proceedings in any court of law"; but the act allows an investigation to be made where the ombudsman is satisfied that it was not reasonable to expect the person aggrieved to go to the courts. We have already seen that in the case of tribunals the ombudsman has been very sparing in use of this discretion to investigate matters that could be taken to a tribunal. The reverse is true of the remedy in the courts: it is rare to find circumstances in which the ombudsman has felt it right to leave the citizen to his remedy in the courts.[69] Why should this be so?

The principle that government must be conducted according to law, which is at the heart of what Dicey called "the rule of law," seems in many ways opposed to the "justice without law" approach which, as we have seen above, was expressed in the 1967 act. In the traditional British approach to law, the courts play a central role; yet, the Parliamentary Commissioner Act deliberately rejects as inappropriate the essential features of decision-making by the courts. This rejection, together with the preference for civil service methods, probably explains many of the initial criticisms of the ombudsman system made by some lawyers.[70] There is still uncertainty as to whether the ombudsman's functions fall within or beyond the scope of the law. Is the British ombudsman a cheap and accessible substitute for the courts, or is he intended to provide protection for the citizen in areas lying outside the jurisdiction of the courts?

In the 1967 and 1971 editions of his book *Administrative Law,* Professor H. W. R. Wade stated that it was the ombudsman's business "to operate beyond the frontier where the law stops." In the 1977 edition, however, the author accepts as inevitable a certain overlap between the ombudsman and the legal system.[71] The view of a leading French administrative lawyer is that in Great Britain the ombudsman was given a residual competence in relation to the courts, in order that he might fill the gaps in the system of judicial control.[72] This difficult question will now be examined in respect of three main matters: procedure; outcome of ombudsman's investigation; and subject matter of disputes and substantive rules that govern ombudsman's findings.

In matters of *procedure,* the methods of the ombudsman and of the courts are almost complete opposites. At the outset, the citizen has the enormous advantage that it costs him nothing to complain to the ombudsman, and at no stage does he run into any liability for the costs should his complaint turn out to be unjustified. The financial limits upon the legal aid scheme are immaterial in this context. What is even more important is that the ombudsman follows an administrative, inquisitorial, and private process of investigation, with full access to departmental files, full power to question civil servants, and the right to expect the cooperation of the department being investigated. The adversary procedure of the courts, conducted at arm's length between the parties through legal intermediaries, could not be more different.

No doubt, the ombudsman's methods enable him to get closer to reconstructing the administrative history of a citizen's case than does high court procedure, notwithstanding that it is now established that the court has power to overrule official claims to withhold evidence in the public interest.[73] Yet, as with judicial proceedings, investigation by the ombudsman involves the collection of information, the resolution (if possible) of disputed issues of fact, the consideration of disputed issues of law, and (when necessary) ascertaining the motives and intentions of the interested parties. Are there circumstances in which the ombudsman should, in order to resolve a specific issue, be able to adopt procedures closer to those of a court? He already has the power (although he does not use it) to take evidence on oath and to permit those answering his inquiries to be legally represented.[74] Should a more formal element be introduced into the process by which, for example, an investigation could be broken down into set stages, say, establishing that the complaint is within jurisdiction, collecting the evidence, making findings of fact, and formulating conclusions? Such changes could enable the complainant to participate more actively in the process but would tend to add to the length of time taken by investigations without an equivalent gain in effectiveness. Two procedural reforms may have more to be said for them.

First, should the ombudsman have power to make a reference to the courts to resolve a point of law that arises during his investigation and on which his conclusions may depend? Such points of law might concern the jurisdiction of the ombudsman himself or the powers of the agency under investigation. An outstanding example of the need for such a procedure is provided by the affair of the increased television license fee in 1975. Although the ombudsman found that there had been serious maladministration by the Home Office, even on the basis that the agency was acting within its powers, the real issue in the case was settled subsequently when one of the aggrieved citizens took the Home Office to court and the court held that the agency had been acting unlawfully.[75] In Denmark the ombudsman may, it seems, ensure the provision of legal aid to a citizen in circumstances when a judicial remedy would be appropriate.[76]

Second, should the ombudsman have power to require an agency to maintain the status quo pending the completion of his investigation? Under the 1967 act, an investigation by the ombudsman does not affect the power or duty of an agency to take further action with respect to the subject matter of the investigation, and the ombudsman has no executive power to intervene.[77] It is undoubtedly valuable for the agency to have continuing authority to deal with the complainant's affairs, since when a complaint is discovered to be justified, remedial action can be taken rapidly without waiting until the ombudsman completes his investigation. But is it within the spirit of the 1967 act that an agency should have authority to take immediate action to implement a decision (for example, to demolish a listed building or, as in the Edinburgh Airport case, to construct a new runway) when that decision is currently being investigated by the ombudsman?[78] If such action is irrevocable or can be revoked only at considerable loss to public funds, the value to be obtained from the ombudsman's eventual report becomes merely academic. Such circumstances are probably exceptional, but where they arise, should the ombudsman have power to go to the court to seek a temporary injunction against irreparable action being taken by the agency?

So far as the *outcome* of an investigation is concerned, whenever the ombudsman reports that the individual's complaint is justified, the way in which the citizen obtains a remedy is governed by the 1967 act. The act prevents the ombudsman himself from making an award of a particular remedy to the citizen, but the ombudsman is concerned to see that an "acceptable" or "reasonable" outcome results; financial compensation is only sometimes a suitable outcome. If an injustice caused by maladministration is not remedied, he may make a special report to parliament on the case. As the annual report of the ombudsman for 1977 makes clear, the system of complaint, investigation, and report provides numerous opportunities for the agency to consider whether to provide a remedy.[79] In one case, the Inland Revenue agreed to restitution of the tax involved in a complaint more than a year after the ombudsman had reported, during which time the Select Committee of the House of Commons had endorsed the ombudsman's call for a financial remedy.[80] In such rare cases of agency obduracy, should the ombudsman have power to require the payment of financial compensation to the citizen? This extension of the ombudsman's powers would not require him to become involved in the executive decision-making of the agency, any more than a court becomes involved in the running of an agency when it declares the damages the agency should pay. In 1968, the ombudsman was at pains in the Sachsenhausen case to leave the Foreign Office with the responsibility of reviewing the complainants' claim.[81] Today, his political authority is much greater than in 1968, but it possibly needs to be reinforced in law.

As regards the *subject matter* of the individual's disputes with the administration and the *rules* that should govern the result, how much overlap is there between the jurisdiction of the courts and the British ombudsman? At one extreme, the citizen may merely allege rudeness and minor inefficiencies such as a lost file or a wrongly addressed letter. At the other extreme, the citizen may be asserting a legal right that is flatly rejected by the agency. In between, many complaints may involve mixed aspects of maladministration and legality. One reason for this is the principle, described recently by a judge as a commonplace in matters of public administration, that "sound administration must rest on a sound legal basis."[82] It follows that an essential element in a report by the ombudsman on a citizen's complaint is that the legal framework of the agency's action should be made clear, if only as background to an assessment of the administrative acts under review. Such questions as the following need to be answered: What were the legal powers of the agency in the matter? What constraints were placed upon the agency by acts or by statutory instruments? How far were the policies pursued by the agency required by the law? Did the law require or permit the exercise of discretion in the circumstances of the case?

But are legal rules merely the framework within which a matter is administered, no more than a "threshold question," which has to be answered at the outset but can thereafter be safely forgotten? Or may legal rules go on to influence and possibly determine the nature of the administrative decision itself? In the past, administrative law was sometimes identified with the narrow rules of *vires,* of jurisdiction. But the trend in the case-law today goes beyond this, and the courts appear to be using their powers to get closer to the merits of administrative decisions. In one influential decision, the House of Lords has held that a decision wrong in law may constitute an excess of jurisdiction.[83]

From recent decisions in the area of town planning and compulsory purchase, it is clear that British courts are no longer applying a narrow test of *vires* in their scrutiny of agency decisions. While not denying that it is the agency's task to make a decision on the merits of the case, the courts have shown that they are capable of passing judgment on the administrative assessment of the situation. As Lord Denning said in 1965, referring to the statutory right to apply to the court for review of a clearance order under the Housing Act,

Under this section it seems to me that the court can interfere with the Minister's decision if he has acted on no evidence; or if he has come to a conclusion to which on the evidence he could not reasonably come; or if he has given a wrong interpretation to the words of the statute; or if he has taken into consideration matters which he ought not to have taken into account, or vice versa; or has otherwise gone wrong in law.[84]

When it is remembered that the ombudsman may not question the merits of a discretionary decision taken with-

out maladministration by an agency, the criteria set out by Lord Denning are not very different from those observed by the ombudsman when he is dealing with a complaint against a departmental decision to refuse a planning appeal or to confirm a compulsory purchase order.[85]

Another important example of expanding judicial interest in the administrative process is to be found in the broadening of the legal doctrine of "natural justice" into that of "fairness."[86] The duty of administrators to act fairly is a theme that runs through most of the ombudsman's casework. He is also aware of the need to observe natural justice when certain decisions of special significance to an individual are taken, for example, the decision that someone is not a fit and proper person to be permitted to control an insurance company.[87] The ombudsman has said of one such case, "I took the view that if the exercise of (this) power is to be, and seen to be, free of arbitrariness, the person whose fitness is in doubt should be told clearly the reasons why the Department are considering his fitness and be given a full and fair opportunity of answering the case."[88] The principle is one established by a vast body of court decisions; its application to the case in question depended upon the ombudsman's special powers.

But it is above all with the review of discretionary decisions that both the courts and an ombudsman are much concerned. On the judicial side, the trend of such decisions as *Padfield* v. *Minister of Agriculture*[89] and *Secretary of State for Education and Science* v. *Tameside Council*[90] has not yet been halted. Notwithstanding Section 12(3) of the 1967 act, which has been quoted above, by far the greater part of the ombudsman's casework has concerned administrative discretion.[91] According to K. C. Davis, "A public officer has discretion whenever the effective limits on his power leave him free to make a choice among possible courses of action or inaction."[92] Of discretion in this sense, Professor Jowell has remarked that discretion is rarely absent and rarely absolute.[93] (Possibly administration *is* discretion?) The examples of official discretion given by Davis could be reproduced many times over from the ombudsman's reports since 1967—to give only four examples, the making of discretionary grants and subsidies to industry and agriculture; the backdating of war pensions; the withdrawal of authorizations to garages for Ministry of Transport testing of cars; and the reimbursement of their costs to successful objectors at public inquiries.

These are all examples of overt discretions arising out of legislation. In some cases (for example, in immigration control and the supplementary benefits scheme), appeal against the exercise of official discretion lies to a tribunal. But despite the recommendation contained in Part II of the Whyatt Report in 1961, that a general tribunal should be established to hear miscellaneous appeals from discretionary decisions taken in agencies, no government since 1961 has attempted to tackle this problem in any systematic way. It seems impossible to explain in terms of general principle why it is that some discretionary decisions are subject to an appeal to a tribunal and why many (probably the majority) are not. Consequently, in the absence of any right of appeal, many disappointed citizens bring their grievances over such decisions to the ombudsman. In such cases, the role of the ombudsman is not to make a fresh decision on the facts, and he may feel himself constrained by Section 12(3) of the 1967 act to record that, in the absence of maladministration, he is not permitted to question the merits of the decision. But what he does is to review the circumstances in which the first decision was taken, to check that all relevant material was taken into account and irrelevant factors were excluded. He thus can satisfy himself (and possibly the complainant) that the first decision was not vitiated by maladministration. Sometimes such grievances get to the ordinary courts, whose approach is not all that different.[94]

Overt discretion vested in agencies usually leads to the making of administrative rules, so officials may pursue reasonably consistent policies in accord with the aims of current policy. More often than not, these rules will not be made in the form of statutory instruments but will have a less formal and often rather uncertain status. Both the courts and the ombudsman have been concerned with the problems that arise from this phenomenon of modern government. These problems include such questions as how should such rules be made? Should the rules be kept secret or made publicly known? In what form should they be published? Should the rules be subject to any form of parliamentary control or scrutiny? How should such rules be reviewed and if necessary amended? How binding are such rules upon officials who are called upon to make decisions in individual cases? Must the agency leave to officials a discretion to depart from the rules in exceptional circumstances? How are such rules to be interpreted in difficult cases? Are such informal rules capable of being interpreted by a court or of creating a legal entitlement on the part of the citizen?[95]

On this last point, it was the view of the Foreign Office legal advisers in the Sachsenhausen case that the "Butler rules," by which compensation was to be distributed to U.K. citizens who had been the victims of Nazi persecution, were not capable of being interpreted by anyone except the Foreign Office. By this view, the rule could not give rise to a right to receive compensation on the part of anyone who believed on good grounds that he had satisfied the conditions laid down in the rules.[96] In that case, the report of the ombudsman showed with good sense that he rejected this autocratic claim by the Foreign Office. Despite the legal advice on which that claim was based, it is far from certain that administrative rules have no legal effect, are incapable of creating rights, and cannot bear judicial review and interpretation.[97] In the Compton Bassett case, which also arose out of internal administrative rules, the different problem arose of whether it was desirable for the executive secretly to amend rules that it had already made known to parliament. The government eventually accepted somewhat reluctantly that where an administrative rule had been announced in parliament, subsequent changes of significance should also be announced there.[98]

Another potentially vast area of administrative discretion is discovered once it is conceded that agencies have power in favor of the citizen to waive or depart from provisions of statute, for example, by waiving the payment of tax that is due in law,[99] or by not requiring the individual to satisfy one of the conditions that in law must be observed before a social security benefit is payable.[100] Discretion of this kind is exercised in respect of Section 86 of the Road Traffic Act of 1972. This act specifies the circumstances in which a fee for a driving test that does not take place may be refunded, but, as the ombudsman has told us, "to avoid inequities arising from too rigid an interpretation of the Road Traffic Acts, the Department drew up, in 1969, with the approval of ministers, and in consultation with the Treasury, a list of exceptional circumstances in which forfeiture could be waived on an extra-statutory basis."[101] This may often be not so much an extrastatutory discretion as a contrastatutory discretion. Despite the established practice of tax concessions by the revenue departments, that may be made either on a "class" basis or on an individual basis, the legality of such acts is often far from clear.[102] But the ombudsman's reports reveal that such practices are widespread. Not surprisingly, he has had more occasion to pick his way through this thicket of nonlaw than the courts have had. But on occasion, agencies are still heard to deny that they have any discretion of this kind to exercise.

There is also the area of what a lawyer would describe as "administrative estoppel," which is of concern to both the ombudsman and the courts. When is an agency free to depart from a decision that has already been made in favor of the citizen? When is an agency bound in taking a decision by statements previously made by officials, whether with or without due authority? Is the agency always free to change its mind, or to disavow the official upon whose statement a citizen has relied? In these circumstances, the ombudsman may well hold that injustice will be caused to a citizen unless the agency takes full account of any previous official actions. The courts, too, have recognized that in such circumstances considerations of equity and fairness may outweigh the letter of the law.[103]

Finally, there is the widening expanse of governmental liability, that is, the liability of agencies to compensate individuals for harm caused to them directly or indirectly through some negligent or other culpable act of administration. At common law, individual Crown servants were and are personally liable for their unlawful acts. The Crown Proceedings Act of 1947 imposed liability on the Crown to be sued in tort "as if it were a private person of full age and capacity," requiring departments to assume vicarious liability for the Crown servants employed in the departments. Notwithstanding the reference to the liability of a "private person," the effect of the 1947 act has been to impose liability on departments for acts that are directly related to the Crown's public duties and could scarcely be performed by a private person. The House of Lords decision in *Dorset Yacht Co.* v. *Home Office*,[104] which held the Home Office liable for the negligence of borstal officers in failing to supervise borstal boys, who thereupon escaped and damaged private property nearby, is the most prominent of recent judicial decisions establishing liability for administrative negligence. It has been followed by *Anns* v. *Merton Borough Council,* which held a local authority liable for the negligence of their staff in failing properly to exercise a statutory power to inspect the foundations of houses in the course of construction.[105] These two cases have extensive implications for public agencies, whose statutory powers may include the regulation and control of private business activities such as insurance companies,[106] or who may issue a public warning about the possible danger of certain methods of building construction and thereby make properties unsaleable.[107]

A significant development in the law of negligence was made earlier in *Hedley Byrne & Co.* v. *Heller and Partners,* where the House of Lords held that there might be liability for financial loss caused through reliance on a negligent misstatement.[108] Although the case concerned a banker's reference given in the course of private business, it would seem that an individual who relies to his detriment on incorrect statements made to him by an official in the course of the latter's duties may have a remedy both against the official and his employing authority.[109] This surely provides a legal basis for the many cases in which the ombudsman has caused agencies to make *ex gratia* payments to individuals who have been misled by incorrect advice from officials.[110] Developments in the law of tort could also lead to an agency being held liable to an individual for financial loss caused to a citizen through unreasonable delay in the exercise of statutory powers. On this matter the casework of the ombudsman[111] is ahead of the case-law of the British courts.

Sometimes investigation by the ombudsman may indicate that an agency has acted unlawfully. In a case concerning the removal of documents from an accountant's office in the course of a Value Added Tax investigation, the ombudsman stressed that he had no authority to judge matters of law, but the report leaves no room for doubt that his own conclusion was that some of the documents had been taken illegally.[112] This raises once again the interaction between an individual's right to sue for damages in the courts and his right to complain of maladministration to the ombudsman. The most acute difficulties in this respect are raised by complaints about the treatment of patients in the National Health Service.[113] While the National Health Service ombudsman may well consider that his office was not created to make it easier for an action for damages to be brought against hospital authorities, should a complainant be required to give an undertaking not to sue, as a condition of the ombudsman's conducting an investigation?[114] If the ombudsman's investigation does disclose substantial grounds on which liability should be accepted by the Health Service authorities, should this report be made the basis of a legal claim?

There is, moreover, an urgent need for more analysis of the relationship between legal liability and the making of *ex gratia* payments. Traditionally in English law, liability has been based upon fault, and the Crown Proceedings Act of 1947 observes this tradition. There is, however, room for much argument as to what constitutes sufficient fault, in particular whether an agency can be liable for administrative errors that occur from negligence, malice, or other improper motive. There are indeed some areas of public law where it can be argued that a public authority's liability should not depend on proof of fault at all.[115] It is therefore a matter of considerable interest to discover the approach taken by the ombudsman, on a complaint that an error by an immigration officer had caused an individual loss of earnings for a period of nearly six weeks: "I do not myself accept, as a general rule, that, when an officer makes a mistake which cannot be attributed to malice, prejudice or gross negligence on his part, but which is clearly contrary to departmental policy, and that mistake directly causes a member of the public to suffer a financial loss, his department should not accept financial responsibility."[116] On the facts in that case, however, there had been "no more than a human error, made at a time when immigration officers generally were under very considerable strain in applying the new Immigration Rules," and the ombudsman did not criticize the Home Office for deciding not to pay compensation for the loss of earnings.

CONCLUSION

This discussion of the relationship between the ombudsman and the courts shows that many problems of administrative law that are in the course of receiving judicial answers are at the same time coming before the ombudsman, there to be answered for his own purposes. For the time being, and subject to the rather unlikely possibility of a radical reform that might bring the administrative work of the courts and that of the ombudsman together into a single institution, parallel processes exist, each having certain advantages and disadvantages relative to the other. Each system has acquired and is acquiring experience that could be valuable to the other.

Hitherto, the ombudsman's discretion to investigate complaints that might be the subject of a remedy in the courts has been generously exercised, and it is hoped that this situation will continue. Even though the authority of a court may be needed to establish the principle that a government agency is liable for incorrect advice given to the citizen by an official, this is no reason why every citizen who complains that he received incorrect advice should be forced to sue the department before he can expect any redress.

The two forms of procedures, courts and ombudsman, are in fact likely to remain very different, and so is the constitutional status of the two systems, although there may be a need for a few key links between the two to be established. But it would be unfortunate if the substantive rules and principles developed by the two systems of control were to differ sharply. One hierarchy of broadly consonant norms is needed, rather than two separate hierarchies of conflicting norms. Already, as in respect of natural justice and fairness, there may be much more common ground than is sometimes supposed. For what both systems are concerned with is the proper regulation of government's treatment of the citizen. Principles of good administration may look different from the rules of law to which we are accustomed, and are likely to be phrased in terms of duties imposed on the administration. But just as the courts can protect the citizen's right to enforcement of the law in matters that directly affect him, so can the ombudsman be a valuable means of protecting the citizen's interest in, or right to, good administration.

NOTES

1. Ronald Dworkin, *Taking Rights Seriously* (London: Duckworth, 1977), p. 205.

2. Ibid., p. 198.

3. See Sir Guy Powles, "Ombudsmen and Human Rights Commissions," *Review of International Commission of Jurists*, No. 21 (December 1978): 31.

4. Immigration Appeals Act 1969, implementing the Wilson Report on Immigration Appeals, Cmnd. 3387, 1967.

5. See the *Internationale Handelsgesellschaft* case [1972] C.M.L.R. 255 and the *Nold* case [1974] C.M.L.R. 338.

6. Hansard, H.L.Deb., vol. 208, col. 605 (1 April 1958).

7. Mr. Crossman at H. C. Deb., vol. 734, col. 42 (18 October 1966), and Lord Gardiner at H. L. Deb., vol. 279, col. 1364 (8 February 1967).

8. W. N. Hohfeld, *Fundamental Legal Conceptions* (New Haven, Conn.: Yale University Press, 1919).

9. In 1971, the report by JUSTICE, *Administration under Law* (London: Stevens), proposed the enactment of Principles of Good Administration, to apply to government departments, local authorities and nationalized industries.

10. *4th Report of Select Committee on P.C.A.*, H.C. 615 (1977–78), p. viii.

11. Cmnd. 2767, 1965, paras. 2 and 4.

12. See the Whyatt Report, *The Citizen and the Administration* (London: Stevens, 1961), Part II, recommending the creation of a general tribunal to hear a miscellany of appeals from discretionary decisions by departments. The recommendation has never been accepted by government.

13. In 1973, the existence of the P.C.A. with power to request a review of departmental decisions was stated in parliament by a minister to be one reason why it was unnecessary to provide by legislation for a right of appeal against the power to ban an individual from conducting insurance business. See *2nd Report of Select Committee on P.C.A.*, H.C. 524 (1976–77), pp. xi and 28–41; and *Report of P.C.A. for 1976*, H.C. 116 (1976–77), p. 47.

14. E. C. S. Wade, *Law of the Constitution*, 10th ed. (London: Macmillan, 1959), p. 199. For a perceptive study of changing Anglo-Saxon attitudes in this respect, see S. A. de Smith, *The New Commonwealth and Its Constitutions* (London: Stevens, 1964), Chapter 5.

15. See H. W. R. Wade, "The British Ombudsman: A Lawyer's View," *Administrative Law Review*, vol. 24, p. 137. This comment remains valid despite the appointment of a practising lawyer, C. M. Clothier, Q.C., as P.C.A. from January 1979. But is it coincidence that phrases like "the balance of probability" seem to appear more often in his reports than previously? See, for example, *4th Report of P.C.A.*, H.C. 351 (1979–80), p. 48.

16. Court decisions have already been made on the powers of the Local Commissioners for Administration: *Re a Complaint against Liverpool City Council* [1977] 2 All E.R. 650. See also *R. v. Local Commissioner for Administration, ex p. Bradford Council* [1979] Q.B. 287, which has dicta relating to the formulation of complaints to the P.C.A.

17. Parliamentary Commissioner Act, 1967, s.5(5); *In re Fletcher's Application* [1970] 2 All E.R. 527.

18. *Introduction to the Philosophy of Law* (New Haven, Conn.: Yale University Press, 1959), p. 63.

19. Ibid., p. 68.

20. W. A. Robson, *Justice and Administrative Law*, 2d ed. (London: Stevens, 1947), p. 35; and cf. Pound, *Introduction to the Philosophy of Law*, p. 65.

21. For example, *7th Report of P.C.A.*, H.C. 664 (1977–78), pp. 192, 199, 202, 222, 226, 254, 260.

22. In 1978, an index by subject matter of decisions published during 1978 was made available on request from the P.C.A.'s office: H.C. 205 (1978–79) p. 6. In 1980, when only selected reports on cases were being published, each quarterly report contained a brief list of departments investigated, the earlier proposal for a continuing subject index having been abandoned.

23. See, by G. Marshall, "Maladministration" [1973], *Public Law* 32; and "Techniques of Maladministration," *Political Studies* 23 (1975):183.

24. Quoted by L. N. Brown and P. Lavirotte in "The Mediator: A French Ombudsman?" (1974) 90 L. Q. R. 211, 213.

25. *Report of P.C.A. for 1968*, H.C. 129 (1968–69), pp. 84, 85, 125; and *Report of P.C.A. for 1970*, H.C. 261 (1970–71), p. 10.

26. See for example, *1st Report of P.C.A.*, H.C. 35 (1975–76), pp. 116–143, 214; *1st Report of P.C.A.*, H.C. 126 (1977–78), p. 8.

27. See in particular the difficulties resulting from new rights to compensation given by the Land Compensation Act of 1973: *6th Report of P.C.A.*, H.C. 598 (1977–78) and *1st Report of Select Committee on P.C.A.*, H.C. 91 (1978–79).

28. See, for example, in respect of war pensions, *Report of P.C.A. for 1977*, H.C. 157 (1977–78).

29. For example, *1st Report of P.C.A.*, H.C. 35 (1975–76), pp. 165 and 226.

30. See note 21 above.

31. A. Legrand, *L'Ombudsman Scandinave* (Paris: Rehon and Durand-Auzins, 1970), p. 406.

32. Evidence of D. W. Williams to Select Committee on P.C.A., H.C. 444-v (1977–78), p. 119.

33. *First Report, June–December 1977*, H.C. 359 (1977–78).

34. For example, in the Hunterston development case, *3rd Report of P.C.A.*, H.C. 241 (1974–75), p. 166, and in the invalid tricycle affair, *6th Report of P.C.A.*, H.C. 529 (1974–75) p. 162.

35. National Health Service Reorganisation Act of 1973, Sched. 3, para. 1. The restriction was considered by the Select Committee on the P.C.A. in the report on the independent review of hospital complaints, H.C. 45 (1977–78). This restriction as such does not apply when the P.C.A. is examining complaints against the Ministry of Defence about medical treatment received by civilians in military hospitals (for example, *7th Report of P.C.A.*, H.C. 664 [1977–78], p. 20) or complaints by prisoners about their medical treatment while in prison. But the P.C.A. may take the view that a matter of pure clinical judgment involves no element of maladministration. In July 1980, a government decision on the clinical judgment exception was still awaited: *3rd Report of Select Committee on P.C.A.*, H.C. 406 (1979–80), p. xiv.

36. For example, the current policy of Inland Revenue on remission of unpaid tax brought about by official error (see R. Gregory and P. G. Hutchesson, *The Parliamentary Ombudsman*, 1975, pp. 573–586) and the changed policy regarding the starting date for arrears of war pensions which arose from Captain Horsley's case (*2nd Report of P.C.A.*, H.C. 587, 1970–71). For the latest statement on tax remission, see H.C. Deb., Vol. 973, col. 180, W.A. (7 November 1979).

37. *1st Report of P.C.A.*, H.C. 35 (1975–76), p. 157; *5th Report of P.C.A.*, H.C. 524 (1977–78), p. 173.

38. For example, regarding the use of typewriters by prisoners: *5th Report of P.C.A.*, H.C. 406 (1972–73), p. 129; *Report of Select Committee on P.C.A.*, H.C. 268 (1974), p. x;

and *2nd Report of Select Committee on P.C.A.*, H.C. 488 (1975–76), p. v.

39. Isolated cases do occur, for example, *7th Report of P.C.A.*, H.C. 664 (1977–78), p. 151.

40. *2nd Report of Health Service Commissioner*, H.C. 160 (1976–77), p. 58; and *2nd Report of Select Committee on P.C.A.*, H.C. 372 (1977–78), p. v.

41. M. Lerhard, ed., *The Danish Ombudsman 1955–69* (Copenhagen: Schultz, 1972), pp. 62–63.

42. Cf. Legrand, *L'Ombudsman Scandinave*, p. 513.

43. By s.11(3) of the 1967 act, a minister may exclude from the P.C.A.'s reports material the disclosure of which would be "prejudicial to the safety of the State or otherwise contrary to the public interest."

44. For example, *Report of P.C.A. for 1967*, H.C. 134 (1967–68), p. 74.

45. See Gregory and Hutchesson, *Parliamentary Ombudsman*, pp. 593–99.

46. *R. v. Chief Immigration Officer, ex p. Salamat Bibi* [1976] 3 All E.R. 843.

47. Judgment of the Court, 21 February 1975, series A, vol. 18.

48. *Report of P.C.A. for 1970*, H.C. 261 (1970–71), p. 124; and *Yearbook of European Convention on Human Rights*, 1970, p. 730.

49. *6th Report of P.C.A.*, H.C. 665 (1975–76), p. 143.

50. This impact is discussed in D. J. Harris, "The Application of Article 6(1) of the European Convention on Human Rights to Administrative Law," *British Yearbook of International Law 1974–75*, vol. 47, 157.

51. Gregory and Hutchesson, *Parliamentary Ombudsman*, Chapter 11.

52. Cmnd. 218, 1957, p. 9.

53. For example, *1st Report of P.C.A.*, H.C. 37 (1975–76), pp. 94, 129; *1st Report of P.C.A.*, H.C. 126 (1977–78), p. 109; Gregory and Hutchesson, *Parliamentary Ombudsman*, pp. 226–30.

54. Parliamentary Commissioner Act of 1967, s.5(1).

55. See, for example, K. Bell, *Research Study on Supplementary Benefit Appeal Tribunals 1975* (H.M.S.O.); and M. Adler and A.W. Bradley, *Justice, Discretion and Poverty* (London: Professional Books, 1976).

56. On delay by tribunals, see *4th Report of P.C.A.*, H.C. 351 (1979–80), p. 31. On the ambiguous position of county court officials, see the same report, p. 60.

57. For example, *1st Report of P.C.A.*, H.C. 37 (1975–76), p. 78.

58. Ibid., p. 74.

59. Note 64 below.

60. *1st Report of P.C.A.*, H.C. 37 (1975–76), p. 83.

61. Parliamentary Commissioner Act of 1967, s.12(3).

62. See, respectively, *1st Report of P.C.A.*, H.C. 2 (1974) p. 140; and *3rd Report of P.C.A.*, H.C. 223 (1976–77), p. 192.

63. For example, *1st Report of P.C.A.*, H.C 37 (1975–76), p. 90.

64. Tribunals and Inquiries Act 1971, s.1(1)(c).

65. For example, *1st Report of P.C.A.*, H.C. 37 (1975–76), p. 62.

66. In *R.* v. *Environment Secretary, ex p. Ostler* [1977] Q.B. 122. Ostler's case failed because of the six-week rule. After investigation by the P.C.A., Ostler recovered compensation for the costs of his abortive pursuit of a legal remedy: *3rd Report of P.C.A.*, H.C. 223 (1976–77), p. 40; and *2nd Report of Select Committee on P.C.A.*, H.C. 524 (1976–77), pp. x, 16–18.

67. See respectively, *R.* v. *Home Secretary, ex p. Phansopkar* [1976] Q.B. 606; *Congreve* v. *Home Office* [1976] Q.B. 629; *R.* v. *Barnsley Council, ex p. Hook* [1976] 3 All E.R. 452; *Laker Airways Ltd.* v. *Department of Trade* [1977] Q.B. 643.

68. For the new procedure of application for judicial review, see Rules of Supreme Court, new Order 53 (S.I. 1955 of 1977); discussed by J. Beatson and M. H. Matthews, *Modern Law Review* 41 (1978):437.

69. D. Foulkes, "The Discretionary Provisions of the Parliamentary Commissioner Act 1967," *Modern Law Review* 34 (1971):377, 380–84; Gregory and Hutchesson, *Parliamentary Ombudsman*, pp. 230–241.

70. For example, H. Street, *Justice in the Welfare State* (London: Stevens, 1968), Chapter 5.

71. H.W.R. Wade, *Administrative Law*, 4th ed. (Oxford: Clarendon Press, 1976), pp. 73–86. Cf. C. Harlow, "Ombudsmen in Search of a Role," *Modern Law Review* 41 (1978):446.

72. G. Braibant, "Les Rapports du Mediateur et du Juge Administratif," *Actualité Juridique, Droit Administratif* (1977):283.

73. *Conway* v. *Rimmer* [1968] A.C. 910.

74. Parliamentary Commissioner Act of 1967, ss. 7(2) and 8(2).

75. *7th Report of P.C.A.*, H.C. 680 (1974–75); *Congreve* v. *Home Office* (above, n. 65).

76. M. Lerhard, *The Danish Ombudsman 1955–69*, p. 78.

77. Parliamentary Commissioner Act of 1967, s. 7(4). The one exception to this under the 1967 act was that the P.C.A. had power to direct that an alien or Commonwealth immigrant be readmitted to the United Kingdom for the purposes of his investigation. But this power seems never to have been used, and it is uncertain whether the power still exists, since the former legislation on aliens and Commonwealth immigrants has been replaced by the Immigration Act of 1971.

78. In the Edinburgh Airport Case (*1st Report of P.C.A.*, H.C. 2 [1974] p. 140), the government's decision to proceed with construction was taken to the prime minister by objectors and was raised in parliament, but without success: H.C. Deb., vol. 861, col. 1417 (29 October 1973).

79. H.C. 154 (1977–78), Chapter 4.

80. The case was first reported in *5th Report of P.C.A.*, H.C. 496 (1975–76), p. 194. For a case of obstinacy in the National Health Service, see *3rd Report of Select Committee on P.C.A.*, H.C. 406 (1979–80), p. xiii.

81. Gregory and Hutchesson, *Parliamentary Ombudsman*, Chapter 11.

82. Roskill L.J. in *Congreve* v. *Home Office* (above).

83. *Anisminic Ltd.* v. *Foreign Compensation Commission* [1969] 2 A.C. 147.

84. *Ashbridge Investments Ltd.* v. *Minister of Housing* [1965] 3 All E.R. 371, 374.

85. For typical cases, see *1st Report of P.C.A.*, H.C. 37 (1975–76), pp. 42 and 65. And see comments on the Nigg Bay decision, *Report of P.C.A. for 1976*, H.C. 116 (1976–77), p. 7.

86. Leading decisions include *Re H.K.* [1967] 2 Q.B. 617; *Wiseman* v. *Borneman* [1971] A.C. 297; *R.* v. *Liverpool Corporation* [1972] 2 Q.B. 299; *Maxwell* v. *Department of Trade* [1974] Q.B. 523.

87. *Report of P.C.A. for 1976*, H.C. 116 (1976–77), App. B; and *2nd Report of Select Committee on P.C.A.*, H.C. 524 (1976–77), p. xi.

88. *Report of P.C.A. for 1976*, H.C. 116 (1976–77), p. 5.

89. [1968] A.C. 497.

90. [1977] A.C. 1014.

91. See also the Whyatt Report, *The Citizen and the Administration* 1961, Part II; and J. Jowell, "The Legal Control of Administrative Discretion" [1973] *Public Law* 178.

92. *Discretionary Justice: A Preliminary Inquiry* (Urbana, Univ. of Illinois Press, 1971), p. 4.

93. [1973] *Public Law* 178, 179.

94. For example, *R.* v. *Minister of Transport, ex p. Males* [1970] 3 All E.R. 434.

95. The case-law includes *R.* v. *Port of London Authority, ex p. Kynoch* [1919] 1 K.B. 176 and *British Oxygen Co.* v. *Board of Trade* [1971] A.C. 610.

96. Gregory and Hutchesson, *Parliamentary Ombudsman*, p. 461.

97. Consider, for example, *R.* v. *Criminal Injuries Compensation Board, ex p. Lain* [1967] 2 Q.B. 864.

98. Note 44 above.

99. For example, note 78 above.

100. For example, *1st Report of P.C.A.*, H.C. 37 (1975–76), p. 94.

101. *1st Report of P.C.A.*, H.C. 37 (1975–76), p. 88.

102. *R.* v. *Customs and Excise Commissioners, ex p. Cooke* [1970] 1 All E.R. 1068. In *1st Report of Select Committee on P.C.A.*, H.C. 91 (1978–79), the official evidence distinguishes between *ex gratia* payments (justifiable by the exceptional circumstances of a case) and extra-statutory payments (not within the terms of a statute but broadly in line with it), but states that payments cannot be made directly contrary to a statute. For additional criticism of extrastatutory tax concessions, see *Vestey* v. *I.R.C. (No. 2)* [1979] 2 All E.R. 225.

103. The case-law includes *Robertson* v. *Minister of Pensions* [1949] 1 K.B. 227; *Re 57 Denton Road, Twickenham* [1953] Ch. 51; and *Lever Finance Ltd.* v. *Westminster Council* [1971] 1 Q.B. 222.

104. [1970] A.C. 1004.

105. [1977] 2 All E.R. 492.

106. See report of Tribunal of Inquiry into the collapse of the Vehicle and General Insurance Co., H.L. 80, H.C. 133 (1971–72); and *4th Report of P.C.A.*, H.C. 485 (1975–76) concerning the Nation Life Insurance Co.

103. *1st Report of P.C.A.*, H.C. 126 (1977–78), p. 51.

108. [1964] A.C. 465.

109. *Ministry of Housing* v. *Sharp* [1970] 2 Q.B. 223.

110. For example, *4th Report of P.C.A.*, H.C. 290 (1972–73) p. 4.

111. Note 24 above.

112. *1st Report of P.C.A.*, H.C. 126 (1977–78) p. 14.

113. Report of Select Committee on P.C.A. on the independent review of hospital complaints, H.C. 130 (1977–78).

114. For example, *1st Report of Health Service Commissioner*, H.C. 130 (1977–78) p. 88.

115. C. Harlow, ''Fault Liability in French and English Public Law,'' *Modern Law Review* 39 (1976):516.

116. *1st Report of P.C.A.*, H.C. 37 (1975–76) p. 156.

CHAPTER 8

THE OMBUDSMAN AND FREEDOM OF INFORMATION IN CANADA

INGER HANSEN, Q.C., PRIVACY COMMISSIONER, CANADIAN HUMAN RIGHTS COMMISSION

ATTITUDES TO PERSONAL information rights used to be rather casual. I remember that my father enlisted my help in tracing our ancestors in the Danish Public Archives by going through registers of births, marriages, and deaths. At no time did it occur to me that our research might be an invasion of privacy of members of our family. In my early years, I also submitted to medical treatment without ever considering whether I might have a right to read or comment on the doctor's file concerning me, or whether he had a right to pass my data to others without my knowledge or consent. Later in life, I paid unemployment insurance premiums and taxes, and I gave away a copy of my income tax return in order to obtain a loan from a bank for the purpose of opening a law practice. I filled out an application for a passport and obtained credit after having revealed my financial circumstances. I became the proud owner of "plastic money," and I seldom questioned the correctness, completeness, relevancy, or currency of the information others kept in their files about me. Not until the late 1970s did the question or the need for protection of personal information enter my consciousness.

I do not think I was alone in this casual treatment of my personal data. Others, I am certain, felt the same way. But today, many of us have encountered the frustrations of trying to straighten out computer error. We are aware that information is collected about us almost everywhere, and we are anxious because the ability to store, manipulate, and transfer data has increased dramatically. We now know that the technology exists to store an infinite amount of data, to transmit it almost instantaneously and to store it "forever." We are conscious of the need to limit the information we give away about ourselves, but we have not quite come to grips with how this may be achieved. We worry, as well, about our personal data being stored in other countries. But we are also afraid to say "no" or even "why" when someone asks for personal data.

Many of us are ill at ease because we have to give up personal data to get benefits or services, and we fear losing control over the data we give away. We know we cannot run away from our past, nor from our medical, marital, and professional records, from evidence of our spending habits, whether of money or time. It can all be retrieved at the touch of a button, we suspect. We tolerate having so much information about ourselves collected and stored because it makes things easy. And we enjoy the benefits of communal living, easy credit, extensive medical records and instant flight reservations. We know we cannot have them, unless we are prepared to give up some of our privacy in return.

I believe that people have greater opportunity today to control what information they give, to whom and for what

---

Taken from an address to the Second International Ombudsman Conference, Jerusalem, October 27, 1980.

purpose. We have greater awareness of our right to know. We are more conscious of the cost/benefit ratio of giving away information about ourselves. There are laws granting data protection in some jurisdictions. The idea that we ourselves must guard our privacy by handling our own data with care is taking hold. On the other hand, scientific discovery dependent on numerical computations has made hitherto undreamt of advances, thanks to computer technology. Without computers, there would probably have been no trips to the moon, no truly accurate research into diseases with environmental or genetic cause and many other benefits that we take for granted today. Computers are not inherently evil and the advent of computers has made the provision of access to information possible on a large scale.

Sweden has had the right of access to nonclassified government data since the 1930s. "Freedom of Information," that is, access to general government records, is viewed by many people as essential to democracy. The demands for "freedom of information" and "privacy" overlap and occasionally clash. Both have been made with increasing intensity in many parts of the world. Needless to say, governments have resisted the demand to see everything on various grounds, such as the need to protect criminal and other investigations, the personal privacy of third parties, corporate privacy (trade secrets and information that renders the corporate body involved less competitive), and the safety and security of the nation itself.

Canada is trying to grapple with the question of secrecy and rights to information and privacy. Some parliamentarians and private individuals and groups have actively promoted the cause of freedom of information for a long time. Many Canadian provinces have legislation that deals with the right of access to records in specific areas, such as credit or medical records. Two provinces, New Brunswick and Nova Scotia, have passed freedom of information laws; other provinces are investigating the possibility of passing such laws. Two successive federal governments have introduced bills in the Canadian parliament to provide general rights of access to government information. The latest was introduced on July 17, 1980. If enacted, it will provide for access to general government information. The bill also provides for extensive amendments to the existing federal personal data protection law. Here, I will describe the existing data protection law and my experience as a specialist ombudsman, a reviewer of complaints from persons who say they have not been accorded their rights under the present laws. I will also outline the provisions of the proposed legislation and indicate differences between the old and the new.

DATA PROTECTION NOW IN EFFECT

The Canadian Human Rights Act, Part IV of which deals with personal data protection, came into force on March 1, 1978. As of that day, individuals have had the right to examine and obtain copies of records concerning themselves that are used for administrative purposes and are held by federal government departments and institutions. A person also has the right to know the uses to which the records have been put since March 1, 1978, to challenge the correctness of the information, or to require a notation on file when the correction is not accepted.

To a degree, Part IV protects individuals against the passing of information from one government department to another or to third parties. Subsection 52(2) provides:

Every individual is entitled to be consulted and must consent before personal information concerning that individual that was provided by that individual to a government institution for a particular purpose is used or made available for use for any non-derivative use for an administrative purpose unless the use of that information for that non-derivative use is authorized by or pursuant to law.

There are no secret banks of information in Canada. However, of the approximately fifteen hundred information banks containing personal information, twenty-two are not subject to the rights of access, knowledge of use, correction, and notation just outlined. In accordance with a provision in the act, a minister may obtain a cabinet order "closing the bank" on the grounds that disclosure of information in it would harm relations with other countries or governments, the safety of Canada, or prevention of crime. The protection against the passing of information in Subsection 52(2) still applies.

Shortly after taking office, I received several complaints in respect of some of the closed banks and met initial resistance when we sought to investigate those complaints. We now have access to all closed banks for investigatory purposes. I insisted that if access were not granted, it would be impossible to assure members of the public that information had not been placed in the closed information banks by inadvertence or in bad faith. I should mention that the existing law is not clear as to whether investigators and the privacy commissioner have the right of access to the closed banks, but I am encouraged to see that the right to audit closed banks is explicit in the bill now before parliament.

In respect of all the other data banks, documents or parts of documents may be exempted with the authority of the minister concerned. Exemptions may be claimed only for reasons stipulated in the act, as follows:

. . . where, in the opinion of the Minister, knowledge of the existence of the record or of information contained therein

(*a*) might be injurious to international relations, national defence or security or federal-provincial relations;

(*b*) would disclose a confidence of the Queen's Privy Council for Canada;

(*c*) would be likely to disclose information obtained or prepared by any government institution or part of a government institution that is an investigative body

(i) in relation to national security,

(ii) in the course of investigations pertaining to the detection or suppression of crime generally, or

(iii) in the course of investigations pertaining to the administration or enforcement of any Act of Parliament;

(*d*) might, in respect of any individual under sentence for an offence against any Act of Parliament

(i) lead to a serious disruption of that individual's institutional, parole or mandatory supervision program,

(ii) reveal information originally obtained on a promise of confidentiality, express or implied, or

(iii) result in physical or other harm to that individual or any other person;

(*e*) might reveal personal information concerning another individual;

(*f*) might impede the functioning of a court of law, or a quasi-judicial board, commission or other tribunal or any inquiry established under the *Inquiries Act;* or

(*g*) might disclose legal opinions or advice provided to a government institution or privileged communications between lawyer and client in a matter of government business. (Sec. 54)

. . . the Governor in Council may make regulations

(*d*) prescribing any special procedures or restrictions deemed necessary with regard to examination of medical records of an individual, including psychological reports concerning that individual, and, if deemed appropriate, procedures that would preclude examination of such records and reports by the individual where, in the opinion of a duly qualified medical practitioner, examination thereof by the individual would be contrary to the best interests of the individual. (Sec. 62)

PROCEDURE FOR GAINING ACCESS

In order to gain access to his or her own personal file, a person may examine the Index of Federal Information Banks at a post office. This index lists the fifteen hundred personal information banks that have been identified as containing personal information used for administrative purposes. The particular information banks in which a person is interested are selected from the index. An application form must be completed, giving the particular number assigned to the bank in the index, and it must be mailed to the government department concerned. The address of each government department is in the index.

If all goes well, individuals should receive the informa-tion requested within thirty days. Because of the amount of information on file, an individual will sometimes be invited to attend at a convenient place to review the file rather than be furnished with copies. The same thing may happen if the file is in French and the individual's choice of language is English, or vice versa. Individuals are entitled to have translations of their personal information. However, for reasons of economy, they may be asked to select those documents of which a translation is necessary.

Responsibility for administering the personal information rights rests on each federal government department and institution covered by the legislation. One cabinet minister is designated as the minister responsible for the general coordination of personal information rights and for the publication at least once a year of the index. Each department has a high-level official as privacy coordinator, who is responsible for the department's delivery of information rights to the public.

Some critics have suggested that having to select which file an individual wishes to search is too complicated. That criticism seems to overlook the possibility that if the government established a central information system much privacy would be lost because there would be no protection against passing information from one department to another. If data were held in a centralized system, public servants would have to decide which banks a particular individual ought to search. That, too, might not be acceptable. But let me give you three examples from the index by way of illustration:

15655
Taxation Rulings Subject Matter Files

The purpose of the bank is to file correspondence from and to taxpayers on matters related to the Income Tax Acts and Regulations. It contains correspondence received from individuals wherein an interpretation of a section, subsection, etc., of the Income Tax Act or another law related thereto is requested, and Revenue Canada Taxations's reply. This bank is used for records retention and maintenance only. Records acquired in the course of investigations of a taxpayer's affairs, information obtained on a promise of confidentiality, and legal opinions obtained or advice provided to Revenue Canada Taxation by the Department of Justice will be exempted from access by virtue of Section 54(c)(d)(e) and (g) of the Act. Access to a record will be provided upon proof of identification including name, address, signature and social insurance number. In some instances correspondence may be filed in the name of the taxpayer's representative. In these cases the name and address of the representative should also be included on the Record Access Request Form. The subject matter and date of the requested correspondence is also required. Records in this bank are maintained for seven years.

15235
Customs Intelligence Records

The purpose of this bank is to assist in the enforcement of the Customs Act and other Acts pertaining to Customs. Broad categories of data include criminal history (smuggling contraband), demographic considerations, commodity information, cooperation and liaison with other law enforcement bodies. This information is used primarily to notify Customs Officers of likely means of conveyance and methods of smuggling goods and of individuals and/or Companies who are suspected of or who have committed infractions under the various government Acts administered in whole or in part by Departmental officials. Files are retained for an indefinite period. *Records in this bank are exempt from access under Section 53(b)(ii) of the Human Rights Act.*

22410
Orchestra Singer's Records

The purpose of this bank is to maintain a record of singers who have performed or are available for performing with the National Arts Centre Orchestra. It contains names, addresses, telephone numbers, audition information and related correspondence. Information on file is retained indefinitely.

As you will see, a description of the information bank follows the pattern of indicating the purpose of the bank, its contents, and its life span. But, to return to the question of an individual having to select the information banks, it is obvious that if one is not an orchestra singer or a smuggler, one would have no interest in searching those banks.

COMPLAINTS

The privacy commissioner is appointed by the governor in council, holds office for a fixed term, and during that term can be dismissed only by the governor in council on address to both the House of Commons and the Senate. Individuals who allege that they have not been accorded the rights to which they are entitled under Part IV of the Canadian Human Rights Act may lodge a complaint with the privacy commissioner who is under a statutory duty to investigate every complaint.

The privacy commissioner has no power to reverse decisions but makes quasi-judicial findings as to whether an individual has been denied a right under the act. Recommendations may be made to the responsible minister, and findings and recommendations must be conveyed to the complainant. They may eventually be included in the annual report on the activities of the privacy commissioner, which must be delivered to the minister of justice for tabling in the House of Commons.

The law requires that the investigation of complaints be conducted in private, and no one is entitled as of right to a hearing before the privacy commissioner. The act also demands that any government institution or person that may be adversely affected by a report or a recommendation made by the privacy commissioner shall be given full and ample opportunity to answer adverse allegations or criticisms before findings or recommendations are made. Those involved are entitled to be represented by counsel.

The privacy commissioner is authorized in the same manner as a superior court to compel the attendance of witnesses and the production of documents and has the right of access to premises occupied by a government institution concerned in an investigation. Restrictions may be placed on the privacy commissioner by the governor in council in the interest of national defense or security, but no such restrictions have been imposed.

The mandate of the privacy commissioner resembles that of a parliamentary ombudsman. It calls for impartiality until a finding of facts and law has been made and thereafter may require advocacy on behalf of a complainant, based on the finding. Part IV contains no direct mandate to advocate improvement of the law or attitudes concerning access to information, and there is no mandate to deal with administrative decisions taken on the basis of the data. Nevertheless, changes to the law or policies occur as the secondary result of representations or recommendations made by the privacy commissioner, after receipt and investigation of specific complaints.

PRIVACY COMMISSIONER'S WORKLOAD

During 1979, the first full year of operation of the office, we completed the investigation of 347 complaints. Half of these complaints were from penitentiary inmates who complained that they had experienced considerable delays in exercising their right of access to several information banks. Each complainant made approximately 2.5 complaints. During the first eight months of 1980, investigation of approximately 170 complaints was undertaken, and the average complaint per person dropped to 1.5 complaints. Originally, the types of complaints made by individuals were recorded immediately after the first contact. That proved totally inaccurate and caused many subsequent changes. We therefore hold statistics in abeyance until after a particular person's complaints have been completed and until after we have developed some criteria for recording complaints. The complaints are divided into those that concern access, use, exemptions, and delay. Complaints of different categories from the same individual are counted separately. Complaints, whether or not of the same category, lodged by the same individual but against several departments or institutions, are recorded as one for each category and one for each department or institution. But complaints of the same category regardless of the number, lodged by one individual against one department or institution, are counted as one only, unless the results require separate reports.

This was necessary both for ease of recording and for avoiding distortion of statistics. A few examples will illustrate the point. An individual may complain about delay in gaining access to a record and, having gained access, may complain that a correction was not accepted. The same department is involved, but two investigations are necessary. In another instance, an individual may object to certain exemptions (in one case there were over seventy), but they all involve the same record. In essence, only one investigation is necessary, and therefore only one complaint is recorded. The nature of the work and the time needed for investigation are reflected in case synopses provided in the annual report.

The chief privacy investigator directs the work of four other investigators. There are four support staff members, but we receive administrative and personnel services from the Canadian Human Rights Commission and advice from its legal counsel.

In addition to the complaints, we receive a large number of inquiries from the public. These are handled by the investigators. While some may believe this is a waste of investigators' valuable time, I am convinced that the best people must be "up front." If inexperienced people staff the telephones where the first contact with members of the public takes place, chaos will result, and that chaos will have to be sorted out later causing even greater waste of time. Besides, it is obvious to us that members of the public are pleased that they can get through right away to a person who understands and is prepared to do something. The number of inquiries handled totaled 611 in 1978, 683 in 1979, and 435 for the first eight months of 1980.

We currently have a backlog of 155 complainants (or an estimated two hundred complaints). Some of these have been active for a long time because they are complex and involve sensitive issues. We estimate that if we did not receive any more work, it would take us approximately eight months to complete the pending work. I intend to make representations for more resources to the Treasury Board.

EVALUATION

An ombudsman must conduct investigations fairly, to ensure that all complainants receive that to which they are entitled. That same principle applies to an information commissioner. A complaint to the office is often resolved at the administrative level because the problem is one of failure of communication or clerical error. But occasionally the privacy commissioner may directly challenge ministerial decisions.

Not everyone has accepted the new law with open arms, but thoughtful people are accepting the need for a proper balance between the individual's right to know and the government's right to protect collective interests and the privacy of other individuals.

The greatest problem facing public servants and members of the public is to overcome attitudes that have been built up over the years. Some administrators in the federal service were noticeably shocked when they realized that, as a result of Part IV of the Canadian Human Rights Act, a promise of confidentiality to referees could no longer be given. Some have suggested that information will become bland, that subjective opinions will be given orally instead of in writing. This will likely happen. However, in the long term privacy legislation will lead to more honesty and to proper documentation in support of administrative actions. It is hard to imagine that managers will be able to justify administrative decisions based exclusively on records kept in their heads. Enactment of information laws will result in more concise reports, and investigative reports will relate facts to support conclusions. In addition, if an assessment of an individual cannot be put in writing, it does not normally deserve to have a lasting effect on that person's life.

It will no doubt take time for many federal administrators to realize that government policy in relation to personal information was in fact reversed when the new law came into effect. Before that date, the government of Canada released personal information only in response to a court order or else in its sole discretion (and the courts did not have total access). The individual who wanted access to government files would usually have to establish a good case in order to obtain disclosures. Since the enactment of Part IV of the Canadian Human Rights Act, the onus is on the minister who is responsible for giving reasons, specifically founded in law, why the information should not be disclosed to an individual who wants to see his personal data held by the Canadian government. It was a good start.

ACCESS TO INFORMATION ACT AND PRIVACY ACT

In July 1980, the secretary of state of Canada, the Honorable Francis Fox, introduced a Bill (C–43) in the Canadian House of Commons. The bill is in two parts: one would provide general access to government information; the other would replace the provisions concerning personal information rights now contained in the Canadian Human Rights Act, Part IV. Generally speaking, the bill was well received by the media and by the opposition parties. The government news release stated that the bill is based on the "principle that government information should be available to the public, that necessary exemptions to the right of access should be limited and specific, and that decisions on the disclosure of government information should be reviewed independently of government.''

The second part of the bill, the one that deals with personal information rights, reaffirms the right of individuals to gain access to and to correct personal data concerning themselves, and it expands the rights in the existing legislation. For instance, in Part IV of the Canadian Human Rights Act, individuals were only entitled to gain access to information used for the purpose of administrative decisions. Under the new bill, individuals will have the right of access to any of their personal information, provided it can be found.

As was the case in the existing privacy legislation, the right of access to public and personal information is not absolute. Information obtained in confidence from other governments, other countries, and the Canadian provinces could be withheld, although it might be disclosed with the consent of the other governments. Information that might damage international relations, national defense, or the safety of Canada, and information concerning criminal investigations, can still be withheld. Personal information (as defined in the bill) and confidential, corporate, or union information would be protected from disclosure. Finally, cabinet documents, internal advice within the government, and papers relating to the government's negotiating positions could be withheld from disclosure.

Furthermore, personal information would be protected from disclosure except

(a) for the purpose for which the information was obtained or compiled by the institution or for a use consistent with that purpose;

(b) for any purpose in accordance with any Act of Parliament or any regulation made thereunder that authorizes its disclosure;

(c) for the purpose of complying with a subpoena or warrant issued or order made by a court, person or body with jurisdiction to compel the production of information;

(d) to the Attorney General of Canada for use in legal proceedings involving the Crown in right of Canada or the Government of Canada;

(e) to an investigative body specified in the regulations, on the written request of the body, for the purpose of enforcing any law of Canada or a province or carrying out a lawful investigation, if the request specifies the purpose and describes the information to be disclosed;

(f) under an agreement or arrangement between the Government of Canada or an institution thereof and the government of a province, the government of a foreign state, an international organization of states or an international organization established by the governments of states, or any institution of any such government or organization, for the purpose of administer-

ing or enforcing any law or carrying out a lawful investigation;

(g) to a member of Parliament for the purpose of assisting the individual to whom the information relates in resolving a problem;

(h) to officers or employees of the institution for internal audit purposes, or to the office of the Comptroller General or any other person or body specified in the regulations for audit purposes;

(i) to the Public Archives for archival purposes;

(j) to any person or body for research or statistical purposes if the head of the government institution

(i) is satisfied that the purpose for which the information is disclosed cannot reasonably be accomplished unless the information is provided in a form that would identify the individual to whom it relates, and

(ii) obtains from the person or body a written undertaking that no subsequent disclosure of the information will be made in a form that could reasonably be expected to identify the individual to whom it relates;

(k) to any government institution for the purpose of locating an individual in order to collect a debt owing to Her Majesty in right of Canada by that individual or make a payment owing to that individual by Her Majesty in right of Canada; and

(l) for any purpose where, in the opinion of the head of the institution,

(i) the public interest in disclosure clearly outweighs any invasion of privacy that could result from the disclosure, or

(ii) disclosure would clearly benefit the individual to whom the information relates.

The procedure for reviewing complaints from individuals who allege that they have not been granted the rights spelled out in the act would involve two stages. First, there would be appeal to an information commissioner or a privacy commissioner. Each commissioner (or one holding both mandates) would function as a parliamentary ombudsman. Almost unlimited power of access to government information would be granted to the commissioners, and they would have the authority to compel the production of witnesses and documents. The commissioners would make recommendations but would not have power to order a reversal of a decision. Either the individual or the commissioners would be able to refer questions to the federal court of Canada.

Second, the court would be empowered to examine the records and to hear arguments from all parties. Where exemptions involve possible injury to defense or international relations, the court would have the power to order the release of the documents, if it decided that the minister did not have reasonable grounds for refusing access. In other cases, the court would be empowered to substitute its opinion for that of the minister involved.

Both commissioners would be required to file annual reports with the House of Commons, and a parliamentary committee would be designated to conduct a permanent review of the administration of the act.

I am particularly pleased to see that the bill provides that the commissioners and the staff working in the office of the commissioners would not be compellable witnesses before a court; that the commissioners would have authority to examine closed information banks; and that the privacy commissioner is released from also serving as a human rights commissioner. (My experience is that the two offices cannot be merged—the one demands that you work as an activist, and the other that you act impartially and quasi-judicially. I have experienced conflict in fulfilling my duties in the dual role.)

The commissioners' appointments would be with the approval of parliament, that is, with the agreement of all political parties. The term is for seven years during "good behavior." The commissioners would have the rank and powers of deputy ministers and would be paid a salary equal to that of a judge of the federal court.

Let us now turn to the most important topic: what does this all mean to ombudsmen?

ACCESS TO INFORMATION—THE ROLE OF THE OMBUDSMAN

Ombudsmen should be concerned with the development of information rights. Their offices may be affected in various ways:

1. Access to their files may be granted to the public.

2. Authority to gain access to information relevant to their investigations may be limited or expanded by new laws.

3. Their workload may increase.

4. They may become subject to control by a data commission.

5. They may be appointed to investigate complaints from individuals who allege they have not been accorded information rights to which they are entitled under law.

The Files

Legislation may grant access by clients or by the public in general to records held by ombudsmen. On the assumption that this could happen, they should consider what exemptions they believe necessary to protect the integrity of their investigations. For example, they may need protection from disclosure of investigative techniques or sources of information. They may wish to train their staff to change their report-writing to make the task of disclosure easier. Furthermore, the arrangements of reports may have to be changed to separate facts from conclusions, something persons without special training find

hard to do. They may also wish to stress that their staff should not make judgments which they do not have the professional credentials to reach. For example, if their investigators (not being psychiatrists) report that the "complainant suffered from delusions," they may want it changed to "the complainant insisted there were little electronic listening devices installed in his brain," so that the readers may draw their own conclusions. They may have to instruct staff to refrain from scribbling gratuitous comments on files. Finally, they may wish to insist that only one person or problem be dealt with in each document because this saves claiming exemptions to protect the privacy of the one who has not asked for the records. Finally, they may wish to establish a regular schedule for destruction of data held by the ombudsman's office.

Right of Access

Most ombudsmen have extensive powers to compel the production of evidence. If legislation is proposed in their jurisdiction, they may wish to make representations to ensure that their authority to obtain evidence not be diminished by any new laws. This could happen accidentally, or otherwise, depending on how exemptions are phrased in the law. Ombudsmen may be faced with legislation that provides them with access to exempted information for purposes of investigating complaints, but at the same time, prohibits them from disclosing the information. This is the case under Part IV of the Canadian Human Rights Act (and the new bill).

The privacy commissioner is now able to investigate, to ensure that nothing has been unlawfully withheld from a complainant in a totally closed information bank. However, if a complaint cannot be substantiated, the ombudsman is faced with having to report to the complainant: "You have been fairly dealt with, but I cannot tell you why. . . ." Nevertheless, the benefits of having access for investigatory purposes become obvious in cases where information that has been withheld is released (by the department) as a result of representations or recommendations from the ombudsman's office to a minister. If an information commissioner did not have access to closed banks, administrators could simply hide documents, or documents could be placed in the inaccessible information banks in error. Of course, it is possible that legislation might increase the ombudsman's ability to obtain information and thus make his or her lot a little easier.

Workload

It is also possible that the public's right of access to information will increase the ombudsman's workload. Matters that would have gone unnoticed without access to files will become the subject of complaints. Moreover, it may be useful for an ombudsman's preliminary assessment of a complaint about maladministration to have the client seek access to his or her records, and bring the information to the ombudsman office. This would be particularly useful in jurisdictions where the ombudsman is compelled to give notice before being entitled to commence even a preliminary inquiry into a complaint.

Data Commission

Some jurisdictions provide for the control of the collection, use, and transmission of data. The control is usually in the hands of independent data protection commissions. It is possible that legislation will require the ombudsman to obtain a license to collect data and that the Data Protection Commission may impose conditions for that purpose. For example, the Norwegian Data Act, the Law Concerning Registers of Persons (Personal Information Data Banks), provides *inter alia* that the Norwegian Data Commission give advice and guidance concerning privacy and security of data to those who intend to establish data banks containing personal information. The commission may "express itself both as a result of complaints and on its own initiative concerning the use made of information contained in such registers" (translation mine). Consent from the king, that is, the government, is required for the establishment of electronic records in all cases, and consent is required to collect, regardless of how stored,

1. information about race, political, or religious opinions;

2. information that a person has been suspected, charged, or convicted of an offense;

3. information about a person's health or use of intoxicants;

4. information about sexual relations;

5. other information about family and similar relationships concerning genealogical or civil status, financial status between spouses, or responsibility for dependents.

To fulfill its mandate, the Data Commission has authority to obtain the necessary information, has access to data banks, and can perform tests it deems necessary. The duty to keep data confidential, that is, privilege against disclosure, cannot be claimed against requests from the Data Commission.

The Generalist Ombudsman as Information Ombudsman

All ombudsmen are already involved in solving problems of access to information. If a case of maladministra-tion has occurred because information has not been given to an individual, the ombudsman concerned will surely speak up. There is no reason why the task of investigating complaints about access to information cannot be handled by existing ombudsmen in their respective jurisdictions. Indeed, the ombudsman of New Brunswick, Canada, Joseph Bérubé, has recently taken on such duties under a new law. Ombudsmen's offices are excellently equipped to handle information complaints. The administrators with whom the ombudsman would deal, in relation to information complaints, would probably be the same. The way in which complaints are handled would be similar, if not the same.

In addition to dealing with complaints concerning administrative actions related to the rights in Part IV, the privacy commissioner is charged with reviewing ministerial decisions to withhold information from applicants. The minister, no doubt, acts on the advice of administrators when claiming exemptions from disclosure, but if I find that an individual has not been accorded a *legal right* established by Part IV, I have a statutory duty to report to the minister and to the complainant. I may also include the finding in my annual report to parliament. Granting authority to an ombudsman to investigate ministerial decisions or failure to grant legal rights does not, in my opinion, create any difficulties for an ombudsman, but authorizing an ombudsman to *reverse* ministerial decisions might not be desirable. The traditional, almost unlimited, authority for ombudsmen to investigate and to act informally when investigating complaints has worked well, precisely because an ombudsman has neither judicial nor political authority. Giving decision-making authority to an ombudsman or an information commissioner may have popular appeal. Indeed, in Canada, ombudsmen are sometimes called toothless tigers, and movements are afoot from time to time to give them "more clout." I disagree with such suggestions.

If an ombudsman is given authority to reverse decisions, the ombudsman must develop judicial distance. The easy resolution of complaints through informal methods will become rare, if not impossible. Once an ombudsman has the attributes of a court, negotiations and mediation at lower administrative levels will become infrequent. Administrators may become defensive and may insist that cases be put in writing and be formally presented. There will be fewer opportunities to present the complainant's case orally in order to ascertain facts known only to administrators. Positions will become polarized too soon. Furthermore, if an ombudsman has decision-making power, there should be procedural (and therefore time-consuming) safeguards for public servants who may be adversely affected by the ombudsman's decisions.

My objection is not to judicial review but to clothing

the ombudsman with judicial powers. Indeed, if the final decision on access is to rest with the courts, I would favor granting authority to the information commissioner to refer issues to the court on behalf of a complainant, so that important issues may be finally reviewed by the courts, even if the complainant cannot afford a lawyer.

As previously mentioned, the legislation proposed to parliament in 1980 provided for appeal to the courts *after* an individual has sought the assistance of the information commissioner or the privacy commissioner, and the commissioners as well as complainants would have the right to take cases to court. The cases that do go to court will eventually provide a useful set of precedents to assist in the informal solution of complaints. In my opinion, only 5 percent of the cases I have dealt with would warrant examination by lawyers and the courts.

CONCLUSION

Most people are in favor of freedom of information and personal information rights until they realize that the principles may apply to information they prepared. It takes time to get used to a complete reversal of principles. It also takes time and effort to learn to write objective reports. People are anxious because information that was prepared or collected long before information rights were incorporated in law may become available. Information laws have a retroactive effect because it is difficult to make the date of proclamation of the law the cutoff point. If the information collected before that date is still available on file, it is subject to disclosure.

It was interesting to discover that police forces and the military in Canada adjusted more quickly to the new laws than did other departments. I should add that our penal institutions experienced the same administrative nightmare as a result of our privacy laws as they did in the United States. Prisoners' requests for access have not been fulfilled because, as the department keeps telling them, "the volume of requests exceeds the capacity to respond."

New rights mean new problems. It is obvious that many new challenges for ombudsmen, for lawyers, managers and employees, businesses and their customers, will have to be faced as a result of legislation of information rights. I think there is no turning back. I am in favor of as much disclosure of information as possible. But I also believe in balancing disclosure with protection of the privacy of others and with the general public interest and the safety of society as a whole.

CHAPTER 9

THE OMBUDSMAN IN HEALTH CARE INSTITUTIONS IN THE UNITED STATES

MILDRED MAILICK, School of Social Work, Hunter College

Access to human, personalized, and comprehensive health care is an issue of increasing concern in society. Beginning with the 1950s, the health care system has undergone a period of rapid change. Highly sophisticated medical research and rapid technological advances have altered diagnostic processes and the types of treatment provided to patients. The medical encounter has become less personal. In some situations, it is marked by the use of elaborate equipment in the hands of highly skilled and specialized technicians who are accountable to physicians or hospitals rather than to patients. In other cases, nursing and custodial care are provided away from home in institutional settings often by unskilled, unlicensed personnel who respond only in a limited way to the personal needs of the individual patient. In both situations, a sense of mutual alienation affects the patient and the providers of care.

Acute care hospitals reflect many of these problems. In recent years, they have grown larger and infinitely more complex. While patients eagerly seek the capabilities and the assembled expertise concentrated in the hospital, they often experience the hospital as a confusing and dehumanizing labyrinth. In the outpatient care facilities (clinics and emergency rooms), patients may lack the information and skills necessary to deal successfully with the system in order to locate and receive indispensable services. In addition, hospital functionaries, compartmentalized into relatively isolated specialized services, may themselves have inadequate capacities to communicate, coordinate, and negotiate across departmental and specialty lines.

Hospitalized patients are acutely aware of their dependency on health care personnel. They perceive them, either correctly or not, as having the power to provide or withhold services crucial to their personal and survival needs. They often may feel vulnerable because of acute physical discomfort precisely at a time when they are stripped of their usual social anchorings. They may lack cues so as to be able to assess the reciprocal rights and expectations that are appropriate to the hospital setting. The short-term nature of the hospital stay and the patient's urgent wish for immediate medical care ordinarily help a good many to tolerate a temporary loss of a sense of identity and control, although not without some emotional pain.

In long-term care institutions (nursing homes, skilled nursing, and intermediate care facilities), the preemption of control of patients by the institution can be much more pervasive. Institutional personnel have almost complete jurisdiction over the quality of life of physically and/or mentally frail individuals, and in some cases such control extends to survival itself. Many patients, especially the elderly, must live out their lives in these "total" institutions. The frequent isolation of patients from friends and relatives adds feelings of powerlessness and despair.

In this medical context, who speaks for the patient? In the absence of a market mechanism, there is obviously the need for some kind of corrective procedure that is available to patients and that offers a countervailing force to the power of the providers of care. Some mechanisms are already in place, although they do not necessarily always work effectively.

121

Traditionally, patients, as other citizens, have recourse to the courts to obtain redress for wrongdoing. The dramatic rise in medical malpractice suits attests to the increased use of this mechanism in cases of alleged medical mismanagement, especially where irreversible damage has occurred. Access to legal redress, however, is more effective for some groups of patients than others. The poor, members of minority groups, and those in long-term care facilities have less access to the remedies provided by the courts. Relatively few members of these groups find their way to legal advisers because of barriers of culture, language, or information. Moreover, resorting to legal reparation is often less than fully effective when the patient claims damage because of abuses in the quality of life or care rather than because of medical wrongdoing. Complaints such as punishment of the patient, overmedication, physical abuse, or unprofessional behavior on the part of the institutional staff are difficult to define in exact terms and equally difficult to document. Attorneys may be reluctant to bring these cases to trial except when they involve extreme situations.

Furthermore, legal suits often take many years to settle. For nursing home patients, this presents a special problem. The plaintiffs may die before action is taken. Or, if they survive, they may potentially be placed in considerable jeopardy. The accused may continue to have tremendous power over the accuser unless the patient can be moved to a new facility for protection. This is often physically dangerous for the frail or elderly and, indeed, may be totally unrealistic when no adequate alternative facility is available.

Society recognizes that the patient is not adequately protected by the courts alone. Government tries to use its power to regulate, inspect, audit, and license. In addition, quasi-governmental organizations are invested with power to certify or accredit. Most of these types of external control are directed at monitoring the physical plant and the conditions for proper treatment in the institution as well as the qualifications of the providers of service. However, these agencies exercise only periodic control over the institution. Few manage to assess the actual care and treatment of patients.

Most hospitals maintain a series of self-regulating internal mechanisms of control alongside of those imposed from the outside. Some control mechanisms such as the professional standards review organizations are necessary in order to qualify for government grants and reimbursements. Other controls, such as medical audits and tissue committees, help the institution to identify practices that may fall below established standards of performance. Nursing homes have fewer such mechanisms, although some are beginning to recognize that self-regulation may be wise in order to stave off the imposition of further external controls.

Internal mechanisms of control essentially set standards for practice and evaluate medical decision-making and skill. As in the case of legal action, they are important, but they have limitations as an effective recourse for the patient. They are retrospective in approach, evaluating individual cases in order to accumulate data to improve future practice. They cannot be activated by or on behalf of the individual patient who currently may be receiving poor treatment, nor are the deliberations of the committee available for the patient's use.

Thus, while the courts, government regulation and inspection, and mechanisms of internal control provide tools for periodic assessment, they do not effectively respond to the complaints of individuals. Ombudsman-like mechanisms have been developed that do respond to patient complaints, although, like the health care field itself, they tend to be fragmented, lack comprehensive scope, and are unevenly administered. They differ from the classical model of the ombudsman, but they do have certain similarities as well. They possess in common the characteristic of responding to the complaints of patients and of attempting to redress individual grievances. They differ in the degree of autonomy they possess, the methods they use, the population groups they serve, and their level of effectiveness. While ombudsman programs are found in a variety of health settings, they most commonly serve two groups of patients at high risk: those in nursing homes and in acute general hospitals.

OMBUDSMAN PROGRAMS FOR LONG-TERM CARE POPULATIONS

The plight of the nursing home patient reached national attention during the middle 1970s. Congressional hearings and documented reports of substandard care and abuse shocked the public and created enormous pressure for the passage of new legislation to protect the rights of the frail and elderly in long-term care institutions. However, developing an effective legislative program to meet this group's needs is an inherently difficult undertaking. First, the patient population is physically ill, debilitated, and sometimes confused. They make poor complainants and even poorer spokespersons on their own behalf. Many of their complaints, while possibly or probably justified, cannot be documented; others have little basis in fact but may refer to problems that the patient may have difficulty in articulating. Often, those receiving complaints may respond to the mental state of the patient rather than judging the actual validity of the complaint. Second, the patient population is reluctant to complain for fear of possible retaliation by the staff in the form of inattention to needs, harassment, or abuse. This fear permeates all medical institutions, but is most pervasive in long-term care facilities. It may deter complaints even in the most extreme situations. Third, the patient population is often isolated from the outside world with few visitors whom they trust to advocate on their behalf. Fourth, the patient population may be unaware of their rights and what they can expect and demand from the institution and its staff. The Patient's Bill of Rights, which many states require to be posted in nursing homes, defines rights, but education is needed for the document to be effectively interpreted to the patient.

With all of these problems, ombudsman programs do provide one avenue for the resolution of individual or collective complaints of this population group. The ombudsman acts as a liaison, listening to the problems of the patients and interceding for them with the nursing home administrators and with public agencies. The ombudsman provides contact for the isolated patient, facilitates communication with the functionaries of the institution, and provides information to the patient about his rights.[1]

Enabling Legislation

In 1972, the Health Services and Mental Health Administration of the Department of Health, Education, and Welfare awarded contracts to four states and one national organization to develop model nursing home ombudsman programs.[2] A year later, the program was turned over to the Administration on Aging (AoA), and in 1975 all states were offered grants to develop similar programs. However, the funding was significantly lower than what had been provided to the model programs and was insufficient to establish workable programs without considerable fiscal participation of the states themselves. The Comprehensive Older Americans Act Amendments passed in 1978 defined the functions and responsibilities of the ombudsman and made it obligatory that each state submit a plan for the establishment of a long-term care ombudsman program.[3] The law provided that each state could operate the program itself or contract with an appropriate public or nonprofit agency that was not responsible for licensing or otherwise associated with long-term care facilities. The responsibilities of the program were to investigate complaints of older individuals about administrative action adversely affecting their health, safety, and welfare; to monitor the development of legislation, regulations, and policies in relation to long-term care facilities; to provide information to public agencies about older residents of long-term facilities; and to provide and promote organizations and volunteers participating in the ombudsman program.[4] Each state was free within the guidelines of the law to develop its own program, and all fifty states have submitted plans to the AoA. Variation in the programs centers on key issues of auspice, access, statutory authority, scope, and staffing patterns.

The classical ombudsman is protected from bureaucrat-

ic pressures through sponsorship by an executive, an organization, or a legislative body that is outside the system he investigates. The effectiveness of his office is dependent upon his independence and capacity to be objective. Some states have lodged their ombudsman programs in the Office of Aging and some in the Department of Health; others are located outside of the regular department and report directly to the governor of the state. A few states contract out their programs to voluntary agencies or community groups. As might be expected, each arrangement has both values and drawbacks. Greater independence is achieved by locating the program under the auspice of a community-based agency, but this is countered by increased problems of communication and cooperation with public agencies. Making the ombudsman accountable to the governor ensures independence and prestige and is closest to the traditional ombudsman concept. Least desirable is lodging the program in either the Department of Aging or Health, where it can become dominated by and confused with the department's regulatory and inspection activities or neglected in favor of other functions.

Access and Statutory Authority

Access is another key issue in which the programs in the various states differ. The law requires that each state "establish procedures for appropriate access . . . to long-term care facilities and patient records,"[5] but does not specify what is meant by the term "appropriate." A range of interpretations has been developed. In some states such as New Jersey, the ombudsman has legal access to all facilities and records. In others, such as New York, access is not guaranteed, and the ombudsman must gain the agreement of the management of the facility in order to enter. Incentive to allow access is based upon the institution's fear of adverse publicity.[6] However, when access is dependent upon the cooperation of the institution, it tends to make the ombudsman program less effective. Not only can the ombudsman be barred from the facilities that have the worst practices, but even if access is gained, the ombudsman tends to remain only as long as he maintains the good-will of the administration. This leads to a lessening of ability to be a truly independent critic of the nursing home.

Access to patient records is an unresolved issue in a number of states. The 1978 amendments require "appropriate access" to the resident's records, again leaving in doubt the exact meaning of the term.[7] Some states have interpreted it to allow the ombudsman to review patient records without restriction. Others require the written consent of the patient before giving the ombudsman permission to read records. While the intent of the latter interpretation is to safeguard the privacy of the patient, its effect is to disclose to the staff of the institution that the patient has made a complaint to the ombudsman. This effect conflicts with the intention of the law, which clearly aims to protect the patient's anonymity.[8]

Questions about statutory authority follow similar patterns. The traditional ombudsman has no powers of enforcement and depends upon the influence of his office to gain resolution of problems. In most states, the ombudsman has no statutory authority or right to prosecute. In a few, he has subpoena power and can initiate suits.[9]

Scope

Scope is a third issue about which there is variability in state programs. The 1978 amendments broadened the definition of long-term care facilities to include any skilled or intermediate care institution, nursing home, or other adult care home. However, because of insufficient funding, many programs extend their services only to nursing homes. Each state must allocate 1 percent of its AoA federal allocation, or $20,000 per year (whichever is greater), to the ombudsman program.[10] Some states have allocated substantial additional funds to the ombudsman program, but many make only minimal supplementary allocations.

Individual programs have responded to budgetary restrictions by focusing their efforts on a selected number of nursing homes, restricting the geographic area in which they work intensively, or constricting the categories of complaints to which they will respond. Each state program makes some choices, recognizing that within the confines of a limited budget the greater the scope, the less the intensity of the effort in each facility.

Staffing

The 1978 amendments strongly support the training and utilization of volunteers and the development of citizens' organizations as part of the ombudsman program.[11] While variation exists in staffing patterns as to the balance between paid and volunteer workers, most programs that depend on continual monitoring of nursing homes require a large cadre of volunteers. The volunteer ombudsman is assigned to a specific nursing home in order to identify problems, attempt to resolve them, and prevent them from reappearing. Experience suggests that nursing home patients are extremely fearful and need to get to trust the ombudsman before being willing to ask questions or activate complaints. The volunteer ombudsman gains visibility, builds relationships with the patients, and establishes channels of communication with the staff. The ongoing presence of the ombudsman in the nursing home facilitates the complaint process. The pa-

tient's anonymity is shielded by the ombudsman who may talk to a dozen patients on any one visit. Telephone calls and letters of complaint that may be intercepted are thus avoided. Many patients who are too debilitated or handicapped to activate their own complaints can eventually express their dissatisfaction to someone whom they have grown to trust. The fact that the volunteer ombudsman visits regularly reduces the threat of retaliation, although it does not eliminate it.

There are advantages and disadvantages to the use of volunteers. They expand the scope of the ombudsman program and forge a link between the residents and the community. However, volunteers require constant recruitment and training, they vary in their ability to judge quality of care, and they may have insufficient skills in investigating complaints and in keeping appropriate records. While many of the patients' complaints do not need a high level of expertise to resolve, some require greater resourcefulness and skill. Some programs train their volunteers to identify those types of situations that they are unable to handle and turn them over to a professional worker.

Programs that depend more heavily on paid professional workers cannot provide the intensive observation of the volunteers. They usually encourage complaints by means of well-organized educational campaigns and the use of twenty-four hour a day "hot lines." This type of program requires a greater amount of capacity and initiative on the part of the patient or family and offers less protection to the complainant. In general, the complaints to the programs using hot lines and paid ombudsmen tend to be concerned with more serious abuses, whether by virtue of the fact that the patients are less likely to be motivated to call them with minor complaints or whether, as professionals, they are more skillful in uncovering serious abuse and mistreatment.

Types of Complaints

Complaints, regardless of the type of program, tend to overlap, but they generally fall into three categories: quality of life, quality of care, and infringement of rights. Quality of life complaints center around problems in the life space of the patient which, while not constituting violation of statutory regulations, may be troublesome or uncomfortable. These would include loss of clothing, inadequate laundry facilities, stolen property, lack of appropriate recreation, rudeness of the staff, and so on. Quality of care complaints have to do with inadequate medical treatment or nursing care, overmedication, the inappropriate use of physical or chemical restraints, or unsuitable diet. Infringement of rights complaints include violations of the right of patients to have their beds retained for them during hospitalizations, to have an accounting of their monies on a regular basis, to have reasonable visiting hours, and to have the institution maintain standards set by the health and sanitary codes. The Patient's Bill of Rights codifies some of these rights and encourages their enforcement.

Complaints reach the ombudsman in one of several ways. In programs where a volunteer ombudsman is assigned to a particular facility, he usually visits several times a week and receives complaints directly from patients or from their families. The volunteer ombudsman can also pursue independent observations of conditions or practices in the institution which he perceives as creating problems. Staff members will sometimes enlist the aid of the ombudsman in obtaining certain benefits for a patient or in changing some aspect of the patient's situation. When the program depends upon paid workers and complaints are received by "hot line" or letter, the complaints are logged and are responded to within a set period of time, usually forty-eight hours. Here the ombudsman must negotiate entry into the facility, investigate the problem, and attempt to resolve it.

The guiding principles in resolving the problems are to solve the problems at the lowest level of authority possible; to protect the complainant from possible retaliation; to substantiate the complaint if possible, but not to discount those that cannot be proved; and to refer to the appropriate agency those situations where possible legal action should be taken. Many of the quality of life problems are resolved fairly easily, but others need continuing monitoring and negotiation. Some quality of care problems require long and complicated negotiations in which the interest of the administrator, the staff member, the union, and the patient are all represented.[12]

Evaluation

It is difficult to generalize about the success of the nursing home ombudsman programs in the United States since each state program differs in some dimensions from others. Some critics contend that ombudsman programs are successful only in those situations where the officials being monitored are already responsive to complaints. However, where there is injustice or contempt for patients and their rights, a more powerful corrective mechanism is needed.[13] Except in those few states where access to the facility is mandated, ombudsmen are probably most effective in better functioning nursing homes. They probably do not even gain admittance to those institutions where the administrators and staff are most avaricious and malevolent and where the grossest violations of patients' rights and quality of care are likely to exist. In these cases, redress of grievance requires mechanisms with

more statutory clout. Generally, it is clear that ombudsman programs are most useful and effective when they deal with less severe complaints. In addition, their very existence acts as a deterrent to some abuses, encourages the aggregation of data about conditions in long-term care facilities, and, as a result, has some effect on legislative reform. Alone, ombudsman programs are insufficient, but joined as they are in many states by other health agencies such as health consumer organizations, groups of relatives of institutionalized patients, residents' councils, state prosecutors, and regulatory agencies, a considerable degree of surveillance and control is achieved. However, the piecemeal nature of these overseeing groups allows for fragmented control, with the likelihood that the most vulnerable groups of patients are underserved.

PATIENT REPRESENTATIVES IN ACUTE, SHORT-TERM HOSPITALS

Hospital services represent the largest single category in the cost of health care in the United States, and each year, more than one out of every ten persons enters a hospital as an inpatient.[14] The patients using the services of the hospital are markedly different from those who use nursing homes. They are younger, and while perhaps suffering from a variety of chronic illnesses, they are admitted for an acute problem for which treatment is expected to have some impact. They stay in the hospital for a relatively short period of time, on an average of 7.6 days per admission.[15] While in the hospital, they are dependent on the staff for meeting their personal and survival needs, but their access to the outside world and their short stay tend to make them less vulnerable than nursing home patients. In spite of this difference, research suggests that patients in short-term hospitals also fear retaliation. In one study, two-thirds of the patients refrained from expressing their needs or criticisms to physicians and nurses for fear of being considered troublemakers. Many felt they needed to make few demands of them in order to ensure they would get a response in an emergency. They were less reticent, however, in talking about their complaints to those who had no direct care responsibilities.[16]

In addition to a sense of powerlessness and jeopardy, the patient has a number of other problems in dealing with the hospital. The size and complexity of the modern hospital require that the patient cope with a large number of service components that are not necessarily well coordinated. More than fifty separate occupations carry out their duties within the hospital setting.[17] The patient may be perplexed about what each can be expected to do. In teaching hospitals, he must, in addition, respond to a confusing number and variety of house staff, interns, medical students, and other students. While most hospitals require that name tags be worn by personnel as identification, some patients do not understand the purposes that each has, and they feel bombarded by the number of people who enter their room asking the same questions and making similar examinations. Thus, the patient needs someone with knowledge of the hospital system to provide him with information when he needs it, to listen to his complaints, and, if necessary, to intercede for him in seeking resolutions to problems.

Many hospitals have established patient representative programs and have invested in them responsibility to meet these needs. In simplest form, patient representatives have been described as "persons who serve as liaison between patients and the hospital." Indeed, this is how they were defined in a survey conducted by the American Hospital Association in the early 1970s.[18] A more specific definition was developed by the Society of Patient Representatives which, with minor revisions, still serves as a working description.

The patient representative's primary assignment is to serve as the liaison between patients and the institution as a whole and between the institution and the community it serves. They provide a specific channel through which patients can seek solutions to problems, concerns and unmet needs.

As the patient's advocate they enable patients and families to obtain solutions to problems by acting in their behalf with administration or any department or service, coordinating among departments if necessary and recommending alternative policies and procedures in order to improve service to patients.
As the institution's direct representative, they interpret its philosophy, policies, procedures and services to patients, their families and visitors.[19]

While sometimes called ombudsmen, patient representatives differ in significant ways. Most important, the ombudsmen traditionally are based outside of the system in which they intercede, acting as a countervailing force to institutional power. The patient representative is an employee of the hospital, often reporting to the chief executive officer and, therefore, is not an independent critic. A closer analogy to the patient representative would be a company union which, while providing certain benefits to its members, is essentially an instrument of management. However, if the hospital is viewed as a microcosm of the larger society, the role of the patient representative is similar to that of the ombudsman. He is highly visible and accessible to the patients, his mandate is limited to problems arising out of the bureaucratic workings of the hospital system, he investigates problems based on patient complaints, and he derives most of his effectiveness from his capacity to move freely about the

hospital, using his position of prestige and his neutrality within the system to make recommendations. He usually has no power to manage or coerce changes. In effect, the hospital has institutionalized the role of an ombudsman but has placed constraints on the scope of his actions. He is allowed to be an independent critic, but only as long as he does not disrupt the system.

Functions of Patient Representatives

The patient representatives serve a variety of the hospital's needs. They provide a patient-based source of information about patient care problems which supplements more standard data normally received from departmental administrators. They may point to problems of which the hospital staff are unaware or for which institutional bias creates blind spots. Because they are usually located outside of the regular departmental hierarchy, they have the advantage of a somewhat more objective view of the care given to patients, and therefore can sometimes encourage a new look at problems in the hospital. They seldom have sole responsibility for major system change, but they can act as a catalyst when other conditions in the hospital are favorable.

Patient representatives also mediate between the patient and the institution. They encourage compliance by informing the patient of the hospital's rules and expectations and conversely by acquainting him with his rights within the institution. The patient's complaints are promptly investigated, resolved when possible, and, when not, explanations are given. When a patient suffers damage or major inconvenience, the patient representative may have the power to cancel bills, order extra nurses, or offer other conciliatory measures. Most administrators hope that the reduction in conflict accomplished by these actions diminishes the patient's propensity to sue the hospital.[20]

While these functions of the patient representative program are useful to the hospital, they do not preclude the provision of service to patients. Almost all patient representative programs are capable of solving lower level systems problems that make up the bulk of patient complaints. In most cases, the rules are "bent" to meet the patient's need without changing the system. The more effective programs also provide feedback about the complaints which then is used in administrative decision-making. The advantage of hospital-based patient representatives as opposed to outside critics is that they have greater knowledge of the hospital's services and better capacity to use both formal and informal channels to resolve problems for the patient. The bulk of the complaints that are received by the patient representative are better handled in this way. However, the very presence of this corrective mechanism within the hospital may serve to discourage more serious complaints by redefining them in more innocuous terms or by keeping them from being articulated. Certainly, when a patient's complaint is against the hospital's interest, he is well advised to seek legal assistance and advocacy from outside the hospital.

Historical Development and Current Characteristics

A few patient representative programs began as early as the 1950s under titles such as ombudsman, patient care coordinator, patient advocate, or patient service coordinator. Many programs were short-lived and succumbed to budget cuts. In the early stages, individual patient representatives functioned in the same geographical areas, unaware of each other's existence. Beginning in the early 1970s, stories about their activities started to appear in local newspapers.[21] The first article written for a professional journal appeared in 1969, and in the early 1970s there was a burgeoning of reports in nursing, social work, and hospital administration journals.[22] A Society of Patient Representatives was formed and affiliated with the American Hospital Association in 1971. Membership in the society rose from ninety-three in 1971 to over eight hundred in eight years. A nationwide survey of patient representative programs conducted in 1976 showed that over 80 percent of the patient representative programs were established after 1970.[23] Within a ten-year period, they have experienced a phenomenal rate of growth, especially in view of the cost containment measures that most hospitals have instituted. They are now found in one out of every four hospitals.

The nationwide survey also revealed that patient representative programs were most likely to be located in large, voluntary, urban teaching hospitals. Most of them (almost three-fourths) are small programs, employing two or fewer persons. One-third use volunteers, usually to augment the activities of a paid worker. While there are some common characteristics and functions such as responding to complaints and giving information, the programs seem to fall into three categories. The *grievance* programs are the largest group and the type that most closely resembles ombudsman. Their main function is to respond to complaints about quality of life and quality of care, investigate and resolve systems problems, channel data about patient care and system dysfunction to hospital administrators, and monitor potential malpractice cases. The *hospitality* programs respond principally to quality of life complaints, relate mostly to problems about the personal comfort of the patient (food and housekeeping), and attend to other amenities that are so often overlooked in hospitals. *Personal service* programs provide counseling services to

the patient helping to make discharge plans and referrals. The patient representatives, as a group, are as diverse as the programs in which they work. Eighty percent are women, and, according to the 1976 survey, only 43 percent have a baccalaureate or higher degree. No educational requirements have been established for the job.[24]

In a study in the New York area of seven hospitals with patient representative programs, there was considerable variation in the way they were established, their auspice, their characteristic functions, and their effectiveness. Six of the seven programs were financed by hospital funds and one by a private foundation. Three of the seven were grievance programs, although two used volunteers to augment the paid staff and to perform some hospitality functions. Three were hospitality programs, using volunteers as their main source of personnel. A fourth functioned only in the emergency room of the hospital performing hospitality functions. The program was financed by an outside foundation, had difficulty gaining access to the hospital staff, and without the support of the administrator of the hospital it had little impact. Those programs with strong support from the hospital's administrators were generally more effective both in resolving the problems of the patients and in acting as critics of the system. Two of the patient representatives had power invested in their office. The other five derived their power from the support of the administrators or from the medical board. All of the programs initially encountered opposition from the lower echelons of the hospital staff which gradually diminished as it became clear that the patient representative would not or could not jeopardize the system or disrupt the major processes of the hospital.[25]

Evaluation

Criticisms of patient representative programs have been raised on a number of issues. First, it is suggested that patient representatives frequently respond only to minor problems and that good patient relations are not significantly affected by their resolution, nor are they effective in uncovering major problems or making system changes.[26] A second criticism is that patient representatives help to keep a dysfunctional system operating by "patching up" cracks in the organization. Many consider it to be a "bandaid" approach, one that does not deal with causes of problems or real system change. Third, as an employee of the hospital with responsibility to central administration, the patient representative can hardly be a true ombudsman, an independent critic of the hospital, or an unequivocal advocate of the patient's interests.

It is clear that a community-based health ombudsman program for patients in short-term hospitals is necessary in order to augment the hospital-based patient representative programs. Great Britain has such a system, founded in 1973. It protects citizens in a broad range of health matters, monitors administrative procedures of the National Health Service, and responds to quality of care complaints in both short-term and long-term institutions.[27]

While there are a number of community-based health advocacy groups in the United States, they are more concerned with affecting public policy than with advocating for individual patient complaints. In addition, most of these organizations are concerned with a single patient group, such as those suffering from diabetes or kidney disease, and do not serve the general public or take a special interest in the hospital. They have no statutory authority or right of access to institutions. What is needed is an extension of the nursing home ombudsman program to cover all health care institutions and all age groups. Such a comprehensive program would offer a partial answer to the question of who speaks for the patient.

NOTES

1. Ellen Sullivan, "Corrective Mechanisms for Upgrading Care in Institutions for Aged" (New York: Center for Policy Research, 1979, unpublished study).

2. M. Hochbaum and F. Galkin, *Patients and Their Complaints* (New York: American Jewish Congress and Community Action and Resources for the Elderly, 1977), p. 6.

3. The Older Americans Act, P.L. 89–73, 42 U.S.C. SS 3001 et seq. 1965; amended 1978, P.L. 95–478.

4. #307 (a) (12) (A) (i) (v).

5. #307 (a) (12) (B).

6. Sullivan, "Corrective Mechanisms."

7. #1321.43 (d) (2).

8. *National Senior Citizens Law Center Washington Weekly* 5, No. 35 (September 7, 1979):4.

9. Sullivan, "Corrective Mechanisms."

10. Ibid.

11. #307 (a) (12) (A) (iv).

12. Sullivan, "Corrective Mechanisms."

13. Richard Cloward and Richard Elman, "Poverty, Injustice and the Welfare State, Part 1, An Ombudsman for the Poor," *The Nation* 202 (February 28, 1966):230–35.

14. U.S. Department of Health, Education, and Welfare, Public Health Service, *The Nation's Use of Health Resources*, Publication No. (PHS) 80–1240 (Washington, D.C.: U.S. Government Printing Office, 1979), p. 52.

15. Ibid., p. 52.

16. D. L. Tagliacozzo and H. O. Mauksch, "The Patient's View of the Patient's Role," in E. G. Jaco, ed., *Patients, Physicians and Illness,* 2d ed. (New York: Free Press, 1972), pp. 162–75.

17. John Knowles, "The Hospital," in *Life and Death and Medicine,* A Scientific American Book (San Francisco: W. H. Freeman and Company, 1973), p. 94.

18. American Hospital Association, "Special Survey on Selected Hospital Topics" (1974, unpublished).

19. Society of Patient Representatives, "A Descriptive Definition" (Chicago: n.d., unpublished).

20. Alexandra Gekas, "Good Patient Relations Can Help Abate Potential Risk Situations," *Hospitals, J.A.H.A.* 52 (November 1, 1978):86.

21. S. J. Harris, "Humanizing the Hospitals," *Chicago Daily News,* November 6, 1973; A. State, "Sinai Hospital Smooths the Way for Patients," *The Detroit Jewish News,* August 10, 1973; J. Pesco, "Patient's Friend," *McCalls,* February 1973; "The Patient's Friend," *Time Magazine,* August 30, 1971.

22. Ruth Ravich and Helen Rehr, "Ombudsman: A New Concept in Voluntary Hospitals," in *Human Services and Social Work Responsibility* (New York: National Association of Social Workers, 1968), pp. 303–10; J. Stolkanske, "Is a Patient Counselor Worth the Investment?" *Group Practice* 20 (June/July 1971):200–23; Ruth Ravich, Helen Rehr, and Charles Goodrich, "Hospital Ombudsman Smooths the Flow of Services and Communication," *Hospitals* 43 (March 1969):56–60; Sister Mary Modesta, "Patient Relations Representative Bridges the Gap," *Hospital Progress* 51 (September 1970):30–32; G. Annas and J. Healy, "The Patient Rights Advocate," *Journal of Nursing Administration* 4 (May/June 1974).

23. Mildred D. Mailick, "Models of Patient Representative Programs," in M. Mailick and H. Rehr, eds., *In the Patient's Interest: Access to Hospital Care* (New York: Prodist, in press).

24. Ibid.

25. Mildred D. Mailick, "Professionals View Patient Representatives," in Mailick and Rehr, eds., *In the Patient's Interest.*

26. Barbara Rubin, "Medical Malpractice Suits Can be Avoided," *Hospitals, J.A.H.A.* 52 (March 16, 1978):58.

27. Margaret Stacey, "Consumer Complaint Procedures in the British National Health Service," *Social Science and Medicine* 8 (1974):429–39.

BIBLIOGRAPHY

Anderson, S.V. "Developing the Ombudsman's Role in Health Care Services." *Public Affairs Report* 15, No. 6 (1974) (Bulletin of the Institute of Governmental Studies, University of California, Berkeley), 6 pp.

———. "The Ombud and Health Services." *Journal of Health and Human Resources Administration* 2, No. 1 (August 1979): 88–107.

Stacey, F. A. "The Machinery for Complaints in the National Health Service." *Public Administration* 43 (Spring 1965):59–70.

CHAPTER 10

THE MILITARY OMBUDSMAN IN ISRAEL

HAIM LASKOV, Soldiers' Complaints Commissioner

Adult Israelis, with few exceptions, serve in the Israeli Defense Forces (IDF) for an appreciable period of their working lives, first in compulsory national service, then in the reserves, and finally in the Home Guard. They can be called at any time to spend varying periods away from home subject to military discipline. They learn to switch roles quickly and smoothly. Compared with other defense forces, their conditions of service are austere and the compensation meagre. Yet, they serve willingly and with good heart. They act like a citizens' army, bringing to their military service much the same attitudes and behavior of their civilian life. They are unimpressed with rank, uniforms, and medals. They know their rights and jealously guard them. Their officers, too, have little time or patience for the ceremonial and care much for their charges. They realize that in order to succeed the military organization must be based on human values no less than on military ones. Although there are instances of maladministration, they are exceptional. More important, the military machine is prepared to right wrong when such is shown. Deficiencies cannot be avoided, but IDF officers and ranks are ready to improve things where they can.

THE SOLDIERS' COMPLAINTS COMMISSIONER

Ever since the establishment of the IDF, soldiers have been free to lodge complaints against fellow soldiers or their superiors, through the proper channels of command. Soldiers are also allowed to complain directly to the military advocate general, to the military advocate of the air force, navy, and of the commands and, with regard to the criminal offenses, to the Military Police Investigation De-

partment. These procedures of submitting complaints are still open to soldiers and have in no way been affected by legislation regarding complaints.

In the course of the deliberations that took place in 1970 in the Knesset (Israeli Parliament) prior to the establishment of the Office of the Commissioner for Complaints from the Public, there arose the question of dealing with soldiers' complaints relating to the rules of the service and the conditions of the service or discipline. It was agreed that, in addition to the existing military routine orders regarding complaints, there was a case for establishing a statutory procedure for handling complaints but not necessarily by the commissioner for complaints from the public. It was considered undesirable that complaints from the military should be examined and decided upon by a civilian body, which was unacquainted with military procedure, not keenly aware of military administration order and discipline, and not acting within the military organization. On the other hand, the minister of defense felt that an office of a Soldiers' Complaints Commissioner (SCC) within the military organization should not be part of the military establishment and that it should be entirely independent of the military chain of command. The proposal to unite the office of the SSC with that of the military advocate general was therefore rejected, and it was decided to create a separate office.

The government proposed to the Knesset that the Military Justice Law should be amended with the addition of a new part (Part 11) which would detail the powers of a military ombudsman and the right of soldiers and their close relatives to complain to the ombudsman. Its proposal was tabled on July 14, 1972, and debated three days later. It was approved in principle and submitted to the

Foreign Affairs and Security Committee of the Knesset for detailed examination and final drafting. The law was finally approved and published on August 1, 1972, and came into force on November 1, 1972. On August 13, 1972, General Haim Laskov, one of the former chiefs of staff of the Israeli Defense Forces, was nominated as the first soldiers' complaints commissioner.

The Knesset signified its regard for the SCC not only by the top priority it gave to the passage of the law establishing the office, but much more significantly by the unanimous support which the spokesmen of all parties gave to the law. Each one of them welcomed the proposed law, hailing it as an important step in safeguarding the rights of the soldiers without infringing on the efficiency of military command and discipline. It was decided that the SCC should be nominated by the minister of defense to underline the necessity of giving the post to a person well versed in military matters and procedure and having extensive personal command experience. It was stressed that only such a person could win the confidence of the military authorities and soldiers alike, knowing him to be well qualified to examine complaints, to decide impartially on them, and at the same time safeguarding morale and good discipline. On the other hand, in order to emphasize the function of the SCC as safeguarder of the civil rights of the soldiers, the minister of defense was required by the law to consult the minister of justice, before nominating the SCC. Furthermore, in order to retain parliamentary control, the nomination of the SCC was made subject to the approval of the Foreign Affairs and Security Committee of the Knesset. The tenure of office was decided to be five years, with full power to renominate the incumbent. It was also decided that the SCC should report annually and whenever he believed necessary directly to the minister of defense and to the Knesset committee.

The functions of the SCC were aptly described by the minister of defense in the Knesset debate:

This proposal has been drafted in order to give remedy to soldiers in active service, when they think, as individuals, that justice has not been done to them. Not that the general orders are wrong, not that the policy is wrong, not that the Israeli Defense Forces are too tough, but when the individual, a certain soldier, thinks that he does not get his full rights, that he is wronged within the existing rules, and he complains about it.

This view, which was upheld by the majority of the Knesset, limits the powers of the SCC to the function of treating individual complaints, but it also gives the SCC full authority to see to it that within the scope of existing orders and policies, full justice is done to the individual as a free citizen in a democratic army, limited only by the demands of military efficiency and discipline. It was fully recognized that, by fulfilling this function, the SCC aids the individual soldier, upholding his rights and instructing him in his duties, if it appears that his complaint is unfounded. At the same time, the SCC enforces good order, military discipline, and military efficiency by bringing to the attention of the military authorities infringements of orders, wrongs done to soldiers, and other improper conduct, and by advising them how, in his opinion, these deficiencies may be corrected. But all this is without power to interfere and order such correction directly, for these powers remain in the hands of the military authorities, although it is clear that in practice, the SCC's recommendation is disregarded only rarely and in exceptional cases.

It was in order to give force to this definition of the SCC's scope of activity that the Knesset decided not to accord the SCC powers to initiate examinations without having received a written complaint. For the same reason, the SCC was not empowered to investigate anonymous complaints. Nor was he authorized to examine complaints addressed to other authorities, for it was felt that the SCC's scope of activity should be limited to examining those complaints that soldiers or their near relatives addressed to him directly. On the other hand, the Knesset ruled that the SCC should be obliged to examine any soldier's complaint fulfilling the conditions set out in law and not being outright vexatious or bothersome. The SCC was compelled to examine all such complaints, even if they seemed to him on the face of it unfounded or trifling.

By according the SCC full powers of investigation, including the power to subpoena witnesses, both civilian and military, and to force them to give evidence, even under oath, and fining witnesses who do not comply, the Knesset provided the SCC with the necessary power to conduct his own effective investigation in order to clarify any point raised in the complaint. In this, the SCC was made independent of the help of police or military authorities. The Knesset also provided that in conducting these investigations, the SCC should be free from any legal restriction usually imposed on investigation on grounds of procedure or admissibility of evidence, and he should investigate the complaint in any way he may think fit. The act further laid down that "no court shall entertain an application for relief against decisions of findings of the SCC in matters of complaints."

The SCC's special position was further stressed by the Knesset's decision to add to the proposed law a provision establishing that the SCC, in fulfilling his duties, was to be completely independent of any authority but the law, and in this he was placed in a position similar to that of a judge. But the SCC's functions were limited to examining soldiers' complaints and advising all concerned, including the military authorities, on the results of his examination and the way to improve any deficiency discovered. His decision did not establish or deny rights that might be claimed in a court of law, nor was the SCC permitted to deal with complaints on matters decided by or pending before any civil or military court or disciplinary officer.

By incorporating the law dealing with soldiers' complaints into the Military Justice Law, the lawmakers expressed their intention to modify the act containing all the provisions for dealing with offenses in the armed forces. They added a special part dealing with the examination of soldiers' complaints pertaining to acts that were not offenses in themselves but that nevertheless were or might become harmful to good order and discipline. Of course, the SCC's examination might sometimes disclose misconduct amounting to an offense. If so, the SCC was to report it to the military advocate general to deal with according to other provisions of the Military Justice Law. But this was only an incidental part of the SCC's work. The main portion was not the criminal, but the usual, mostly even well-meant behavior of officers and men, which caused, justly or not, a feeling in the heart of this or that soldier that he had been wronged. The SCC's major task was to encourage anyone who thought himself wronged to come forward, write his complaint, and have it impartially examined, assuring him that what could be straightened out and corrected would be done in an amiable spirit and in accordance with the letter and spirit of the law.

THE SCC'S HANDLING OF SOLDIERS' COMPLAINTS

In order to give a clear picture of how the SCC and his staff handle complaints, it may be useful to discuss in detail the conditions that any complaint must fulfill, in order to be entitled to examination under the Military Justice Law (Part 11) and the modes of examining such complaints.

Who May Submit a Complaint?

Anyone who considers himself aggrieved by an act (including an omission or delay to act) that took place while the aggrieved person was a soldier on active service in the IDF may submit a complaint to the SCC. (Under this act the aggrieved can be either a member of the standing forces or a reservist on active duty.) The next of kin of an aggrieved person may also submit a complaint, and if there are no such relatives, any person requested by the soldier to submit the complaint may do so.

Against Whom May a Complaint Be Directed?

The complaint must relate to an act committed by a soldier on active duty or by a civil employee of the IDF. It does not matter if, after the act complained against has occurred, the soldier or employee ends his service or work with the army. The relevant time is the time the act took place, and not the time the complaint was submitted.

If the complaint knows the identity of the person complained against, he is obligated to identify the said person in the complaint. But sometimes a soldier complains against an act performed by a military authority or unit and is unable to name the person directly responsible for the act. In this case, the complainant states such details as he knows, and the SCC investigates the matter and ascertains the person or persons responsible for the act, in order to examine the complaint according to the law.

How a Complaint Is Submitted

The complainant must include as many details as possible in his complaint, sign the complaint with his own hand, and state his name, rank, personal number, and army's post number. If the complaint is not submitted by the aggrieved person himself, the complainant must also state his name and address. The complaint is then forwarded directly to the SCC, not through the regular military channels. A soldier may add to his complaint any relevant document he may think desirable to bring to the SCC's attention. But a military document may be added only if it was lawfully in the complainant's hands for personal use.

If, in the opinion of the complainant, the complaint contains any information classified as secret or top secret, it must be handed over in a closed envelope to the official in charge of the office of the aggrieved person's unit. The envelope is then forwarded to the SCC, unopened, through proper military postal service, according to the army orders pertaining to the forwarding of classified material. A complaint by a prisoner or detainee must be delivered to the officer in charge of the military confinement installation, in a closed envelope, and the said officer must forward it, unopened, to the SCC.

Against What Acts May a Complaint Be Submitted?

The law defines the conditions which must be fulfilled in order that the act referred to may constitute a proper subject matter for a complaint. Only if all of the subsequently mentioned conditions are fulfilled is the complaint eligible for the SCC's examination.

1. The act complained against is directly injurious to or directly withholds a benefit from the aggrieved soldier.

2. The act relates to the rules of the service, the conditions of the service or discipline.

3. The act is contrary to any enactment or to army

orders, or is done without lawful authority, or is contrary to sound administration, or involves an excessively inflexible attitude or flagrant injustice.

Complaints Not to Be Examined

The law states several kinds of complaints that the SCC may not examine. This refers mainly to complaints connected with judicial decisions or the investigation of offenses.

The law also prescribes that the following complaints shall be examined only if the SCC finds a special reason justifying his examination of the complaint:

1. A complaint on a subject matter on which a decision has been given, and the law accords, against such a decision, a right to contest, to object, or to appeal to any authority other than the SCC. The object of this restriction is to induce the complainant to make full use of his legal rights before turning to the SCC.

2. A complaint submitted after a year or more has elapsed since the act complained against was done or since the act became known to the complainant.

3. A complaint submitted after 180 days have elapsed from the date on which the aggrieved person ceased to be a soldier.

The time limit is intended to emphasize that the SCC generally handles only complaints submitted with due diligence, soon after the act complained against has happened. But if he thinks that there is a special reason for doing so, it is in his discretion to examine certain complaints, even though the time limit has been infringed or though there exists a right to contest, to object, or to appeal against the decision complained against.

The Powers of the SCC in Examining a Complaint

In order to facilitate the examination of complaints, the law provides that the SCC and any persons empowered by him in that behalf have full powers of investigation like those accorded to the chairman of a court of inquiry. These powers include the right to subpoena witnesses, to have them testify even under oath, and to demand the production of all kinds of evidence. The person complained against and his superior are required to submit their views on the complaint, in writing, within the period prescribed by the SCC.

Army orders require each soldier to assist the SCC in the performance of his duties and to abstain from any act that may cause delay or interfere with the submitting of a complaint or with the examination thereof.

Procedures of Examination

When a complaint is submitted, the SCC first ascertains if it fulfills the requirements of the law, as stated above. As necessary, the SCC or his representative conducts a preliminary investigation, looking into the files of the general headquarters and of other relevant headquarters, in order to uncover the real facts of the case. At this stage, the proper military authority quite often rectifies the subject matter of the complaint, thus obviating the need for further action by the SCC.

But if the complaints necessitate further examination, fulfilling all the conditions demanded by the law, the SCC proceeds to the next stage. This stage consists in sending a copy of the complaint or the complaint itself to the person complained against, and to his superior, providing them with a suitable opportunity to answer the complaint. The SCC sometimes also brings the complaint to the attention of some higher authority and asks for its views. If these answers are satisfactory and no further point is to be elaborated on, the examination is terminated and its results summed up. Sometimes, however, there remain topics to be clarified, even after the above-mentioned answers have been received. If this is so, an investigator from the SCC's staff is charged with the case; he interrogates witnesses and, if necessary, visits the unit of the complainant and informs himself on all aspects of the case. All statements of the complainant himself and of the other witnesses are taken down in writing, and if the SCC thinks it fit, any witness may be asked to confirm the truth of his statement under oath. After all evidence has been gathered, the case is summed up.

Discontinuance of Examination

The SCC is obliged to discontinue his examination if in the course of it he discovers evidence that would have justified not initiating the examination in the first place, if it had been known beforehand. Furthermore, he may discontinue the examination if the matter to which the complaint relates has been rectified or if the complainant has withdrawn the complaint.

Results of Examination

If the complaint has been found to be justified, notice to such effect, stating the reason for that decision, is given to the complainant, the person complained against and his commanding officer, as well as to an officer empowered in that behalf by the chief of the general staff of the IDF.

In the notice, the SCC may set out a summary of his findings and point out the need to rectify any defect revealed by the examination and the manner in which it should be rectified. A senior staff officer of the Adjutant General Branch of the IDF has been appointed to see that the SCC's recommendations are carried out after having received due notice of them. This officer must report to the SCC within two months on all steps taken in the consequence of these recommendations. Army orders require the rectification of any defect pointed out by the SCC. Only the chief of general staff himself is empowered to decide not to act upon the SCC's recommendation, but in this case he must be prepared to explain the reasons for this course of action to the minister of defense and to the Foreign Affairs and Security Committee of the Knesset.

If the complaint has been found to be unjustified, if examination has been discontinued, or if the SCC has from the beginning decided there are due reasons not to examine the complaint, notice to such effect, stating the reasons for this decision, is given to the complainant. The person complained against and his commanding officer are also duly informed of any discontinuance of the examination or of it having been found unjustified. The notice may set out a summary of the SCC's findings.

Army orders provide that no disciplinary action shall be taken against a soldier whose complaint has been found to be unjustified. The SCC may inform the military advocate general on the case only if he is convinced that the complaint was false on purpose, thereby violating provisions of the criminal law. The military advocate general will initiate appropriate legal steps if he thinks it fit.

Duty of Secrecy

The law requires that the SCC and all his assistants keep secret any information reaching them in their official capacity. They may disclose such information only in the course of carrying out their duties under the law in examining complaints. Thus, the complainant rests assured that any information given by him in the complaint or divulged in the course of the examination will not reach unauthorized persons. This privilege to privacy in the matter will be absolutely upheld as far as compatible with the necessity for full and impartial examination of his complaint.

Annual Report

For each year ending March 31, a report is submitted to the minister of defense and the Parliamentary Committee for Foreign Affairs and Defense. The aims of the report are to comply with the law (Section 557) to keep the minister of defense and the Parliamentary Committee for Foreign Affairs and Defense informed about objective procedures of the SCC; to record the activities and changes in the office of the SCC; and to document statistically the office activities with illustrations of cases.

THE ORGANIZATION OF THE SCC

In investigating complaints, the SCC has involved as many military personnel as necessary as part of a public and educational process. A soldier who complains is a good soldier. Even if it causes inconvenience to others, his right to complain creates a duty in others to respond. Soldiers should know how people feel and what causes bad feelings that detract from performance. On the other hand, publicity outside the military should be avoided so that complainants are not labeled publicity seekers, although the office should be publicized within the military as much as possible so that soldiers will know their rights.

The Office of the Soldiers' Complaints Commissioner is staffed by regular national service and reserve service officers and other ranks. The office itself is divided into three sections: the Examiners' Department, the Legal Department, and the SCC Secretariat. The Examiners' Department is headed by a full colonel, eight lieutenant colonels and two majors, and three captains and lieutenants. Most of the examiners have field experience. Their mission is to examine each complaint as to what happened, recommend findings, sum up if justified, and recommend how to right the wrong. The Legal Department is headed by a full colonel legally qualified, and eight legal officers. They advise the SCC and examiners as to the law in general and each grievance in particular, check the findings of each case if according to the process of law, and draft the final findings for each case. The SCC Secretariat is headed by a major, one lieutenant, and administrative and clerical staff. Its tasks are to coordinate the flow of documents, typing, registration, posting, and lectures on the act to military units. The manning of the Examiners' Department and the Legal Department facilitates the application of field experience and legal approach to each grievance directed to the SCC.

Each grievance is registered, legally classified if within the jurisdiction of the SCC, then classified as to the characteristic of the complaint, serialized, and acknowledged. If the grievance is not within the SCC's jurisdiction, the complainant is notified by letter explaining that the complaint will not be examined. When the complaint lacks evidence, relevant information, or signature, a complete complaint is requested. Statistical data are being computerized in order to maintain control as to the flow and handling of grievances.

Data are updated in three phases: day of arrival, commencement of day of examination, and day of termination. The following computer reports are in use:

- Weekly report in alphabetical order

- Two monthly reports—examination still open

- Six monthly reports on:
  Complaints per unit.
  Subject of grievances.
  Complainants.

- Report on request for:
  Statistics according to subjects.
  Statistics according to arms of service command and corps.
  Names of those against whom complaints were launched.
  Lead time taken to complete examination.

- Annual reports. Statistics for annual report.

Every three months, a stocktaking is carried out, including the complaints still being examined, and sample spot checks are made.

The examination of complaints closely follows legal requirements. Nevertheless, examiners are aware that the whole subject of complaints can become quite emotional.

At times, for instance, it is difficult to be definite about negligence, sloth, exaggeration, or omission. Examiners must have full and direct knowledge of the unit's mission and the background of the complainant as well as the person or persons against whom the complaint has been directed and the interpersonal relations that obtain in the unit. These data are vital to ensure that the conclusions and recommendations are within the limits set down by the law and that they be fair and free from bias. Within these boundaries, a sense of urgency has to be maintained and coupled with the constant aim to right the wrong.

After preliminary examination of a complaint to check whether it is within the SCC's jurisdiction, the details are verified. If the character of the grievance is technical—pertaining to documents—the procedure is to verify the grievance in relation to the evidence contained in the document and to arrive at conclusions and recommendations. If the grievance is not technical, the examining officer analyzes it, describes the act or omission, specifies what he believes made the feeling of grievance critical, and prepares letters to the person against whom the grievance has been directed and to the commanding officer of both. If the written evidence received is sufficient to arrive at conclusions and recommendations, the case is summed up and sent to the Legal Department.

If the written evidence is not sufficient, that is, if it still lacks evidence or if contradictions remain, the next step is

Table 10.1
Complaints Investigated by the Soldiers' Complaints Commissioner, Israel, 1972–1980

	1972–73	1973–74	1974–75	1975–76	1976–77	1977–78	1978–79	1979–80	TOTAL
Total complaints	2,669	7,224	11,056	9,620	8,543	10,080	9,375	8,390	66,597
Enlisted men	1,194	2,627	3,808	3,802	3,678	3,765	3,829	2,829	25,532
Regulars	192	647	1,527	1,167	1,037	1,350	1,251	1,414	8,585
Reservists	718	2,276	4,047	3,084	2,546	3,415	3,180	2,887	22,153
Next of kin	595	1,674	1,674	1,567	1,282	1,550	1,115	1,260	10,687
Solution without investigation	—	2,604	3,080	3,367	2,211	2,649	2,769	2,783	20,095
Investigation of technical grievances	1,130	2,339	4,147	2,630	1,938	2,691	2,617	2,880	20,372
Investigation by correspondence	408	881	1,683	2,074	2,110	1,747	1,426	1,216	11,545
Investigation as court of inquiry	88	184	339	254	211	196	190	166	1,628
Grievance completed	2,258	6,008	9,249	8,325	6,470	7,283	7,002	7,045	53,640
Justified	539	1,295	2,804	2,349	2,273	2,389	969	1,057	13,675
Unjustified	245	379	651	893	823	876	990	947	5,804
Not within jurisdiction	1,432	4,080	5,520	2,804	1,787	2,559	3,054	2,538	23,774
No cause	—	—	—	1,769	1,303	1,194	595	1,091	5,952
Investigation closed, grievance settled	42	254	274	510	284	265	1,394	1,412	4,435
Redirected to judge advocate	—	—	—	608	531	756	1,104	966	3,965

to conduct the examination as a court of inquiry. Once findings are verified and cleared by the Legal Department, the SCC, after studying the case, informs the aggrieved soldier whether his grievance has been found to be justified, partially justified, or unjustified. If the complaint has been found to be unjustified, this is explained in the findings and the matter is closed. If the complaint has been found to be partially or completely justified, the findings will indicate what shortcomings in existing procedures or processes have to be corrected, the agency to implement the correction, and the authority to verify and report completion to implementation. The SCC also communicates his final findings to the soldier or soldiers against whom the grievance was directed, their commanding officer, and the senior officer appointed by the chief of staff to see that the SCC's recommendations are carried out.

IMPACT

The office of the SCC became operational on November 1, 1972, and has continued to develop procedures and organization to suit the variable factors affecting soldiers' grievances. It got off to a fitful start. In its first complete year of operation (April 1, 1973, to March 31, 1974), almost 32 percent of the complaints were found deficient and were returned to the complainant with due explanation. Another 12 percent were found to be in the jurisdiction of other authorities, whereupon these complaints were transmitted to the proper authorities. The remaining 56 percent were examined by the SCC. Of these, in only 3 percent of all complaints received was it found necessary to institute a full-fledged examination with interrogation of witnesses by an investigator. In all other cases, the examination was satisfactorily concluded on the ground of the files of the military authorities and if need be, on the ground of the explanations given in writing by those concerned. Of the complaints examined by the SCC, more than 61 percent were found to be justified complaints and 36 percent unjustified. In the remaining 3 percent, the examination was discontinued, usually because the subject matter was rectified or because the complainant withdrew his complaint. In almost all of the cases in which the complaint was found to be justified, it was recommended that the defect be corrected, and the recommendation was accepted and acted upon by the military authorities. The results for 1972–80 are given in Table 10.1; further information on the subjects of the complaints and the identity of the complainants is found in Table 10.2.

The SCC's considerable activity and the relative number of complaints addressed to him demonstrate that the soldiers of the IDF have confidence that the SCC is independent and that the SCC's recommendation that a wrong be redressed will be duly acted upon. Furthermore, the SCC has succeeded in securing the full cooperation of the IDF commanders in his efforts to hold impartial examinations and to carry out his recommendations. But, more important still, the commanders believe that permitting the men free and undisturbed access to the SCC by complaint is good for the units' morale. Thus, every soldier who thinks himself wronged may address his complaint directly to the SCC without fear of reprisal. One may note with satisfaction that the full cooperation of all ranks has been achieved.

In Israel, the SCC's activity has added to the IDF's moral strength and has helped keep maladministration or excess under control. It is perhaps more important to maintain the army's spiritual and moral strength. The aim of the Israeli Parliament in establishing the office of the SCC was to create an authority charged with safeguarding the soldier's civic rights, building up his moral strength, and improving army administration—without impairing efficiency and military discipline. The SCC has fulfilled these expectations, thereby not only fortifying the army's democratic spirit, but also improving its fighting quality by making it a morally stronger army.

Table 10.2
Subjects of Complaints Investigated by the Soldiers' Complaints Commissioner, Israel, 1979–1980

SUBJECT	NUMBER OF COMPLAINTS
Medical treatment	773
Payments	1,039
Personal equipment	123
Commander and subordinate relations	741
Statutory privileges	1,212
Conditions of individual service	669
National service	302
Regular service	156
Reserve service	1,450
Operational maladministration	78
Technical maladministration	58
Confinement	28
Religious matters	32
Women service	1
Grievances not within the jurisdiction	1,728
Total	8,390

CHAPTER 11

THE OMBUDSMAN IN CORRECTIONAL INSTITUTIONS

A. THE CORRECTIONS OMBUDSMAN IN THE UNITED STATES

STANLEY V. ANDERSON, University of California, Santa Barbara

Chief Justice Warren Burger once said that "every penal institution must have . . . the means of having complaints reach decision-making sources through established channels, so that the valid grievances can be remedied and spurious grievances exposed."[1] This chapter is mainly about one such channel—the ombudsman institution in prisons. It examines two kinds of offices, one in which the ombudsman stays behind his desk and the other in which he ventures into the field. The original offices in Scandinavia handle complaints from prisoners much as they do other complaints. Grievances are received and investigated mostly through correspondence.[2] During the past six years, a new kind of office has sprung up in North America, one whose work is limited to places of incarceration. Prison ombudsmen do most of their work face-to-face, inside the prisons.

This study stems from the failure of two correctional ombudsman proposals in 1971. The first was embodied in a bill adopted by the California Legislature but vetoed by then Governor Ronald Reagan.[3] The second was a proposal to rebellious Attica inmates put forward by the commissioner of the New York State Department of Correctional Services, Russell Oswald, but never implemented.[4] Opposition to the proposals in California and New York cannot be explained by mere partisan labels. The ombudsman idea cuts across the ideological spectrum and has been identified with both major political parties in the United States.[5]

Because there were no ombudsman offices anywhere at that time whose field of responsibility was limited to places of incarceration, the justification for the California proposal had necessarily to be based considerably upon speculation. As an ombudsman for corrections has existed in Minnesota since 1972 and a deputy for prisons has operated in the Iowa ombudsman office since 1973, the best way to allay the misgivings of those who fear that an ombudsman in prison might be disruptive is to present the experience of these new offices.

The experience is reassuring. Indeed, the presence of an ombudsman has benefited management as much as the inmates. The ombudsman has been a useful control device for upper echelons, while employees down the line have been able to use the ombudsman as a means of focusing attention on their pressing problems. Thus, the ombudsman office is not just another layer of bureaucracy, but is instead a monitor for bureaucracy. It is an instrument for controlling the quality of quality-control instruments. Grounded in the common law case-by-case method, it is much more effective in policing day-to-day administrative activity than courts, legislators, or governors. The complaints that properly pertain to an ombudsman office are those related to administrative action. It screens other matters and refers them to prison officials, legal aid offices, public defenders, and social service agencies. Without these alternative resources, the ombudsman might drown in a deluge of requests.

THE IDEA OF A CORRECTIONAL OMBUDSMAN

Only one criminologist has made the prison ombudsman an integral part of his approach.[6] Otherwise, the ombudsman notion cuts across the current strands of debate in penology, and the ombudsman institution is congenial to any humane philosophy of imprisonment. While an atmosphere of prison reform is not essential to the operation of an ombudsman office, it is conducive. In a climate of prison reform, each new program or service provides a new possible subject of controversy. Because the correctional ombudsman idea itself is a reform measure, with a primary focus on the grievances of individual prisoners, it is part of the ferment that currently surrounds prisoners' rights and remedies.

Formerly, in some American state prisons, an inmate had to take his hat off at a respectful distance and ask permission to speak to a guard by saying "Sir!" During the nineteenth century, many convicts were not allowed to communicate with one another, let alone with the outside world. Until fairly recently in this country, it might be said that prisoners had neither rights nor remedies. They were slaves of the state, completely subject to the warden and his subordinates. Individual institutions were autonomous, and there was no appeal to a higher authority. The past twenty years have seen the emergence of rights and the development of remedies. In contrast to the "slave of the state" doctrine, we are moving toward the position that "A prisoner retains all the rights of an ordinary citizen except those expressly, or by necessary implication, taken from him by law."[7]

A crucial initial step in the process of translating rights into reality is to open lines of communication outside the prison walls. Most states have followed the example set by the federal Bureau of Prisons in allowing inmates to correspond with friends and family and in permitting prisoners to write "uncensored and unopened letters to public authorities, the courts, and members of the House and Senate."[8] Normally, an inmate may send a "kite" to any official within a given prison. Among the other authorities to whom an inmate may write are those in the chain of command above the warden, that is, the head of the Department of Corrections and the head of the umbrella agency that may house the department. This avenue is valuable, but it "does not assure a convict that his grievance will be evaluated by a thoroughly impartial authority."[9]

While appeals to elected officials outside the system add impartiality, the office-holders contacted usually lack the capacity to carry out an independent investigation.[10] Moreover, some legislators who otherwise welcome constituent complaints may not want to be bothered with convicts. One governor's aide said that he always waited several weeks or more to reply to an inmate letter because a prompt answer would generate a spate of letters from the inmate and his companions. The aide said that he did not want to encourage "pen pals."

An aggrieved inmate who is frustrated by the reaction of the executive and legislative branches is likely to turn to the courts for judicial redress. In the past twenty years, there has been a veritable flood of litigation in two main areas: post-conviction appeals and challenges to the conditions of incarceration.[11] The second area stems from the discrediting of the hands-off doctrine, which held that the "courts are without power to supervise prison administration or to interfere with ordinary prison rules or regulations."[12] The gates in the dam of this kind of judicial abstention have been opened by the newly construed constitutional prohibition against cruel and unusual punishments[13] and the recent reinterpretations of the meaning of the due process and equal protection clauses.[14] Whatever the reasons, prisoners now petition more than ever before. Although the flow for prisoner redress has stabilized, the volume of complaints remains high.[15] There is some reason to believe that too many complaints to the courts are frivolous, and, in two states, Maryland and North Carolina, prisoner litigation has been curtailed in the state courts by interposing a mandatory administrative procedure that includes an opportunity for a hearing before an Inmate Grievance Commission. At the federal level, however, the U.S. Supreme Court has directed the district courts to take cases from prisoners, even though state remedies have not been exhausted, pursuant to the Civil Rights Act of 1871, which protects against "the deprivation of any rights, privileges, or immunities secured by the Constitution and laws."[16]

If the tide of lawsuits cannot be stemmed, it must be channeled. The underlying problem is one of screening papers that have not been prepared by lawyers.[17] A special committee of the Federal Judicial Center, composed of five federal judges, has made the following preliminary recommendations for handling prisoner complaints:

centralized processing by expert "intake" or "writ" clerks

subsequent screening by law clerks or magistrates

assigning all complaints from one prisoner to a single judge

the use of a standardized complaint form[18]

There is no evidence that ombudsman offices have reduced inmate litigation, but they do assist in the screening process. In Iowa, for example, the deputy ombudsman for corrections gave sealed and confidential testimony in chambers in a federal suit filed by an inmate at the Iowa State Penitentiary.[19] In Connecticut, a federal judge referred a complaint to the correctional ombudsman "with instructions to investigate and report its findings to the court."[20] This particular dispute was resolved without requiring further action by the court.

Overall, the direct interplay between court and ombudsman has been minimal. While there is some overlap of functions, which is probably wholesome, each has its own distinct role to play. An ombudsman could not effectively attack a grossly deficient prison system, as a federal judge did in Arkansas.[21] According to a study sponsored by the American Bar Association on the Arkansas case:

[T]he number of, and consequent level of supervision by free world employees increased significantly, thereby improving inmate safety. The general level of sanitation improved markedly. Significant strides were made in reducing racial discrimination and race relations improved as a result. Health services and recreation were expanded considerably. Corporal punishment was stopped, and a measure of procedural regularity was introduced into prison discipline.[22]

An ombudsman might have been able to cope with one or two of these problems, but he would not have been able to attack them all at the same time. Thus, the courts can help to establish the basic preconditions for the successful operation of a prison ombudsman office.[23] By the same token, ombudsmen should handle minor complaints that have a potential for clogging the courts. (We do not know if those who complain to an ombudsman would otherwise have gone to court, and we do not know if those who go to court would have been satisfied with an ombudsman.) For substantial relief of the regular courts, it seems to be necessary to set up an administrative court. Such tribunals can have an ombudsman component, as they do in Maryland and North Carolina.

THE INSTITUTIONALIZATION OF CORRECTIONAL OMBUDSMEN

In transferring the ombudsman institution to the New World, the development of specialized prison offices has clearly been the most significant innovation. There are now six correctional ombudsman offices in the United States: in Minnesota (since 1972), Connecticut (1973), Iowa (which added a prison deputy in 1973), Kansas (1975), Michigan (1975), and Oregon (1977). In terms of size, only Michigan is on a par with Sweden, the most populous of the Scandinavian countries. The prison population of Michigan, however, is proportionally much greater, and the inmates are concentrated in a single institution which is the largest in the United States and perhaps the largest in the world.

Appointed by then Governor Wendell Anderson upon nomination by a broadly based ten-member Ombudsman Commission, Theatrice Williams has served as ombudsman for corrections in Minnesota since July 1972. Williams is black, the son of a Mississippi sharecropper. He holds a Master's degree in social work from the University of Pennsylvania and had previously been director of a community center in Minneapolis. The prison ombudsman idea was one of many proposed by David Fogel during his brief tenure as commissioner for corrections in Minnesota. According to Fogel, "Initial anxiety melted when each of the state's institutional administrators and their executive staff met, analyzed, and modified the proposal."[24] The result was a law enacted by the Minnesota Legislature in 1973, creating the Office of Ombudsman for the Minnesota State Department of Corrections. The statute was amended in 1976 to make the office permanent, by repealing the previous automatic expiration date of July 1977. These amendments also gave the ombudsman subpoena power and immunity from suit or compulsory testimony, while extending the jurisdiction of the office to include regional facilities (but not local jails).

The ombudsman serves "at the pleasure of the Governor" (Minn. Stats. 241.41). Except for the manner of appointment and the absence of a fixed term, the Minnesota ombudsman office differs from other ombudsman offices only in that its jurisdiction is limited to correctional matters. Indeed, with these important exceptions, the Minnesota law is taken in great part from Walter Gellhorn's Annotated Model Ombudsman Statute (see Appendix A).[25] It costs about $210,000 a year to run the office. Initially, it was partly supported by grants from the U.S. Law Enforcement Assistance Administration and the Bush Foundation. For their first two years, the ombudsman offices in Iowa and Nebraska were also supported by grants, in their case, from the U.S. Office of Economic Opportunity.

In addition to the ombudsman and his deputy, the office has three field investigators and a research analyst—men and women of diverse ethnic backgrounds, with Bachelor's or Master's degrees in the social sciences or in social work. Two former staff members were ex-offenders, as was one of the ten interns who have passed through the office. The six professional staff members serve about eighteen hundred inmates in eight adult and juvenile institutions and another twenty-three hundred parolees. Half of the work of the office is directed to the nine hundred men held in the maximum security prison at Stillwater, about twenty miles from the ombudsman's office in Saint Paul.

Prison inmates in Minnesota have access to the telephone, but it is just as easy to lodge a complaint directly with a representative of the ombudsman's office on the premises. At first, "the overwhelming majority of the complaints were written and came through the mail."[26] Now, only about 20 percent are initiated in writing, while 30 percent are started by telephone and 25 percent are made in person. The remaining 25 percent are indirect referrals, which often lead to an interview.

The ombudsman has received an average of 150 complaints a month. Levels reached over the first seven years were as follows:

> 935 (1972–73)
>
> 1,026 (1973–74)
>
> 1,299 (1974–75)
>
> 1,171 (1975–76)
>
> 1,250 (1976–77)
>
> 1,188 (1977–78)
>
> 1,733 (1978–79)

During most of these years, there were two complaints for every three inmates, which put Minnesota ahead of other correctional ombudsmen (see Table 11.1). In screening complaints, the Minnesota ombudsman does not apply a strict test of exhaustion of remedies:

Complainants are encouraged to utilize existing resources at the various institutions or within the Department of Corrections to

Table 11.1
Correctional Complaints to Ombudsmen

AREA	NO. OF COMPLAINTS PER INMATE
Minnesota	1 for every 1.5
Iowa	1 for every 5
Hawaii	1 for every 9
Denmark	1 for every 13
Sweden	1 for every 17
Norway	1 for every 20
Nebraska	1 for every 30
New Zealand	1 for every 40

resolve their grievance. The problem with this, as a hard and fast rule, is that the resources for resolving grievances are not well defined. As the resources are better defined and the complainants gain confidence in them, the Ombudsman can become more insistent upon their use.[27]

The subject matter of inmate complaints in Minnesota is much the same as that found in other ombudsman jurisdictions. The 1,130 cases whose consideration was concluded in 1975–76 were categorized as follows:

221 Rules	101 Legal
210 Parole	24 Records
162 Program	17 Threats
109 Placement	7 Discrimination
107 Property	66 Miscellaneous.[28]
106 Medical	

When he concludes his investigation, the ombudsman does not characterize complaints as justified or unjustified. He does claim that he is able to find a satisfactory resolution, in whole or in part, about 75 percent of the time (see Table 11.2). The complainant's perceptions of satisfaction have been somewhat less sanguine. In a 1973 survey conducted by the Law School at the University of Minnesota, half of the inmates at Stillwater Prison felt that the ombudsman had helped them,[29] while a 1974 appraisal carried out by the Governor's Commission on Crime Prevention and Control showed that "less than half (45.5 percent) of inmates at all the institutions were satisfied with the Ombudsman's efforts on their behalf."[30] Part of the inmates' lack of enthusiasm was attributed to the absence of a formal procedure for notifying clients of the conclusion of the ombudsman's investigation. (This lapse has since been corrected.) The Crime Commission study also found that administrators were "basically satisfied with the Ombudsman's performance," while staff personnel "were supportive."[31] It concluded that "Generally speaking, it seems that those who were initially *least* enthusiastic about the concept (administrators and guards) are now the most satisfied with his efforts, while those who were originally *most* enthusiastic about the concept (inmates) are now least satisfied with his efforts."[32]

The Crime Commission study also recorded that "[t]he Ombudsman has made fifty-six policy recommendations and approximately one-half of these have been implemented."[33] Twenty-two of the fifty-six (including twelve of the first fourteen) had to do with procedures governing parole hearings, grievance mechanisms, and disciplinary decisions. Among recent recommendations that have been rejected is one that would have had the Department

Table 11.2
The Minnesota Ombudsman for Corrections

RESOLUTION	CASE RESOLUTION	
	Cases	Percentage
Full	821	68.3
Partial	96	8.0
None	39	3.2
Withdrawn	71	5.9
Dismissed	107	8.9
Referred	68	5.7
Total	1,202	100.0

SOURCE: *1977–78 Annual Report*, p. 17.

of Corrections "create a judicial subdivision that would be responsible for administering the disciplinary hearings at all adult institutions." Another would have required that "the prison maximum custody classification committee be chaired by a staff member from the Department of Corrections central office."[34]

The ombudsman's successful intervention in crisis situations has helped to establish his credibility:

In October, 1972, T. Williams and Commissioner Fogel were able to secure the release of a guard who was being held hostage, after four hours of talk with three inmates, two of whom had previously had contact with the ombudsman.

In 1973, the ombudsman's investigation of a fight between several black and white inmates at St. Cloud Reformatory established that the origins of the dispute were not racial[35] and thereby helped prevent the incident from escalating into a major racial conflict.

In 1973 and 1974, the ombudsman's investigation of a series of inmate suicides helped allay misgivings that the deaths might have been racially motivated killings.[36] In the most dramatic of these, Mr. Williams recorded the dying statement of an inmate who had taken poison and set his cell on fire.

These explosive incidents reveal a new dimension of prison ombudsman activity: that of riot prevention and control. Former Governor Anderson states that "one of the main reasons I appointed an Ombudsman for the prisons is that if you're going to avoid Attica-type riots, you have to have a channel for inmates to express grievances so they don't feel they have to riot."[37] The cooling function can be specific, as in the occurrences just related, but it can also be general. Stillwater Warden Bruce McManus alludes to the latter when he says: "The Attica thing scared everybody in corrections. These joints are impersonal, but the Ombudsman gives prisoners a little indi-

vidual attention. If nothing else, it provides a catharsis for the men."[38]

Relations between McManus and Williams reached a low point in March 1973, following the use of tear gas in the segregation block while Deputy Ombudsman Melvyn Brown was inside. McManus still denies Williams's charge that excessive force was used. Since then, Warden McManus has stated:

I was uptight. He was uptight. And our staff fought him. We went from suspicious holding off to a serious confrontation. But I think Williams learned a lot. He and I have learned a lot together. [Williams has a] willingness to see both sides. He's a straight professional . . . an honest man. . . . At least he understands our problems and how we think. He may not buy it, but he understands.[39]

Minnesota Corrections Commissioner Kenneth Schoen goes even further in praising the ombudsman office, saying, "I don't know how we operated without it."[40]

Crisis intervention is dramatic, but the more pervasive impact comes from numerous uncelebrated contacts. The 1,132 complaints considered by the Minnesota correctional ombudsman during 1975–76 were lodged by 693 different individuals. This represents an average of 1.6 complaints for each complainant. Only about fifty of the nearly seven hundred complainants—one out of fourteen—could be called querulants, defined as those who complain four or more times a year. Even the most persistent complainer averaged less than one complaint a month.

Many more matters are handled informally. According to Paul Keve: "The [Minnesota] experience has shown the great importance of starting the program with a patient, tolerant, adaptive, low-key approach that will encourage the Ombudsman's credibility in the view of both inmates and staff."[41]

The first time we met, Williams told me that one prison reform group had been quite disappointed at his refusal to join with them in a frontal attack on the Minnesota prison system. Similarly, in Iowa, when asked if he would demolish walled prisons, prison deputy ombudsman Raymond Cornell replied, "I am not by nature a man who seeks to destroy." Like general-purpose ombudsmen, those who specialize in prisons are incrementalists.

COMPARATIVE PERSPECTIVE

In population, the two largest ombudsman jurisdictions mentioned to this point have been Sweden with 8 million and Michigan with 9 million inhabitants. It is a substantial jump to the appointment of a prison ombudsman in Canada, with a population of 22.5 million inhabitants. There are about eighty-five hundred inmates in federal institutions, under sentences of two years or more. (Shorter sentences are served in provincial jails.) This inmate population is smaller than that in Michigan, but it is spread over a much vaster territory. Except for a greater interval between visits to prisons, necessitated by the greater distances, the operation of the Canadian correctional investigator is virtually indistinguishable from that of the prison ombudsman offices in the United States. Structurally, however, the office is precarious, as it depends upon an annual renewal by the solicitor general. It should be made into a statutory office. The Canadian experience suggests that prison ombudsmen could function effectively in American states of comparable population, such as California or New York. In California, however, there are nearly twenty-five thousand prison inmates. Can an ombudsman handle three times as many potential clients as there are in Canada?

There are four basic ways to attack the problem of size: (1) having more than one ombudsman, as with the plural offices in Sweden, Finland, and recently in New Zealand; (2) decentralization, as exemplified by the regional ombudsman offices in the Canadian provinces of Alberta (branch in Calgary) and Quebec (branch in Montreal) and again recently in New Zealand (branches in Auckland and Christchurch); (3) specialization, of which military ombudsmen and prison ombudsmen are the foremost examples; and (4) filtering, by denying the public direct access to the ombudsman. This last technique, used in France and Great Britain (each with a population of more than 50 million inhabitants), requires that complaints be forwarded by members of parliament. Great Britain has since retreated from this line. Medical care was excluded from the purview of the parliamentary commissioner for administration (PCA) when the office was founded in 1967. Later, when the PCA was given a separate and additional assignment as Health Service commissioner in 1973, he was empowered to receive complaints directly from the public. This is a far superior solution. But, if specialization alone is insufficient to carry the burdens of size, then some other means should be found than the erection of artificial barriers.

Decentralization is such a device. The Health Service ombudsman has separate mandates for England, Scotland, and Wales. The Stormont in Northern Ireland established its own commissioner for complaints in 1969. In Britain, then, as in Canada, we find both specialization and regionalization. The same tack might be followed elsewhere. In New York, for example, the prison ombudsman proposal of the Correctional Association of New York would have divided the state into four regions. Decentralization should not be carried too far, however. There should not be a separate office for each prison:

"[L]iving, working, eating on a daily basis with the staff, the Ombudsman would become but one more person working at the prison."[42]

In the structure of their prison work, there are four main types of statutory ombudsmen in the United States:

General purpose offices (Alaska, Hawaii, and Nebraska).

General purpose office, with specially designated prison deputy (Iowa).

Correctional offices, with the ombudsman appointed by the governor (Minnesota and Oregon), the legislature (Michigan), a special board (Kansas), and a private philanthropic institution (Connecticut).

Inmate Grievance Commissions, with an executive director who functions as a correctional ombudsman (Maryland and North Carolina).

All of the ombudsmen whose jurisdiction is limited to corrections hold office at someone else's pleasure. Perhaps the caution implicit in this limitation can be attributed to the particularly sensitive nature of prison administration. There is an understandable reluctance to do anything that might undermine security. For three reasons, however, a tenured prison ombudsman would not threaten security: (1) careful selection; (2) removability for cause; and (3) the fact that the ombudsman cannot compel obedience to his recommendations.

What is missing is a prison ombudsman removable only for cause who serves a set term, as other ombudsmen do. As with judicial appointments, tenure in office is meant to buttress independence. None of the removing agencies has yet interfered with the work of a prison ombudsman, but a new governor in Minnesota or a different majority in the Michigan Legislature, for example, could bring instability or loss of independence. While the lack of a term of years is precarious, it is also open-ended and could lead to the retention of a relatively ineffectual ombudsman simply because the employment had no date of termination. It is easier not to renew an appointment than it is to fire someone. On either count, the prison ombudsman statutes should be amended to provide fixed terms for incumbents.

Great care has been exercised in the selection of prison ombudsmen. It took a year or more to seek, screen, and select the office-holders in Connecticut, Kansas, and Michigan. Less time elapsed in Minnesota—about five months—but a nominating panel was used composed of six members appointed by the governor (including at least one woman and two representatives of racial minorities) and the following office-holders of their designees: the commissioner of corrections, the attorney general, the state public defender, and the commissioner of human rights.[43]

Jails have been excluded from this chapter on the assumption that conditions are so bad that an ombudsman could not function.[44] Basic reforms would have to come first; order would have to replace chaos. This may have been accomplished in Connecticut, where the six regional jails, called correctional centers, are under the jurisdiction of the Department of Corrections. So far, Correctional Ombudsman James Bookwalter has gone to work in only one of the six, the largest, in Hartford. He receives proportionally fewer complaints from the jail inmates, and his investigations are more frequently terminated by the discharge of the complainant. Perhaps the ombudsman should complete his investigations even though the complainant has left. The work of ombudsmen in jails deserves further study. The statewide offices in Iowa and Hawaii have jurisdiction over jails, as do the Canadian provincial ombudsman offices. The urban ombudsmen in Jackson County, Missouri, and Seattle, Washington, appear to have been effective in monitoring their county or city jails. The New York City Board of Correction has been carrying out an ombudsman function in addition to its other duties.[45]

The American contribution to the correctional ombudsman is not in the invention of specialized offices as such. That had already been done with the establishment of military ombudsman offices in Sweden (1915), Norway (1952), West Germany (1957), and Israel (1972). The peculiar American contribution is in bringing the ombudsman to the inmate. This is now done mainly by correctional ombudsmen and deputies who visit prisons frequently—at least once a week to maximum security institutions and once a month to most others—in order to carry out their investigations. By concentrating on prisoners, correctional ombudsmen have for the first time effectively extended the outreach of the ombudsman office to poor people. Otherwise, the main beneficiaries have been members of the middle class.[46]

Presence on the premises is what defines the work of prison ombudsmen and what distinguishes their work from the prison work of other ombudsmen. Being on the scene alters the way in which complaints and inquiries are received and handled. Reception is changed in several ways. First, the threshold of effort required to lodge a complaint or make an inquiry is reduced by the face-to-face or telephonic availability of the ombudsman. Second, an inmate's reluctance to complain is lessened by the protection against retaliation that is implicit in the ombudsman's continued presence. Third, the complainant is more likely to express his grievance at an early stage when rectification is still possible.

Prison ombudsmen take full advantage of their mobility within the walls. They have direct and immediate access to records, inmates, staff, and warden. They can approach problems at the operational level. This style facilitates the handling of simple requests for service, information, or referral, and allows the ombudsman to concentrate his efforts on more serious or difficult cases.

Three of the prison ombudsmen in the United States—in Maryland, Michigan, and North Carolina—are lawyers, but the others and their deputies are not. Only one—Preston Barton in Kansas—is a professional criminologist. Despite the variety of their backgrounds and despite the structural kaleidoscope of their offices, the workings of the correctional ombudsman offices have been remarkably similar. By definition, they differ from the traditional general purpose offices in singling out the complaints of prisoners for special attention. This attention is compensatory: it helps to put the inmate on a footing comparable to that of an ordinary citizen in his dealings with government.

Inmate, guard, administrator, warden, commissioner, legislator, governor: there is substantial support for the ombudsman among all of these, but it seems to grow on the way up the hierarchy. Both popularity and success can be illuminated by contemplating the following different but interrelated ways of viewing an ombudsman office:

—It is the interposition of the third-party principle into the resolution of grievances, so that no man is the judge of his own case. In the prison context, with a nudge from the courts, ombudsmen have for the first time made officials accountable to an external arbiter.

—It provides a speedy and inexpensive way of limiting administrative discretion which heretofore has been largely uncontrolled.[47] Ombudsmen make a significant contribution to the development of fair standards and fair procedures within prisons. The creation of an ombudsman or ombudsman-like office has been concurrent with the formal upgrading of internal grievance procedures in Kansas, Maryland, Michigan, North Carolina, and Wisconsin.

—It is a vehicle for crisis intervention. As already noted, ombudsmen can be helpful in preventing or controlling prison violence.

—It is a sensitive feedback relay that is triggered by complaints and inquiries to identify salient information and communicate it to appropriate supervisory and policy-making officials.

—Finally, the ombudsman symbolizes the use of reason and moral persuasion rather than force. This is very civilized—and civilizing!

NOTES

1. "We Refuse to Be Responsible for the People We Imprison," address to the National Conference of Christians and Jews, Philadelphia, November 1972, reprinted in American Bar Association Commission on Correctional Facilities and Services, *Thoughts on Prison Reform*, 1975, p. 20.

2. See Stanley Anderson, "Ombudsmen and Prisons in Scandinavia," *Nordisk Tidsskrift for Kriminalvidenskab* 66, No. 3–4 (1978): 211–46.

3. See Timothy L. Fitzharris, *The Desirability of a Correctional Ombudsman* (Berkeley, Calif.: Institute of Governmental Studies, University of California, 1973). See also Brian Taugher, "The Penal Ombudsman: A Step Toward Penal Reform," *Pacific Law Journal* 3 (1972): 166–89.

4. See Russell G. Oswald, *Attica: My Story* (New York: Doubleday, 1972), p. 119. See also Tom Wicker, *A Time to Die* (New York: Quadrangle, 1975), pp. 176, 308.

5. See Stanley Anderson, *Ombudsman Papers: American Experience and Proposals* (Berkeley, Calif.: Institute of Governmental Studies, University of California, 1969), pp. 29–32.

6. See David Fogel, "Overseeing Fairness: The Ombudsman," in *"We Are the Living Proof": The Justice Model for Corrections* (Cincinnati, Ohio: Anderson, 1975), pp. 230–36. At p. 235, Fogel notes: "An Ombudsman is still another strata [*sic*] of the multi-tier conflict resolution system we are constructing in this chapter."

7. *Coffin* v. *Reichard*, 143 F.2d 443, 445 (6th Cir. 1944), *cert. denied*, 335 U.S. 887 (1945). The "slave of the state" doctrine was articulated in *Ruffin* v. *Commonwealth*, 62 Va. (21 Gratt) 790, 796 (1871).

8. Walter Gellhorn, *When Americans Complain: Governmental Grievance Procedures* (Cambridge, Mass.: Harvard University Press, 1966), p. 148.

9. Ibid., p. 150.

10. But see Manfred von Nordheim and Richard W. Taylor, "Prisoners' Right to Petition West German Legislatures for Redress of Grievances," *Political Science Discussion Papers* 4 (Kent State University, Summer 1972): 51–60.

11. Total civil filings in the U.S. district courts were slightly more than doubled during seventeen years from 1960 to 1976, inclusive. During the same period, prisoner petitions (both civil rights and habeas corpus petitions are included among civil filings) increased ninefold, from 2,177 to 19,809 (4,780 from federal prisoners and 15,029 from state prisoners). From 1975 to 1976, the increase of prisoner petitions was only 2.6 percent, and these petitions declined as a percentage of all civil filings from 18 percent to 15.2 percent. See *1976 Annual Report of the Director*, Administrative Office of the U.S. Courts, pp. 93–96.

Habeas corpus petitions in the superior courts of the state of California trebled during the ten years from 1966 to 1976, from approximately three thousand to nine thousand. From 1975 to 1976, they increased only 1.5 percent. See Judicial Council of California, *1977 Annual Report of the Administrative Office of the California Courts*, p. 198.

12. *Banning* v. *Looney*, 213 F.2d 771 (10th Cir.), *cert. denied*, 348 U.S. 859 (1954).

13. U.S. Constitution, Eighth Amendment. See *Holt* v. *Sarver*, 309 F. Supp. 362 (E. D. Ark. 1970). (Arkansas penitentiaries must either close or improve sanitation and medical conditions and eliminate overcrowding, segregation, and the use of inmates as guards.)

14. U.S. Constitution, Fifth and Fourteenth Amendments. See *Morrissey* v. *Brewer*, 408 U.S. 471, 33 L.Ed. 2d 484, 92 S. Ct. 2593 (1972) (upon revocation of parole, the individual must be given some opportunity to be heard) and *Wolff* v. *McDonnell*, 418 U.S. 539, 41 L.Ed.2d 935 (1974) (in prison disciplinary hearings, the accused must be given written notice of charges, an opportunity to call witnesses, and written findings of fact). But see *Baxter* v. *Palmigiano*, 47 L.Ed.2d 810 (1976). (In prison disciplinary hearings, the accused need not be assigned counsel or be given the right of confrontation, and adverse inferences may be drawn from his silence.)

15. The Administrative Office of the California courts comments upon the growth and decline of habeas corpus petitions in the state courts of appeal as follows: "The beginning of the upward trend coincided with the United States Supreme Court decision in *Morrissey* v. *Brewer* . . . , and would appear to be attributable to . . . that decision. The current decrease suggests that the effects of that decision have been assimilated." See *1977 Annual Report*, p. 186 (footnote omitted).

16. 42 U.S.C. Section 1983. See *Monroe* v. *Pape*, 365 U.S. 167 (1961) and *Burrell* v. *McCray*, 516 F.2d 357 (4th Cir.), *cert. denied*, 48 L. Ed. 2d 788 (1976). See also "Comment: Exhaustion of State Administrative Remedies in Section 1983 Cases," *University of Chicago Law Review* 41 (1974): 537–56, and "Comment: 42 U.S.C. Section 1983, Prisoner Petitions—Exhaustion of State Administrative Remedies," *Arkansas Law Review* 28 (1975): 479–90.

17. In addition to permitting access to "jailhouse lawyers" (*Johnson* v. *Avery*, 393 U.S. 483, 21 L. Ed.2d 718, 89 S.Ct. 747 1969), prison authorities must provide law libraries or the assistance of lawyers or law students (*Bounds* v. *Smith*, 52 L.Ed.2d 72 1977). See generally Bruce R. Jacob and K. M. Sharma, "Justice After Trial: Prisoners' Need for Legal Services in the Criminal-Correctional Process," *Kansas Law Review* 18 (1970): 493–628.

18. See John H. Wood, Jr., "Federal Prisoner Petitions," *St. Mary's Law Journal* 7 (1975): 501.

19. *1975 Report to the Governor of Iowa and the Sixty-Sixth General Assembly, Second Session, by the Iowa Citizens' Aide*, pp. 5–6.

20. Complaint No. 62A/100/05, *Ombudsman Quarterly Report: Second Quarter, Third Year* (July 1, 1976; mimeo), p. 8.

21. *Holt* v. *Sarver*, 309 F. Supp. 362 (E.D. Ark, 1970); *aff'd* 442 F.2d 304 (9th Cir. 1971).

22. M. Kay Harris and Dudley P. Spiller, Jr., *After Decision: Implementation of Judicial Decrees in Correctional Settings* (Washington, D.C.: Resource Center on Correctional Law and Legal Services; mimeo, November 1976), p. 20.

23. Arkansas has not taken advantage of this opportunity. In a letter to me dated January 5, 1977, Assistant Attorney General Robert A. Newcomb says: "In light of the fact that the Supreme Court had failed to rule that exhaustion of state remedies is a necessary prerequisite to the filing of a 42 U.S.C. Section 1983 suit, this office has decided not to seek legislation implementing

an inmate grievance procedure . . . similar to the one existing in Maryland and North Carolina.'' This bears out the observation in ''Comment: Exhaustion,'' *University of Chicago Law Review* 41 (1974), at p. 556, that a modified requirement of exhaustion ''would act as an incentive for state agencies to provide complete interim relief during the state administrative process, so as to assure an opportunity to correct their own errors.''

24. *''We Are the Living Proof''*: *The Justice Model for Corrections* (Cincinnati, Ohio: Anderson, 1975), p. 232. See *A Proposal to Establish an Experimental Ombudsman for the Minnesota Department of Corrections* (Minneapolis: University of Minnesota, November 15, 1971; mimeo, 51 pp.).

25. The Gellhorn statute may be found in Stanley Anderson, ed., *Ombudsmen for American Government?* (Englewood Cliffs, N.J.: Prentice-Hall for the American Assembly, 1968), pp. 159–73 and in Appendix A of this volume.

26. *A Report on the First Six Months of Operation of the Ombudsman for the Minnesota Department of Corrections* (January 1973), p. 7.

27. *Ombudsman for Corrections: 1972–73 Annual Report*, p. 3. But see n. 31 (below).

28. Definitions of these categories are supplied in the *1973–74 Annual Report*, pp. 4–5, and in the *1974–75 Annual Report*, p. 4. A case summary from each category is provided in the *1974–75 Annual Report*, pp. 6–10, and in the *1975–76 Annual Report*, pp. 11–19. Otherwise, the ombudsman does not supply case notes in his annual reports.

29. Dennis Goldenson, *An Evaluation of the Minnesota Corrections Ombudsman Program* (July 23, 1973; typescript, 33 pp.).

30. Gerald Strathman, *Minnesota Ombudsman for Corrections: An Evaluation Report* (November 1974; mimeo, 55 pp.), p. 2.

31. Staff did not feel that the ombudsman was ''fulfilling his responsibility concerning staff grievances.'' See *An Evaluation Report*, p. 2. In 1974–75, the ombudsman received twenty-four complaints from staff members. Here, the ombudsman is more insistent that he not become involved until ''all other channels have been utilized,'' particularly ''union and civil service assistance.'' See *1974–75 Annual Report*, p. 3.

32. *An Evaluation Report*, p. 3. (Emphasis in original.)

33. *An Evaluation Report*, p. 2. The fifty-six recommendations are listed at pp. 47–50. The ombudsman made forty-three recommendations in 1975–76. At the end of the year, two of these were pending and twelve had been rejected. The remaining twenty-nine were accepted, one only partially. See *1975–76 Annual Report*, pp. 28–30.

34. *1975–76 Annual Report*, p. 29. See also Ombudsman for Corrections, *Presentation on Prisoners' Rights, Grievance and Disciplinary Procedures at Stillwater State Prison* (April 5, 1973; mimeo, 11 pp., plus appendices).

35. See the *Ombudsman's Investigation Report of the August 5, 1973, Incident at the State Reformatory for Men at St. Cloud* (November 1, 1973; typescript, 27 pp.).

36. See the *Ombudsman's Investigation Report of the Deaths of John Love and Thomas Durham* (December 12, 1973; typescript, 14 pp.) and *Investigation of the Deaths of Rick Fultz and James Martin* (May 1, 1974; typescript, 21 pp.).

37. Quoted by Bryce Nelson, ''Prisoners' Ombudsman a Sympathetic Listener,'' *Los Angeles Times*, October 1, 1972, p. A–13.

38. Quoted by Michael W. Fedo, ''Prison Ombudsman: The Minnesota Experience,'' *America* 128 (May 5, 1973): 410.

39. Quoted by Edgar May, ''Prison Ombudsmen in America: They Listen to Both Sides,'' *Corrections Magazine* 1 (January/February 1975): 48.

40. Ibid., p. 47.

41. *Prison Life and Human Worth* (Minneapolis: University of Minnesota Press, 1974), p. 153.

42. Howard Lesnick, ''Grievance Procedures in Federal Prisons: Practices and Proposals,'' *University of Pennsylvania Law Review* 123 (1974): 29.

43. See Executive Order No. 14 (February 3, 1972), which is appended to the Minnesota Ombudsman for Corrections' annual reports, *supra*, notes 27 and 28.

44. See generally Ronald Goldfarb, *Jails: The Ultimate Ghetto* (New York: Anchor Press/Doubleday, 1975).

45. See *1974 Annual Report of the New York City Board of Correction*, p. iii: ''During 1974, the Board received and acted upon over 390 inmate requests and complaints and resolved countless problems varying greatly in complexity.'' See also Steve Gettinger, ''The Board of Correction: Prison Watchdog Agency,'' *Corrections Magazine* 2 (June 1976): 36–37.

46. See John E. Moore, ''Ombudsmen and the Ghetto,'' *Connecticut Law Review* 1 (1968): 248.

47. See generally Kenneth Culp Davis, *Discretionary Justice* (Baton Rouge, La.: Louisiana State University Press, 1969). See also James A. Jablonski, ''Controlling Discretionary Power in Prison Organizations: A Review of the Model Act,'' *Washington University Law Quarterly* (1973): 563–606.

B. OMBUDSMANSHIP IN CORRECTIONS: THE POWER OF PRESENCE ON THE PRISON PREMISES

PRESTON N. BARTON II, CORRECTIONS OMBUDSMAN, KANSAS CORRECTIONS OMBUDSMAN BOARD

ALTHOUGH THERE IS no way to determine with any certainty that all the work an ombudsman does in prison makes a difference, the odd reality is that the very existence of the ombudsman in a prison is the difference. In order for an ombudsman to effectively handle complaints in a prison, he must be physically present. It is this very presence on the premises that justifies his existence. As Professor Stanley Anderson has declared: "Presence on the premises is what defines the work of prison Ombudsmen," and as Sir Guy Powles, former New Zealand ombudsman, has put it: "One cannot know the inmate and his problems, unless you know his keepers and their problems; you cannot know the prison superintendent and his problems until you see the physical institution and are made aware of its problems."

Here is an agency that has statutory authority to be present within the walls of a prison, which has been traditionally prohibited to outsiders. Here is an outside agency whose staff does not have a vested interest in the survival of the prison bureaucracy, but rather in the treatment of individuals—both employees and prisoners. Here is an agency that can speak out with a separate voice on important issues, events, and programs—a voice that until recently has not existed. Here is an agency that is often present when events are occurring, and thus does not have to depend entirely upon someone else's version in order to understand what has happened. I refer not to the politician or official who from time to time makes the headlines by crying out against the conditions of prisons after having made a brief tour of a prison, but to a staff that has developed a finely tuned ear and a well-focused eye on the inner workings—and not mere appearances—of a prison. This

is what we have come to call the *Power of Presence on the Premises*.

Generally, prisons have always operated in such a manner that free people have very limited knowledge of the day-to-day events inside a prison. There are moments when society's attention is focused on the institution. Such times occur when there are an excessive number of escapes or when there is an unusually high degree of violence within an institution. From time to time, private citizens and public officials conduct inquiries.

The questionable meaningfulness of such inquiries is illustrated by the work of a gubernatorial appointed committee in 1908 and 1909 in Kansas in response to allegations of mistreatment of prisoners in the Kansas State Penitentiary. Noted editor William Allen White commented on its work: "The substance of the report on the penitentiary is to the effect that the warden hasn't done anything to be ashamed of, but he shouldn't do it again."[1]

How does the atmosphere of the institution change with the reality that on any one day it is likely there will be an outsider walking around within the walls? How does this affect the attitudes and behavior of institutional staff and inmates?

RESPONSE FROM ADMINISTRATORS AND LINE STAFF

One policy in the state of Kansas, which is a carryover from an earlier era, gives us a clue to the answer to this question. In Kansas prisons today, prisoners are allowed to possess a tape recorder only if it does not have the capacity to record. The only apparent explanation for this policy is that the administration fears that what correctional staff members say will be recorded to be used against them. This policy is now being strongly questioned.

It is clear that the institutional staff members perceive us (much as the tape recorder) as an intrusion to doing the work the way they believe it should be done. To minimize the sense of intrusiveness, as well as to ensure all aspects of an issue are known, we go to the correctional staff members involved in a complaint to get their side of the issue and, more important, to give them an opportunity to take responsibility for solving the problem and thus, possibly avoid having to go to their supervisors for the solution. The approach of investigating and resolving complaints at the lowest possible level within the institutional chain of command is quite different from that used by the majority of ombudsman offices.

Using this approach, I find that institutional staff members have considerable pride in their work and believe they are doing a good job. One of the most difficult tasks is to convince them that there is indeed a problem in their area of responsibility. Once this has been accepted, however, institutional staff members are often eager to find a solution to the problem. Unless a policy issue is involved, a goodly number of complaints can be resolved in such a low-keyed manner. The solution is designed by the very person who must make it work, rather than having it mandated from above on down through the organizational chain of command. This approach requires a heavy emphasis on skills in communication and communications facilitation. It is often useful to have the complainant and the other party meet jointly with the ombudsman staff member. This meeting should take place only after very careful preparation on the parts of all three parties and with the understanding that the ombudsman staff member is in charge and may stop the proceedings at any time.

Some of the more satisfying complaints that have been resolved are those that have also resulted in a change in the relationship between inmate and institutional staff member or between line staff member and supervisor. The parties learn something about one another, especially that they can communicate with each other in a more meaningful way. The complainant in a case that is successfully resolved can come to view the other party as a potential resource to whom to turn when future problems arise and, therefore, not have to depend upon an outside resource, such as the ombudsman, to be made available. This approach combines the investigative process and the resolution process. If after going to the appropriate institutional staff member the problem has not been resolved, the issues are then taken up the chain of command until a resolution is effected.

There are a number of drawbacks to attempting to re-

solve a complaint at the lowest possible level within the organizational hierarchy. One of the primary issues is its time-consuming nature. It works very well if line staff and line supervisors are able to resolve the issue, but it takes a good deal of time if the complaint must be taken very far through the organizational chain of command. We, however, always reserve the option of bypassing the chain of command, if the nature of the complaint requires a more rapid response. This style also tends to leave senior administrators in the dark about the activities of the ombudsman office. It can result in their belief that we are not useful or productive. Or it can provoke a good deal of suspicion and paranoia on their part as to what we are doing and what we may know. This undesirable side-effect can be significantly reduced by holding frequent meetings with top administrators to discuss, in generalities, the nature of the work being done by the ombudsman staff. Doing this also provides a forum in which we can provide significant information to the administrators which they have missed by not being involved in resolving a number of complaints. It is hoped that they will utilize the feedback information in the development of policies and in making other key management decisions.

Line staff and administrators often present themselves in a manner that strongly conveys they have given extensive thought to a decision and see absolutely no need for rethinking it. In the prison environment with a very thin balance of control between inmates and staff, administrators are very often reluctant to amend a policy decision once it has been made. Although they may acknowledge it was not the best decision, administrators often defend their position of holding the line for fear of "losing face"—of losing their power position with the inmates. The fear is that the administration would appear indecisive. Worse, it might appear that the institution is being run out of the ombudsman office. It demonstrates weakness. We, in fact, do all we can to ensure that the ombudsman office does not seem to be the power behind the warden. If we do decide against the administration's position, however, I have little patience or regard for the administration's concern with "losing face."

RESPONSE FROM COMPLAINANTS

While such an approach presents the least possible threat to institutional staff, it does involve some risk-taking on the part of the inmate or staff complainant. What we say to the complainant is that we will make his complaint known to the person about whom he is complaining and give that person the opportunity to tell the other side of the issue. This approach needs to be utilized when the problem affects only one complainant and specific identifying information about him is needed for resolving the complaint. If, however, a number of persons are affected by a particular policy, our source of information is not relevant. For the individual complainant, this screening mechanism helps us gauge how serious the complainant is in pursuing a matter to a meaningful resolution and shows he is not merely seeking to "get the other guy." By planning such a thorough approach to resolving the complaint, we also communicate to the complainant that we are taking the complaint seriously.

When the ombudsman representative presents an inmate's problem to a staff member or a staff member's problem to his supervisor, it is presented as the concern of the ombudsman office. This is done deliberately to diffuse the sense of antagonism and conflict among those people who must live and work together. We can afford to use this approach only as long as we retain our sense of being outsiders. The ombudsman representative redefines the problem to fit within his sense of what needs to be addressed. The ombudsman representative must make the complaint his own concern and present it to the administration in that manner.

Prison administrators frequently want to know more about the individual making the complaint and less regarding the situation being complained about. The administrator wishes to discredit the complainant rather than focus attention on the problem. Inmates have also objected to this approach. We are taking control away from them by reformulating a complaint and the means of resolution to fit our own frame of reference. This usurping of control is difficult to accept by inmates who already retain little control over their lives. To counterbalance this feeling, we attempt to involve inmates as much as possible in resolving their complaints. With only rare exceptions, we give them the final say in whether or not a complaint is to be pursued further, at any phase during the investigation and resolution process.

Those of us who handle inmate complaints receive a lower percentage of unfounded complaints than do those ombudsmen who handle complaints from the general public. This observation is tentative because the statistics among various ombudsman offices are not uniform. The differences, however, do appear to be significant in this area. In attempting to understand this discrepancy, two possible explanations come to mind, both rooted in the phenomenon of institutionalization. First, it appears that prospective complainants would have more knowledge and exposure to the ombudsman office by virtue of the closed communication system within an institution than would the citizen complainant in a free community. Thus, the potential institutional complainant will self-screen out a number of complaints that would not be appropriate or substantial. Second, the lower percentage of unfounded complaints within the prison setting can be explained by the need of persons not to "use up" potentially valuable resources for the future, when there are so few resources available, compared to those that would be available in a free community.

It is not uncommon for a complainant to work especially hard at getting our attention and in finding ways to ensure that we will pursue a complaint. One approach is that of sensationalizing the situation to get us "hooked" into it. What is helpful here is to differentiate between the content of the complaint and the strategy of complaining. A very familiar strategy is to "put down" the competence or character of a person who occupies the position that would normally be the resource available to solve that problem. For example, an inmate complainant will go to great lengths to tell me why the counselor would not possibly be able to help him, although the situation is clearly one in which the counselor should be involved.

EFFECTS ON OMBUDSMAN STAFF

This style of complaint handling has a number of effects on both staff and ombudsman. I spend most of my day reading correspondence or listening to people telling me about all the things that have gone wrong. How do we keep from being cynical, from becoming perpetual pessimists? Our approach to complaint handling and our presence on the premises bring the ombudsman staff into direct contact with the day-to-day violence and risk to one's person that is ever present in an institution. This, on the one hand, makes us a bit more open to hear what institutional staff members and inmates may be telling us about their fears. The shared common experiences over time can enhance our credibility. The danger, on the other hand, is that our sense of objectivity can slip away.

As an outsider, the ombudsman's representative is very much alone in his day-to-day activities within an institution. As a member of one work group, he is working within another work group's territory. His work is one of continuous exploration and discovery of foreign turf. He can never fully know the institution. What he does know most intimately are those aspects of institutional life that are dysfunctional. He seldom has the opportunity to enjoy and be fully aware of those aspects of institutional life that work well and that have meaning to the staff and inmates. His caseload of problems is too great to take time for that. Because he is not part of the communications system of the institution and because he is not present every day, he can never know everything that is going on within the institution. He is the outsider on the inside.

New ombudsman representatives struggle with this sense of aloneness. Some align themselves with the inmates, identifying with the inmates' sense of being victimized by the system and overlooking the constructive approaches that complainants could take to resolve their own problems. Other ombudsman representatives have sought out the support of institutional staff members. It becomes reassuring to them that they can get direct information about how things should be working, even though this information is very often distorted to the advantage of the institutional staff members. In time, the ombudsman representatives come to rely too heavily upon what institutional staff tell them, without doing their own work to find out information on a firsthand basis. Thus, the overwhelming sense of being a stranger is reduced by aligning oneself to either the inmate population or the institutional staff. At the same time, the unique and precious difference that an outsider can offer is lost.

There is a third approach for the ombudsman representative: to become well grounded in the ombudsman concept and function, to hold on to that as though one's life depended on it—indeed, one's effectiveness does. By maintaining a continuous sense of curiosity and a healthy sense of questioning everything one hears, the ombudsman representative can retain his own sense of difference as an outsider and thus still be able to bring about change—to resolve the complaint.

CONCLUSION

The correctional ombudsman makes a significant commitment of time, energy, political risk, and sometimes personal physical risk. What does an ombudsman office or a governmental unit have at stake in making such a commitment? Why would a group of politicians want to create a corrections ombudsman? Or why would a general jurisdiction ombudsman elect to devote the ever scarce resources of his office to such an endeavor? Conversely, why do so many not make this commitment?

Governments have a considerable stake in keeping prisons quiet. Inmates do not have a vote. They are not even liked by those citizens in the society who do have a say in their government. Indeed, they have deliberately been removed and isolated from the rest of the society. But it has been a long accepted truism that the manner in which a society perceives and treats its prisoners reflects its regard of the worth and dignity of each individual citizen. The meaning of society's treatment of prisoners goes far beyond its mere expression of nonacceptance of these few persons whom it confines. The same may be said about such groups as psychiatric patients, the elderly (especially those in nursing homes), the severely handicapped, and welfare recipients.

While the quality of life varies considerably from prison to prison, there are the overriding common elements of institutionalization and the loss of freedom. Those who run the prison, of course, have an enormous amount of control over those confined. For me as an ombudsman, the central issue is the degree of visibility which the rest of government and the community, as a whole, have of the exercise of this control.

NOTE

1. Harvey R. Hougen, ''The Impact of Politics and Prison Industry on the General Management of the Kansas State Penitentiary, 1883–1909,'' *Kansas Historical Quarterly* 53, No. 3 (Autumn 1977):317.

BIBLIOGRAPHY

Fitzharris, T. L. *The Desirability of a Correctional Ombudsman.* Berkeley, Calif.: Institute of Government Studies, University of California, 1973, 114 pp.

Raphael, A. ''Ombudsman and Prisons: The European Experience.'' *Corrections Magazine* (January–February 1975).

Tibbles, L. ''Ombudsmen for American Prisons.'' *North Dakota Law Review* 48 (Spring 1972): 383–441.

CHAPTER 12

THE CAMPUS OMBUDSMAN IN NORTH AMERICA

DONALD C. ROWAT, Carleton University, and
GEOFFREY WALLACE, University of California,
Santa Barbara

THE INSTITUTION OF ombudsman has spread to the campuses of North America. Most ombudsmen were appointed in response to the student disturbances of the late 1960s to deal with student complaints against university administration and with their educational grievances. Many were retained because university administrators and student union councils found them useful in correcting administrative mistakes and ascertaining the needs of troubled students. In Stanley Anderson's words,

Institutions of higher learning are ideal for the implementation of the ombudsman idea. They are bureaucracies served for the most part by able and intelligent employees who apply complex laws, regulations, rules and practices to a myriad of services and situations. Inevitably, errors occur and misunderstandings arise. As civilized institutions, colleges and universities are dedicated to consultation, correction, and cure. The ombudsman is a fail-safe device for grappling with unsolved residues.[1]

In this chapter, Donald Rowat describes the peculiar nature of the campus ombudsman, while Geoffrey Wallace focuses on the current situation in the state of California.

THE NATURE OF A CAMPUS OMBUDSMAN*

In recent years, the office of ombudsman has been created at a number of universities in Canada. The idea of appointing an officer to look into complaints against the university bureaucracy is so new that various versions of the office have been created. The time is therefore ripe to examine some of the main questions concerning the nature and functioning of this new institution.

In general, it is needed because of the tremendous growth of big bureaucracy in the modern world. This subject has several aspects. One is what one might call the arrogance of office. Officials very quickly develop this attitude if they have been in office a very long time. Another is the many minor errors that occur in a big bureaucracy, often unintentionally. The third important aspect is that the individual feels lost when he is facing a gigantic bureaucracy. He therefore needs someone to turn to in whom he has confidence, someone whom he trusts as being independent and natural, who has the power to investigate his case to see if he has been treated fairly.

The courts and other traditional appeal procedures have been inadequate to remedy the thousands of minor grievances that people are confronted with when administrations make decisions. At the end of World War II, as the welfare state advanced and the bureaucracies grew in size, democracies were living on their past reputations for the rule of law. We in the English-speaking countries have always prided ourselves on the fact that our liberties are protected by the courts and the rule of law. But unfortunately we are worse off than the dachshund in the famous anonymous rhyme:

---

*By Donald C. Rowat, abstracted from *CAUT Bulletin* ACPU (September 1980): 17–19.

There was a dachshund, one so long he hadn't any notion
How long it took to notify his tail of emotion.
And so it was that, though his eyes were filled with tears and sadness
His little tail went wagging on because of previous gladness.

We, too, are wagging our tails because of previous gladness about our reputation for the rule of law, without realizing that the tremendous growth in bureaucracy should have filled our eyes with tears and sadness. The rule of law is no longer adequately protecting the ''little man'' in his dealings with the administration. The ombudsman may therefore be regarded as a very important new invention in the machinery of democratic government that helps to remedy this situation.

Let us now consider more specifically the application of the ombudsman idea to universities. Those of us who have been promoting the ombudsman plan—and I have been at it now for almost twenty years—ought to be careful to look into our own backyards. We may be like Robert Stanfield when he was interviewed during his trip to Jerusalem. He reportedly said, ''If you think the Middle East is a mess, you should see my backyard.'' Although we may be thinking about the worldwide spread of the institution and the need for it in the various governments of the world, those of us in the universities who are promoting this idea ought to look into our own backyards. We would find that very much the same reasoning, very much the same arguments, hold true with respect to university administration. We are now confronted with what is called the ''multiversity,'' an institution with thousands of students, a huge bureaucracy, and a great capacity for officials to act in an arbitrary fashion and certainly to make mistakes. We also find that the appeal procedures in most of the universities are rather cumbersome and difficult to pursue. Hence, the student finds himself lost when confronted with the huge bureaucracy of the university administration.

Universities Paternalistic

An additional important factor in the case of universities is that they are essentially, at least historically and traditionally, paternalistic organizations. They tend to take a paternalistic attitude toward the students, and characteristic of appeal procedures in a university is that an appeal is made within the same bureaucracy that made the decision in the first place. This is an undesirable arrangement that the ombudsman institution helps to remedy. It provides an outside, independent authority who investigates the case and decides on the fairness of the decision that was made.

Because of the great need in the university milieu for the independence, neutrality, and objectivity of the office, it should be set up in a formal way so as to ensure its independence from the university administration. Preferably, it should be provided for in the law that governs the university rather than in the bylaws of its board or senate or by action of the president. The office will thereby be completely independent of the university administration and have its own source of law. The same sort of argument has been made about a governmental ombudsman. It is said that he should be provided for in the Constitution of a country rather than by ordinary law, and certainly not by executive action. Short of provision in a university charter, perhaps the next best way of providing for the office would be in the bylaws of the board of governors. But the board of governors, composed mainly of outside lay members, tends to be dominated by the president, and therefore its bylaws are likely to be slanted in favor of the administration.

One mistake that can easily be made in creating the office in the universities is to turn it into what has been called an executive office. In the United States at the state level, a number of state governors have been impressed with the popularity of the ombudsman idea and have said, ''Oh yes, our state needs an ombudsman. I'll therefore appoint an ombudsman.'' So he appoints one of his political friends as the ombudsman. It is perfectly clear that such an executive ombudsman, whose office is not set up by law and who is not responsible to the legislature, is very likely to side with the administration in any crucial decision. Similarly, a number of university presidents in the United States have said, ''Oh yes, an ombudsman is a good idea for universities, so I'll appoint my ombudsman.'' And so the university president appoints as ombudsman an administrator who does not have the interests of the students at heart and who is very likely, through his experience and training, to side with the administration or the professors in any dispute or complaint. Therefore, one thing that ought to be guarded against in creating the office for universities is an executive ombudsman. The institution should be clearly independent of the administration.

Pay Peanuts, Get Monkeys

Because of student interest in the idea, there is the opposite problem—a student-dominated ombudsman. The students' council may become interested in the plan, and so they appoint somebody who naturally turns out to be a student or a recently graduated student. The difficulty with this kind of plan is that the ombudsman then becomes a kind of advocate for the student's case, instead of being an independent officer at a senior enough level to carry some clout with the administration and to inspire enough confidence for his recommendations to be adopted. He is arguing a case for the student rather than being an independent investigator who is trying to make a neutral judgment about whether the university has made the right decision.

Instead of these opposite extremes—the executive ombudsman and the student ombudsman—the proper role of the university ombudsman, if it follows the classical plan, is to be in the middle. The only way this can be assured is to have a completely joint office. The legislation or bylaws that set up the office should provide that the university and the students share the control and cost of the plan, and that the ombudsman be appointed by a joint committee of the university administration and the students. Even in a so-called joint plan it is very easy, because of the paternalistic nature of the university, for the administration to arrange to have the predominant voice. Students have to be very careful in joining such a plan to make sure it is really a 50-50 plan. They must insist that they participate in the creation and control of the office and in the appointment of the ombudsman, and in particular they must be willing to pay half of the costs of the office. If the university is paying all or most of the cost, it is likely to exert an undue influence on the office. Students should also make sure that the office is well enough financed to do the job it is expected to do. As someone said recently in the *Globe and Mail*'s ''quote of the day.'' ''If you pay peanuts, you get monkeys.''

Ombudsman Plans Vary

One of my former students, Ms. Nutter-Hoffman, who was the assistant ombudsman at Carleton, has recently completed an honors essay on the university ombudsman in Canada. Although it was an incomplete study, it did show some very interesting comparative differences. The offices that she identified as genuine ombudsman plans in the classic pattern were the ones at Dalhousie University, the University of Quebec in Montreal, Concordia, Carleton, and the University of Toronto. The grandfather of all these plans was not covered by the Hoffman essay—the one originally organized at Simon Fraser University during the time of student radicalism in the late 1960s. It is essentially a student-run plan. One was also set up at the University of Alberta very soon after an ombudsman was appointed for the province in 1967. It was created by a bylaw of the board of governors, had a very good basic structure, and provided for joint administration of the plan and a joint appointment. It was studied by Karl Friedmann, formerly at the University of Calgary and now

ombudsman for British Columbia. At that time, he and a colleague wrote an article for the Canadian Association of University Teachers *Bulletin* based on this plan and discussing the nature of and need for university ombudsmen in Canada. They thought that the plan for the University of Alberta was a rather good one. Yet, when the first ombudsman's term came to an end, the plan was abandoned. Perhaps one of the reasons was that it was given the job of handling complaints from both the students and the staff. But we cannot be sure why the plan failed until someone writes up its history. Students at the University of Ottawa ran an ombudsman-like office for a few years, and there may be one or two other campus ombudsmen in Canada not covered by the Hoffman study.

There are considerable variations among the plans that now exist in Canada. After examining these variations, one can pose some key questions about the nature of campus ombudsmen. One is: Should the ombudsman be a former university administrator, a professor, or a student, or none of these? For instance, when the plan was created at Carleton University, I do not think the students realized its limitation. The initiative was taken by the students' council and, although they provided for the appointment of the ombudsman by a joint committee of students, administrators, and professors, the office was described and advertised in such a way, and the pay was put at such a level, that it would have been impossible for an experienced administrator or a professor to become the ombudsman. Although they did not specify that the ombudsman had to be a student or a very recent graduate, it became an unwritten requirement. As a result, there has been a succession of ombudsmen at Carleton who were either students or recent graduates.

Off-Campus Investigations

A second question to be posed is: Should the campus ombudsman deal with nonuniversity problems? The plans vary considerably in this respect. When the office was created at Carleton, I was at first rather critical of the fact that the university ombudsman took on noncampus problems because I thought it was a mixing of functions and was likely to downgrade the real purpose, which was to investigate complaints against the university administration. But I have somewhat changed my view after watching this office in operation over a period of years. The ombudsman institution at Carleton has managed successfully to combine investigating complaints against the university administration with handling off-campus problems. So one finds the ombudsman at Carleton dealing with all kinds of off-campus problems—landlord-tenant relations, immigration, and so on. These do not bear on a student's direct relations with the university but are nevertheless serious problems for many. Experience at Carleton shows that an ombudsman who deals with off-campus problems must have a good arrangement for quick legal advice.

A third question is: Should the ombudsman also deal with complaints from the faculty and support staff? When campus ombudsmen were first created, many people thought that it should be made an all-university institution. Since the university is a community, the ombudsman should handle complaints from anyone in that community. The faculty have complaints just as civil servants have complaints, and it is characteristic of the governmental ombudsman plans to receive complaints from civil servants against their superiors. So, it was thought, why not have a plan that will allow faculty to complain against their superiors within the university administration? However, there are problems with mixing student and employee complaint functions. As mentioned, this may have been one of the reasons why the plan foundered at the University of Alberta. The Canadian Association of University Teachers has been dealing with the problems of faculty as employees for a long time. It has set up a very efficient tenure committee, and most universities have well-developed appeal procedures for faculty grievances. So there is not the same need for an ombudsman to handle such grievances. It may be an undesirable mixing of functions to provide that the university ombudsman should deal with complaints from both the faculty and students, and may distort or downgrade the function of looking after complaints from students. On the other hand, a campus ombudsman could usefully handle minor faculty complaints that fall outside the normal appeal procedures. And often the support staff members have no other suitable procedure for handling their complaints.

Jurisdiction over Universities

A fourth question to be raised is: Should the provincial ombudsmen have jurisdiction over the universities? It is interesting that in Hawaii, which has a state university, the state ombudsman does have jurisdiction over the university, so he is able to investigate complaints from the students or staff against the university administration. The ombudsmen in Nova Scotia and New Brunswick (Nova Scotia from the beginning and New Brunswick more recently) have had their scope extended to cover local governments. Similarly, one could ask: Since the universities are important public institutions, why should not the provincial ombudsmen's scope be extended to

them? This could be done in addition to having a university ombudsman. The role of a provincial ombudsman would be to collaborate with the university ombudsman and to take on the more serious cases—in particular those that require somebody who is absolutely independent from the university to conduct an investigation. There is now a movement to create provincial laws on administrative procedure which require due process in all provincial activities. In Ontario at least, the new law on administrative procedure appears to apply to universities as state emanations. One can argue that the role of a provincial ombudsman should be extended to cover complaints against the universities in order to ensure procedural due process in university administration. The administrative court systems in Western Europe cover the universities. In West Germany, for instance, a doctoral student can appeal to an administrative court on the ground that he was dealt with unfairly in his comprehensive examinations.

Whatever may be the best answer to these questions, there is little doubt that campus ombudsmen are needed in today's monstrous multiversities in order to help students who have become hopelessly entangled in bureaucratic redtape through no fault of their own—and usually through no intentional fault of the university administration. For this reason I hope that before too long, through the initiative of either the students themselves, university senates, or enlightened university administrations, the office will have been created at the vast majority of universities in Canada.

THE CALIFORNIA UNIVERSITY AND COLLEGE OMBUDSMAN*

California has a tradition of ombudsman offices in most of its major educational institutions. There are reasons why these offices were established and why they have survived. California has more people in public education than the entire population of New Hampshire. The system is arranged in three tiers: the university, the state colleges and universities, and the community colleges. This is a vast bureaucracy with centralized governance for the University of California and the state colleges and universities. The university has nine campuses and the state colleges and universities have eighteen, while the community college system has over one hundred.

During the years 1965–70, the campuses had problems of polarization, disruption, and open conflict. Students and faculty rallied against federal decisions and levied similar charges against the educational system. Polariza-

*By Geoffrey Wallace, University Ombudsman, University of California, Santa Barbara.

tion preceded noteworthy changes in typically quiet college communities. Berkeley experienced repeated confrontations with police and students. James Rector was killed by police during one demonstration. In Santa Barbara, Dover Sharp, an innocent janitor, was killed by a pipe bomb at the Faculty Club. Kevin Moran was shot and killed by police. The Bank of America branch building was burned to the ground. Over one thousand arrests of students were made during four major riots. Los Angeles experienced similar problems. In this climate, students and faculty explored proposals for mitigating this inimical, dangerous polarization.

Between 1968 and 1973, students introduced proposals for the office of ombudsman on all campuses of the two major systems.[2] They were concerned with the impersonal treatment of students in multiversities, the arbitrary nature of many actions and decisions, the remote monolithic quality of California education, and the anxiety and stress that were involved in succeeding in education. The 1960s taught some members of the educational community rage, but it did not drastically alter the bureaucratic nature of education. Students perceived the ombudsman office as a possible means of giving those who were treated impersonally or unjustly an agency designed to mediate their conflict.

President Clark Kerr had espoused the notion of using reasoned persuasion as opposed to pure coercion to get things done.[3] Likewise, the peace movement had established an intellectual framework for appreciating the role of resolving conflict with reason rather than force or power. Academic experts on the ombudsman, such as Professors Stanley Anderson and John Moore at the University of California, Santa Barbara, were also influential advocates. Faculty felt that a person mutually acceptable to all constituencies would not be a threat to them if the office did not have decision-making authority. The faculties of Berkeley, Los Angeles, Santa Barbara, Irvine, and Riverside accepted the office within two years of its first proposal. The state college system responded to the suggestion by providing funds on every campus for an ombudsman office.

The offices established in California had (1) *independence,* through structural safeguards; (2) *impartiality;* (3) *accessibility;* but (4) *no sanctioning power.* The positions were filled by candidates with expertise in the nature of the institution and the constituents. The offices were allowed to take complaints from students in all cases, but varied in accepting staff and faculty complaints. Thus, the ombudsmen at Los Angeles, Riverside, and Santa Barbara accept complaints from staff, faculty, and students, the ombudsman at Berkeley deals only with student grievances, while the office at San Diego deals with staff complaints. The California state campuses pri-

marily take student complaints. Most of the incumbents come from faculty ranks, but the campus ministry is another frequent source. The campus ombudsmen can initiate action by their own motion, they can access records in their investigation, and they may publicize the findings of investigations at their discretion. By national standards, they are well paid and experienced in campus affairs. Care was taken to select incumbents creditable to all parties.

Complaint workloads vary from one hundred per year to two thousand. Complainants are primarily students (over 75 percent statewide) who meet face to face with the ombudsman (or deputy) who investigates the matter and reports back to the complainant. University constituencies prefer direct contact to formal, written, impersonal contact. While some initially viewed the university ombudsman as an institution which they hoped would cure systemic ills such as impersonal treatment, pressure, or arbitrary actions, the office has survived and has succeeded as a marginal assistance to the aggrieved. The office has provided an agency that gives substantive assistance and emotional first aid to those who are injured by the educational bureaucracy in California. To some extent, the office was established to eliminate injustice; yet it survived by mitigating injustice. The university ombudsman is the one office that combines emotional expression of the stress and pressure of education with substantive efforts by an expert to resolve any inequities. The office provides one-stop improvement. It is established to be parsimonious in resolution. It does not become another part of the maze. It is the point where an issue can be unraveled and resolved.

In the separation, specialization, and fragmentation of the university, the ombudsman office as it exists in California universities has proven capable of dealing with the whole range of issues that affect human beings. Problems have facets that touch on various agencies. When an individual is least able to function, the greatest demands are often imposed. When individuals are most stressed, they are often least able to mobilize their full capabilities. Ombudsmen have been particularly useful in these situations and in such student concerns as police-student relations, distributive justice, and equal access in education, issues of national policy, sexual harassment, and the self-serving image of bureaucracies. Students have rarely used other formal grievance systems. They find the ombudsman office a sympathetic place where they can be upset without embarrassment and have their problems discussed with promise of action. But they have also come to recognize its limitations as a marginal correction agency; it is not a system reformer. Reasoned persuasion is the only weapon it has, but that seems sufficient for individual grievances. For systemic problems such as housing, unequal educational opportunity, or racism, the ombudsman office can only remind people constantly.

People are better educated and have greater potential if they know what has happened in their education and if they have played some role in it. They must start taking part in the democratic world, a world in which they are free and responsible. Ombudsmen try to teach people how they are being handled. They say, "This is how the organization is structured; this is how it is working; this is what it is saying to you." And they transliterate sometimes: "These are your possibilities. How do you feel? How will anger work toward resolving your problem? How will indifference work toward resolving it? What will happen if you just let it go on the way it is going?" Often the result is an exchange that sounds like a Platonic dialogue: "Is this your sense of authority? Is this your idea of a desirable world? Is this the role you choose to play?" In a domestic problem, they might say, "Is this your sense of friendship?" Such questions arise every day. Ombudsmen have an opportunity to provide a tutoring process through which people reach greater understanding.

Institutions cannot appoint a person to handle every problem that arises. The ombudsman fills that vacuum; he is the person one goes to when no one else will deal with this problem. If the person whom complainants have seen is less concerned with institutional mores than the well-being of the complainants, the ombudsman office can help the institution come to terms with its own constituents, the students. Systems like universities have an al-most infinite number of internal conflicts. The ombudsman is charged with handling many of the problems and conflicts associated with large, complex, and often impersonal bureaucratic institutions.[4]

NOTES

1. S. V. Anderson, "Public School Ombuds Offices," *California Journal of Teacher Education* 7, No. 3 (1980): 26.

2. Minutes, Student Body President's Council, UC/CSCU.

3. Clark Kerr, *Uses of the University* (New York: Harper, 1963), pp. 22–23.

4. "Ombudsman on the Campus," *The Center Magazine* 13, No. 4 (July/August 1980): 19–23.

BIBLIOGRAPHY

Buccieri, C. H. "Campus Troubleshooter Resetting His Sights." *College and University Business* 45 (1968): 51–53.

_____. "Ombudsman: New Troubleshooter on Campus." *College and University Business* 44 (1968): 52–55.

Friedmann, K. A., and Barker, B. M. "Ombudsmen in Universities." *CAUT* (Canadian Association of University Teachers) *Bulletin* 20 (Spring 1972): 43–60.

Institute for Local Government and Public Service. *The Ombudsman in Higher Education: Advocate or Subversive Bureaucrat?* Chico, Calif.: 1969, 68 pp. (typed).

Rowland, H. R. "The Campus Ombudsman: An Emerging Role." *Educational Record* 50 (Fall 1969): 442–48.

CHAPTER 13

AN AMERICAN SCHOOL OMBUDSMAN

JAMES WINEINGER, WICHITA PUBLIC SCHOOLS
DISTRICT OMBUDSMAN

ACCORDING TO GEORGE WOLKON and Sharon Moriwaki, the ombudsman institution has therapeutic value[1] in cooling immediate anger, discharging discontent, and establishing tranquility by removing grievances. The complaints process helps the parties clarify motives and perceptions. It brings them together and teaches them coping skills. It fosters "an environment conducive to mutual learning by stimulating effective communication."[2] It works well in institutions of higher education where, as Stanley Anderson points out, the students are "the cream of the crop," volunteers, "generally law abiding, often altruistic, sometimes idealistic."

They have all the advantages of motivation and means, of optimism growing from accomplishment, and they tend to come from affluent, articulate, and supportive segments of society. By way of contrast, many pupils in school are like prison inmates . . . sentenced to a long term of years in an often highly controlled and quite coercive structure with significant elements of anti-social behavior among age-peers.[3]

Would a school ombudsman work as well or at all in such an environment? There are fewer school ombudsmen offices in North America than campus ombudsmen, and like them they essentially support the system rather than advocate system change, although they do deal occasionally with significant issues, such as denial of individual rights, cruelty, racism, and discrimination. General purpose ombudsman offices deal with complaints by pupils and their parents, school employees, and school administrators who feel themselves aggrieved by education bureaucracies. Rarely have ombudsman offices been established just to deal specifically with complaints arising from public school systems. Wichita is such a case.

In September 1972, an experimental school ombudsman program was sponsored by the Wichita League of Women Voters. It was financed by a grant from the U.S. Department of Health, Education, and Welfare. The office was suspended in June 1974 but revived in January 1976. It arose out of a drastic desegregation program that was implemented in 1970. The cross-busing plan required most of the city's black student population to attend schools out of their immediate neighborhoods, while white students were selected on a birthdate lottery basis to fulfill their integration obligation with a one-year assignment to an Assigned Attendance Area (AAA) school. A statistically significant number of students suspended from secondary schools during the 1971–72 school year for "unacceptable" behavior were black. In fact, blacks represented nearly 43 percent of those suspended (2,455 of the total 5,764), although they constituted only 13.6 percent of the total secondary student population.

BACKGROUND DEBATE

During the school year 1972–73, the League of Women Voters (LWV) recognized and formulated the need for an ombudsman office. The group felt that the minority isolation in northeast Wichita had been intensified by the adoption of the cross-busing desegregation plan. Many discussions were held with local school officials about the creation of an office to handle complaints from parents and other patrons. The school officials maintained that as each principal served the public as his/her own ombudsman there was no need for an "independent" resource. The LWV proposed to alleviate the feelings of isolation and powerlessness within the black community by requesting the establishment of a school ombudsman service. It claimed that the board of education was incapable of providing such a service itself because it lacked the time, staff, and funds to handle parent complaints and that minority women in particular were uncomfortable in dealing with the white, male-dominated superintendent's office. Black students more than any others needed help in coping with their school-related problems.

LWV member Van Wilson led the effort to seek federal government funding of an ombudsman project to demonstrate its usefulness to the community and to school district officials. Her proposal was successful, and funding was provided through the Emergency School Assistance Act which aided school districts in implementing integration plans. The league planned a community-based advisory committee of twelve members to supervise and evaluate the ombudsman project. The committee, consisting of representatives from the local education authority, the Young Women's Christian Association, Urban League, Juvenile Court, G. I. Forum, and Legal Aid Society, together with six high school students, selected Robert Wright, a high school mathematics teacher, to be ombudsman for one year while on leave of absence.

Some leaders in the black community criticized Wright's appointment because he was white. The National Education Association also objected because teachers could go to the ombudsman office instead of taking their grievances to the association. There was professional concern that complaints could be made against teachers without their knowing the identity of their accusers. Gradually, opposition subsided, and much publicity was generated to get the new office known in the community. Brochures were distributed in grocery stores, shopping centers, and churches, with special attention to areas with high minority concentrations.

At the end of his year in office, Wright returned to teaching, and Rex Kreig, a student at Wichita State University who had worked with Wright as a volunteer, was selected to fill the position of school ombudsman for the second year of the project grant (1974–75). That year proved to be a difficult period for the ombudsman program. Kreig was be less acceptable than Wright to school officials. The media frequently identified him as a source of controversy, and he had difficulty working with the Advisory Committee. The end result was that the board of education became disenchanted with the idea of an ombudsman and voted in the spring of 1975 not to endorse the project with local funds. However, a new board member, John Frye, was elected in April 1975, and he supported the project. He reversed the action of the previous board when he took office in July, and Unified School District 259 agreed to assume funding for the ombudsman program.

At this point, the board of education instructed its attorney, Bob Foulston, to work with Robert Wright to draft a (board) policy to spell out functional guidelines for an ombudsperson (due to a concern that "ombudsman" might be interpreted as sexist). The original structure of the Advisory Committee was expanded slightly, with the board replacing the LWV. At first, the superintendent was reluctant to approve the new arrangement but later conceded that the ombudsperson would report to the ombudsperson advisory board and the final say would rest with the board. It was felt that if the ombudsperson were responsible to the superintendent, the program would lose its effectiveness. Accordingly, the superintendent was allowed to make recommendations to the board of education concerning only the employment or termination of the ombudsperson, not the behavior or actions of the incumbent. The director of the Pupil Services Division would serve as liaison with the ombudsperson for personnel and supply matters. The Advisory Committee opened the search late in 1975 and finally selected a former school social worker, Jim Wineinger, who reopened the office on January 12, 1976, in the newly constructed City Hall building. With certain modifications, Wineinger continued to follow the working arrangements set by ombudsman Wright and adapted his policy to reflect the composition of the Advisory Committee. The committee has met monthly to receive his reports, discuss issues raised by members, and otherwise provide direction and assistance to the ombudsperson.

THE SCHOOL OMBUDSMAN'S OPERATIONS

Ever since the board of education began funding the office, the ombudsman has worked out of the City Hall building instead of a store front near the core area of downtown Wichita. The ombudsman spends much of his time outside the office gathering information, visiting with parents, students, and school employees, mediating concerns, and working with school personnel. At first, the school district was skeptical and defensive, but its attitude has since shifted to growing openness and acceptance. It is common now for a school staff member to call upon the ombudsman to intervene or assist in working with a particular family where the school has previously experienced difficulty. His primary function is to be an independent resource for patrons who have complaints, suggestions, or questions regarding the public school system. Much of the work involves clarifying school policy, mediating conflicts between school staff and parents and students, and interpreting educational jargon.

The Advisory Committee ensures that the ombudsman

complies with the guidelines (Board of Education Policy P2250.00). This representative body has been largely composed of enthusiastic and energetic members. An attempt is made to maintain a balanced representation by sex and ethnicity. Although specific names of complainants and school personnel are not given to the Advisory Committee in its monthly meetings, individual members raise many questions about the nature of complaints, implications about the accumulation of certain kinds of concerns, and the actions taken by the ombudsman.

Parents represent the largest client group of the ombudsman. During the past four years, approximately 80 percent of all contacts with the ombudsman office have been initiated by parents of students attending a Wichita public school. Of the remaining 20 percent, approximately 12 percent were originated by a citizen or agency-related person, with students and employees of the school district being responsible for the remaining 8 percent. Although the school ombudsman can officially become involved only in matters relating to the public schools in Wichita, a number of inquiries and questions are received from smaller school districts surrounding Wichita. The ombudsman normally reviews with patrons of these smaller districts the manner in which similar investigations would be conducted to resolve their problem if they lived in Wichita. The ombudsman refers them to the Kansas commissioner of education if they are not satisfied with their attempts to resolve the concern on their own local level.

Upon receipt of a complaint from a patron of U.S.D. 259, the ombudsman will normally contact the administrator or administrative office most directly involved with the student/patron. After checking by phone with this person, usually a principal, a determination is made regarding the necessity to visit at the school, or to take other action. Frequently, after the initial contact with the school principal and a "reading" of this response has been made, the ombudsman reports back to the complainant and a plan is developed, that is, whether to arrange a conference at the school between the parent, student, principal, and other school resource people as required, along with the ombudsman, or jointly plan other suitable action.

Because of the delicate nature surrounding complaints about school personnel and because of the fact that the ombudsman is permitted by policy to investigate complaints against employees without disclosing the name of the patron, his primary function has been to delineate the specific grievances and communicate them directly to the employee about whom the complaint has been registered. Notification, again, will have been to the supervisor or administrator about the general nature of the grievance, along with an inquiry about similar or other complaints involving this particular employee. Following the discussion with the employee about whom the complaint has

been lodged, recommendations are made to both the complainant and the employee. The guidelines for the ombudsman office, specified in Policy P2250.00, identifies the steps normally utilized in responding to complaints registered. If recommendations at the most direct or immediate level do not produce a suitable resolution to the problem, other action will be taken. The ombudsman considers each complainant as having a justified or justifiable complaint. An investigation is always made on the assumption that a genuine grievance exists. A real effort has been made not to categorize complaints into boxes such as trivial, critical, serious, or very serious. The ombudsman has sought to respond to each inquiry or complaint in a timely manner and with sincerity.

Upon the conclusion of an investigation into an allegation of injustice, a summary of findings along with a recommendation is made to both the complainant and appropriate school personnel. The following case will serve as an illustration: A parent of a multiple-handicapped elementary school child complained about the physical abuse her daughter was receiving at the hands of other students attending the comprehensive school that housed their special education program. After talking with administrators both at the school building and in the central office, a meeting was arranged to review the problem along with the individual education plan for the student. The information pointed to the fact that the student was eliciting much of the abusive behavior on the part of other students by seeking their approval/acceptance through inappropriate ways, that is, hitting, kicking, and spitting at them. A plan including closer monitoring of the student's informal activities and interchanges with peers was drawn up. Positive reinforcement was to be given for acceptable approach behavior on the part of the multiple-handicapped student to other students. It was further recommended to the parent that effort be expended to provide opportunities for the child to interact with children in the community, outside the school setting, for the development of social skills. A recommendation was also made that the school counselor work with the student and perhaps involve this student in a small group to seek a more positive self-image and gain skills in communication and interaction with peers. In a followup contact with the parent, it was learned that the student's experience at school was much more positive; the abusive reactions of peers had virtually been eliminated.

In some cases, the complainant might not be totally satisfied with the results or findings of the ombudsman. For example, if a student was suspended for behavior that was administratively interpreted as disruptive to the educational process, it is highly unlikely that a review of the matter by the ombudsman would result in early readmission. First, Kansas laws do not provide for an appeal against a short-term suspension. Second, board of education policies authorize administrators to make the determination between "disruptive or disrespectful" behavior and acceptable behavior. Naturally, common sense or good judgment is a key for an administrator to effectively work with students to minimize inappropriate behavior. At any rate, a parent who complains that a school administrator has acted unfairly or too severely is likely to find little satisfaction when the ombudsman reports that the suspension cannot be reversed and that no process for an appeal exists. The ombudsman tells patrons that they have the option of contacting board of education members personally, and they may also contact the Ombudsperson Advisory Committee if dissatisfied with his actions.

THE NATURE OF COMPLAINTS

Most complaints originate because of misperceptions, misunderstandings, and various other forms of communication breakdown. Needless to say, emotions are frequently intense between parents and school personnel, and it is imperative that the ombudsman be an expert balancing artist on the proverbial tightrope. An illustration of this situation can be extracted from cases centering around the issue of disciplinary action taken in response to unacceptable student behavior. Frequently, upset parents contact the office about "unreasonable" action taken by administrators in response to the misbehavior of their children. Tempers and emotions may be very high. In some cases, the parent has contacted school personnel and has concluded that the real problem is the administration's reaction to the student's behavior. Correspondingly, school personnel may also be at an emotional brink because of the type and/or frequency of the student behavior in question—for example, smoking, fighting, class cutting, and truancy. Principals sometimes report that parents are nonsupportive of *any* corrective action when it applies to their child.

Other cases include curriculum items, special education concerns, cross-busing, transportation service, grades, and requests for assistance of many varieties. Curriculum items have generally centered upon a need to establish a course or program or for the improvement of an existing one. Many times this type of case has involved a concern about/with a particular teacher or other school district employee. Special education cases have steadily increased both numerically and in the proportionate amount of ombudsman services. Questions are extremely varied, time consuming, and at times complex. Parents request assistance in understanding the total process: identification, comprehensive evaluations, staffings, due process hearings, development of individualized educational plans, as well as many other auxiliary issues related to special education services.

Cross-busing continues to generate cases because of the need to select students for the district's integration program. Annually, one thousand students are compulsorily bused to a school other than their neighborhood school to help achieve an equitable racial balance or ratio within each comprehensive attendance center. The board of education has established a Deferment Review Committee to act upon parent requests for students to be exempted from this integration program. In 1979, a total of 379 requests were reviewed, with 209 deferments being granted. Essentially, the ombudsman office has served two functions in cross-busing cases. First, information has been provided to complainants. Second, the ombudsman has accompanied parents to appeal hearings with the committee to assist with deferment requests.

Complaints about actual transportation services frequently involve concerns about late buses, erratic driver behavior, overcrowded buses, disciplinary action taken for rule infractions by bus riders, and an assortment of other related problems. Normally, the function of the ombudsman has been to reinforce or document the patron's registered concern with phone calls and letters to appropriate school district and bus company officials. The school district employed a new bus contractor in 1978 after management problems caused many interruptions of service from the former transportation contractor. Complaints to the ombudsperson increased even more with the new contractor during the first year of operation.

Concerns regarding grades and credits typically require a review of a student's permanent record, a meeting with school personnel involved with course evaluation, interpretation of credits earned outside of this district, or school staff members involved with communications to students concerning required courses and the number of units of credit required for graduation. Again, the primary function of the office has been to assist patrons in working through their concerns by joining them in conferences with school officials and seeking to mediate when communications have broken down.

The number of inquiries dealt with by the revised ombudsman office has varied from 196 (1975–76) to 530 (1978–79) with an annual average around 450, the overwhelming majority (over 95 percent) being made by telephone. Only two out of three have been complaints, but they have been liberally spread among elementary schools (40 percent), junior high schools (30 percent), and senior high schools (15 percent) and have concerned, in order of magnitude, behavioral/suspensions/expulsions, special education problems, personnel, busing and transportation, enrollment, grades, and transfers. The major patrons, as expected, have been parents, but students and employees have also availed themselves of the ombudsman services.

The following are sample cases taken from the 1979–80 school year.

Special Education Placement: Parents requested assistance in receiving special education services for their seven-year-old son. Through inquiries of central office administrators, I learned placement procedures were underway. Three days later, a specific program placement was confirmed via a conference call.

Acceleration: Parents requested assistance in securing advanced grade placement for their child. I reviewed policy relating to detention and acceleration and advised the parents to work directly with the building principal. After considerable debate, the student was accelerated one grade level.

Transportation: A parent called to express concern and frustration about the removal of bus service for hazardous purposes to an elementary school. I advised parents to work with the principal and the director of elementary education to seek a satisfactory supervision plan for their children before and after school.

Expulsion: Parents were concerned that their twelfth grade son was not allowed to participate in any type of educational program. Upon reviewing the original problem that led to the expulsion, the hearing that upheld the administrative recommendation to expel, and the pending process to relocate students experiencing this type of problem, I suggested that the parents work with the director of secondary education and the pupil welfare and attendance coordinator. The student was finally permitted to attend, following the establishment of a review panel to process concerns such as this one.

Grades: A parent complained about the unfair grading and negative attitude of her son's English teacher. I agreed to coordinate a meeting with the teacher, principal, parent, our intern student, and me. The parent and teacher were extremely defensive and hostile towards one another. I suggested that the principal closely monitor the classroom situation and serve as the communications contact point for the parent. Although the grade was unchanged, a workable classroom climate and communication system were initiated.

SATISFACTION OF COMPLAINANTS

The School Ombudsperson Advisory Committee annually conducts surveys of individuals who have registered complaints with the ombudsman. Between 45 and 65 percent of respondents have replied, and the results are summarized in each annual report. Since 1978, an additional survey has been sent to school employees with equally positive responses. In 1980, the response was 86 percent positive and 8 percent negative. The committee and the board of education have expressed satisfaction

with these results, particularly in light of the fact that many people do not complain until they have become highly frustrated or emotionally upset. Even when the ombudsman has been unable to totally satisfy a patron, effort has been made to communicate sincerely and politely with the complainant. This has been reflected in the comments made in the surveys, many of which have been most complimentary about the usefulness, professionalism, and competency of the office.

Interestingly, the 1980 survey of patrons revealed that 60 percent learned of the office by word of mouth compared with 16 percent through the brochure, 14 percent through the media, and 11 percent through telephone book listing. Only 50 percent expressed satisfaction, while 27 percent made no comment and 22 percent were not totally satisfied, many feeling that "the Ombudsperson's hands are tied by the system." Over 86 percent of the respondents were white. Again, many expressed personal satisfaction with the office, particularly in bridging the gap between a bureaucratic school system and frustrated parents and students who found it unresponsive, insensitive, and uncaring about individual needs. To some, the office was the only positive aspect of the Wichita educational system. To others, the office offered good service for people with problems who did not know where to look for help or who kept running into "chain of command" problems.

Nonetheless, it is disconcerting that only five hundred complaints are received from the Wichita public school system. Clearly, there must be many more people who have cause to complain and could be helped by the ombudsman office. Companies that have employees distraught over some school occurrence involving their children could benefit by working through the office. Real estate firms might direct newcomers with school-age children to it. Elderly persons with legitimate concerns about the quality of education could call the office. In recent years, the office has seen fewer complaints involving discipline and behavior problems and grades and credits, and more requests to help parents with transportation difficulties and special education evaluations, and to supply information about alternative education programs. In the winter of 1980, complaints were received about cold classrooms and late buses. However trivial these may seem, they are important to pupils and their parents, and it would be better if more complaints like these were made. Certainly, the office could handle them and provide more followup.[4]

NOTES

1. G. H. Wolkon and S. Moriwaki, "The Ombudsman Programme: Primary Prevention of Psychological Disorders," *In-*

ternational Journal of Social Psychiatry 19 (Autumn/Winter 1973): 220–25.

2. S. V. Anderson, "Public School Ombud Offices," *California Journal of Teacher Education* 7, No. 3 (Summer 1980): 27.

3. Ibid., pp. 27–28.

4. R. Curry, "Ombudsman Paid Not to Take Sides." *The Wichita Eagle Beacon,* January 27, 1981, 4z.

BIBLIOGRAPHY

Anderson, S. V. "Public School Ombud Offices." *California Journal of Teacher Education* 7, No. 3 (Summer 1980): 25–33.

Barham, F. E. "The Educational Ombudsman: A Study of the Ombudsman in American Public Schools." Unpublished doctoral dissertation, University of Virginia, 1973.

APPENDIX A

ANNOTATED MODEL OMBUDSMAN STATUTE

WALTER GELLHORN, COLUMBIA UNIVERSITY

A BILL
To establish the Office of Ombudsman

in . . . .

[Enactment clause in locally appropriate form]

Section 1. *Short title.* This Act may be cited as The . . . . .
. . . . [insert name of state, city, or other entity] Ombudsman
Act.

COMMENT. The ''foreign-sounding word'' *ombudsman* has gained
wide usage in America and many other countries. Its distinctiveness
makes it preferable to more usual official titles such as ''commissioner'' or ''director.'' The position, new in American experience,
deserves a new identification.

Section 2. *Definitions.* As used in this Act, the term

(a) ''Administrative agency'' means any department or other governmental unit, any official, or any employee of . . . .
. . . . . . [state, city, or other entity involved] acting or purporting to
act by reason of connection with . . . . [again insert
name of state, city, or other entity]; but it does not include (1) any court
or judge or appurtenant judicial staff, (2) the members, committees, or
staffs of the . . . . [insert name of the legislative
body, e.g., City Council] or (3) the . . . . [insert
title of chief executive] or his personal staff.

COMMENT. Traditional immunization of courts against extra-judicial
scrutiny argues against permitting an American ombudsman to inquire into a judge's behavior. Legislators and the chief executive are
directly answerable to the electorate; their conduct in office tends in
any event to be conspicuous and subject to continuous political examination. Other elected officials (such as, in some jurisdictions, members of regulatory bodies, law enforcement officials, and educational
administrators) are less immediately involved in policy making and
are engaged chiefly in administrative matters indistinguishable from
those performed by non-elected officials generally. Their inclusion
within the reach of the Ombudsman Act therefore seems desirable.
If a state bill were to be drafted, a fourth exception should be considered, as follows: ''(4) any instrumentality of any political subdivision

of the state.'' This would make clear that the state ombudsman should
avoid dealing with municipal and county affairs, if state superinten-
dence of local officialdom is deemed undesirable. In a state-wide bill
prudence may also dictate a fifth specific exclusion to make indisput-
able that interstate bodies such as the Port of New York Authority or the
Delaware River water resources board are not meant to be reached,
though this specificity is perhaps not really needed: ''(5) any instrumentality formed pursuant to an interstate compact and answerable to
more than one state.''

(b) ''Administrative act'' includes every action (such as decisions,
omissions, recommendations, practices, or procedures) of an administrative agency.

Section 3. *Establishment of office.* The office of Ombudsman is hereby established as an independent agency of . . . .
[insert name of state, city, or other entity]

COMMENT. Whether the Ombudsman can be a wholly independent
entity or must instead be included within the Executive or the Legislative Branch depends upon the local constitution or charter. Organizational detachment is the desired estate if it can be achieved
constitutionally.

Section 4. *Appointment.* The . . . . [insert title
of chief executive] shall appoint the Ombudsman, subject to confirmation by two-thirds of the members of each chamber of the
. . . . [insert name of legislative body] present
and voting.

COMMENT. In foreign countries the ombudsman has been elected by
the legislature. The governmental structure in those countries differs,
however, from the American pattern. Appointive officials, whatever
their nature, are customarily chosen in American jurisdictions by the
Chief Executive, subject sometimes to legislative confirmation. The
present proposal contemplates confirmation by an unusually substantial vote in both chambers (if two exist) rather than in the Senate alone.
This is intended to stress the ''nonpolitical'' nature of the appointment
and to reflect the need for the general acceptability of the person
chosen. Whether the required majority be two-thirds of those voting

Reproduced with permission from The American Assembly, *Ombudsman for American Government?*, Stanley Anderson, ed., (Englewood Cliffs, N.J.: Prentice-Hall, 1968), pp. 159–73.

or some other figure can, of course, be fixed in accord with local preference or precedent.

Some persons favor direct legislative selection, without participation by the Executive. Thus, a Florida bill proposes simply that the ombudsman is to be "appointed by agreement of the president of senate and the speaker of the house subject to confirmation by a majority of the members of each chamber of the legislature." A Connecticut bill provides that one or more candidates "shall be selected by the judiciary committee and reported to the general assembly," after which the ombudsman is to be "elected by a vote of either a majority of each major political party or a two-thirds majority of the general assembly." A more elaborate plan has been advanced in California. It envisages a "Joint Legislative Committee on Administrative Justice" composed of three members of each house from both political parties. From a list prepared by a blue ribbon commission, the committee is to nominate the ombudsman by an absolute majority vote, and the nominee is to be "appointed to the office of Ombudsman by concurrent resolution of the Legislature."

All the plans emphasize the desirability of "de-politicalizing" the selection process.

The California plan contemplates that the joint committee will have a continuing existence and will be available for consultation by the ombudsman "as he deems necessary to the execution of his powers and duties." No matter how the office of Ombudsman may be filled, some such provision in the legislature's own internal organization would be desirable so that the ombudsman can have a regular point of contact when needed.

Section 5. *Qualifications*. The Ombudsman shall be a person well equipped to analyze problems of law, administration, and public policy, and shall not be actively involved in partisan affairs.

COMMENT. Efforts to define the qualities sought in an ombudsman tend to result in a catalogue of human virtues, leading one person to remark that if ever such a man were found, he would instantly be cast in bronze rather than appointed to a mundane office. Experience abroad points clearly to the desirability of the ombudsman's having a legal background because he must deal with many grievances that hinge on analysis of statutes and rulings. Requiring any specific experience or absolutely excluding any category of persons (for example, those who have recently been legislators or have held other office) seems undesirable. The consensus of opinion that will presumably support legislative confirmation should be an adequate barrier against unsuitable nominees.

Section 6. *Term of office*. (a) The Ombudsman shall serve for a term of five years, unless removed by vote of two-thirds of the members of each of the two chambers of the . . . . [insert name of legislative body] upon their determining that he has become incapacitated or has been guilty of neglect of duty or misconduct;

COMMENT. The Ombudsman should be secure, but not absolutely untouchable. The proposed provision would adequately guard against casual threats. An alternative would be to provide simply that the Ombudsman shall serve out his term, unless "impeached by the [legislature] in accord with the procedures prescribed by the constitution." The likelihood of removal is extremely slim, in any event.

(b) If the office of Ombudsman becomes vacant for any cause, the Deputy Ombudsman shall serve as Acting Ombudsman until an Ombudsman has been appointed for a full term.

COMMENT. Whether the term of office should be more or less than five years is not demonstrable. Abroad, no term exceeds four years. Here, some persons believe that the detachment of the Ombudsman from the Chief Executive will be accentuated if a vacancy does not automatically coincide with the inauguration of a new mayor or governor. Some advocate an even longer term than five years. The length of the term is not very important. If the institution proves its worth, tinkering with the Ombudsman's independence would be so politically perilous as to be altogether unlikely. To guard against sudden attacks upon an incumbent, removability should be made difficult, as has been done in this draft. As for vacancies, a stopgap until a permanent appointment can be made for a full term is preferable to an appointment merely for the balance of the unexpired term, as others have sometimes suggested.

In New Zealand the incumbent Ombudsman continues serving beyond the expiration of his term, unless and until a successor has qualified. Although this assures continuity of Ombudsman services, it means that the hold-over Ombudsman has no security of tenure, a circumstance that may at least theoretically expose him to undesirable pressures.

Section 7. *Salary*. The Ombudsman shall receive the same salary, allowances, and related benefits as the chief judge of the highest court of . . . . [name of state]

COMMENT. Setting the Ombudsman's pay and perquisites at the level of the highest ranking judge will give the new office a desirably high prestige, will eliminate wrangling now and in the future about the appropriate dollar amount of the Ombudsman's salary, and will avoid the obsolescence that would soon occur if the desired salary were to be precisely stated. If the Ombudsman is connected with a governmental subdivision rather than with the state itself, some other comparison would be appropriate.

Section 8. *Organization of office*. (a) The Ombudsman may select, appoint, and compensate as he may see fit (within the amount available by appropriation) such assistants and employees as he may deem necessary to discharge his responsibilities under this Act;

(b) The Ombudsman shall designate one of his assistants to be the Deputy Ombudsman, with authority to act in his stead when he himself is disabled or protractedly absent;

(c) The Ombudsman may delegate to other members of his staff any of his authority or duties under this Act except this power of delegation and the duty of formally making recommendations to administrative agencies or reports to the . . . . [insert title of chief executive] or the . . . . [insert name of legislative body].

COMMENT. This section gives the Ombudsman a free hand in staffing his office, without even the restraints of civil service and classification acts. The highly personal nature of the Ombudsman's work, coupled with its essentially experimental nature, justifies giving this leeway to so highly placed and, by hypothesis, responsible an official. For the same reasons the Ombudsman has been given a free choice about assigning duties and subdelegating powers, with the single limitation that when criticisms or proposals for change are to be voiced in a formal manner, only the Ombudsman himself may be heard (except when the Deputy Ombudsman is in full charge during the Ombudsman's disability or protracted absence).

Section 9. *Powers*. The Ombudsman shall have the following powers:

(a) He may investigate, on complaint or on his own motion, any administrative act of any administrative agency;

COMMENT. The power to investigate should be stated unqualifiedly, though later sections will indicate the grounds that justify action by him and will thus suggest the occasions on which investigation would be suitable. Experience abroad shows that efforts to define jurisdiction have caused much laborious and essentially unproductive hairsplitting; a more general grant of power to investigate will eliminate some "legalistic" analysis in the beginning of the Ombudsman's work, but his own discretion will lead him to set sensible boundaries to the areas within which he will investigate, lest he be crushed by the burden of unproductive work.

(b) He may prescribe the methods by which complaints are to be made, received, and acted upon; he may determine the scope and manner of investigations to be made; and, subject to the requirements of this Act, he may determine the form, frequency, and distribution of his conclusions and recommendations;

COMMENT. Some foreign statutes require that complaints be written. Leaving matters of this kind to the Ombudsman's choice in the light of experience is preferable. Similarly, giving the Ombudsman power to shape his own investigations is desirable; any implication that he should utilize the same method at all times should be avoided, as should any requirement of formal hearing of an adversary nature. If a proceeding for the taking of testimony were in fact to occur, it should be perceived as an element of an investigation rather than as a proceeding in the nature of a trial. Hence its content need not necessarily be the same as would normally be demanded in a formal adjudicatory hearing.

(c) He may request and shall be given by each administrative agency the assistance and information he deems necessary for the discharge of his responsibilities; he may examine the records and documents of all administrative agencies; and he may enter and inspect premises within any administrative agency's control.

COMMENT. Experience elsewhere suggests that the Ombudsman will be given ready access to official papers or other information within the administrative agency. Cooperative working relationships have been readily established so that the Ombudsman's need for documentary material has not conflicted with the administrators' continuing need to use the same material. As for inspection of administrative offices and installations, this draft gives the Ombudsman power to inspect but imposes no duty to do so routinely, as has been required of the Ombudsmen in several Scandinavian countries.

(d) He may issue a subpoena to compel any person to appear, give sworn testimony, or produce documentary or other evidence the Ombudsman deems relevant to a matter under his inquiry.

COMMENT. Every existing Ombudsman statute provides very broadly for the use of compulsory process in order to obtain needed information. In point of fact, however, the subpoena power has virtually never been used abroad, since information has been freely given. Concern has nevertheless been expressed in this country that wide-ranging inquiries into public administration might lead to burdensome demands. Hence Section 18, below, takes pains to stress protections for witnesses, even though the occasions for bringing them into play are likely to be very few indeed.

(e) He may undertake, participate in, or cooperate with general studies or inquiries, whether or not related to any particular administrative agency or any particular administrative act, if he believes that they may enhance knowledge about or lead to improvements in the functioning of administrative agencies.

COMMENT. If foreign experience is an accurate guide, work on individual complaints will chiefly preoccupy the Ombudsman's energies and attention. Nonetheless, he should be clearly empowered to address himself to general problems (some of which, indeed, may not be reflected at all in current complaints) and should be free to work not only with other governmental bodies, but also with non-governmental research enterprises which, in the United States much more than in most other countries, provide a great deal of the manpower, insight, and enthusiasm that underlie governmental improvements.

Section 10. *Matters appropriate for investigation.* (a) In selecting matters for his attention, the Ombudsman should address himself particularly to an administrative act that might be

1. contrary to law or regulation;

2. unreasonable, unfair, oppressive, or inconsistent with the general course of an administrative agency's functioning;

3. mistaken in law or arbitrary in ascertainments of fact;

4. improper in motivation or based on irrelevant considerations;

5. unclear or inadequately explained when reasons should have been revealed;

6. inefficiently performed; or

7. otherwise objectionable;

COMMENT. The statute desirably details the kinds of administrative acts whose occurrence has chiefly generated demands for the Ombudsman system. This draft sets them forth as guides, not as limitations. The Ombudsman is told to devote himself to these types of problems, but he need not feel himself confined to them if the catalog later be found to be incomplete. Subsection (3) refers to acts that rest on arbitrary ascertainments of fact. Very clearly, the Ombudsman must not attempt to be a super-administrator, doing over again what specialized administrators have already done and, if he disagrees, substituting his judgment for theirs. In some instances, however, the propriety of an administrative act may rest wholly on a factual determination that in turn rests on an excessively flimsy foundation. As in cases that go to courts for review, the Ombudsman should not regard as "arbitrary" anything and everything with which he disagrees; but he should be in a position to say, in essence, that reasonable men would not have found the facts in the way the administrator did.

Subsection (5) is not intended to create a new legal requirement that findings of fact and conclusions of law accompany every administrative act. It means merely that official actions should be understandable and, usually, should be explained when those affected by them seek fuller understanding. Experience abroad shows that this is one of the areas most fruitfully cultivated by Ombudsmen.

Subsection (6) refers to administrative acts that may lie within the zone of legality, but might nevertheless be subject to improvement in the future. Thus, for example, the form of decision given by a Scandinavian administrator to old age pensioners caused later distress because the pensioners read into it some hopes that were not justified by existing law. The Ombudsman found nothing improper in the decisions that had been made, but suggested some purely stylistic changes that eliminated the bewildering "officialese" previously in use.

Subsection (7) uses a catch-all phrase, "otherwise objectionable." This will perhaps emphasize the Ombudsman's concern with such matters as rudeness and needless delay, both of which bulk large among citizens' grievances.

(b) The Ombudsman may concern himself also with strengthening procedures and practices which lessen the risk that objectionable administrative acts will occur.

COMMENT. Subparagraph (b) makes clear that the Ombudsman should have a large and continuous interest in "preventive medicine" rather than solely in trying to abate a difficulty after it has arisen.

Section 11. *Action on complaints.* (a) The Ombudsman may receive a complaint from any source concerning an administrative act. He shall conduct a suitable investigation into the things complained of unless he believes that

1. the complainant has available to him another remedy or channel of complaint which he could reasonably be expected to use;

2. the grievance pertains to a matter outside the Ombudsman's power;

3. the complainant's interest is insufficiently related to the subject matter.

4. the complaint is trivial, frivolous, vexatious, or not made in good faith;

5. other complaints are more worthy of attention;

6. the Ombudsman's resources are insufficient for adequate investigation; or

7. the complaint has been too long delayed to justify present examination of its merit.

The Ombudsman's declining to investigate a complaint shall not, however, bar him from proceeding on his own motion to inquire into the matter complained about or into related problems;

COMMENT. The duty to act on every complaint should not be imposed, partly because the dimensions of the work burden cannot be exactly predicted and partly because some complaints will show on their face that they are unlikely to lead to productive findings. The above listing leaves the Ombudsman free to reject complaints, but does not bar his making inquiries. Specifically, he need not reject a complaint because another judicial or administrative remedy exists. Normally, one may suppose, the Ombudsman will insist that matters proceed through regular channels. Explaining to a complainant the steps he can take to obtain review will usually suffice. But assuredly some cases will arise in which the burdens of expense and time are realistic barriers to a complainant's pursuing the theoretically available remedies. In those instances access to the Ombudsman should not be precluded. Subsection (1) leaves the avenue open, but the traffic is still subject to control.

Another policy choice is reflected in Subsection (3) which does not require that every complaint be based on a claimed invasion of a strictly personal interest. This permits a complainant to bring to the Ombudsman's notice a matter of public rather than purely private concern. But if the complainant's concern with the subject matter is too attenuated, the Ombudsman may choose not to investigate.

Subsection (7) does not contain an explicit "statute of limitations" on complaints, though the Ombudsman is left free to reject those based on stale claims or ancient grudges. In Sweden complaints must be acted on if filed within ten years of the events in question; Denmark, New Zealand, and Norway, by contrast, require rejection of any complaint pertaining to occurrences beyond the preceding twelve months. Neither extreme seems desirable. The present draft lays down no rule in this respect, but allows the Ombudsman to pick his way at the outset. Later, in the light of experience, he may wish to promulgate some rules of his own, as is allowed by Section 9 (b), above.

(b) After completing his consideration of a complaint (whether or not it has been investigated) the Ombudsman shall suitably inform the complainant and, when appropriate, the administrative agency or agencies involved.

COMMENT. A decision not to investigate a complaint does not mean that it has been altogether ignored. For example, the Ombudsman and the agency involved may regard the complaint as an adequate equivalent of a petition for administrative review of which the complainant has not yet availed himself; the Ombudsman may in such a case simply forward the complaint to the appropriate appellate authority, advising the complainant that this has been done in his behalf. In other instances very extensive legal analysis may be undertaken preliminarily, leading to the conclusion that no grievance could be found to exist. In such a case the Ombudsman may be expected to write an explanatory opinion that, if foreign experience is duplicated in this country, will in the generality of instances prove wholly persuasive to the complainant. Flatly requiring the Ombudsman to state reasons whenever he decides not to investigate should, however, be avoided. Numerous complaints show on their face that they are psychopathic rather than governmental in nature. The Ombudsman's judgment must be relied upon to determine the suitable response in those instances. All practicing Ombudsmen do in fact take great pains to communicate fully and frankly with complainants, in general. This is particularly true as to cases whose merits have been explored. The Ombudsman's findings and reasoning have powerfully shaped public opinion as well as official attitudes. Conclusions adverse to a complainant's position deserve to be well explained, as has been done consistently by all foreign Ombudsmen.

Some proposals have explicitly required that if a complaint has reached the Ombudsman through a member of the legislature, the Ombudsman must report his findings and recommendations (if any) to the legislator who had forwarded his constituent's complaint. Undoubtedly the Ombudsman, guided by ordinary tact and prudence, would routinely furnish to legislative intermediaries copies of his explanations to complainants and affected officials; making statutory provision for simple courtesy seems unnecessary. If anything more is intended by the suggested requirement that the Ombudsman "report" to a legislator who has forwarded a constituent's complaint, the requirement should be resisted. The Ombudsman should not be perceived as a staff aide whose activities may be directed by individual legislators, to whom he must then report back.

(c) A letter to the Ombudsman from a person in a place of detention or in a hospital or other institution under the control of an administrative agency shall be immediately forwarded, unopened, to the Ombudsman.

COMMENT. A provision of this nature has commonly been included in ombudsman statutes. It provides a measure of psychological assurance that everyone may have ready access to the Ombudsman without fear of reprisal.

Section 12. *Consultation with agency.* Before announcing a conclusion or recommendation that criticizes an administrative agency or any person, the Ombudsman shall consult with that agency or person.

COMMENT. No provision need be made for giving specific notice that the Ombudsman has decided to investigate, if he does so decide. He will inescapably be in communication with the administrative agency when he needs its information or opinions. Formalities should be avoided lest a small organization be overborne by essentially ceremonial requirements.

At the point of announcing his conclusions, however, the Ombudsman should guard against his own mistakes by consulting those whom his findings may hurt. The requirement that he consult will not substantially impede his work, but will be a protection for all concerned against unwitting errors in fact, judgment, or expression.

Section 13. *Recommendations.* (a) If, having considered a complaint and whatever material he deems pertinent, the Ombudsman is of the opinion that an administrative agency should 1) consider the matter further, 2) modify or cancel an administrative act, 3) alter a regulation or ruling, 4) explain more fully the administrative act in question, or 5) take any other step, he shall state his recommendations to the administrative agency. If the Ombudsman so requests, the agency shall, within the time he has specified, inform him about the action taken on his recommendations or the reasons for not complying with them;

COMMENT. Though the Ombudsman will rarely have reason to make a recommendation if he does not find an error in what the administrative agency has done or neglected to do, he should remain free to suggest improvements in method or policy even when the existing practice may be legally permissible. Thus he may facilitate one agency's learning about and taking advantage of the experience of another.

Section 13 (a) contemplates no entry of judgment, as it were, but simply the expression of opinion by the Ombudsman. He is not a superior official, in a position of command. He cannot compel a change in an administrative act. His recommendation may, however, induce an agency to exercise whatever power it may still possess to right what the Ombudsman points out as a past mistake. Bearing in mind that consultation under Section 12 will precede recommendation under Section 13, one may safely predict that rashly critical opinions will not be expressed.

(b) If the Ombudsman believes that an administrative action has been dictated by laws whose results are unfair or otherwise objectionable, he shall bring to the . . . . [name of legislative body]'s notice his views concerning desirable statutory change.

COMMENT. This subsection makes clear that the Ombudsman's duty extends beyond simply finding that an administrator acted in accord with existing statutory law; if the law itself produces unjust results, he should bring this to legislative notice. He is not meant to be a general social reformer, but he does have an obligation to take note of statutory provisions that cause unexpectedly harsh administration.

Section 14. *Publication of recommendations.* The Ombudsman may publish his conclusions, recommendations, and suggestions by transmitting them to the . . . . [title of chief executive], the . . . . [name of legislative body] or any of its committees, the press, and others who may be concerned. When publishing an opinion adverse to an administrative agency or official he shall (unless excused by the agency or official affected) include the substance of any statement the administrative agency or official may have made to him by way of explaining past difficulties or present rejection of the Ombudsman's proposals.

COMMENT. Bringing his views into the open is the Ombudsman's sole means of gaining the public's support. This section permits publication even when an agency has accepted a recommendation. Publicity may be needed to call other administrators' attention to current developments and also to remind the public at large that the Ombudsman is functioning for the citizenry's benefit. Publicity, however, occurs at the end and not at the beginning of discussions with the agency involved. Persuasion is the chief instrument in gaining administrative agencies' favorable response to suggestions. Only when persuasion fails will the Ombudsman begin to think about mobilizing the force of public opinion. To guard against one-sidedness, the Ombudsman is required to disclose the criticized agency's or official's view of the matter along with his own, when the two views differ.

Section 15. *Reports.* In addition to whatever reports he may make from time to time, the Ombudsman shall on or about February 15 of each year report to the . . . . [name of legislative body] and to the . . . . [title of the chief executive] concerning the exercise of his functions during the preceding calendar year. In discussing matters with which he has dealt, the Ombudsman need not identify those immediately concerned if to do so would cause needless hardship. So far as the annual report may criticize named agencies or officials, it must also include the substance of their replies to the criticism.

Section 16. *Disciplinary action against public personnel.* If the Ombudsman has reason to believe that any public official, employee, or other person has acted in a manner warranting criminal or disciplinary proceedings, he shall refer the matter to the appropriate authorities.

Section 17. *Ombudsman's immunities.* (a) No proceeding, opinion, or expression of the Ombudsman shall be reviewable in any court;

COMMENT. Subsection (a) precludes judicial review of the Ombudsman's work. This preclusion simply recognizes that the Ombudsman issues no orders and takes no steps that bar anyone from pursuing preexisting remedies.

(b) No civil action shall lie against the Ombudsman or any member of his staff for anything done or said or omitted, in discharging the responsibilities contemplated by this Act;

COMMENT. Subsection (b) extends to the Ombudsman's office the immunity from harassment by lawsuit that is shared by judges and many other officials. It does not preclude criminal prosecution were serious misconduct ever to be brought to light; moreover, Section 6 provides for removal from office were the Ombudsman to be found miscreant.

(c) Neither the Ombudsman nor any member of his staff shall be required to testify or produce evidence in any judicial or administrative proceeding concerning matters within his official cognizance, except in a proceeding brought to enforce this Act.

COMMENT. Subsection (c) saves the Ombudsman's office from the awkwardness of interrupting its on-going work in order to testify about matters concerning which it may have received information (often given in confidence). The subsection does not, however, preclude the Ombudsman's testifying in proceedings needed to enforce the Act, such as an action to compel compliance with a subpoena or a prosecution against a violator under Section 19, below. The subsection does prevent his being used as an adjunct to private litigation.

Section 18. *Rights and duties of witnesses.* (a) A person required by the Ombudsman to provide information shall be paid the same fees and travel allowances as are extended to witnesses whose attendance has been required in the courts of this state;

(b) A person who, with or without service of compulsory process, provides oral or documentary information requested by the Ombudsman shall be accorded the same privileges and immunities as are extended to witnesses in the courts of this state, and shall also be entitled to be accompanied and advised by counsel while being questioned.

(c) If a person refuses to respond to the Ombudsman's subpoena, refuses to be examined, or engages in obstructive misconduct, the Ombudsman shall certify the facts to the . . . . [insert name of suitable court]. The court shall thereupon issue an order directing the person to appear before the court to show cause why he should not be punished as for contempt. The order and a copy of the Ombudsman's certified statement shall be served on the person. Thereafter the court shall have jurisdiction of the matter. The same proceedings shall be had, the same penalties may be imposed, and the person charged may purge himself of the contempt in the same way as in the case of a person who has committed a contempt in the trial of a civil action before the court.

COMMENT. Subsection (c) describes the manner of enforcing subpoenas through independent judicial examination of the matter. The procedure here proposed is derived from California Government Code 11525. In all probability, the need to enforce subpoenas will not in fact arise. Information already in the possession of an administrative agency will be freely accessible to the Ombudsman. Information in a complainant's possession will of course be gladly supplied. Occasions on which data must be dragged from reluctant third parties are not likely to occur.

Section 19. *Obstruction.* A person who willfully obstructs or hinders the proper exercise of the Ombudsman's functions, or who willfully misleads or attempts to mislead the Ombudsman in his inquiries, shall be fined not more than $1,000.

COMMENT. If the enactment be by a municipality, counsel should determine whether the local legislature has power under state law to create an offence punishable by fine. Counsel must determine in each state whether necessity exists for indicating the court in which proceedings are to be brought, and upon whose initiative.

Section 20. *Relation to other laws.* The provisions of this Act are in addition to and do not in any manner limit or affect the provisions of any other enactment under which any remedy or right of appeal is provided for any person, or any procedure is provided for the inquiry into or investigation of any matter. The powers conferred on the Ombudsman may be exercised notwithstanding any provision in any enactment to the effect that any administrative action shall be final or unappealable.

Section 21. *Appropriation.* There are hereby authorized to be appropriated such sums as may be necessary to carry out the provisions of this Act.

COMMENT. The appropriations section must be shaped in accord with local practice and fiscal regulations. In some jurisdictions it need not be included in an organic statute like the one now proposed. In other jurisdictions a specific amount may have to be shown as the appropriation.

If inclusion of an appropriation section is not absolutely necessary, its omission is recommended.

Section 22. *Effective date.* This Act shall take effect immediately.

THE INTERNATIONAL BAR ASSOCIATION OMBUDSMAN FORUM

In 1967, the American Bar Association (ABA) through its Section of Administrative Law created an Ombudsman Committee. Two years later, it adopted a resolution favoring the ombudsman concept on the state and local level and recommending experimentation at the federal level, which was amended in 1971 to authorize the Section of Administrative Law to present the ABA's views and to encourage the establishment of ombudsman offices. The chairman of the Ombudsman Committee, Bernard Frank, issued his first annual survey of ombudsman developments throughout the world until in 1980 the survey was assumed by the International Ombudsman Institute. In 1974, he wrote the committee's Model Ombudsman Statute for State Governments.

In 1971, Frank wrote an article entitled "The Ombudsman—A Challenge" for the *International Bar Journal* (November, pp. 32–39) in which he discussed the definition of the ombudsman, existing ombudsmen and ombudsman-like institutions, proposals for ombudsman systems, the reasons for the office, its principal elements, and an evaluation, and concluded with a challenge to the International Bar Association (IBA) to concern itself with the ombudsman concept. At its meeting in Brussels in April 1972, the IBA Council agreed to appoint an Ombudsman Committee after ascertaining that the International Commission of Jurists did not have such a committee. In April 1973, Frank was appointed chairman of the Ombudsman Committee, a position he held along with that on the ABA Ombudsman Committee, until 1980. In that role, he was instrumental in establishing an advisory board which included ombudsmen who were not members of bar associations, an academic advisory board, and a member organization liaison (between bar associations and the committee). At its Vancouver Conference in August 1974, the IBA supported the ombudsman concept. Thereafter, Frank issued regular bulletins that promoted the ombudsman community

until the International Ombudsman Institute was established. His bulletins and annual surveys constitute a detailed history of the recent development of the ombudsman institution.

In 1975, the Canadian Provincial Conference adopted a recommendation made in prior reports to the IBA Council that an Ombudsman Center be established at a university. The World Ombudsman Steering Committee also adopted the recommendation and endorsed the establishment of the International Ombudsman Institute at the University of Alberta when the First International Ombudsman Conference met in Edmonton in September 1976. Its board of directors included several ombudsmen and the chairman of the IBA Ombudsman Committee who developed close relations with the new institute. Eventually, in 1980, many of the functions performed by Bernard Frank were assumed by the institute. Vice-Chairman Alex Weir, solicitor to the Alberta ombudsman, took over the chair from Frank at the August 1980 IBA Berlin Conference and the Alberta ombudsman became executive director of the institute. Previously, the Canadian representative on the IBA Council proposed that the Ombudsman Committee become an IBA Section to improve its status and obtain IBA funds for its ombudsman promotional activities, but there had been some resistance by the Ombudsman Committee which was reluctant to lose its unique status.

The proposed change from Ombudsman Committee to Ombudsman Section was preceded by an amendment to the 1974 IBA resolution to include local government ombudsman offices and approaches to include the Soviet Prokuratura, although it did not comply with the type of ombudsman that the IBA promoted. It was hoped that all ombudsman offices throughout the world would participate in the IBA ombudsman projects. At the 1980 Berlin Conference, the Ombudsman Committee had seventy-four members (twenty-nine from Canada, twenty from the United States, sixteen others from countries with ombudsman-like offices and nine members from nine countries without an ombudsman), the Ombudsman Advisory Board had ninety-five members, all ombudsmen or former ombudsmen from twenty-nine countries, the Academic Advisory Board had thirty-eight members from fourteen countries, and thirty-nine member organizations of the IBA had designated members to serve as liaisons with the Ombudsman Committee.

At the IBA Council meeting held in Lisbon in May 1981, Arthur Maloney, QC, presented the case for ombudsman section status to give recognition to the committee's unique status within the IBA and to enable the committee to establish a financial basis. The council decided to rename the committee the "IBA Ombudsman Forum" whose primary goal would continue to be the promotion of the institution of classical ombudsman. The new forum extends the work of the former committee, maintains close links with ombudsman offices throughout the world and the International Ombudsman Institute, and associates with the work of the International Juridicial Organization, World Habeas Corpus, and Human Rights Internet. At the invitation of the Association of Law Societies of South Africa, it sponsored in March 1982 a seminar on the ombudsman as part of its promotional activities. Its current address is 1630 Phipps-McKinnon Building, 10020-101A Avenue, Edmonton, Alberta, Canada T5J 3G2.

THE INTERNATIONAL OMBUDSMAN STEERING COMMITTEE

RANDALL IVANY, ALBERTA OMBUDSMAN

The International Ombudsman Steering Committee originated at the First International Ombudsman Conference held in Edmonton, Alberta, Canada, from September 6 to September 10, 1976. It was agreed at that time that a Steering Committee of classical Ombudsmen be formed. The composition of the Steering Committee was as follows: from the Southern Region, Justice Moti Tikaram, Fiji; Oliver Dixon, Western Australia; and Judge Frederick Chomba, Zambia—from the European Region, Nordskov Nielsen, Denmark; Aimé Paquet, France; and Lieselotte Berger, Germany—from the North American Region, Frank Flavin, Alaska, United States of America; and Dr. Randall Ivany, Alberta, Canada, as the chairman. At first, the third representative from North America was held in abeyance pending discussion of who should be invited to attend the next conference. Ultimately, Arthur Maloney, QC, of Ontario, became the third member from the North American Region.

Part of the terms of reference for the Steering Committee recommended that the Second International Ombudsman Conference should be held three to four years from 1976, and that the said conference should be held at one of the three following cities: Jerusalem, Sydney, or Stockholm. The terms of reference basically dealt with the proposals for the Second International Conference, that upon the determination of the venue of the next international conference, that an ombudsman from the host country or state, or his designate, become a member of the Steering Committee. Thus was added Dr. I. E. Nebenzahl of Israel. It was further suggested that the Steering Committee act as a liaison between the ombudsmen until the international conference was held in 1980 in Jerusalem.

Perhaps the most important matter outside of the planning of the Second International Ombudsman Conference has been the establishment of the International Ombudsman Institute at the Faculty of Law, University of Alberta, Canada. The official opening of this institute was held in Jerusalem during the course of the Second International Conference. During the course of the conference, it was decided that the International Ombudsman Steering Committee should be replaced by a Consultative Committee of Ombudsmen from various regions to assist in the planning of the Third International Ombudsman Conference.

APPENDIX D

THE INTERNATIONAL OMBUDSMAN INSTITUTE

RANDALL IVANY, Alberta Ombudsman

The International Ombudsman Institute was established in 1978 at the University of Alberta, after years of discussion and planning. As early as 1969, Dr. Bernard Frank, chairman of the Ombudsman Committee of the International Bar Association, raised the idea of a university center at the Bangkok World Conference on World Peace Through Law. Dr. Frank approached many organizations with the purpose of promoting the establishment of such a center. Among the groups approached were the Canadian ombudsmen at their annual conference in September 1975. In cooperation with Dr. Randall Ivany, ombudsman for Alberta, a formal submission by the University of Alberta's Faculty of Law was prepared and presented to the then existing International Ombudsman Steering Committee in May 1977. The proposal was accepted, and the International Ombudsman Institute was established.

The International Ombudsman Institute is incorporated as a nonprofit organization under the Canada Corporation Act. Some of its objects are to promote the concept of ombudsmanship and to encourage its development throughout the world; to encourage and support research; to develop and operate educational programs associated with ombudsmanship; and to collect, store, and disseminate information about the institution of ombudsman.

As of the end of 1981, the board of directors of the International Ombudsman Institute was as follows:

Judge Joseph E. Bérubé, ombudsman for New Brunswick

Oliver F. Dixon, former ombudsman for Western Australia

Dr. Bernard Frank, former chairman of the International Bar Association Ombudsman Committee

Dr. Myer Horowitz, president of the University of Alberta

Dr. Randall Ivany, ombudsman for Alberta

Frank D. Jones, QC, dean of law, University of Alberta

Ulf Lundvik, former chief parliamentary ombudsman for Sweden

Baroness Serota, chairwoman, Commission for Local Administration in England

Sir Justice Moti Tikaram, ombudsman for Fiji

Dr. Jacques Vontobel, ombudsman for the city of Zurich, Switzerland

Judge Ulf Lundvik is the president of the International Ombudsman Institute, Dr. Bernard Frank is the vice-president, and Dr. Randall Ivany is the acting executive director.

PUBLICATIONS

1. *The International Ombudsman Institute Newsletter*. Six issues a year are published, and the newsletter is distributed to all members.

2. *Court Cases of Interest to the Ombudsman Institution*. An annual publication of legal decisions involving ombudsman offices throughout the world.

3. *The International Ombudsman Institute Occasional Paper Series*. A series of papers on topics related to the Ombudsman Institution.

4. Publication of, or assistance in publishing, proceedings of various international and regional ombudsman conferences. To date, these include the International Bar Association Ombudsman Committee Sydney, Australia Conference, the United States Association of Ombudsmen Third Annual Conference Proceedings, and the Sixth Annual Conference of Canadian Legislative Ombudsmen.

5. Publication of the annual *Ombudsman and other Complaint-Handling Systems Survey* in conjunction with the International Bar Association Ombudsman Committee.

6. Publication for the Commonwealth Secretariat of a directory of Commonwealth Ombudsman Offices and related materials.

7. Publication of an annual comprehensive bibliography on the ombudsman. The bibliography is a computerized data base, and searches may be done for specific subject areas, authors, titles, and so on.

8. Assistance in the publication of major works on the ombudsman.

RESOURCE CENTER

1. A comprehensive library of annual reports for ombudsman offices throughout the world.

2. A representative library of monographs, articles, and papers on the Ombudsman Institution.

3. A collection of legislation for ombudsman offices throughout the world.

4. A comprehensive listing of ombudsmen throughout the world.

5. A profile data program for each office of legislative and executive ombudsmen throughout the world.

6. Sponsorship of seminars.

7. Ombudsman/scholar-in-residence program. To date, there have been three ombudsmen-in-residence: Sir Guy Powles, former chief ombudsman of New Zealand (1978); Judge Ulf Lundvik, former chief parliamentary ombudsman for Sweden (1979); and Ramawad Sewgobind, ombudsman for Mauritius (1980).

The International Ombudsman Institute is always willing to respond to requests for information. Contact should be made with the institute at:

International Ombudsman Institute
Law Centre
The University of Alberta
Edmonton, Alberta, Canada
T6G 2H5

THE HANSARD SOCIETY

MAXINE VLIELAND, Secretary of the Hansard Society

The Hansard Society for Parliamentary Government was founded during World War II by Stephen King-Hall, an independent member of parliament and well-known broadcaster, at a time when the British people were aware of the importance of preserving parliamentary democracy at home and were concerned about the reintroduction of democracy to Europe after the war. King-Hall's original intention was to set up daily Hansard reports of parliamentary debates, but the Hansard Society, as it came to be called, soon developed much broader aims and extended its activities to political education and research. It has always tried to strengthen parliamentary institutions by encouraging public interest in them. Membership is drawn from members of parliament of all parties as well as from academics, journalists, and businessmen. It has wide support among schools, university students, and the general public.

In a fast-changing world, the society seeks to adapt and extend its activities to reflect public opinion and political trends while remaining an unbiased and comprehensive source of comment on the country's political organization and the functioning of its parliamentary democracy. During the 1950s, an important aspect of its work was fostering the ideals of parliamentary democracy in the emerging nations of Africa and Asia. More recently, it has tended to focus on the strengths and weaknesses of parliamentary institutions.

The society organizes essay competitions, seminars, and lecturers. Each year it runs a very thorough course on British political, economic, and financial institutions for foreign diplomats. It has recently held two high-level international conferences, one on referendums and the other on the ombudsman system. After ten years' experience with the ombudsman, it seemed appropriate to hold a review and to ask what had been learned, comparing the British experience and that elsewhere. The conference, held in September 1978 at Ditchley Park, was attended by ombudsmen from Fiji, Mauritius, France, and Sweden, and by the former New Zealand ombudsman. The British delegation, led by the parliamentary commissioner and the chairman of the Commission for Local Administration in England, was composed of members of parliament, lawyers, academics, and representatives of local authorities. The participants reviewed experiences and took up wider issues such as the role of the ombudsman in the defense of citizens' rights.

THE UNITED STATES ASSOCIATION OF OMBUDSMEN

LAWRENCE B. GUILLOT, FORMER PRESIDENT, USAO

The United States Association of Ombudsmen (USAO) was formed in 1977 to provide a forum for exchange between ombudsman offices of the classical type in the United States, many of which had been established in the early and mid-1970s. Prior to its formation, there had been sporadic regional and academic conferences, but no centralized way of keeping in touch one with another. Much of what they knew of each other was through Bernard Frank's annual survey of ombudsman offices for the International and American Bar Associations, and through the work of Stanley V. Anderson and John E. Moore, with publications and conferences sponsored by the Institute of Governmental Studies at the University of California, Berkeley.

An attempt was made in the fall of 1975, by a not-for-profit institution calling itself the Ombudsmen Foundation, to hold a nationwide ombudsmen conference with the participation of every kind of ombudsman and complaint-handling office, governmental at all levels, business, educational, health, and other specialties. A year later, in September 1976, a number of U.S. ombudsmen meeting at the first international ombudsman conference in Edmonton, Alberta, in Canada, decided that the time was right for a professional association of practicing ombudsmen in the United States. Those present from the United States were Frank Flavin of Alaska, Herman Doi of Hawaii, Paul Meyer of Seattle/King County in Washington, Lawrence Guillot of Jackson County, Missouri, Preston Barton, Kansas correctional ombudsman, academics Stanley Anderson and Larry B. Hill, and Bernard Frank of the International Bar Association. A decision was made to hold a national U.S. conference the following year and to incorporate a United States Association of Ombudsmen.

The Seattle/King County office hosted the first conference in August 1977. At the end of that conference, the USAO was officially formed and officers elected. Articles of incorporation were filed on October 6, 1977, in the state of Alaska. Bylaws were drafted, reviewed by the board of directors in April of the following year, and formally adopted on October 1, 1978. Suc-

ceeding national conferences were held in Dayton, Ohio, in 1978, in Minneapolis, Minnesota, in 1979, in Detroit in 1980, and in Minneapolis in 1981. The USAO board usually met several times a year, and ongoing activities of the association were carried on between meetings.

PURPOSES AND ACTIVITIES

As a not-for-profit organization with a 501(c)(3) tax status, the USAO has wide general educational, scientific, and charitable purposes. Specifically, however, its stated purpose is to assist existing ombudsmen and ombudsman organizations to improve the operations of their offices throughout the United States and to promote and encourage the establishment of ombudsman offices at national, state, and local levels throughout the United States.

In the first few years of its existence, using only the resources of existing offices and the time of its officers, the USAO has been able to begin work on model legislation, sponsor a newsletter, the *Clarion*, sponsor the annual conference, start a membership directory, draft a grant application for educational materials, and encourage professional exchange between offices and between ombudsman offices and governmental leaders. The annual conferences are open to anyone seriously interested in promoting the ombudsman concept.

The USAO has taken its stand on what it considers to be the kind of ombudsman concept worth promoting in Article VI of its bylaws. Not surprisingly, this section of the bylaws was the subject of some heated controversy at annual conferences in the first several years of the USAO's history.

While conferences have been open, voting membership in the USAO has been restricted to "only Ombudsmen or public officials performing the Ombudsman functions," and such voting membership is restricted to "one member per Ombudsman jurisdiction." Furthermore, such members must meet the following standards:

1) a governmental official created by constitution, charter, legislation or ordinance;

2) an official whose independence is guaranteed through (a) a defined term of office and/or (b) appointment by other than the executive and/or (c) custom;

3) an official of high stature;

4) an official with the responsibility to receive and investigate complaints against governmental agencies;

5) freedom of the official to investigate on his or her own motion;

6) an official who may exercise full powers of investigation to include access to all necessary information both testimonial and documentary;

7) the ability of the official to criticize governmental agencies and officials and to recommend corrective action;

8) an official with the power to issue public reports concerning his or her findings and recommendations;

9) an official who is restricted from activities constituting a personal, professional, occupational or political conflict of interest; and,

10) an official with freedom to employ and remove assistants and to delegate administrative and investigative responsibilities to them.

These standards for an ombudsman office relate very closely to the American Bar Association and International Bar Association resolutions for ombudsman offices and to the International Ombudsman Conference Steering Committee definition of an ombudsman.

BOARD OF DIRECTORS AND OFFICERS OF THE USAO

The first board of directors was elected by those present at the Seattle conference in 1977. Once elected by the general membership, the board of directors elects its own officers. Members of the board of directors serve a two-year term. No director shall serve for more than four continuous years. The first board of directors (1977–79) and the offices they held were Bonnie Macaulay of Dayton/King County, Ohio, president; Lawrence Guillot of Jackson County, Missouri, vice-president; Paul Meyer of Seattle/King County, Washington, secretary-treasurer; T. Williams, Minnesota correctional ombudsman; and Frank Flavin of Alaska.

In 1979, Paul Meyer resigned at the end of his tenure in Seattle. After the 1979 elections, the board of directors created a second vice-president and separated the offices of secretary and treasurer. The persons elected in 1979 and the offices they held on the board were Lawrence Guillot, of Jackson County, Missouri, president; T. Williams, Minnesota correctional ombudsman, vice-president; William Angrick II, Iowa, vice-president; Bonnie Macaulay, Dayton/Montgomery County, Ohio, treasurer; and Preston Barton, Kansas correctional ombudsman, secretary. In February 1980, Guillot resigned as Jackson County ombudsman and consequently resigned from the USAO board. He was succeeded by Frank Flavin, Alaska, and when he failed to be reappointed as Alaskan Ombudsman in 1981, by William Angrick, Citizens Aid/Ombudsman, Des Moines, Iowa.

MEMBERSHIP

At the end of 1981, the USAO had twenty-three voting members, each of the practicing ombudsmen representing an office that met the criteria of Article VI. Roughly one hundred other members, all of them nonvoting, were staff persons in these ombudsman offices, other ombudsmen not meeting the criteria of Article VI, other types of complaint handlers, and persons interested in the ombudsman concept.

The ombudsman offices that were represented with voting members were as follows: Alaska state ombudsman; Anchorage, Alaska, municipal ombudsman; Berkeley, California, municipal ombudsman; Guam ombudsman; Hawaii ombudsman; Iowa ombudsman; Kansas correctional ombudsman; Wichita, Kansas, school ombudsman; Lexington/Fayette, Kentucky, urban county ombudsman; Montgomery, Maryland, county public school ombudsman; Ann Arbor, Michigan, school ombudsman; Michigan correctional ombudsman; Detroit, Michigan, municipal ombudsman; Minnesota correctional ombudsman; Jackson County, Missouri, ombudsman; Nebraska ombudsman; New Jersey office of the ombudsman for the institutionalized elderly; Jamestown, New York, municipal ombudsman; New York City municipal ombudsman; Dayton/Montgomery County, Ohio, municipal ombudsman; Oregon correctional ombudsman; Puerto Rico ombudsman; and Seattle/King County, Washington, ombudsman. Not members, but apparently eligible for membership, were the offices of the Wichita, Kansas, municipal ombudsman and the Jamestown, New York, municipal ombudsman.

Honorary memberships were voted to Bernard Frank in 1978 and to Stanley V. Anderson in 1980.

CONFERENCES

The first USAO conference was held in Seattle, Washington, on August 1–3, 1977. In addition to the many meetings of ombudsmen in small groups, by jurisdictional areas and for social, get-acquainted purposes, there were a number of substantial papers presented. They included an overview on the ombudsman as a citizen participation device by Larry B. Hill, a review of the work of ombudsmen in prisons and jails by Stanley V. Anderson, a presentation on ombudsman procedures, standards, and case evaluations by Lawrence Guillot, the powers of the ombudsmen in investigations by Arthur Maloney, a comparison between the Israel ombudsman and the U.S. concept by Gerald Caiden, the ombudsman role of superintending the police by John E. Moore, and the public accountability of the ombudsman by Brenda Danet. These papers were gathered together by Larry B. Hill and are to be published, together with other materials, in a volume entitled *American Ombudsmen: Evaluations and Prospects* (University of Oklahoma Press, forthcoming).

The second USAO conference, held in Dayton, Ohio, on October 1–5, 1978, was of a very practical bent. Sessions were largely devoted to case studies, round robin discussions of common problems by jurisdictional areas, and workshops on topics such as investigative approaches and techniques, recordkeeping and report writing, caseload management, public information, privacy, and confidentiality.

The third USAO conference, held in Minneapolis, Minnesota, on August 5–8, 1979, had as a theme: "The Ombudsman as Communicator, Investigator and Change Agent." Jerie M. Pratt delivered a paper on "The Ombudsman as Communicator." Sidney L. Willens presented a paper and a handbook on "The Ombudsman as Investigator." Each was followed by extensive workshops arranged by jurisdictional areas. A final presentation on "The Ombudsman as a Change Agent" was made by Charles W. Whalen, Jr. A large part of the conference was given over to specially called meetings dealing with conflict and tensions about the nature and structure of the USAO. Formal *Proceedings of the Third Annual USAO Conference* were prepared by the participants, edited by Lawrence Guillot, and are available through the International Ombudsman Institute.

CONFLICTS OVER THE OMBUDSMAN DEFINITION AND VOTING MEMBERSHIP

The annual "Ombudsman and Other Complaint-Handling Systems Survey," published in 1979 jointly by the International Bar Association and the International Ombudsman Institute, listed eighteen ombudsman offices in the United States. The same publication detailed how there were in the United States about fourteen correctional ombudsmen, four school ombudsmen, about a hundred and thirty college and university ombudsmen, a number of health program and business ombudsmen, and between a hundred and a hundred twenty-five ombudsmen and complaint handlers at various levels of federal, state, and local government. This imbalance between the number of ombudsman offices of the classic independent type and variations on the concept creating executive ombudsmen and other types of complaint handlers, with or without the ombuds-

man title, reflects the fascination in the United States with the ombudsman concept and either confusion on how it should be structured or reluctance to bestow the classical powers on such an office.

Since the United States Association of Ombudsmen has both a restricted voting category of membership based on the classical concept and a policy of open participation at conferences, it has been sometimes a laboratory and sometimes a debating ground about the advantages and disadvantages of the classical structure and legislation. The proceedings of the third USAO conference epitomize the debate.

The founders and board of directors of the USAO have decided to live with the tension, in hopes of producing growth for the ombudsman institution in the United States. Voting membership in the organization is still restricted to one incumbent ombudsman from each of the ombudsmen institutions in the United States that meets the criteria outlined earlier in Article VI of the bylaws. Regular meetings of the board of directors and the annual meeting of the voting membership are held to decide on the ways the ombudsman concept and its advantages can be promoted throughout the United States. The annual conferences, local conferences, exchanges between offices, and publications are available on an open basis to anyone interested in the ombudsman concept and institution.

ORGANIZATIONAL CONTACT

Because of its modest resources, there is no permanent office or independent staff for the USAO. Activities are carried on entirely by its membership and the board of directors. Anyone wishing to contact or obtain further information from the USAO should write to any ombudsman office in the United States or William Angrick, Citizens Aid/Ombudsman, 515 East 12th St., Des Moines, Iowa 50319.

SELECTED BIBLIOGRAPHY

Abraham, H. J. "People's Watchdog Against Abuse of Power." *Public Administration Review* 20 (1960): 152–57.

Andreas, D. M. *Ombudsmen for Local Government*. Saint Catharines, Ont.: Brock University, 1971. 140 pp.

———. "Ombudsmen: Supervisors of Bureaucracy." In Donald C. Rowat, ed. *Provincial Government and Politics: Comparative Essays*. Ottawa: Carleton University Bookstore, 1973.

Ascher, C. S. "The Grievance Man or Ombudsmania." *Public Administration Review* 27 (1967): 174–78.

Bader, H., and Brompton, H. B. *Problems of the Ombudsman: The Case of Austria's Proposed People's Advocate*. Northridge: Department of Political Science, California State University, 1973. 17 pp.

Bagchi, Ajoy. "Redress of Public Grievances." *Journal of the National Academy of Administration (India)* 15, No. 2–3 (April–September 1970): 67–80.

Beral, H., and Sisk, M. "The Administration of Complaints by Civilians Against the Police." *Harvard Law Review* 77 (1963): 499–519.

Berger, R. "Administrative Arbitrariness and Judicial Review." *Columbia Law Review* 65 (1965): 55–95.

Bexelius, A., and Powles, G. "The Ombudsman: Champion of the Citizen." *Record of the Association of the Bar of the City of New York* (June 1966): 385–411.

Bockman, E. J. "Ombudsman: Quis Custodiet Ipsos Custodes." *Municipal Reference Library Notes* 10 (1966): 165–71.

Boim, L. "'Ombudsmanship': Redress of Grievances in the Polish People's Republic." *Annuario di Diritto Comparato e di Studi Legislativi* 41 (1967): 205–47.

Bradley, A. W. "The Redress of Grievances." *Cambridge Law Journal* 37 (1962): 82–98.

Burbridge, C. T. "Problems of Transferring the Ombudsman Plan." *International Review of Administrative Sciences* 40 (1974): 103–108.

Caiden, N. J. "The Ombudsman and the Rights of the Citizen." *Australian Quarterly* 36, No. 3 (1964): 67–77.

———. "Ombudsmen for Under-Developed Countries? Pre-Conditions for an Ombudsman." *Public Administration in Israel and Abroad* 8 (January 1968): 100–15.

Carey, John. "Procedures for International Protection of Human Rights." *Iowa Law Review* 53 (1967): 291–324.

Carlson, R. J., ed. *University of Illinois Assembly on the Ombudsman: Final Report of Regional Assembly*. The American Assembly of Columbia University and Institute of Government and Public Affairs, University of Illinois at Urbana-Champaign, May 1969, 39 pp.

Chapman, B. "The Ombudsman." *Public Administration* 38 (1969): 303–10.

———. *The Profession of Government: The Public Service in Europe*. London: Allen and Unwin, 1959.

Cheng, H. Y. "The Ombudsman System in Evolution: Can It Be Adapted to Commonwealth Developing Countries?" M.A. Thesis, Carleton University, Ottawa, 1977. 114 pp. (typed).

Cloward, R. A., and Elman, R. M. "Poverty, Injustice and the Welfare State—Part I: An Ombudsman for the Poor?" *The Nation* (February 28, 1966): 230–35.

Cohen, L. H. "The Parliamentary Commissioner and the 'M.P. Filter'." *Parliamentary Affairs* (Autumn 1972): 204–14.

Colan, F. T. "The Ombudsman, or the Myth of the White Knight." *Social Studies* 64 (October 1973): 202–10.

Collins, T. A. "An Ombudsman for Local Government." *Indiana Legal Forum* 1 (1968): 376–97.

Commonwealth Secretariat. *Ombudsman in The Commonwealth*. London: Commonwealth Secretariat, 1980. 34 pp.

Acknowledgment for this bibliography and for materials supplementing chapter bibliographies is made to Priscilla Kennedy of the International Ombudsman Institute, which maintains a complete bibliography on the ombudsman and related subjects.

Compton, E. "The Administrative Performance of Government." *Public Administration* (Spring 1970): 3–14.

Conference of Australasian and Pacific Ombudsmen, Wellington, New Zealand, November 19–22, 1974. *Official Record of Proceedings,* and *Supplement.* Wellington: Office of the Ombudsman, 1975. 214 pp.

Conference on the Ombudsman, Vancouver, B.C., 1970. *Proceedings of the Conference on the Ombudsman.* Held in Vancouver, B.C., March 20–21, 1970. 84 pp.

Cooper, F. E. "The Need for an Ombudsman in State Government." *Prospectus* 1 (April 1968): 27–44.

Council of Europe. *Meeting of the Legal Affairs Committee with the Ombudsmen and Parliamentary Commissioners in Council of Europe Member States, Paris, 18–19 April 1974.* Strasbourg: Council of Europe, 1974, Documents AS/Jur/Omb. (25) 1–17, pp. 1–139.

Cramton, R. C. "A Federal Ombudsman." *Duke Law Journal* (April 1972): 1–14.

D'Alemberte, T. "Ombudsman, A Grievance Man for Citizens." *University of Florida Law Review* 18 (Spring 1966): 545–52.

Danet, B. "Toward a Method to Evaluate the Ombudsman Role." *Administration and Society* 10 (1978): 335–67.

De Smith, S. A. "Anglo-Saxon Ombudsman?" *Political Quarterly* 33 (1962): 9–19.

———. *Judicial Review of Administrative Action.* London: Stevens and Sons, 1977. 486 pp.

Dolan, P. "Creating State Ombudsmen: A Growing Movement." *National Civic Review* 63 (May 1974): 250–54.

Drake, C. "Ombudsman for Local Government." *Public Administration* (Summer 1970): 179–89.

Frank, B. "The Ombudsman—A Challenge." *International Bar Journal* (November 1971): 32–39.

———. "The Ombudsman and Human Rights." *Administrative Law Review* 23 (April 1970): 467–92.

———. "The Ombudsman—Revisited." *International Bar Journal* (May 1975): 48–60.

———. "The Tanzanian Permanent Commission of Inquiry—The Ombudsman." *Denver Journal of International Law and Policy* (Fall 1972): 255–79.

Friedmann, K. A. *Complaining: Comparative Aspects of Complaint Behaviour and Attitudes Toward Complaining in Canada and Britain.* Beverly Hills, Calif.: Sage Publications, 1974. 67 pp.

Fry, G. K. "The Sachsenhausen Concentration Camp Case and the Convention of Ministerial Responsibility." *Public Law* (Winter 1970): 336–57.

Gellhorn, W. *Ombudsmen and Others: Citizens' Protectors in Nine Countries.* Cambridge, Mass.: Harvard University Press, 1966. 488 pp.

Ginsbury, G., and Stahnke, A. "The Genesis of the People's Procuratorate in Communist China, 1949–1951." *China Quarterly* 20 (October–November 1964): 1–37.

Greenstein, I. R. "A Study of Campus Ombudsman," Masters Thesis, University of Maryland, 1977. 86 pp.

Gregory, R. "Bureaucracy observed." *New Society,* January 11, 1973, pp. 58–60.

Gwyn, W. B. "The Discovery of the Scandinavian Ombudsman in English-Speaking Countries." *West European Politics* 3, No. 3 (1980): 317–38.

———." 'JUSTICE' and the Ombudsman: A Case Study of Policy Formulation Within a Non-Coercive Public Interest Group." In *Perspective on Public Policy-Making,* Tulane Studies in Political Science 15, pp. 95–140.

Hadi, M. A. "Extension de l'ombudsman: triomphe d'une idée ou deformation d'une institution?" *International Review of Administrative Sciences* 43 (1977): 334–44.

Hagan, J. E. "The Suitability of the Ombudsman System for Ghana." M. A. Thesis, Carleton University, Ottawa, 1970, 120 pp. (typed).

———. "Whatever Happened to Ghana's Ombudsman?" *Transition* 40 (December 1971): 28–32.

Haider, S. M. "Ombudsmen: Plea for Reform in Law and Public Administration." In S. M. Haider, ed. *Public Administration and Police in Pakistan.* Peshawar: Pakistan Academy for Rural Development, 1968.

Hamilton, R. H. "Can You Fight City Hall and Win?" *Public Management* 49 (October 1967): 269–75.

———. "Ombudsman or What?" *National Civic Review* 57, No. 3 (1968): 132–37. Reprinted in *Congressional Record* 114, No. 51 (March 27, 1968): E2376–E2378.

Hansen, J. *Die Institution des Ombudsman.* Frankfurt am Main: Athenäum Verlag GMBH, 1972.

Hartke, V. "Ombudsman." *California Western Law Review* 10 (Winter 1974): 325–58.

Hill, L. B. *Ombudsman, Bureaucracy and Democracy.* Norman, Okla.: Department of Political Science, University of Oklahoma, forthcoming.

———. "The Transference of the Institution of Ombudsman, with Special Reference to Britain." M.A. Thesis, Tulane University, New Orleans, 1966. 168 pp. (typed).

Hurwitz, S. *The Experience of Parliamentary Commissioners in Certain Scandinavian Countries.* Background paper for the U.N. Seminar on Judicial and Other Remedies Against the Illegal Exercise or Abuse of Administrative Authority. New York: Doc. T E 326/1 (40–7), United Nations, 1959, 28 pp. (mimeo.)

———. "The Folketingets Ombudsman." *Parliamentary Affairs* 12 (1959): 199–208.

———. "The Scandinavian Ombudsman." *Political Science* 12 (1960): 121–42.

India, Lok Sabha. *Ombudsmen in Various Countries.* New Delhi: Lok Sabha Secretariat, undated (1968?). 93 pp.

Jackman, L. "Ombudsman for Caribbean Governments." *Journal of Administration Overseas* 13, No. 4 (October 1974): 536–44.

Jacomy-Millette, A. "Is the Institution of the Ombudsman Applicable to Africa? Legislation and First Results." *Canadian Journal of Africa Studies* 8 (1974): 145–53.

———. "Note sur l'Ombudsman africain." *Revue Générale de droit* 2 (1971): 123.

Jolliffe, E. B. "The Inevitability of the Ombudsman." *Administrative Law Review* 19 (1966): 99–102.

Kass, B. L. *Ombudsman: A Proposal for Demonstration in Washington, D.C.* Washington, D.C.: Washington Center for Metropolitan Studies, 1968, 40 pp.

————. "We Can Indeed Fight City Hall: The Office and Concept of Ombudsman." *American Bar Association Journal* 53 (March 1967): 231–36.

Kersell, J. E. "Parliamentary Ventilation of Grievances Arising Out of the Operation of Delegated Legislation." *Public Law* (1959): 152–68.

Kimicha, M. "The Ombudsman and the Permanent Commission of Enquiry." *Journal of Administration Overseas* 12, No. 1 (January 1973): 46–50.

King, D. B. "The Consumer Ombudsman." *Commercial Law Journal* (September 1974): 355–60.

Kirchheiner, H. H. *Ombudsman en Democratie.* Alphen aan den Rijn: Samson, 1971.

Kjekshus, H. "The Ombudsman in the Tanzania One-Party System." *African Review* 1, No. 2 (September 1971): 13–29.

Klesment, J. *The Ombudsman and Related Systems of Governmental Supervision in Scandinavian and Other Countries.* Washington, D.C.: Library of Congress, European Law Division, June 19, 1961. 29 pp. (mimeo).

Lawson, F. H. "An Inspector-General of Administration." *Public Law* (Summer 1957): 92–95.

Legrand, A. *L'Ombudsman Scandinave. Etudes comparées sur le contrôle de l'administration.* Paris: Librairie générale de Droit et de Jurisprudence, Bibliothèque de Science Administrative, 1970.

Lewis, N., and Gateshill, B. *The Commission for Local Administration: A preliminary appraisal.* London: Royal Institute of Public Administration, 1978. 68 pp.

Linden, A. M. "Tort Law as Ombudsman." *Canadian Bar Review* 51 (1973): 155–68.

McClellan, G. B. "The Role of the Ombudsman." *University of Miami Law Review* 23 (1975): 463 et seq.

MacLeod, I. G. "The Ombudsman." *Administrative Law Review* 19 (1966): 93–98.

Mang'enya, E. A. M. *The Permanent Commission of Enquiry (Ombudsman).* Dar es Salaam: Tanzania Government Printer, 1970.

Martin, R. "The Ombudsman in Zambia." *Journal of Modern African Studies* 15, No. 2 (June 1977): 239–59.

Mazuran, M. J. *The Ombudsman and City Governments.* School of Public Administration, University of Southern California, Summer 1967, 53 pp. plus appendices. (mimeo.)

Middleton, K. W. B. "The Ombudsman." *Juridical Review* 5 (1960): 298–306.

Minattur, J. "Ombudsman—A Many Splendored Thing." *Law Quarterly* (1971): 246–63.

————. "Ombudsman in Developing Countries." *Supreme Court Journal* (India) (1970): 21 et seq.

Mitchell, J. D. B. "Administrative Law and Parliamentary Control." *Political Quarterly* (1967): 360–74.

————. "The Ombudsman Fallacy." *Public Law* (1962): 24–33.

Moore, J. E. "Ombudsmen and the Ghetto." *Connecticut Law Review* 1 (1968): 244–48.

————. *Ombudsmen and the Ghetto.* Berkeley, Calif.: Institute of Governmental Studies, University of California, 1968. 245 pp.

Mortati, C. *L'Ombudsman (il difensore civico).* Torino: Unione Tipografico—Editrice Torinese, 1974. 307 pp.

Murray, C. H. "The Grievance Man: In Scandinavia." *Administration* 8 (1960): 231–37.

Nader, R. "An Answer to Administrative Abuse." *Harvard Law Record* (December 20, 1962): 13, 15.

Napione, G. *L'Ombudsman: il controllore della publica amministrazione.* Milano: Giuffre Editore, 1969. 283 pp.

Newman, F. C. "Natural Justice, Due Process and the New International Covenants on Human Rights." *Public Law* (Winter 1967): 274–313.

————. "Ombudsman and Human Rights: The New U.N. Treaty Proposals." *University of Chicago Law Review* 34 (Summer 1967): 951–62.

Norton, P. M. "The Tanzanian Ombudsman." *International and Comparative Law Quarterly* 22 (October 1973): 603–31

Nyagah, S. *The Ombudsman; Constitutional and Legal Processes for the Protection of the Citizen from Administrative Abuses.* Lower Kabete, Kenya: Kenya Institute of Administration, 1970. 36 pp.

Orfield, L. B. "The Scandinavian Ombudsman." *Administrative Law Review* 19 (1966): 7–74.

Osew, E. A. "The Role of a Parliamentary Commissioner (Alias Ombudsman)." *Review of Ghana Law* 1 (1969): 45–54.

Patterson, A. D. "The Ombudsman." *U.B.C. Law Review* 1 (April 1963): 777–81.

Payne, J. E. "Ombudsman Roles for Social Workers." *Social Work* 17 (January 1972): 94–100.

Peck, P. W. "The Ombudsman in Slotsholmen." *Public Administration* 44 (1966): 333–46.

Peel, R. V., ed. *The Ombudsman or Citizen's Defender: A Modern Institution.* Philadelphia: American Academy of Political and Social Science, 1968. 238 pp.

Powles, G. R. "The Citizen's Rights Against the Modern State and Its Responsibilities to Him." *Public Administration* 23 (1964): 42–68.

————. "Ombudsmania." *Parliamentarian* 50, No. 1 (1969): 69–72.

Pugh, I. "The Ombudsman—Jurisdiction, Powers and Practice." *Public Administration* 56 (1978): 127 et seq.

Reuss, H. S., and Anderson, S. V. "The Ombudsman: Tribune of the People." *Annals of the American Academy of Political and Social Science* 363 (January 1966): 44–51.

Roche, R. "The Ombudsman Proposals: A Critique." *IBAR* 2 (October 1980): 29–57.

Rowat, D. C. *The Ombudsman: Citizen's Defender.* London: Allen and Unwin; Toronto: University of Toronto Press; Stockholm: Norstedt; 2d ed., 1968. 384 pp.

————. *The Ombudsman Plan; Essays on the Worldwide Spread of an Idea.* Toronto: McClelland and Stewart, 1973. 315 pp.

————. "Ombudsmen for North America." *Public Administration Review* 24 (1964): 230–33.

————. "The Problem of Administrative Secrecy." *International Review of Administrative Sciences* 2 (1966): 99–106.

_____. "Recent Developments in Ombudsmanship." *Canadian Public Administration* 10 (1967): 35–46.

Sandler, A. "The Ombudsman." *Vital Issues* 17, No. 6 (1968): 1–4.

Sargant, T. "The Ombudsman and One-Party States in Africa." *Journal of African Law* 8, No. 3 (1964): 195–97.

Sawer, G. "The Jurisprudence of Ombudsmen." *Public Administration* 48 (Summer 1970): 179–89.

_____. *Ombudsmen*. 2d ed. Melbourne: Melbourne University Press, 1968. 50 pp.

Scott, S., ed. *Western American Assembly on the Ombudsman: Report*. Berkeley, Calif.: Institute of Governmental Studies, University of California, 1968. 36 pp.

Shukla, V. S. "The Ombudsman Hysteria." *Supreme Court Journal* (India) (May 1967): 84–96.

Silver, I. "The Corporate Ombudsman." *Harvard Business Review* (May–June 1967): 77–87.

Singh, B. "Rise and Progress of Ombudsman—The Citizens' Defender." *International Journal of Legal Research* 4 (December 1969): 127–43.

Southeastern Assembly on the Ombudsman. *Our Kind of Ombudsman: A Symposium*. [L. Harold Levinson, ed.] Gainesville, Fla.: Public Administration Clearing Service, University of Florida, 1970. 73 pp.

Stacey, F. A. *Ombudsman Compared*. Oxford: Oxford University Press, 1978. 256 pp.

Steenbeck, J. G. *The Parliamentary Ombudsman in Sweden, Denmark and Norway*. Haarlem: 1964. 230 pp.

Taylor, R. W., and von Nordheim, M. "The Ombudsman: A Symposium." *The Administrative Law Review* 19 (November 1966): 6–106.

Tibbles, L. "The Ombudsman: Who Needs Him?" *Journal of Urban Law* 47 (1969–70): 1–67.

United Nations. *Remedies Against the Abuse of Administrative Authority—Selected Studies*. New York: United Nations, 1964. p. 167.

_____. *Seminar on Judicial and Other Remedies Against the Abuse of Administrative Authority, with Special Emphasis on the Role of Parliamentary Institutions*. Stockholm, June 12–25, 1962. New York: Doc. ST/TAO/HR/15. iii, 34 pp.

_____. *Seminar on Judicial and Other Remedies Against the Illegal Exercise or Abuse of Administrative Authority*. Kandy, Ceylon, May 4–15, 1959. New York: Doc. ST/TAO/HR/4. 99 pp.

Utley, T. E. *Occasion for Ombudsman*. London: C. Johnson, 1961. 160 pp.

Vontobel, J., et al. "The Ombudsman in Switzerland." *Verwaltungs Praxiz* (December 1974): 369–90.

Washington. Legislative Council. Committee on State Government. *The Ombudsman in Scandinavia. Advantages and Disadvantages . . . for State Government*. 32 pp. (mimeo).

Weeks, K. M. "How the Ombudsman Works to Help Citizens." *Cleveland Bar Association Journal* 38 (1967): 122–23, 125–26.

_____. *Ombudsmen Around the World: A Comparative Chart*. 2d ed. Berkeley, Calif.: Institute of Governmental Studies, University of California, 1978. 163 pp.

Wennergren, B. *Protection of the Citizen in Administrative Procedures*. Brussels: International Institute of Administrative Sciences, 1968.

Wheare, K. C. *Maladministration And Its Remedies*. London: Stevens, 1973. 172 pp.

_____. "The Redress of Grievances." *Public Administration* 40 (1962): 125–28.

Whyatt, J. *The Citizen and the Administration: The Redress of Grievances*. London: Stevens, 1961. 104 pp.

Williams, D. W. *Maladministration: Remedies for Injustice*. London: Oyez, 1976. 232 pp.

Witherspoon, J. P. *Administrative Implementation of Civil Rights*. Austin, Tex.: University of Texas Press, 1968.

Wolfensberger, W. *Citizen Advocacy and Protective Services for the Impaired and Handicapped*. Toronto: National Institute on Mental Retardation, 1973. 277 pp.

Wolkon, G. H., and Moriwaki, S. "The Ombudsman Programme: Primary Prevention of Psychological Disorders." *International Journal of Social Psychiatry* 19 (Autumn/Winter 1973): 220–25.

Zweig, F. M. "The Social Worker as Legislative Ombudsman." *Social Work* 14 (1969): 25–33.

INDEX

CONTRIBUTORS

ANDERSON, STANLEY V., is professor of political science at the University of California, Santa Barbara. He graduated from the University of California, Berkeley, obtaining his Ph.D. in 1961. He has practiced at the California State Bar and has taught public law. From 1969 to 1973, he was principal investigator in the Ombudsman Activities Project, and since 1977 he has been chairman of the Ombudsman Committee, Administrative Law Section of the American Bar Association. He has published extensively on the institution of ombudsman.

BARTON, PRESTON N., II, has been corrections ombudsman and executive secretary of the Kansas Corrections Ombudsman Board since 1975. He is a graduate in social work of Temple University and the University of Pennsylvania. He has been a staff member of the army correctional facility at Fort Riley, Kansas, and the Pennsylvania Prison Society, and has taught at the University of Kansas School of Social Welfare.

BRADLEY, A. W., has been professor of constitutional law at the University of Edinburgh since 1968 and dean of the Faculty of Law since 1979. He has taught at Cambridge University and the University of East Africa, and he has been a member of the Law and Social Services Committee of the Social Science Research Council. He was responsible for the ninth edition of *Constitutional and Administrative Law* by E. C. S. Wade and G. G. Phillips.

CAIDEN, GERALD E., is professor of public administration at the University of Southern California. He graduated from the London School of Economics and Political Science, obtaining his Ph.D. in 1959. He has taught in universities in Canada, Australia, Israel, and the United States. He has published extensively in the field of public administration and has acted as consultant, researcher, and administrator to a wide variety of public organizations.

GUILLOT, LAWRENCE B., was director/ombudsman of the Jackson County Office of Human Relations and Citizens Complaints (1973–80) and president of the United States Association of Ombudsmen (1979–80) before he resigned to develop a third-sector public service corporation. He graduated from North American College and Gregorian University in Rome. He has been an active Catholic priest and educator, and active in community affairs as a member of a planning commission and school district commission.

GWYN, WILLIAM B., has been professor of political science at Tulane University since 1969. He is a graduate of the University of Virginia and the University of London where he obtained his doctorate in 1956. He has written extensively about the institution of ombudsman.

HANSEN, INGER, is privacy commissioner of the Canadian Human Rights Commission. She graduated from the University of British Columbia and practiced law in Vancouver until 1969 when she joined the Legal Department of the Ministry of the Solicitor General. In 1973, she was appointed the first Canadian correctional investigator (penitentiaries ombudsman) before assuming the job of privacy commissioner in 1977.

HILL, LARRY B., is a professor of political science at the University of Oklahoma.

IVANY, RANDALL, has been the ombudsman of Alberta since 1974. He has been chairman of the International Ombudsman Steering Committee since 1976 and is executive director of the International Ombudsman Institute. He is a graduate of Wycliffe College and an ordained Anglican priest in which capacity he served in various locations until elected dean of Edmonton in 1969. He has been active in community affairs and voluntary work.

KIRCHHEINER, H. H., is district court judge in Amsterdam. He graduated in law at the State University of Leiden before assuming a career in judicial administration which eventually brought him to the bench in 1952 as district court judge in Alphen a/d Rijn. His doctoral dissertation concerned the democratic foundations of the ombudsman institution. He writes in the field of public law.

LASKOV, HAIM, has been the military ombudsman in Israel since 1972. He has studied at Oxford University and pursued an active public service career in Israel. From 1958 to 1960, he was chief of general staff of the Israeli Defense Forces, and from 1960 to 1972 he was director-general of the Israel Ports Authority. He served on the Agranat Commission of Inquiry following the Yom Kippur war.

MACDERMOT, NIALL, has been secretary general of the International Commission of Jurists since 1970. He was educated at Oxford University and practiced law, becoming QC in 1963. He was a member of the British Parliament (1957–59 and 1962–1970), financial secretary of the treasury (1964–67), and minister of state for planning and land (1967–68). He has been chairman of the Special Committee of International Non-Governmental Organizations on Human Rights, Geneva, since 1976, and he was the minister in charge of the Parliamentary Commissioner Bill.

MAILICK, MILDRED, teaches at the Hunter College School of Social Work, New York. She is a graduate of the University of Chicago and Columbia University School of Social Work. She has been active in social work for many years and has published papers on hospital care.

MALONEY, ARTHUR, practices law in Toronto. He was ombudsman for Ontario from 1976 to 1978. He graduated from the University of Toronto and Osgoode Hall Law School and practiced law. He was appointed QC in 1953 and was elected to the federal parliament, serving from 1957 to 1962.

MIEWALD, ROBERT, is professor of political science at the University of Nebraska, Lincoln. He graduated from the University of Oregon and the University of Colorado and served on the faculty of California State University, Long Beach. He has published extensively in the field of public administration.

NEBENZAHL, IZHAK E., has been state comptroller of Israel since 1961 and commissioner for public complaints since 1971. He studied law and economics at Frankfurt, Berlin, and Freiburg universities, and taught law at Frankfurt University until he went to Israel in 1933. After a career in commerce, banking, and public office, he became chairman of the advisory committee and council of the Bank of Israel in 1957.

NILSSON, PER-ERIK, has been chief parliamentary ombudsman in Sweden since 1978. After graduating in law from Uppsala University, he pursued a judicial career in the Ministry of Justice. From 1972 to 1977, he was administrative chief for the prime minister's office, with special responsibility for legal matters. Then he returned as chief justice to the court of appeal for Northern Sweden. He has been a member of several parliamentary commissions.

PICKL, VIKTOR J., is director of the Austrian Volksanwaltschaft. After graduating in law, he served as a judge, public prosecutor, and commissioner for correctional institutions.

ROWAT, DONALD C., has been professor of political science at Carleton University since 1958. He is a graduate of the universities of Toronto and Columbia and has taught at Dalhousie University and the University of British Columbia. He has published extensively in political science and public administration, and among his many books are *Basic Issues in Public Administration* (1961), *The Ombudsman: Citizen's Defender* (1965), *The Ombudsman Plan: Essays on the Worldwide Spread of the Idea* (1973), *Administrative Secrecy in Developed Countries* (1979), and *International Handbook on Local Government Reorganization* (1980).

SANDLER, AKE, is professor emeritus, California State University, Los Angeles. After graduating from the University of Southern California and the University of California, Los Angeles, he taught political science at California State University, Los Angeles, where he was associate director of the Center for Disarmament and Arms Control. He has published in the field of political science and is a devoted scholar of the ombudsman institution.

SEROTA, BARONESS B., has been chairman of the Commission for Local Administration in England since 1974. She graduated from the University of London. She served on the Hampstead Borough Council (1945–49), the London County Council (1956–65), and the Greater London Council (1964–67). She has been a member of many national commissions and committees in the field of child care, the social services, and the penal system. She was minister of state for health (1969–70), was created a life peer in 1967, and is a governor of the British Broadcasting Corporation.

WALLACE, GEOFFREY, has served ten years as university ombudsman at the University of California, Santa Barbara, where he graduated in sociology. Before his appointment, he handled complaints in five western states for Walter Hickel, then secretary of the interior. He is an intern psychotherapist.

WINEINGER, JAMES, is school ombudsman for the Wichita Public Schools District. He is a graduate of Wichita State University in psychology. He served as a school social worker before becoming ombudsman.